First World War

and Army of Occupation

War Diary

France, Belgium and Germany

9 DIVISION
26 Infantry Brigade
Princess Louise's (Argyll & Sutherland Highlanders)
10th Battalion,
Brigade Machine Gun Company
and Brigade Trench Mortar Battery
9 June 1915 - 11 November 1915

WO95/1768

The Naval & Military Press Ltd
www.nmarchive.com
Published in association with The National Archives

Published by

The Naval & Military Press Ltd

Unit 10 Ridgewood Industrial Park,
Uckfield, East Sussex,
TN22 5QE England
Tel: +44 (0) 1825 749494

www.naval-military-press.com
www.nmarchive.com

This diary has been reprinted in facsimile from the original. Any imperfections are inevitably reproduced and the quality may fall short of modern type and cartographic standards.

Contents

Document type	Place/Title	Date From	Date To
Heading	9th Division 26th Infy Bde 10th Bn Argyll & Sutherland HDRS May 1916-Dec 1917 From 27 Bde 9 Div. To Div 97 Bde		
War Diary	Ploegsteert Area	02/05/1916	06/05/1916
War Diary	Ploegsteert.	06/05/1916	06/05/1916
War Diary	Papot.	08/05/1916	08/05/1916
War Diary	Ploegsteert.	14/05/1916	17/05/1916
War Diary	Papot.	20/05/1916	24/05/1916
War Diary	Ploegsteert Area.	26/05/1916	26/05/1916
War Diary	Papot.	29/05/1916	29/05/1916
War Diary	La Creche Area.	31/05/1916	31/05/1916
Miscellaneous	Casualty Statement. Appendix XIX.		
War Diary	Doulieu Area.	01/06/1916	01/06/1916
War Diary	Morbecque Area.	03/06/1916	03/06/1916
War Diary	Enquin Les Mines.	04/06/1916	14/06/1916
War Diary	St. Sauveur.	14/06/1916	29/06/1916
Miscellaneous	10th Argyll & Suth's High'rs. Casualty Statement for June, 1916		
Heading	26th Inf. Bde. 9th Div. 10th Battn. The Argyll & Sutherland Highlanders. July 1916		
War Diary	Bois De Celestins.	01/07/1916	02/07/1916
War Diary	Grove Town.	02/07/1916	02/07/1916
War Diary	Billon Valley.	04/07/1916	08/07/1916
War Diary	Montauban.	09/07/1916	11/07/1916
War Diary	Talus Boise.	11/07/1916	14/07/1916
War Diary	Longueval.	14/07/1916	19/07/1916
War Diary	Carnoy.	20/07/1916	20/07/1916
War Diary	Sandpit Near Meaulte (Close To Albert).	21/07/1916	22/07/1916
War Diary	Sandpit.	22/07/1916	23/07/1916
War Diary	Vauchelles Les Domart.	23/07/1916	25/07/1916
War Diary	Bruay.	26/07/1916	27/07/1916
War Diary	Estree Cauchie.	28/07/1916	31/07/1916
Miscellaneous	Appendices XXIII & XXIV.		
Map	Longueval 1.5000. Appendix XXII		
Miscellaneous	Casualty Statement July 1916. Appendix. XXIV.		
War Diary	Estree Cauchie.	01/08/1916	09/08/1916
War Diary	Camblain L'Abbe.	12/08/1916	17/08/1916
War Diary	Vimy Ridge.	18/08/1916	23/08/1916
War Diary	Camblain L'Abbe	23/08/1916	31/08/1916
Miscellaneous	10th. Argyll & Suth's. Highlanders. Statement of Casualties, Etc., For August, 1916		
War Diary	Beugin.	01/09/1916	01/09/1916
War Diary	Villers Aux Bois.	02/09/1916	02/09/1916
War Diary	Vimy Ridge Area.	03/09/1916	18/09/1916
War Diary	Camblain Abbe.	19/09/1916	25/09/1916
War Diary	Berlencourt.	30/09/1916	30/09/1916
War Diary	Berlencourt.	27/09/1916	27/09/1916
Miscellaneous		01/11/1916	01/11/1916
War Diary	Berlencourt.	03/10/1916	03/10/1916
War Diary	Frohlan Le Grand.	05/10/1916	06/10/1916

War Diary	Francvillers.	07/10/1916	07/10/1916
War Diary	Albert.	08/10/1916	09/10/1916
War Diary	Flers Line.	10/10/1916	12/10/1916
War Diary	High Wood.	14/10/1916	17/10/1916
War Diary		13/10/1916	19/10/1916
War Diary	Bazentin Le Grand.	20/10/1916	29/10/1916
Miscellaneous	10th Aug. & Suth's. H'rs. Statement of Casualties, Sick, Reinforcements Etc, for October, 1916		
Miscellaneous	Detailed Record Taken Down During Operations. 12/14 Oct 1916	12/10/1916	12/10/1916
War Diary	Detailed Record Taken Down During Operations. 17th to 20th October 1916	17/10/1916	17/10/1916
Heading	26th Herewith War Diary For Nov 1917. Dec.1917		
Miscellaneous			
War Diary	Simencourt.	01/11/1916	09/11/1916
War Diary	Ambrines.	21/11/1916	30/11/1916
Miscellaneous	Casualty. Statement For November 1916. Appendix XXVI.		
War Diary	Ambrines.	03/12/1916	09/12/1916
War Diary	Arras.	10/12/1916	31/12/1916
Miscellaneous	10th (Services) Bn. Argyll & Sutherland Highlanders. Casualty Statement For December, 1916. Appendix XXVII.	01/01/1917	01/01/1917
Miscellaneous	A Form Messages And Signals.	03/02/1917	03/02/1917
War Diary	Arras.	01/01/1917	12/01/1917
War Diary	Maroeuil.	18/01/1917	18/01/1917
War Diary	Ecurie.	15/01/1917	30/01/1917
Miscellaneous	10th. Arg. & Suth'd. Highr's. Casualty Statement for January 1917. App XXVIII.	31/01/1917	31/01/1917
War Diary	Ecurie.	06/02/1917	11/02/1917
War Diary	Hermaville.	12/02/1917	12/02/1917
War Diary	Chelers.	13/02/1917	23/02/1917
War Diary	Marquay.	25/02/1917	26/02/1917
War Diary	Marquay.	21/02/1917	28/02/1917
War Diary	Marquet.	01/03/1917	01/03/1917
War Diary	Etrun.	02/03/1917	02/03/1917
War Diary	St Nicholas.	03/03/1917	10/03/1917
War Diary	Arras.	11/03/1917	21/03/1917
War Diary	Etrun Y Huts.	24/03/1917	31/03/1917
Miscellaneous	Casualty Statement For March 1917	01/04/1917	01/04/1917
Heading	10 A. & S. H. Vol 20 April 1917		
War Diary	Trenches St Nicholas.	01/04/1917	09/04/1917
War Diary	Battle Of Arras.	09/04/1917	17/04/1917
War Diary	Y. Huts.	21/04/1917	21/04/1917
War Diary	Bailleul Aux Cornailles.	21/04/1917	27/04/1917
War Diary	Battle Of Arras.	27/04/1917	30/04/1917
Operation(al) Order(s)	Operation Order No. 1. issued by Lt-Col. H.G. Sotheby, M.V.O. Commanding 10th Argyll & Sutherland Highlanders.		
Miscellaneous			
Miscellaneous	Contact Aeroplanes.		
Miscellaneous			
Operation(al) Order(s)	26th Infantry Brigade Operation Order No. 97	06/04/1917	06/04/1917
Operation(al) Order(s)	26th Infantry Brigade Operation Order No. 96	06/04/1917	06/04/1917
Miscellaneous	March Table for night 8/9th April.	08/04/1917	08/04/1917

Miscellaneous	26th Infantry Brigade Instructions No. 2. Dated 20-3-17. Appendix. 'C'.	20/03/1917	20/03/1917
Miscellaneous	10th Bn. Argyll & Sutherland Highlanders. Operation Orders For The Attack On Athies.	08/04/1917	08/04/1917
Miscellaneous	Headquarters, 9th (Scottish) Division. 8th April, 1917	08/04/1917	08/04/1917
Miscellaneous	Copy of Farewell Messages From:- Lieutenant-Colonel A.F. Mackenzie. C.M.G. M.V.O.	27/03/1917	27/03/1917
Miscellaneous	Copy of Messages from:- Lieutenant-Colonel W.J.B. Tweedie,	30/03/1917	30/03/1917
Miscellaneous	Headquarters, 9th (Scottish) Division. 10th April, 1917	10/04/1917	10/04/1917
Miscellaneous	A Form Messages And Signals.	11/04/1917	11/04/1917
Miscellaneous	Notice.		
Miscellaneous	10th (Service) Bn. Argyll & Sutherland Highlanders. Statement Of Casualties, Sick, Etc., For April, 1917	10/05/1917	10/05/1917
Map			
War Diary	Battle of Arras.	01/05/1917	12/05/1917
War Diary	Bailleul Aux Cornailles.	12/05/1917	31/05/1917
Miscellaneous	10th. Argyll And Sutherland Highrs. Statement Of Casualties, Sick, Drafts, Etc, For May, 1917	31/05/1917	31/05/1917
Miscellaneous	26th Brigade Preliminary Instructions No. 1 For Operations On May 3rd. 1917	30/04/1917	30/04/1917
Miscellaneous	(26th Brigade No. R/58. Dated 30.4.17). Preliminary Instructions No. 1 For Operations On May 3rd. Reference 1/10,000 Map (Attached.) & 1/20,000 Arras, Trench Map.	30/04/1917	30/04/1917
Operation(al) Order(s)	26th. Brigade Operation Order No. 11	02/05/1917	02/05/1917
Miscellaneous	Amendment No. 1 To 26th Brigade Preliminary Instructions No. 1. For Operations On May 3rd 1917	03/05/1917	03/05/1917
Miscellaneous	Message From Brigade.		
War Diary	Laurent Blangy.	01/06/1917	07/06/1917
War Diary	Fampoux.	07/06/1917	08/06/1917
War Diary	Chemical Works Roeux Line.	09/06/1917	12/06/1917
War Diary	Bailleul Aux Cornailles.	13/06/1917	23/06/1917
Miscellaneous	A Form Messages And Signals.		
Miscellaneous	26 Brigade	01/08/1917	01/08/1917
War Diary	Bailleul Aux Cornailles.	01/07/1917	02/07/1917
War Diary	Fossieux Dainville.	06/07/1917	24/07/1917
War Diary	Dainville.	24/07/1917	24/07/1917
War Diary	Berteaucourt	25/07/1917	25/07/1917
War Diary	Ruyaulcourt	26/07/1917	02/08/1917
War Diary	Havrincourt Sector.	02/08/1917	13/08/1917
War Diary	Havrincourt.	15/08/1917	31/08/1917
Operation(al) Order(s)	10th Battalion Argyll And Sutherland Highlanders. Operation Orders No. 112. By Lt.-Col. H.G. Sotheby. M.V.O. Commanding.	18/08/1917	18/08/1917
Operation(al) Order(s)	9th. Divisional Artillery Operation Order No. 141	17/08/1917	17/08/1917
Miscellaneous	Letters of Appreciation to Battalion in connection with Raid on August 18th. 1917	18/08/1917	18/08/1917
Diagram etc	Yorkshire Bank. Sheet 52		
Operation(al) Order(s)	App. Ref. War Diary. 10th. Argyll And Suth. Highrs. 10th. Argyll And Suth. Highrs., Operation Order No. 116, of The 30th. August, 1917. By Major N. McQueen D.S.O., Commdg.,	30/08/1917	30/08/1917
Map	Square K.		
War Diary	Gomiecourt.	01/09/1917	10/09/1917
War Diary	Watou (Belgian).	13/09/1917	13/09/1917

War Diary	Poperinghe.	15/09/1917	16/09/1917
War Diary	Toronto Camp.	17/09/1917	18/09/1917
War Diary	Ypres.	19/09/1917	20/09/1917
War Diary	Ypres Battle.	20/09/1917	21/09/1917
War Diary	Brandhoek Area.	21/09/1917	26/09/1917
War Diary	Ypres.	26/09/1917	27/09/1917
War Diary	Eringhem.	28/09/1917	30/09/1917
Miscellaneous	App. Ref. War Diary. Letters of Appreciation. 10th. Argyll And Sutherland Highlanders.	08/09/1917	08/09/1917
War Diary	Eringhem.	01/10/1917	11/10/1917
War Diary	Paschendaele Ridge Battle.	12/10/1917	13/10/1917
War Diary	Ypres.	14/10/1917	14/10/1917
War Diary	Ypres. (Siege Camp).	14/10/1917	26/10/1917
War Diary	Coudekerque (Dunkirk).	28/10/1917	28/10/1917
War Diary	Nieuport Les Bains.	28/10/1917	31/10/1917
War Diary	Nieuport Bains.	03/11/1917	06/11/1917
War Diary	Oost Dunkirk.		
War Diary	Coxyde Bains.	08/11/1917	22/11/1917
War Diary	Crecky.	22/11/1917	02/12/1917
War Diary	Peronne.	03/12/1917	08/12/1917
War Diary	Gouzeaucourt.	00/12/1917	31/12/1917
Operation(al) Order(s)	26th. (Highland) Brigade Operation Order No. 149	11/10/1917	11/10/1917
Miscellaneous	26th. (Highland) Brigade. Narrative of Operations on October 11th., 12th., And 13th., East of St. Julien. App 3		
Heading	D.A.G. (War Diaries) Base.		
Heading	9th Division 26th Machine Gun Coy. 26th Machine Gun Coy. Feb 1916-Dec 1917		
Heading	26 M.G. Coy Vol 1, 2, 3 Feb 1916 Dec 1917		
War Diary		01/02/1916	01/02/1916
War Diary	Ploegsteert.	01/02/1916	30/04/1916
Miscellaneous	26th Brigade Machine Gun Company.	31/05/1916	31/05/1916
War Diary		01/05/1916	31/05/1916
Miscellaneous	26th Brigade Machine Gun Company.	30/06/1916	30/06/1916
War Diary		01/06/1916	30/06/1916
Heading	26th Bde. 9th Division. War Diary 26th Machine Gun Company. July 1916 Operations On The Somme.		
War Diary		01/07/1916	30/07/1916
Miscellaneous	26th Bde M.G. Co. War Diary-5.7.16-19.7.16	05/07/1916	05/07/1916
Miscellaneous	Notes From Recent Operations.	31/07/1916	31/07/1916
Miscellaneous	26th Infantry Brigade.	30/06/1917	30/06/1917
War Diary		01/08/1916	04/01/1917
War Diary	Gonnelieu.	02/01/1917	29/01/1917
War Diary	Bray. Sur Somme.	30/01/1917	31/01/1917
Miscellaneous	Officer Casualties During January.		
War Diary		05/01/1917	31/03/1917
War Diary	In The Field.	01/04/1917	30/06/1917
Miscellaneous	26th. Infantry Brigade.	01/08/1917	01/08/1917
War Diary		01/07/1917	30/09/1917
Miscellaneous	26th Highland Brigade.	01/11/1917	01/11/1917
War Diary		01/10/1917	31/10/1917
Miscellaneous	A Form Messages And Signals.		
War Diary	The Field.	01/11/1917	30/11/1917
Miscellaneous	26th Highland Brigade.	02/01/1918	02/01/1918
War Diary		01/12/1917	31/12/1917

Heading	9 Div 26 Bde 26 Trench Mortar Bty 1915 June. 1915 Nov.		
Heading	4th Div. IV & VI Div. 26th Trench How 27 Batty. Vol 1 9-30.6.15		
War Diary	IV and VI Divns.	09/06/1915	30/06/1915
War Diary	12 Inf. Bde.	11/06/1915	23/07/1915
War Diary		13/07/1915	13/07/1915
War Diary	S.H.	13/07/1915	13/07/1915
War Diary	W.	16/07/1915	16/07/1915
War Diary	W.F.	16/07/1915	16/07/1915
War Diary	R.	16/07/1915	25/07/1915
War Diary	W.	26/07/1915	29/09/1915
War Diary		04/11/1915	04/11/1915
War Diary	Armentieres.	11/10/1915	17/10/1915
War Diary		11/10/1915	12/10/1915
Diagram etc	Further Details of the German T.M. Bomb Described as a Num Jan in Report.		
War Diary		30/09/1915	04/10/1915
War Diary	'B' Service. Sheet. 28.N.W. I.11.b.5.2. To I.11.d.6.8	30/10/1915	07/11/1915
War Diary	I.11.b.6.3 to I.11.d.1.5.7	10/11/1915	11/11/1915

9TH DIVISION
26TH INFY BDE

10TH BN ARGYLL & SUTHERLAND HDRS

MAY 1916 - DEC 1917

from 27 BDE: 9 DIV.

to 32 DIV 97 BDE

May 1916 – Dec 1917 from 27 Bde 9/5 96/9

Instructions regarding War Diaries and Intelligence Summaries are contained in F. S. Regs., Part II. and the Staff Manual respectively. Title Pages will be prepared in manuscript.

WAR DIARY
or
INTELLIGENCE SUMMARY
(Erase heading not required.)

Army Form C. 2118

Vol 13

10th Argyll & Sutherland Highlanders

Place	Date	Hour	Summary of Events and Information	Remarks and references to Appendices
PLOEGSTEERT Area	1916 May 2		Brigadier General Trotter (27th Brigade) was thrown from his horse and [illegible] and was [illegible] to [illegible] by [illegible] [illegible] Lt Col. W. J. B. Tweedie commanding 27 Bde. during the [illegible] of [illegible] a week	
	3		Enemy appear to have at last discovered the [illegible] [illegible] as at about noon, 2 4.15 shells fell about [illegible] from the [illegible].	
	4		The Battalion has been moved from 27th Brigade to 26th Brigade on the arrangement of the Division, taking the place of [illegible] [illegible] Highlanders. The Battalion remained in Trenches for a further [illegible] of 6 days – During last 6 days, [illegible] [illegible] 3rd South African Regiment have been attached to us for instruction, prior to their joining the Division.	
	5	3.30 pm	Whilst a British [illegible] was [illegible] from [illegible] [illegible] [illegible] [illegible] [illegible] [illegible] [illegible] aeroplane and brought down in flames near HALTE behind Enemy's lines. The 2 [illegible] were seen to fall out. Casualties today 2 killed & wounded.	

1875 Wt. W593/826 1,000,000 4/15 J.B.C. & A. A.D.S.S./Forms/C. 2118.

13-0

9 [illegible]

Instructions regarding War Diaries and Intelligence Summaries are contained in F. S. Regs., Part II. and the Staff Manual respectively. Title Pages will be prepared in manuscript.

WAR DIARY
or
INTELLIGENCE SUMMARY
(Erase heading not required.)

Army Form C. 2118

10th Argyll & Sutherland Highrs

Place	Date 1916	Hour	Summary of Events and Information	Remarks and references to Appendices
PLOEGSTEERT Area	May 6	10.30 am	A disquieting day on the whole - At 10.30 am as the C.O. was conversing with Coy Commanders (also C.O. and Coy Commanders of 9th Scottish Rifles) a machine gun opened on them, bullets striking the ground all round, and though at one time it looked as if it would mean a good bag for the Germans, Casualties were nil.	
		5 pm	In the afternoon we registered with a few Rifle grenades, this caused some annoyance to Boche who retaliated with salvoes of Grenades, Fish Tail Bombs and 7.7 Cm. getting several direct hits on Market Garden behind "A" Coy HQrs - no damage was done, apart from enemy obtaining 2 direct hits on St. YVES AVENUE knocking down parapet.	
		8.30 pm	Gas alarm sounded on our Right - Artillery duel at the same time being heard N Gas did not reach our front.	
			It appears impossible to do any harm with our limited number of Bombs and Grenades - The few we are allowed is merely "playing at war" whatever we send over is retaliated with by 5 times as many and enemy shooting is uniformally good and he generally wounds a few in his retaliation. Casualties today 2 Killed 2 wounded.	

1875 Wt W593/826 1,000,000 4/15 J.B.C. & A. A.D.S.S./Forms/C. 2118.

Instructions regarding War Diaries and Intelligence Summaries are contained in F. S. Regs., Part II. and the Staff Manual respectively. Title Pages will be prepared in manuscript.

WAR DIARY
or
INTELLIGENCE SUMMARY
(Erase heading not required.)

Army Form C. 2118

Place	Date	Hour	Summary of Events and Information	Remarks and references to Appendices
PLOEGSTEERT Area	6		by 5 times as many and Enemy shooting is uniformally Good – we do very small harm to Boche but he generally wounds a few in his retaliation –	
			Casualties today 2 killed 2 wounded –	
	7		Do	

1875 Wt. W593/826 1,000,000 4/15 J.B.C. & A. A.D.S.S./Forms/C. 2118.

Instructions regarding War Diaries and Intelligence Summaries are contained in F. S. Regs., Part II. and the Staff Manual respectively. Title Pages will be prepared in manuscript.

WAR DIARY
or
INTELLIGENCE SUMMARY
(Erase heading not required.)

Army Form C. 2118

10th Arg: Suth: High[rs]

Place	Date	Hour	Summary of Events and Information	Remarks and references to Appendices
Ploegsteert	May 6th	4 pm	Bunhill Row near Battalion Headquarters shelled by 4.2 Enemy Battery at Messines. Considerable damage done to Trolley line and Strand and 1 man killed + 2 wounded	
Papot	8th		Relieved by 9th Scottish Rifles and Battalion goes to Billets at Papot	
			Extending from centre of PICQUET HOUSE locality the left of T.120. It was most violent against HAMPSHIRE T. locality and consisted of 15, 10.5 and 7.7 cm shells, Trench Mortars (minenwerfers) and Rifle grenades. Very large craters were made in certain places, which may have been caused by either 21 cm or heavy Trench Mortars, probably the latter. At 7.40 pm bombardment ceased	

1875 Wt. W593/826 1,000,000 4/15 J.B.C. & A. A.D.S.S./Forms/C. 2118.

Instructions regarding War Diaries and Intelligence Summaries are contained in F. S. Regs., Part II. and the Staff Manual respectively. Title Pages will be prepared in manuscript.

WAR DIARY
or
INTELLIGENCE SUMMARY
(Erase heading not required.)

Army Form C. 2118

10th Argyll & Sutherland Hrs

Place	Date	Hour	Summary of Events and Information	Remarks and references to Appendices
	May 14		It was found impossible to clear the trenches and movement was out of the question.	
			The moment the bombardment ceased, all men who were able to stand, lined the parapet ready to resist a raid.	
			The situation was well in hand.	
			The second bombardment commenced at about 7.50 Pm and continued with unabated violence till 8.45 Pm.	
			It was even more intense than the first bombardment and a much greater proportion of fire was directed against the support lines.	
			Our left and centre groups retaliated vigorously.	
			The 60 Pdrs, 6" guns and Howitzers of Right group assisted in this retaliation, and the flanking section of Right Division enfiladed enemy trenches.	
			The raiders went in 3 parties of about 20 each, reaching our parapet about 9.00 Pm.	
			Surprise in each case seems to have been mutual, as the fire had barely lifted when 2Lt HENRY saw the Germans on the parapet. To use 2Lt Henry's own words "I shot them down like rats and more got in" but a few apparently gained a footing at junction of T.117 & C.T.117	

1875 Wt. W593/826 1,000,000 4/15 J.B.C. & A. A.D.S.S./Forms/C. 2118.

Instructions regarding War Diaries and Intelligence Summaries are contained in F. S. Regs., Part II. and the Staff Manual respectively. Title Pages will be prepared in manuscript.

WAR DIARY
or
INTELLIGENCE SUMMARY
(Erase heading not required.)

Army Form C. 2118

10th Argyll & Sutherland Hrs

Place	Date	Hour	Summary of Events and Information	Remarks and references to Appendices
	May 14		The Lewis Gun did not take part, and has since been found lying buried in the arms of a Lewis gunner, the entire team of the Lewis Guns were killed.	
			Enemy left 13 dead behind of 104th Regt 40th Divn.	
			In German communiqué it is stated they blew in a mine shaft and took 10 Prisoners, neither of which statements is true as we had no mine in that area and all our casualties are accounted for except 5 who there is little doubt are buried in our lines.	
			So the objects of the raid was foiled, the plan being no doubt to find a mine and destroy the shaft.	
			Enemy destroyed a good deal of our trenches which were repaired during the same night and the 2 following days. They must have fired about 4000 shells, the rate of fire at one time being 36 to the minute.	
			Our casualties were about 20 killed and 75 wounded.	
			The Battalion attacked (11th Royal Scots) behaved magnificently.	
			The trenches they hold are on the immediate right of 10th Argylls	

1875 Wt. W593/826 1,000,000 4/15 J.B.C. & A. A.D.S.S./Forms/C. 2118.

Instructions regarding War Diaries and Intelligence Summaries are contained in F. S. Regs., Part II. and the Staff Manual respectively. Title Pages will be prepared in manuscript.

WAR DIARY
or
INTELLIGENCE SUMMARY
(Erase heading not required.)

Army Form C. 2118

Place	Date	Hour	Summary of Events and Information	Remarks and references to Appendices
	May 16		During the Bombardment Enemy heavily shelled S+N 58 and S.2 doing considerable damage but there were only 5 men wounded.	
			Parties from 41st Div are being attached to the Battalion for instruction before taking over the line.	
			Col Tweedie 2/8 Royal Scots attached for 3 days from home.	
	16		Gen. Sir Charles Fergusson (the Corps Commander) visited the Trenches	
	17.		We strafed certain points with Rifle Grenades and Trench Mortars with considerable accuracy. Boche retaliating also shelling S 2 N. 2 men wounded.	
			During night there was a gas alarm but nothing happened on our sector	
			Lt. W. F. FRENCH rejoined 6 May	
			2/Lt. D. M. RAMSAY joined 9 May.	
			Capt R. C. MACFARLANE } 2nd Lt. T. S. GIBSON } joined 14 May.	
			2nd Lt. C. W. GLASS joined 15 May	
			Lt. R. A. COLVIN (Intelligence Officer) was wounded 14 May.	

1875 Wt. W593/826 1,000,000 4/15 J.B.C. & A. A.D.S.S./Forms/C. 2118.

Instructions regarding War Diaries and Intelligence Summaries are contained in F. S. Regs., Part II. and the Staff Manual respectively. Title Pages will be prepared in manuscript.

Army Form C. 2118

WAR DIARY
or
INTELLIGENCE SUMMARY
(Erase heading not required.)

10 Argyll & Sutherland Hrs.

Place	Date	Hour	Summary of Events and Information	Remarks and references to Appendices
Papot	1916 May 20		Battalion relieved in the Trenches by 9th Scottish Rifles, and returned to Billets in PAPOT. Weather since 16th May extremely hot.	
	24	2.25 pm	Aeroplane flew over Billets dropping a Bomb 200 yds from us N.E.	
PLOEGSTEERT area	26	8 am.	Battalion relieved 9th Scottish Rifles in Trenches. Enemy Artillery Active.	
		6 pm.	Owing to the usual shortage of Stokes Gun and Trench Mortar Ammunition, we were able to fire the miserable number of 12 rounds from our Stokes Gun, needless to say Enemy immediately retaliated with 50 Trench Mortars and Rifle Grenades and 80 rounds of 77.cm – Our Barracks received a direct hit – one casualty.	
PAPOT	29		Battalion relieved by 11th Royal West Kent Regiment and returned to Billets in PAPOT. The 10th A & S. H's have now handed over the PLOEGSTEERT TRENCHES, 121, 122, 123 which they have held since 1st Feb, and are leaving them in a very much improved state, ~~than how they were taken over then~~ – At that time there was very little more than a Fire Trench and but little wire – Now S1, S2, S4 have been completed & S3 is a very useful Trench to shelter in under heavy bombardment. Westminster Avenue, St Yves and Lone House Communication Trenches are in good order – Dug outs have been built in Support Lines. Cellars reclaimed & concreted	

1875 Wt. W593/826 1,000,000 4/15 J.B.C. & A. A.D.S.S./Forms/C. 2118.

Instructions regarding War Diaries and Intelligence Summaries are contained in F. S. Regs., Part II. and the Staff Manual respectively. Title Pages will be prepared in manuscript.

WAR DIARY
or
INTELLIGENCE SUMMARY
(Erase heading not required.)

Army Form C. 2118

10th Argyll & Sutherland Hrs

Place	Date	Hour	Summary of Events and Information	Remarks and references to Appendices
PAPOT	1916 May 29		and wells opened up – New Battalion HQ have been built near Dead Horse Corner and are now ready for occupation – Machine Gun emplacements have been built in various positions in the wood and wire laid in every direction – Every path that is used has now Duck Boards laid down. As to the Front line all the Dug Outs have been strongly rebuilt and facing the rear, a Control Trench runs from N to S. Traverses strengthened and the line should be safe from the effect of at least 7.7 Cm. Shells – A great quantity of wire has been put out in front and a commencement made in wiring behind the Parados – Owing to the Support line Trenches being completed it has been possible to thin the Front line and now it is held by 6 Platoons, the remaining 6 Platoons being accommodated in Support lines.	

1875 Wt. W593/826 1,000,000 4/15 J.B.C. & A. A.D.S.S./Forms/C. 2118.

Instructions regarding War Diaries and Intelligence Summaries are contained in F. S. Regs., Part II. and the Staff Manual respectively. Title Pages will be prepared in manuscript.

WAR DIARY
or
INTELLIGENCE SUMMARY
(Erase heading not required.)

Army Form C. 2118

10th Argyll & Sutherland Hrs

Place	Date	Hour	Summary of Events and Information	Remarks and references to Appendices
	1916		APPENDIX XIX attached (Casualty Return)	
			APPENDIX XX " (GAME BOOK)	
			The Game Book shows that our Snipers have not been idle in accounting for Huns during the period in which we have held this Sector.	
LA CRECHE Area	May 31	5.30 am	Battalion left PAPOT for Divisional Rest at ENQUIN LES MINES proceeding by Route march to LA CRECHE area where Battalion billeted for night. (4½ miles)	

W. [illegible] Lt Col
Comdg 10th A & S Hrs

1875 Wt W593/826 1,000,000 4/15 J.B.C. & A. A.D.S.S./Forms/C. 2118.

CASUALTY STATEMENT.

MAY.

APPENDIX XIX

DATE	KILLED	WOUNDED	MISSING	ADMITTED TO HOSPITAL	DISCHARGED HOSPITAL	DRAFTS.
1	1	2		2	2.	
2.		1		2	1.	33.
3.					2.	
4.	1	4			4	1
5.		6		2	3.	46.
6	1	4		1		
7.				3	2.	
8.		2		2	2.	
9.						1.
10.				4	4.	
11.						
12.				2	5	
13		1.			1.	
14		1.		1.	2.	2.
15				1.		
16				2.		
17				2	3	
18		3.			1	
19		1.			5.	
20				1	2.	
21						
22.					1	
23				3	1	1.
24				1.	1.	
25				2.		
26		2		1.		
27				1.		
28					1.	
29				8.		
30						
31				2.		

Instructions regarding War Diaries and Intelligence Summaries are contained in F. S. Regs., Part II. and the Staff Manual respectively. Title Pages will be prepared in manuscript.

WAR DIARY
or
INTELLIGENCE SUMMARY
(Erase heading not required.)

IX

10th Argyll + Sutherland H'rs

Army Form C. 2118

June

Vol 14

Place	Date	Hour	Summary of Events and Information	Remarks and references to Appendices
	1916			
DOULIEU area.	June 1	3.30. pm	Resumed march to Billets in DOULIEU Area (4 miles).	
MORBECQUE area	3	1 pm.	Resumed march to billets in MORBECQUE area (11 miles) marching past in Brigade when Lt. Gen: Sir Herbert Plumer – 2nd Army Commander – inspected the Brigade – It is understood that the 2nd Army Commander was favourably impressed with the appearance and march discipline of the Brigade.	
ENQUIN LES MINES	4	1 pm.	March resumed via AIRE, WITTERNESSE, ESTRÉE BLANCHE arriving ENQUIN LES MINES 7.30. pm (16 miles) – ½ Coy billeted in FLECHINELLE remainder in village. BIRTHDAY HONOURS announced in which the following officers names in the Battalion appeared Lt. Col W. J. B TWEEDIE C.M.G. Major J. C. SCOTT. D.S.O Capt I. M. STEWART Military Cross Capt F. J. D. KNOWLING Military Cross.	

14:0

1875 Wt. W593/826 1,000,000 4/15 J.B.C. & A. A.D.S.S./Forms/C. 2118.

Instructions regarding War Diaries and Intelligence Summaries are contained in F. S. Regs., Part II. and the Staff Manual respectively. Title Pages will be prepared in manuscript.

WAR DIARY
or
INTELLIGENCE SUMMARY
(Erase heading not required.)

Army Form C. 2118

10th Argyll & Sutherld Highrs

Place	Date 1916	Hour	Summary of Events and Information	Remarks and references to Appendices
			Sergt. A. COCHRANE ("A" Coy) awarded Military Medal	
ENQUIN LES MINES.	June 5		The day was devoted to Company Training	
	6		Do.	
			Capt F. J. D. KNOWLING left the Battalion to be attached 27th Brigade for instruction in Staff duties	
			Lt. R. D. THOMSON appointed Regimental Transport Officer vice Capt Knowling -	
			Capt Rev J. E. MOFFETT transferred as Chaplain to 27th Brigade.	
			The remainder of period at ENQUIN LES MINES devoted to Training of which there were two days of Brigade Training.	
	8		Major J. C. Scott D.S.O. left to take command of the combined 6/7 Batt: Royal Scots Fusiliers in the 15th Division	
	10		Brigade Horse Show at which the Battalion won 2 Firsts, 2 Seconds and 3 Third Prizes.	

1875 Wt. W593/826 1,000,000 4/15 J.B.C. & A. A.D.S.S./Forms/C. 2118.

Instructions regarding War Diaries and Intelligence Summaries are contained in F. S. Regs., Part II. and the Staff Manual respectively. Title Pages will be prepared in manuscript.

WAR DIARY
or
INTELLIGENCE SUMMARY
(Erase heading not required.)

Army Form C. 2118.

10th Argyll + Sutherland Highlanders

Place	Date 1916	Hour	Summary of Events and Information	Remarks and references to Appendices
June 14		2 AM	Batt: proceeded by Route March to BERQUETTE – 7 miles – for entrainment to AMIENS, from there marching to ST SAUVEUR – 10 miles.. Billeted in village on banks of RIVER SOMME.	
ST SAUVEUR			Div: now belongs to 13th Corps in 4th Army –	
	16		Officers taken in relays to Trenches near BRAY to visit the position of the proposed Offensive	
			The following are "mentioned" in Despatches in London Gazette of May 15.	
			Lt Col W. J. B. TWEEDIE CMG	
			Major J. C. SCOTT D.S.O	
			Lt + Adjt W. S. STEVENSON	
			C.S.M. D. McLAUCHLAN	
			Sergt A. COCHRANE	
			Lce Corpl R. DUFFIN	
			Trenches have been dug near here, exact replicas of those of ours and the enemy's in MARICOURT – MONTAUBAN area.	
	23.		Trained to CORBIE – 16 miles –	
	24 U. DAY		Preliminary Bombardment to the attack commenced –	
	25		Marched to VAUX SUR SOMME – 2 miles – under canvas.	
	27		Marched to BOIS LES CELESTINS – 5 miles.	
	29		Whilst Batt was drilling a Wild Boar appeared out of the wood – Owing to Bayonets not being fixed at the time the opportunity of pig sticking was missed.	

10th Argyll & Suth'd High'rs

Casualty Statement for June, 1916:—

Date.	Killed	Wounded	Missing	To hospital	From hospital	Drafts.
1st				5	.	
2nd				4		
3rd				3	1.	
4th				8	5.	
5"				.	13.	
6"		1.		1	2	5. Officers.
7"				3	.	
8"				.	1.	
9"				2	.	
10"				1	1.	
11"				.	.	
12"				2	.	
13"				4	3	
14"				1	1	
15"				.	4	
16"				5.	.	1. O.R.
17"	1.			2.	1	
18"					.	
19"					2.	8. O.R.
20"				1.		2. Officers.
21st				1.	.	
22nd				2.	1.	
23rd				.	2.	
24th				.	1.	
25"				1.	.	
26"				3.	.	49. O.R.
27"				1.	1	
28"					.	
29"					.	
30"				1.	1.	

26th Inf.Bde.
9th Div.

10th BATTN. THE ARGYLL & SUTHERLAND HIGHLANDERS.

J U L Y

1 9 1 6

Attached:

Appendices XXIII &
XXIV.

Instructions regarding War Diaries and Intelligence Summaries are contained in F. S. Regs., Part II. and the Staff Manual respectively. Title Pages will be prepared in manuscript.

WAR DIARY
or
INTELLIGENCE SUMMARY
(Erase heading not required.)

Army Form C. 2118.

N/a 9 July

10th ARGYLL and SUTHERLAND Hi'rs

Vol. 15

Place	Date 1916	Hour	Summary of Events and Information	Remarks and references to Appendices
BOIS DE CELESTINS	July 1		The Bombardment prior to the advance which commenced June 24 and should have been completed June 29 was extended for a further period of 48 hours owing to excessive rains but finally culminated at 6 am July 1st when an intense Bombardment started and continued until 7.30. am. when the Infantry attack was launched – On our front 18th & 30th Divisions went over the parapet side by side – Those who saw them say it was done as it would have been on parade, perfect alignment being kept – 18th Division are said to have started kicking a football in front of them! 30th Division encountered little opposition until taking the first German Trench when they had continuous severe fighting before MONTAUBAN was seized at about 10.30 am. and during the day the objective was reached.	
			18th Division on the left encountered serious opposition at the CRATERS and CASINO POINT but nevertheless reached their objective.	
		8 pm	Batt: moved to GROVE TOWN (3 miles) and bivouacked.	
	2		From verbal accounts it appears that enemy expected attack to be made 48 hours previously, when it was originally intended and were unable to understand what was happening – It is supposed that he was caught during a Relief. On going over the Ground many of the Dug outs which are 20 ft deep remained, it was found,	15.0

Army Form C. 2118.

WAR DIARY
or
INTELLIGENCE SUMMARY

(Erase heading not required.)

10th Argyll & Sutherland Highrs

Instructions regarding War Diaries and Intelligence Summaries are contained in F. S. Regs., Part II. and the Staff Manual respectively. Title Pages will be prepared in manuscript.

Place	Date 1916	Hour	Summary of Events and Information	Remarks and references to Appendices
GROVE TOWN	July 2		intact and the inmates fairly safe from Shell fire – this would account for so many being left to repel the attack –	
			Enemy did not appear to relish our Bombs. Most of his Bombs found were found to be of the Cylindrical kind.	
			Our aeroplanes and Kite Balloons hold complete mastery of the air in these parts, hardly one of the enemy's being seen.	
BILLON VALLEY	4		2nd in Command and Adjt visited MONTAUBAN in morning – Lachrymatory shells were falling at junction of MINE ALLEY and MILL LANE, near entrance to MONTAUBAN	
			Batt. received orders to move at 6 pm to BILLON VALLEY (3 miles) – Going very heavy owing to rains – Lewis Gun Teams had hard work pulling carts by hand through mud of X Road – Only one man fell out and he was suffering from pneumonia.	
			1st Line Transport remained GROVE TOWN with 2nd in Command, Assistant Adjutant and 6 Reinforcement officers.	
	5.		Batt. sent parties to reconnoitre way to TALUS BOISÉ, CARNOY and MONTAUBAN. Had usual inspections.	
			Guns of all calibre being moved up and 2nd German line being bombarded previous to next advance.	

2449 Wt. W14957/M90 750,000 1/16 J.B.C. & A. Forms/C.2118/12.

Army Form C. 2118.

Instructions regarding War Diaries and Intelligence Summaries are contained in F. S. Regs., Part II. and the Staff Manual respectively. Title Pages will be prepared in manuscript.

WAR DIARY
or
INTELLIGENCE SUMMARY
(Erase heading not required.)

10. Argyll & Sutherland Highrs

Place	Date 1916	Hour	Summary of Events and Information	Remarks and references to Appendices
BILLON VALLEY	July 5		C.O went to Trenches in afternoon – Early in evening a large number of aeroplanes passed over going towards German lines (possibly a bombing excursion).	
			A French Priest – M. Rudeyski (a Pole) attached to 60th Regiment of Artillery, just arrived from Verdun visited us and asked for some music –	
			arranged a foursome reel and some pipe music for the edification of the French Troops in the Valley.	
	6		Coys on working parties round TALUS BOISÉ Railway.	
			Next day one of the parties returned saying they were given guides of 2 Artillery Officers to point out the place where the lines were to be laid.	
			In the dark they lost touch, so our officer brought the men back a little distance –	
			He then discovered that these two officers who were acting as their guides had been arrested as spies! Consequently no work could be done that night.	
			Every man in the Regt has been served out with 2 detonated bombs – up to date none have exploded!	
			The French Priest, this time accompanied by the Colonel of the Regiment – Col Fontano – returned for a further display of reel dancing.	
			This Battery is one of those who marched 100 miles in 3 days to the relief of Verdun	
			The XXth Iron Corps which crowned itself with glory at Verdun is also on our right.	

2449 Wt. W14957/M90 750,000 1/16 J.B.C. & A. Forms/C.2118/12.

Army Form C. 2118.

WAR DIARY
or
INTELLIGENCE SUMMARY
(Erase heading not required.)

10th Argyll & Sutherland Highrs

Instructions regarding War Diaries and Intelligence Summaries are contained in F. S. Regs., Part II. and the Staff Manual respectively. Title Pages will be prepared in manuscript.

Place	Date 1916	Hour	Summary of Events and Information	Remarks and references to Appendices
BILLON VALLEY	July 6	6.15 pm.	C.O. went to Conference at Brigade office – received first information about forthcoming attack by 26 Brigade on LONGUEVAL.	
	7	2 am.	Party set out to reconnoitre – meeting place was old front line of German Trench where Guides from 12 Royal Scots (27 Brigade) met them. Followed up TALUS BOISÉ Railway, leaving MONTAUBAN which was being shelled, on left – Skirted BERNAFAY WOOD on West side and entered Trench held by "D" Coy, 12 Royal Scots, N. side of WOOD – There are no Germans near here with the possible exception of a few in TRONES WOOD (due E). – Considerably harrassed however by F.O.Os in WINDMILL at LONGUEVAL, and in Chimney at WATERLOT FARM. Returned to BATT H.Q leaving 2nd Lt STOTT and CORP. CAMERON to carry on reconnaissance throughout day and next night – Batt HQ is in midst of a German Battery which has been shelled out and Guns still here. 2nd Lt STOTT came down in afternoon with good report on Ground of our advance – 3 am – 5 am seems most favourable time. He returned to continue his reconnaissance tonight.	
	8	9 am.	Brigade Conference – received further details of advance on LONGUEVAL. "B" & "D" Coys moved off at 2. pm. "B" to occupy front line W of BERNAFAY WOOD "D" on N.E side of MONTAUBAN – at 4. pm remainder of Batt: moved off. H.Q. to N.W Corner of MONTAUBAN – "A" & "C" Coys to open Ground between MONTAUBAN and BRESLAU SUPPORT TRENCH – 8/BLACK WATCH on our right. 7/SEAFORTHS supporting us 5/CAMERONS supporting BLACK WATCH.	

2449 Wt. W14957/M90 750,000 1/16 J.B.C. & A. Forms/C.2118/12.

Instructions regarding War Diaries and Intelligence Summaries are contained in F. S. Regs., Part II. and the Staff Manual respectively. Title Pages will be prepared in manuscript.

WAR DIARY
or
INTELLIGENCE SUMMARY
(Erase heading not required.)

Army Form C. 2118.

10th Argyll & Sutherland Hghrs.

Place	Date 1916	Hour	Summary of Events and Information	Remarks and references to Appendices
	July 8		PERONNE ROAD heavily shelled just as last of Batt crossed it. Coys in position all right – "A" & "C" being in BRESLAU SUPPORT, BACK ALLEY and DUG OUT TRENCH. Established HQ in MONTAUBAN, signalling station being some distance away. This got into communication early with Brigade – only Batt to establish communication before 9 pm. – Rear Coys took up positions of "B" & "D" Quiet night – Received visit from Staff Captain (Capt. Grahame) and Brigade Major (Major Conyers) son of Corps Commander 76 Brigade. Capt Grahame was hit later in CEN[T]RE STREET and died before MO could reach him.	
MONTAUBAN.	9.	[4] am.	C.O. visited "B" Coy who had now established his permanent position with 2 Lewis guns signal communication with "B" & "D" Coys. Intelligence reports of 2nd Lt. CASSIE and STOTT sent to Brigade. They have done continuous good reconnoitring during last 2 days. Shelling light during morning. 2nd Lt. MITCHELL (wounded) to duty.	
		11 am.	All quiet – It is found that the presence of our aeroplanes in the air keeps enemy silent, not being anxious to disclose his new gun positions. Shelling became considerable between 3 and 5 pm becoming very heavy at 5 pm. at which hour Brigade telephoned for C.O. to attend conference.	

2449 Wt. W14957/M90 750,000 1/16 J.B.C. & A. Forms/C.2118/12.

Instructions regarding War Diaries and Intelligence Summaries are contained in F. S. Regs., Part II. and the Staff Manual respectively. Title Pages will be prepared in manuscript.

Army Form C. 2118.

WAR DIARY
or
INTELLIGENCE SUMMARY

(Erase heading not required.)

10. Argyll & Sutherland Highrs

Place	Date 1916	Hour	Summary of Events and Information	Remarks and references to Appendices
MONTAUBAN.	Aug 10.		During afternoon message received that S. End of TRONES WOOD was alone being held and to be prepared for counter attack.	
			On the whole an uneventful day –	
		3.30 am	2nd Lt CASSIE and RAMSAY came to report on their patrols – These 2 officers have done very good work during last 2 nights – 2nd Lt CASSIE succeeded in laying tapes as guides along proposed line of advance. Shelling intermittent throughout day and especially severe during afternoon between 4 and 5 PM – German shelling raised to knock out battery of 18 Pounders which has come into action 30 yds behind HQ but they have not succeeded in frequently hitting HQ. At night started to place MONTAUBAN into a state of defence. Original centre KEEP useless so chose spot further E where there were some cellars and from which shelter might be given to BLACK WATCH if BERNAFAY WOOD were penetrated. Working party unfortunately shelled, 6 casualties including 2nd Lt GLASS (wounded) and 2nd Lt FALCONAR STEWART (wounded at duty). 2nd Lt RAIT was sent to take charge of work and on Adjt's going round later he found work proceeding very well – 2nd Lt RAIT had firm hold on party and with only a few details from Lt GLASS he had succeeded in making quite a sound strong point facing N and E – This officer had never been in action under shell fire previously which was quite heavy at times. No more casualties. Working party worked till dawn about 3.30 am and was shelled returning through CENTRE STREET	

Army Form C. 2118.

Instructions regarding War Diaries and Intelligence Summaries are contained in F. S. Regs., Part II. and the Staff Manual respectively. Title Pages will be prepared in manuscript.

WAR DIARY
or
INTELLIGENCE SUMMARY

(Erase heading not required.)

10th Argyll & Sutherland Highrs

Place	Date 1916	Hour	Summary of Events and Information	Remarks and references to Appendices
MONTAUBAN	Aug 11		Morning hate rather severe – 2nd Lt RAMSAY & CASSIE came to HQ about 3. P.m and made interesting report that they had systematically and thoroughly searched the left road and the whole of the ground in which it is proposed to extend Brigade for attack – 2nd Lt. CASSIE has done exceedingly cool ~~and~~ dangerous work during last three nights and along with 2nd Lt. STOTT has received valuable information for which our patrols amongst others have received thanks of Army Commander and C in C – Little of interest during day – Usual heavy shelling – situation in TRONES WOOD seems to have improved but we do not yet hold N. end. "B" Coy heavily shelled in afternoon from direction of DELVILLE WOOD and had Lewis Gun Team buried, but they were extricated with only 2 slightly wounded – About 3.30 P.m Brigade informed us we should be relieved by 7th Seaforth Highlanders tonight – On sending out message about relief to Coys received following acknowledgement from "B" "Your A D77 received thank the Lord". Capt Lewis has been in a horrid spot and over his scraping in which he lies under the parapet shells fall ceaselessly. The Coy has had constant shelling in a wide trench, originally a German C.T. – without a single dug out –	

2449 Wt. W14957/M90 750,000 1/16 J.B.C. & A. Forms/C.2118/12.

Army Form C. 2118.

Instructions regarding War Diaries and Intelligence Summaries are contained in F. S. Regs., Part II. and the Staff Manual respectively. Title Pages will be prepared in manuscript.

WAR DIARY
or
INTELLIGENCE SUMMARY
(Erase heading not required.)

10th Argyll & Sutherland Highlrs

Place	Date 1916	Hour	Summary of Events and Information	Remarks and references to Appendices
MONTAUBAN	July		BLACK WATCH and SOUTH AFRICAN BRIGADE have had a rough time in front line.	
	11		Owing to relief being effected in daylight we had a few casualties.	
			2nd Lt. W. Y. DRUMMOND killed and 4 men wounded.	
TALUS BOISE			Brigadier said he wished Battalion to have a nights rest before the attack – they however found themselves immediately in front of 8 – 220 French Mortars – Noise worse than ever.	
			However men are very cheerful.	
	12		Nothing of note happened – In afternoon practised battle positions with markers.	
	13		Batt moved up a few yards into VALLEY TRENCH so as to be in position for the advance which is timed for 3.25 am.	
			By 7.30 pm Batt was in forward position in VALLEY TRENCH and VALLEY SUPPORT (the old Hun front line).	
			Heavy shelling again here with Crumps but only one man was hit.	
		8.30 pm	Operation orders arrived (These were discussed ? [illegible] in minute detail).	
		10.30 pm	Adj moved out with covering party and 18 guides to mark out tape lines for Batt to form up in NO MANS LAND.	

2449 Wt. W14957/M90 750,000 1/16 J.B.C. & A. Forms/C.2118/12.

Instructions regarding War Diaries and Intelligence Summaries are contained in F. S. Regs., Part II. and the Staff Manual respectively. Title Pages will be prepared in manuscript.

WAR DIARY
or
INTELLIGENCE SUMMARY
(Erase heading not required.)

Army Form C. 2118.

10th Argyll & Sutherland Highrs

Place	Date 1916	Hour	Summary of Events and Information	Remarks and references to Appendices
TALUS, BOISÉ	July 13	11.30 pm	Batt followed – got tapes laid with assistance of 2nd Lt. D.G. MILLER and Batt filed in position this was completed –	
			Took up position in 9 waves. "A" Coy on left flank, "B" Coy on right flank "C" " " " rear "D" " " " rear	
			HQ and reserve 4 Lewis Guns and 20 Bombers with 9th wave.	
			70 yds between waves.	
			Lay still in position until 3.25 a.m. when Batt began to move forward.	
	14.	3.25 am	Assault commenced and we easily penetrated the enemy's front line. "A" & "B" Coys moving forward, "C" Coy bombing W to assist 27 Brigade. This Coy killed about 100 Germans driving the remainder into the arms of 27th Brigade where they were probably captured. "C" Coy captured a machine gun in action, a well aimed bomb by 2nd Lt LAIDLAW accounting for the whole team – "A" "B" & "D" in a whole moved forward and were caught by our own barrage. This they attempted again and again to penetrate and had practically given up all hopes, when several officers including Lts CASSIE, DE BURGH, MITCHELL and DICKERSON came to the rescue and each collected a party of men and sat down in shell holes until it was obvious that the barrage had lifted. During this barrage a piper accompanied by Lts CASSIE and DE BURGH played "The Regimental March" through the village, the other pipers playing "The Charge"	

Army Form C. 2118.

Instructions regarding War Diaries and Intelligence Summaries are contained in F. S. Regs., Part II. and the Staff Manual respectively. Title Pages will be prepared in manuscript.

WAR DIARY
or
INTELLIGENCE SUMMARY
(Erase heading not required.)

Place	Date	Hour	Summary of Events and Information	Remarks and references to Appendices
	1916			
LONGUEVAL	July 14	4.15 am	We moved again and reached the objective CLARGES STREET (Central Street of LONGUEVAL) and were here again harassed by own Shell Fire – possibly the 220mm French Trench Mortar – This eventually lifted and "A" and "B" Coys started consolidating the front with the assistance of 9th Seaforth Highlanders who arrived later – Between these Coys was a gap (a Street running N+S named "Piccadilly" and in the N. part of this a M.G and Snipers were concealed who continually harassed us – Adjutant and 2nd Lt CASSIE who had led a party up a Trench on the S side of S. continuation of this Street attempted to drive them out with Rifles, a few Rifle Grenades and a Lewis Gun but several of our men were killed and 2nd Lt CASSIE severely wounded and the Snipers remained, killing amongst others 3 - 11th Royal Scots Officers during following morning. Work of consolidation continued and we linked up with 27th Brigade on left and 8th Black Watch on right though we could not quite touch latter owing to Machine Gun fire from [illegible] –	
			In afternoon 8th [illegible] filed through us and took up a N.W. formation in DELVILLE WOOD	
			Later since "A" Coy had no officers and only 40 men left they were relieved by "C" Coy who carried on the work and constructed a strong point on right – "A" and "D" Coys being in rear one in SLOANE STREET and one in old German Front Line, H.Q in front with Signalling Station in rear. By nightfall position was quite strong.	

2449 Wt. W14957/M90 750,000 1/16 J.B.C. & A. Forms/C.2118/12.

Instructions regarding War Diaries and Intelligence Summaries are contained in F. S. Regs., Part II. and the Staff Manual respectively. Title Pages will be prepared in manuscript.

WAR DIARY
or
INTELLIGENCE SUMMARY
(Erase heading not required.)

Army Form C. 2118.

Place	Date 1916	Hour	Summary of Events and Information	Remarks and references to Appendices
LONGUEVAL	Aug. 14.		A Patrol of 50 men under 2/Lt. LEGGATT which was sent out after midnight was caught N of village between 2 machine guns and nearly wiped out – 10 men dribbled back next morning. Casualties during attack and day of 14th. Killed 2/Lt. C.H. DICKERSON Wounded Capt. A.T. NANKIVELL RAMC – (our Medical Officer) " Capt. R.C. MACFARLANE " 2/Lt. J. FALCONAR STEWART (since died of wounds) " 2/Lt. G. CASSIE " 2/Lt. J. S. STOTT " 2/Lt. C. MITCHELL " 2/Lt. H.M. DE BURGH. Missing 2/Lt. E.C. LEGGATT Following wounded but remained at duty Lt. Col. W.J.S. TWEEDIE Captain W.S. STEVENSON 2/Lt. J.L. LAIDLAW Other ranks. Killed 24 Wounded 107. Missing mostly killed 90 Regimental Sergeant Major EADIE was also killed. The experience of the attack seems to show that a barrage of such a period of 40 minutes after an attack has been once launched is an impossible thing to control as far as the Infantry is concerned. Practically the whole of the W side of village was captured and cleaned up while the barrages of our Artillery were still on and parties would have followed a rapid lift from point to point with greater advantage.	

Instructions regarding War Diaries and Intelligence Summaries are contained in F. S. Regs., Part II. and the Staff Manual respectively. Title Pages will be prepared in manuscript.

WAR DIARY
or
INTELLIGENCE SUMMARY
(Erase heading not required.)

Army Form C. 2118.

Place	Date	Hour	Summary of Events and Information	Remarks and references to Appendices
Longueval	15th		Passed comparatively quiet night with no incident to report except the loss of our patrol. Enemy were reported to have attacked strong point on our left front held by Royal Scots on two occasions and to have been driven off. At 11 AM situation unchanged though considerable activity shown on left and British troops were seen entering HIGH WOOD. During the afternoon 138 prisoners taken by the South Africans in DELVILLE WOOD passed through our lines. Cable informs situation was as before, with extraordinarily few casualties in spite of heavy shelling. This was doubtless due to our narrow and concealed trenches. During afternoon received message from S.A. stating they were running short of S.A.A. We sent up all spare bandoliers and sent party back to dump to bring up as much as possible. The enemy had launched a counter attack against them but it met with no success.	
			Patrols were out all night but met with no parties of the enemy.	
"	16th		During the forenoon the 27th Bde. attempted to clear up the situation in N. end of village. Attempts were made to destroy strong points during the morning with STOKES mortars and in the afternoon with 2" Heavy Trench Mortars. Owing to difficulty in locating actual position of these strong points, this was ineffective.	

2449 Wt. W14957/M90 750,000 1/16 J.B.C. & A. Forms/C.2118/12.

Instructions regarding War Diaries and Intelligence Summaries are contained in F. S. Regs., Part II. and the Staff Manual respectively. Title Pages will be prepared in manuscript.

WAR DIARY
or
INTELLIGENCE SUMMARY
(Erase heading not required.)

Army Form C. 2118.

Place	Date	Hour	Summary of Events and Information	Remarks and references to Appendices
			and we continued to be harassed by a few enemy snipers and machine guns. It was decided later to attempt to knock out these points with heavy howitzers.	
			Casualties to date Officers killed 2, wounded 7, wounded to duty 6, missing 1. O.R. 225.	
			On this day 2nd Lt J.L. LAIDLAW was wounded in the head for a second time and later (20th) he died in hospital from the effects of this injury.	
			~~Reconnaissance with heavy ...~~ During this day the enemy was reported to be digging a line SE from FLERS, thus continuing part of a line of trenches already prepared.	
			Under orders from Bde. we systematically searched all houses and dugouts in our area for a second time and reported all clear. Large quantities of new rifles, ammunition, smoke helmets and iron rations were found in one of the cellars.	
Longueval	17th		About midnight wire received ordering withdrawal of most of our troops from front line so that heavies might bombard strong points with safety. This was done with difficulty in the half hour allotted time. During morning Camerons made a second attack on WATERLOT FARM and succeeded in consolidating a line which included it.	
			During afternoon orders were received to relieve S.A. in DELVILLE WOOD, but this could not be carried out and was consequently postponed.	

Instructions regarding War Diaries and Intelligence Summaries are contained in F. S. Regs., Part II. and the Staff Manual respectively. Title Pages will be prepared in manuscript.

WAR DIARY
or
INTELLIGENCE SUMMARY
(Erase heading not required.)

Army Form C. 2118.

Place	Date	Hour	Summary of Events and Information	Remarks and references to Appendices
			Another attempt was made during the evening to drive enemy completely out of LONGUEVAL, this time by the 3rd Division on our left. We were again ordered to hold front trenches very lightly while being bombarded. Draft of 100 men arrived from Base.	
	18th		At 2.45 am the 2nd Gordons, 76 Infantry Bde, attacked N. of LONGUEVAL from west and succeeded in clearing it up to N. edge of wood. During early morning the enemy commenced a heavy bombardment which gradually developed into the most intensive fire which has been experienced by this Division during the present war. Our front trenches were still very lightly held, the majority of the men being in SLOANE ST. and the old front line German trench, both of which escaped the bombardment to a certain extent. About 6 pm on the bombardment slackening B & C Coys. led by CAPTS. WEIR and McQUEEN respectively, counterattacked on our old position and succeeded in driving back a large force of the enemy. At the same time D Coy, who had been sent forward under the very heavy bombardment to support the right of the Brigade, took part in the counter attack on the right which drove the enemy well back through DELVILLE WOOD. In this attack Lieut. R.T. SMITH, a most gallant officer, who was leading D Company, was killed by an enemy sniper, and Lieut. A.B. MURRAY was also killed while rallying a party of men.	

Instructions regarding War Diaries and Intelligence Summaries are contained in F. S. Regs., Part II. and the Staff Manual respectively. Title Pages will be prepared in manuscript.

WAR DIARY
or
INTELLIGENCE SUMMARY

(Erase heading not required.)

Army Form C. 2118.

Place	Date	Hour	Summary of Events and Information	Remarks and references to Appendices
	19th		A little later and while the situation was still unknown, the leading company of the 19th D.L.I. brought up by the Bde Liaison officer 2nd Lt. C.H. RAIT reported and was at once sent forward to support the right of the Brigade which was reported very weak. The second company which arrived was sent to support our own front and to fill any gap on the left, and establish communication on our left. We were already in touch with the Black Watch on the right. The third Company of D.L.I. was also sent forward to support the right of the Brigade, as this flank was still very weak. The fourth Coy was kept in reserve in the old front line German trench. At 8pm. Lt-Col. CONNELL D.S.O. Commdg 6 K.O.S.B. came up to take over, and we began to move across to the E side of LONGUEVAL all our troops which remained viz. our own A.B.T.C. Coys, 2 Coys of D.L.I. and one Coy H.L.I. which had also been sent up to support us. It proved most difficult to get into touch with all these parties, especially since the ground on the other side of the village was unknown to us, but by dawn the relief was carried out, and the whole of the 26 Bde with their supporting companies of D.L.I. and H.L.I. were on the E. side of the village. Dispositions were now as follows —	

Army Form C. 2118.

Instructions regarding War Diaries and Intelligence Summaries are contained in F. S. Regs., Part II. and the Staff Manual respectively. Title Pages will be prepared in manuscript.

WAR DIARY
or
INTELLIGENCE SUMMARY

(Erase heading not required.)

Place	Date	Hour	Summary of Events and Information	Remarks and references to Appendices
			In front line three coys. of [illegible] in support [illegible] line & reserve Lewis guns and Battalion bombers. In support in old German second line through village. A, B & C Coys and one coy. 18th H.L.I. – D Coy were still up in front and some were temporarily formed in DELVILLE WOOD with the South Africans. The remainder of the Brigade was in reserve and withdrawn during the course of the morning to CARNOY.	
			During the day news was received that on the preceding night 17/18th the transport had been heavily shelled. A new type of gas shell was also used and both the Quartermaster Lieut. W.R. WELLER and the Transport Officer 2nd Lt. D. THOMSON were hit twice and died most gallantly. In addition only one man was killed, but 15, including 3 Company QMSgts, were gassed and 17 horses were killed or had afterwards to be destroyed. Sergt. DIXON with great presence of mind sent back word at once and the wagons were brought home and the road cleared as quickly as possible under such conditions.	
			During the morning of the 17th the 53rd Brigade came through our trenches and pushed on into the wood. Fighting activity increased during the day and at 5 pm it was reported that the attack had got as far as PRINCES St, the central ride through the wood, but that casualties had been very heavy.	

2449 Wt. W14957/M90 750,000 1/16 J.B.C. & A. Forms/C.2118/12.

Instructions regarding War Diaries and Intelligence Summaries are contained in F. S. Regs., Part II. and the Staff Manual respectively. Title Pages will be prepared in manuscript.

WAR DIARY
or
INTELLIGENCE SUMMARY

(Erase heading not required.)

Army Form C. 2118.

Place	Date 1916	Hour	Summary of Events and Information	Remarks and references to Appendices
LONGUEVAL	19		During this attack MAJOR W. La T. CONGREVE DSO who had visited us several times in MONTAUBAN was unfortunately killed, thus leaving the 76th Bde without either Brigade Major or Staff Captain.	
			During the afternoon the Brigade Major brought word of a relief and 3 companies were withdrawn, leaving C Coy and the Reserve of Lewis Gunners and Bombers to support the D.L.I. About 10.30pm the 1st R.S.F. began to arrive, but the relief was only partly through when the enemy put a heavy barrage on the South end of the village. Our supporting Coy. was therefore delayed for some time but was eventually brought out intact by Capt. McQUEEN, the relief being completed about 2.30 a.m.	
CARNOY	20th		The Battalion rested in dugouts at CARNOY.	
			Lieut. W.B. MURRAY was buried in the Cemetery here; there were present Brig. Gen. A.B. RITCHIE CMG, Lt. Col. W.R. TWEEDIE CMG, Capt & Adjt. Lieut W.S. STEVENSON, Major H.G. SOTHEBY MVO and the Regimental pipers.	
SANDPIT near MEAULTE (close to ALBERT)		2pm	Marched to SAND PIT (4 miles) where Batt: bivouacked	
	21		Capt J.C.W. ANDERSON reported for duty from 15th Batt;	
			Checked Coy Rolls - and drew packs left behind at CORBIE.	
	22		Inspection by our Brigadier (General A.B. RITCHIE CMG) who thanked Brigade for their services during the month and particularly during fighting round LONGUEVAL	
			2nd Lt. A.J. McNAB and 2nd Lt. J. MACKIE reported from base for duty.	

Instructions regarding War Diaries and Intelligence Summaries are contained in F. S. Regs., Part II. and the Staff Manual respectively. Title Pages will be prepared in manuscript.

WAR DIARY
or
INTELLIGENCE SUMMARY

(Erase heading not required.)

Army Form C. 2118.

Place	Date 1916	Hour	Summary of Events and Information	Remarks and references to Appendices
SANDPIT	July 22.		Brigadier General H P BURN D.S.O lately commanding this Battalion passed through MEAULTE with 152 Brigade – 51st Division to take up position in MAMETZ WOOD.	
			2nd Batt Argyll & Sutherland Highlanders in 33rd Division encamped quite close –	
			7th & 8th Batts also passed through with 51st Division –	
	23rd.	7.30 am.	Moved from SANDPIT by route march for MERICOURT L'ABBE (6 miles) entraining in afternoon for HANGEST – Transport moved by road –	
VAUCHELLES LES DOMART	23rd.	5 pm.	Detrained HANGEST, marched to VAUCHELLES LES DOMART (8 miles) billetted in village – in spite of long march only 2 men fell out and these belonged to new Draft.	
			Batt H.Q. in 16th Century Chateau with Comtesse de St Sauveur	
	24th.		Inspection of complete kit	
	25	4 pm	Moved by Route March to LONGPRE (5 miles). Entraining 7.41 pm	
BRUAY	26	2 am	Detrained at BRYAS with Transport and marched to BRUAY – passing on the way 11th Batt Argyll & Sutherland Highrs belonging to 15th Division. Batt billetted in Town –	

2449 Wt. W14957/M90 750,000 1/16 J.B.C. & A. Forms/C.2118/12.

Instructions regarding War Diaries and Intelligence Summaries are contained in F. S. Regs., Part II. and the Staff Manual respectively. Title Pages will be prepared in manuscript.

WAR DIARY
or
INTELLIGENCE SUMMARY
(Erase heading not required.)

Army Form C. 2118.

Place	Date 1916	Hour	Summary of Events and Information	Remarks and references to Appendices
BRUAY.	Aug 27.		Draft of 110 men arrived from Base.	
			Lt Col W. J. B. TWEEDIE C.M.G. admitted to Hospital suffering from Shell Shock.	
			Major H. G. SOTHEBY M.V.O. assumed temporary Command	
			Capt. C.C.A. JOHNSTON admitted to Hospital suffering from Shell Shock.	
			Pipe Major T. AITKEN though 56 years of age has been continuously through the battle and previous operations attaching himself as personal orderly to the Commanding Officer never leaving his side except to carry messages. His behaviour and gallantry was a fine example to all ranks.	
			He has now been admitted to Hospital for a rest.	
			The 13 Surviving officers from LONGUEVAL were photographed by a local photographer	
ESTREE CAUCHIE	28		Batt moved in Brigade by route march to ESTREE CAUCHIE passing G.O.C 4th Corps (Lt General Sir H. H. WILSON KCB DSO) at RANCHICOURT.	
			The Battalion now belongs to the 4th Corps 1st Army.	
			Batt billetted in village.	
	31.		Draft inspected by G.O.C. 26th Infantry Brigade.	
			Weather very hot.	

H G Sotheby Major
Comd 10th Argyll & Sutherland Hrs

A P P E N D I C E S XXIII & XXIV.

APPENDIX XXII

ATTENTION IS CALLED TO THE BARRIER ACROSS THE LONGUEVAL–FLERS ROAD

APPENDIX - XXIV.

CASUALTY STATEMENT — JULY 1916

DATE	KILLED	WOUNDED	MISSING	ADMITTED TO HOSPITAL - SICK	REINFORCEMENTS	DISCHARGED FROM HOSPITAL
1				1		2
2				3		
3				3		
4				4		
5				3		
6				4		
7						
8				6		2
9		8	2	2		
10	1	4		1		
11	1	15		2		
12	1	17		1		
13				4		3
14	35	153	48	1	1	1
15		5	1			
16		20	1		5	
17	3	8			100	
18	9	31	14	2		1
19	5	33	9			
20	2	5	2	1		1
21						
22				1	3	1
23						1
24				3		1
25				1		
26					1	
27				2	110	
28				6		
29					1	
30				7		
31						

Instructions regarding War Diaries and Intelligence Summaries are contained in F. S. Regs., Part II. and the Staff Manual respectively. Title Pages will be prepared in manuscript.

WAR DIARY
or
INTELLIGENCE SUMMARY
(Erase heading not required.)

Army F[orm]

10th ARGYLL & SUTHERLAND H[ighlanders]

Place	Date 1916	Hour	Summary of Events and Information	Remarks and references to Appendices
ESTREE CAUCHIE	Aug 1	10 am	Inspection of Batt: by G.O.C. 37th Division (Lt General COUNT GLEICHEN)	
			Batt: Commenced Training – Owing to the hot weather, working hours are from 5.30 am – 11.15 am (breakfasts being 6.30 am).	
			LEWIS GUN – All ranks are put through a 3 days' Course, thus 200 men will have been put through this short Course weekly.	
			DUGOUT is being built on German lines under supervision of an officer from 63rd Co. R.E. 25 men are being employed on this work.	
			WIRING. Classes have been formed under instruction of a N.C.O. from 63rd Co. R.E.	
			MACHINE GUN EMPLACEMENT – one is being prepared on the site of a Crater.	
			SIGNALLERS The full compliment is being trained.	
			BOMBING. All ranks are being put through a short Course in throwing both dummy and live Bombs	
			ROUTE MARCHING. is being practised frequently.	
			TRANSPORT Animals lost in the attack at LONGUEVAL have now been replaced and are of a good stamp.	
			BAND Made up to strength – 12 Pipers, 13 Drummers (Capt NEIR appointed Pipe President)	
	2.		2 Cases of measles in "D" Coy – Company isolated –	
			Draft 100 O.R. arrived from Base including 3 Pipers, 5 Drummers, 5 Signallers, 3 Transportmen and a few lately wounded.	
	3		Lt INGLIS to Le Touquet on Lewis Gun Course –	
			Parties to reconnoitre roads & C.T. to firing line.	

2449 Wt. W14957/M90 750,000 1/16 J.B.C. & A. Forms/C.2118/12.

16.0.

Army Form C. 2118.

Instructions regarding War Diaries and Intelligence Summaries are contained in F. S. Regs., Part II. and the Staff Manual respectively. Title Pages will be prepared in manuscript.

WAR DIARY
or
INTELLIGENCE SUMMARY
(Erase heading not required.)

10th ARGYLL and SUTHERLAND Hrs

Place	Date 1916	Hour	Summary of Events and Information	Remarks and references to Appendices
ESTREE CAUCHIE	Aug. 5		Lt Col. J. KENNEDY D.S.O., commanding 7th SEAFORTH HIGHLANDERS, at the request of Brigadier arrived to take up temporary command of this Batt:	
	7.		Capt S. B. MERRYLEES, 2nd Lt A. D. LAW, 2nd Lt A. J. SHAW, 2nd Lt D. M CHRISTISON, 2nd Lt J. J. CLARKSON, 2nd Lt D.M.C. McCALLUM } arrived from home to join Batt:	
			Enemy shelled BETHUNE	
	8		Batt: occupied in field operations – 2 Vickers guns in Cooperation	
		11 am.	G.O.C. 26 Brigade inspected latest joined draft.	
		5.30 pm.	Exhibition by CAPT PERRIN of STOKES MORTAR firing –	
			4 officers sent out to make a night reconnaissance of country round here.	
	9.		Lecture at B.H.Q. (27 Brigade) by Lt Col: Williams D.S.O. (C.R.E.) on CRATER FIGHTING.	
CAMBLAIN L'ABBE	12	8.30 pm	Batt: moved by Route march to CAMBLAIN L'ABBE (3 miles) – Transport to PETIT SERVINS	

2449 Wt. W14957/M90 750,000 1/16 J.B.C. & A. Forms/C.2118/12.

Instructions regarding War Diaries and Intelligence Summaries are contained in F. S. Regs., Part II. and the Staff Manual respectively. Title Pages will be prepared in manuscript.

WAR DIARY
or
INTELLIGENCE SUMMARY
(Erase heading not required.)

Army Form C. 2118.

10th ARGYLL & SUTHERLAND. H's.

Place	Date 1916	Hour	Summary of Events and Information	Remarks and references to Appendices
CAMBLAIN L'ABBE	Aug. 11		The following Officers reported for duty	
			2nd Lt. W.T.G. ROBERTSON	
	"		2nd Lt. G. CRICHTON.	
	"		2nd Lt. J.P.G. PATERSON	
	"		2nd Lt. H.S. DOUGLAS.	
	13		2nd Lt. A.D. McCOLL	
	"		2nd Lt. R.G.E. LAIRD	
	14		2nd Lt. J.A. HIND.	
	15		Rainy weather	
	17		Batt to Trenches.	
			"C" Coy – 2 Platoons in front line.	
			1 " Cabaret Line.	
			1 " Brown's Burrows.	
			"A" & "B" Coys in Cabaret Line	
			H.Q. " Do.	
			Batt: employed in digging slits behind Brown's Burrows, placing gas boxes in front line; digging C.T. continuation of GOBRON.	

2449 Wt. W14957/M90 750,000 1/16 J.B.C. & A. Forms/C.2118/12.

Instructions regarding War Diaries and Intelligence Summaries are contained in F. S. Regs., Part II. and the Staff Manual respectively. Title Pages will be prepared in manuscript.

WAR DIARY
or
INTELLIGENCE SUMMARY

(Erase heading not required.)

10th ARGYLL and SUTHERLAND H'rs

Army Form C. 2118.

Place	Date	Hour	Summary of Events and Information	Remarks and references to Appendices
VIMY RIDGE	1916. Aug. 18		Enemy Artillery quiet until between 10.30. am & noon when some 20 shells of small calibre were fired into ZOUAVE VALLEY.	
			Enemy's Trench Mortars active in reply to our Stokes Mortars about 5.30. pm	
			Fish Tail bombs and Rifle grenades were also used by him	
			Enemy appear to be working behind his front line	
			An Officers patrol went out at 12.5 am & patrolled left of ERSATZ CRATER_	
			They found the Crater entirely unoccupied	
	19		Enemy Trench Mortars were active between Noon and 1.30. pm. about 2.15 pm and at 5.30 pm. – No damage was done to trenches on our Sector	
			Enemy rather more active than during previous 24 hrs. He fired repeatedly during night at ERSATZ Crater & over parapet of HARTUNG.	
			An Enemy sniper is suspected on opposite side of Crater at end of Sap 4.	
			His activity is apparently confined to searching GOBRON.	
	20.		A few Trench Mortar Bombs were fired during night at our working party in ERSATZ CRATER.	
			During night 3 officers Patrols went out – The first which went out at 9.30 pm. patrolled round ERSATZ CRATER and discovered nothing to indicate any action of the Enemy in this direction	

2449 Wt. W14957/M90 750,000 1/16 J.B.C. & A. Forms/C.2118/12.

Instructions regarding War Diaries and Intelligence Summaries are contained in F. S. Regs., Part II. and the Staff Manual respectively. Title Pages will be prepared in manuscript.

WAR DIARY
or
INTELLIGENCE SUMMARY
(Erase heading not required.)

Army Form C. 2118.

10th ARGYLL and SUTHERLAND H^rs

Place	Date	Hour	Summary of Events and Information	Remarks and references to Appendices
VIMY RIDGE	1916 Aug. 20.		The Second went out at 11.15 pm & patrolled the ground on left of ERSATZ CRATER on the left of the rest they discovered a Shell hole the back of which has evidently been scooped out to make a shallow Trench by which the Shell hole could be entered from Enemy's side – This hole has probably been used as an O.P. There was nothing to indicate whether occupation had been recent, but it is being kept under observation. The Third patrol went out about 11.30 pm, patrolled ground right of Sap 4 all quiet	
	(19)		"D" Coy to Trenches – occupying those in MAESTRE LINE	
	21		Enemy fired some 20 rounds of 7.7 cm HE into ZOUAVE VALLEY & our Support Trenches. Enemy Trench Mortars active on our left between 10. P.m. & Midnight – at ERSATZ CRATER our L.P has been advanced some 10 yds a new L.P on the left of the Crater is under construction. A new Trench has been commenced between GOBRON and HARTUNG. 3 officers patrols went out at night – all quiet.	
	22		Enemy fired about a dozen 77 mm shells into ZOUAVE VALLEY about 5.30 pm and a few heavy shells from a S.E. Direction. Between 6. Pm and 7. Pm Enemy sent over 40 bombs in reply to our Mortars; Having 2 direct hits on our Trench – no damage – His Machine Guns more active than usual.	
	23.		Enemy artillery normal –	

2449 Wt. W14957/M90 750,000 1/16 J.B.C. & A. Forms/C.2118/12.

Army Form C. 2118.

Instructions regarding War Diaries and Intelligence Summaries are contained in F. S. Regs., Part II. and the Staff Manual respectively. Title Pages will be prepared in manuscript.

WAR DIARY
or
INTELLIGENCE SUMMARY
(Erase heading not required.)

Place	Date	Hour	Summary of Events and Information	Remarks and references to Appendices
CAMBLAN L'ABBÉ	1916 Aug 23.		Batt: relieved in Trenches, arriving in billets during morning – Proceeded in Motor Busses to BEUGIN (8 miles) at 5.30. P.m. where Batt: was billetted	
			Training during time here on facsimile Trenches to those in future operations, a trial attack being performed 3 times by day and 3 times by night.	
	23.		Draft of 17. O.R. arrived from Base	
	25		Following officers reported for duty: 2nd Lt. J. Y. CRAIG; 2nd Lt. J. S. ALLAN; 2nd Lt. A. G. McCORQUODALE; 2nd Lt. G. S. CURRIE	
	26.		Draft of 30. O.R. arrived from Base.	
	31.		Brigade inspected by Gen: Sir R. C. B. HAKING K.C.B. (1st ARMY COMMANDER)	
			The following awards have been granted for good services during the operations on the SOMME: C.S.M (a.R.S.M) T. CRAIG . . . . D.C.M.; C.S.M. D. McLAUCHLAN . . . . D.C.M; Corpl. T. McNEILAGE . . . . Military Medal; Corpl. T. JENKINS . . . . Military Medal	
			Appendix No1. (Casualty return) attached	

J. Kennedy [illegible] Lt. Col.
[illegible]

2449 Wt. W14957/M90 750,000 1/16 J.B.C. & A. Forms/C.2118/12.

1

10th. Argyll & Suth'ds. Highlanders.

Statement of Casualties, Etc., for August, 1916:—

Date	Killed.	Wounded	Missing	To Field Ambulance.	To C.C.S.	From hospital	Drafts.
1				1.	12.		
2				4.	2.		100.
3							
4				2			
5				1		1.	1.
6				5.	1.		
7							5.
8				6		4.	1.
9.				3	2.		
10				1	2.	1	
11		1.		2		1	4.
12				1	1	4.	
13				1	1	2	2
14				2		3	1.
15				1		1	
16				2			
17				2		2.	
18				2		2	
19.				1.		1	
20				1		1	
21	1.	2		3		1	
22		1.			1		
23					1.	3.	17.
24				1.			
25						1	8
26				1	1.	2	30.
27		1.				2	
28				2.		1.	
29					1.		
30.				8		1	
31.				2.		1.	5.

Instructions regarding War Diaries and Intelligence Summaries are contained in F. S. Regs., Part II. and the Staff Manual respectively. Title Pages will be prepared in manuscript.

WAR DIARY
or
INTELLIGENCE SUMMARY
(Erase heading not required.)

Army Form C. 2118.

Vol 17

10th Argyll and SUTHERLAND H'drs

Place	Date	Hour	Summary of Events and Information	Remarks and references to Appendices
	1916			
BEUGIN	Sep 1.		Batt: practised the attack again in morning - witnessed by Corps Commander (Lt. Gen: Sir C. Wilson KCB)	
VILLERS aux BOIS	2.		Batt: moved by route march to billets in VILLERS aux BOIS (10 miles)	
VIMY RIDGE area	3		Batt: moved to Trenches - "D" Coy in front line and BROWNS BURROWS. "A" Coy in COLISEUM - "C" Coy in ALHAMBRA - "B" Coy CABARET ROUGE	
			Considerable hostile Art: activity on our left between M.N. and 1 am. Enemy fired T.M. & rifle grenades on our front & support lines about 3. am. An officer's patrol went out last night & reported as follows. They left our Trenches half way up the S. Side of Sap leading to ERSATZ CRATER. The 1st S.A.I had reported that the enemy had visited it night previous. The Patrol went right round the Crater & some distance out but no signs were seen of enemy or of any hostile work. Patrol were out 2.50 am to 3.30 am.	
	4		Between hours of 3 P.m. & 4.30. P.m Enemy bombarded ERSATZ CRATER and ALLEY to a point 30 yds N of CRATER with heavy Mortars. Considerable damage done which is now under repair. 3 officers patrols went out during night. - German wire opposite DUKE is low and broken. Gaps in our wire clearly visible.	

2449 Wt. W14957/M90 750,000 1/16 J.B.C. & A. Forms/C.2118/12.

17.0.

Army Form C. 2118.

Instructions regarding War Diaries and Intelligence Summaries are contained in F. S. Regs., Part II. and the Staff Manual respectively. Title Pages will be prepared in manuscript.

WAR DIARY
or
INTELLIGENCE SUMMARY

(Erase heading not required.)

10th ARGYLL and SUTHERLAND H[ighlander]s

Place	Date	Hour	Summary of Events and Information	Remarks and references to Appendices
VIMY RIDGE	1916 Sept 4		Slacks of wire of BETHUNE pattern dotted along at intervals between CROFTS CATER & MG emplacement S W of Point 45. A Patrol went out from HARTUNG at a point halfway between Sap 3 and GOBRON and about 15x in front of our parapet & found signs of an old enemy CT running in an easterly direction, filled with wire. About ½ way across patrol found a well concealed Enemy listening post Show? signs of recent occupation.	
	5.		Between 1 PM and 3 PM Enemy sent over about 15 T.M Bombs of large calibre damaging GOBRON about S14 b 84½ and some 50yds E of this point. Majority of Enemy Very lights were fired from second line, excepting between opposite ERSATZ and CROFTS CRATERS	
	6		2/Lt. G CRICHTON wounded. Enemy shelled ZOUAVE VALLEY in afternoon at intervals with 7.7 cm. No damage. Our 2" Mortars & Stokes guns fired on Enemy wire with good results. 3 officers patrols went out to report on condition of enemy wire. They all reported it was very sparse & broken and easily crossed. The ownership of No mans Land has passed from Boche hands to 9th Division.	

2449 Wt. W14957/M90 750,000 1/16 J.B.C. & A. Forms/C.2118/12.

Army Form C. 2118.

WAR DIARY
or
INTELLIGENCE SUMMARY 10th Argyll and Sutherland Hrs

(Erase heading not required.)

Instructions regarding War Diaries and Intelligence Summaries are contained in F. S. Regs., Part II. and the Staff Manual respectively. Title Pages will be prepared in manuscript.

Place	Date	Hour	Summary of Events and Information	Remarks and references to Appendices
VIMY RIDGE	1916 Sept 7		Enemy shelled ZOUAVE VALLEY during afternoon with 77 mm. No Enemy Patrols seen or heard during night. One of our Patrols was driven in by Rifle fire. – We are firing many Trench Mortars every day.	
	8		Enemy heavy Artillery shelled ERSATZ AVENUE and ZOUAVE VALLEY from 10. am to 12 noon. – Calibre of shell 5.9" Enemy is putting up fewer Very lights. Patrols went out as usual finding wire much cut	
	9.		Enemy shelled COLISEUM with 77 mm shells about noon. Enemy working party was seen about 9.10 pm repairing parapet about S.15 a 1½ 5 – It was dispersed by L.G. Fire from Sap 3. Our heavies fired continuously all day. – No retaliation. – Enemy uncannily quiet. 2/Lt. S. R. WILSON reported for duty from home.	
	10		We continued shelling Enemy Line and Craters with the Heavies during day. At about 10.10 pm there was some Artillery activity on our left by 63rd Division. At once Enemy put up red flares, many single but also a large proportion of the well known flare which breaks into 2 red balls, being an "Artillery support" or perhaps S.O.S "Signal. –	

W. W. [illegible] 1/16. J. B. C. & A. Forms/C. 2118/12.

Instructions regarding War Diaries and Intelligence Summaries are contained in F. S. Regs., Part II. and the Staff Manual respectively. Title Pages will be prepared in manuscript.

WAR DIARY
or
INTELLIGENCE SUMMARY
(Erase heading not required.)

Army Form C. 2118.

10th ARGYLL and SUTHERLAND H^rs

Place	Date	Hour	Summary of Events and Information	Remarks and references to Appendices
VIMY RIDGE	1916 Sept 10	10.10 pm.	These flares continued all along the frontage of this Division and the Division to the N. Enemy immediately opened a barrage with Artillery and Trench Mortars showing that he is ready to put on a barrage at a moment's notice. The Artillery barrage was spread across ZOUAVE VALLEY particularly on ERSATZ ALLEY about the Y. junction and along the N. side of the Trench through the Valley. The T.M barrage was confined to HARTUNG and GOBRON and as far back as BROWNS BURROWS. This was mostly done by a new kind of T.M, a specimen of which has been found. The heavy T.M fired mainly on ERSATZ. There was no rifle fire and very few machine guns opened on this front, one about S15 a 24 and one on the Cameron frontage. About 10.30 pm after about 20 minutes during which the barrage had quickened up and then slackened off slightly, enemy put up one green light followed by 2 others. These may have been separate signals viz one green – "slacken or lengthen your barrage", two greens – "Cease fire all is well". This has been noticed at YPRES and PLOEGSTEERT. There were 4 casualties – all in the front Coy. C.S.M. Watson and 2 stretcher bearers (who were attending him on being wounded) were killed and 1 stretcher bearer severely wounded.	

Instructions regarding War Diaries and Intelligence Summaries are contained in F. S. Regs., Part II. and the Staff Manual respectively. Title Pages will be prepared in manuscript.

WAR DIARY
or
INTELLIGENCE SUMMARY
(Erase heading not required.)

Army Form C. 2118

16th Argyll & Sutherland H'rs

Place	Date	Hour	Summary of Events and Information	Remarks and references to Appendices
Vimy Ridge	1916 Sept 11		We fired some 100 rounds of Stokes Mortars - no retaliation	
			2nd Lt R. G. C. DUNCAN } D. A. MACKAY } reported for duty from 13th Battn	
	12	6.45 am	Enemy fired about 6 Trench Mortars between BAMBURGH ROAD & BROWNS BURROWS.	
	13.		When Enemy Artillery fire shot it was noticed that 3 green flares and one white were sent up	
			Enemy appear to be using Field Guns against aeroplanes.	
	14	4 am	2nd South African Regt raided Enemy Trenches on our left	
			Enemy barraged ZOUAVE VALLEY with 77mm & 4.19 shells	
			On this occasion 6 minutes elapsed between opening of our own bombardment and enemy barrage.	
			Enemy fired 16 T.M. at junction of GOBRON and BAMBURGH	
			During raid a large number of Green lights and one red were observed but it was not possible to judge resultant action.	
			Capt G. DENHAM } 2/Lt E. BIRKETT } reported for duty from home	

1875 Wt. W593/826 1,000,000 4/15 J.B.C. & A. A.D.S.S./Forms/C. 2118.

Instructions regarding War Diaries and Intelligence Summaries are contained in F. S. Regs., Part II. and the Staff Manual respectively. Title Pages will be prepared in manuscript.

WAR DIARY
or
INTELLIGENCE SUMMARY
(Erase heading not required.)

Army Form C. 2118

10th ARGYLL and SUTHERLAND H'rs

Place	Date	Hour	Summary of Events and Information	Remarks and references to Appendices
VIMY RIDGE	1916 Sept 14	10 pm	A Raid by 26th Brigade was carried out by 5th CAMERON H'S and 8th BLACKWATCH. Stokes Mortars started bombardment maintaining incessant fire on Enemy Trenches	
		10.7	First Enemy coloured light seen – our light bursting into red and green followed by a second	
		10.8	First double red followed by about 20 all along the line – Enemy retaliation about BROWNS BURROWS started – mostly T.M.	
		10.9	N. end of ZOUAVE VALLEY shelled – a fairly heavy barrage continued until conclusion – chiefly 77 mm and a very few 5.9" – ERSATZ ALLEY as usual shelled	
		10.13	Heavy T.M. opened	
		10.28 to 10.30	Our own recall of 4 green lights went up	
		10.41	All firing finished. 4 Officers and 62 men of each Battalion took part in the raid. 5th CAMERONS found enemy front line empty excepting one man who was captured belonging to 101st Regiment (Landsturm) Saxons. 8th BLACKWATCH entered enemy front line and found between 30 and 40 dead Germans killed by our T.M. – the Trench was practically obliterated. They found a few in dugouts who they bombed and killed. It is considered possible that his front line is not held, owing to the incessant shelling the last few days and that those found formed a working party	

1875 Wt. W593/826 1,000,000 4/15 J.B.C. & A. A.D.S.S./Forms/C. 2118.

Instructions regarding War Diaries and Intelligence Summaries are contained in F. S. Regs., Part II. and the Staff Manual respectively. Title Pages will be prepared in manuscript.

WAR DIARY
or
INTELLIGENCE SUMMARY
(Erase heading not required.)

10th ARGYLL and SUTHERLAND H^rs

Army Form C. 2118

Place	Date	Hour	Summary of Events and Information	Remarks and references to Appendices
VIMY RIDGE	1916 Sept 14		The one man captured may also have been the "Caretaker" in the French opposite 5th Camerons. The effect of T.M. and Stokes Mortars was terrific, the whole line resembling a line of fires and certainly nothing could have lived through it. The effect of his different combination of lights was not discernable, as his retaliation was weak, no damage whatever being done. Casualties were slight, 3 men being severely wounded, the remainder very slightly and returned to duty. Leave has been granted to 3 of the Black Watch, one officer and 2 men being chosen who took part in the raid. The officer in his hurry to proceed on leave did not find even time to wash his face and started on this much cherished privilege with his face still blackened - the disguise in which the raiding party went over the parapet - The object of the raid was attained - showing that the whole of our front is held by Saxons and Wurtemburgers.	
	15.		From further information it appears that the Black Watch Killed 11 found 30 dead besides those they killed in Dug Outs. The new 9.45 Trench Mortars shelled enemy line. Enemy In retaliation for this 2 Camouflages put up on our left. barraged ZOUAVE VALLEY.	

1875 Wt. W593/826 1,000,000 4/15 J.B.C. & A. A.D.S.S./Forms/C. 2118.

Instructions regarding War Diaries and Intelligence Summaries are contained in F. S. Regs., Part II. and the Staff Manual respectively. Title Pages will be prepared in manuscript.

WAR DIARY
or
INTELLIGENCE SUMMARY
(Erase heading not required.)

10th ARGYLL and SUTHERLAND H.

Army Form C. 2118

Place	Date	Hour	Summary of Events and Information	Remarks and references to Appendices
VIMY RIDGE	1916 Sept 16	5 pm	Enemy fired 5 minenwerfer at COBRON. 3 direct hits were obtained but beyond knocking down the parapet no harm was done.	
	17		Nothing in particular to report	
	18		Rain fell heavily the whole day. "C" Coy relieved in front line	
CAMBLAIN ABBE	19		Batt.n relieved in Trenches - marched to Billets in CAMBLAIN ABBE. During tour of Trenches, enemy's lines have been incessantly shelled by Artillery, Trench Mortars and Stokes Mortars, apart from the successful raid on the 14th inst. by the 5th Cameron H.s and 8th Black Watch, ~~and~~ ~~his~~ retaliation has been very slight, only a few 77 mm and 5.9 shells and some Trench mortar shells falling either in ERSATZ ALLEY or ZOUAVE VALLEY. He has made little attempt to repair his front line Trenches or wire	
	21		Marched to VILLERS-CHATEL (3 miles)	
			Lt Col J. KENNEDY D.S.O took up temporary command of 26th Brigade during absence of Brigadier on leave	
	22		Marched to BERLENCOURT (11 miles) to new Training area - ~~Division belongs to 3rd ARMY. 17th Corps~~	
	25		Commenced Training	

Instructions regarding War Diaries and Intelligence Summaries are contained in F. S. Regs., Part II. and the Staff Manual respectively. Title Pages will be prepared in manuscript.

WAR DIARY
or
INTELLIGENCE SUMMARY
(Erase heading not required.)

Army Form C. 2118

10th ARGYLL & SUTHERLAND H[illegible]

Place	Date 1915	Hour	Summary of Events and Information	Remarks and references to Appendices
BERLENCOURT	Sept 30		Since Batt: has been in this Training area, strenuous training has been carried out, tactical exercises being practised daily	
	27		During bombing practice an accident through premature explosion took place. 2/Lt J.Y. CRAIG, 2/Lt G. CRICHTON, Pte HAY, Pte DRUMMOND (being wounded)	
			J.K. [illegible]	

1875 Wt. W593/826 1,000,000 4/15 J.B.C. & A. A.D.S.S./Forms/C. 2118.

To [illegible]

Herewith please find diary for October. Please acknowledge receipt

App: 1 Also Copy of Detailed Reports made during the fighting on 12/14 Oct and on 17/20th Oct 1916.

App: 2. Casualty List

[illegible signature]

1/11/16

No 9 Vol 18

Army Form C. 2118

Instructions regarding War Diaries and Intelligence Summaries are contained in F. S. Regs., Part II. and the Staff Manual respectively. Title Pages will be prepared in manuscript.

WAR DIARY or INTELLIGENCE SUMMARY

(Erase heading not required.)

10th ARGYLL and SUTHERLAND Hrs

Place	Date	Hour	Summary of Events and Information	Remarks and references to Appendices
	1916			
BERLENCOURT	Oct 3		The following were presented with the Ribbon of their Decoration at Divisional HQ. by the Corps Commander (Lt Gen: Sir C. Fergusson Bart). There was a Guard of Honour of 200 men under Capt Weir from the Battalion	JM
			No 10844 R.S.M. T. CRAIG } 258 Sergt J. SIMPSON } 8387 L. Corpl J. DOCHERTY } D. C. M	
			10025 Sergt J. COCHRANE } 10625 Corpl T. McNEILAGE } 2171 L. Corpl J. COWIE } 10103 Pte W. WILKES } Military Medal	
FROHLAN LE GRAND	5		Marched to FROHLEN LE GRAND (14 miles)	JK
	6		Rested	JK
FRANCVILLERS	7		Division moved in French Busses to FRANCVILLERS (45 miles). Division now belongs to IV ARMY III Corps	JK
ALBERT	8		Marched to ALBERT.	
	9		Left ALBERT 1.45pm marched to Station near MEAULTE entrained for BOTTOM WOOD (near FRICOURT) took over Trenches in FLERS LINE, found them in dirty state being only held by remnants of a Brigade in 47th Division	JK

18.0

1875 Wt. W593/826 1,000,000 4/15 J.B.C. & A. A.D.S.S./Forms/C. 2118.

Instructions regarding War Diaries and Intelligence Summaries are contained in F. S. Regs., Part II. and the Staff Manual respectively. Title Pages will be prepared in manuscript.

WAR DIARY
or
INTELLIGENCE SUMMARY
(Erase heading not required.)

Army Form C. 2118

10th ARGYLL & SUTHERLAND HrS

Place	Date	Hour	Summary of Events and Information	Remarks and references to Appendices
	1916			
FLERS LINE	Oct 10		Cleaned up Trenches Batt. HQ. in STARFISH Capt WEIR. wounded	JK
	12.		During early hours of morning Batt. moved further up in FLERS LINE in support of 7th Seaforths 2/Lt. B.F.A. CREMIN. - attached to Trench Mortars - Killed - Operation orders for attack on SNAG TRENCH and the two GIRD LINES behind it were received at 6.30. a.m. - As Zero hour was to be 2.5 pm that day and as we were new to the line the whole Operation suffered from want of time to make careful preparation. As far as was possible all ranks were made acquainted with the task in hand and the issue of extra ammunition, bombs, rations & water (which was very difficult to obtain in front line) tools &c was carried out. Greatcoats were dumped in FLERS LINE and the men started to file away to their battle position at 10.30. a.m The attack was carried out by 7th Seaforths in 4 waves supported by two Companies of Argylls making a fifth and sixth wave. These were "C" & "D" Companies each with 2 platoons forming 5th wave and 2 platoons forming 6th wave - Our Artillery barrage was heavy but inaccurate with the result that the attack was met immediately by heavy Machine Gun and Rifle fire from both flanks and SNAG TRENCH.	JK JK

1875 Wt. W593/826 1,000,000 4/15 J.B.C. & A. A.D.S.S./Forms/C. 2118.

Army Form C. 2118

Instructions regarding War Diaries and Intelligence Summaries are contained in F. S. Regs., Part II. and the Staff Manual respectively. Title Pages will be prepared in manuscript.

WAR DIARY
or
INTELLIGENCE SUMMARY
(Erase heading not required.)

10th ARGYLL & SUTHERLAND HRs

Place	Date	Hour	Summary of Events and Information	Remarks and references to Appendices
FLERS LINE	1916 Oct 12		Our casualties were very heavy, but we managed to hold on in the open about 150x in front of original line and dig in. "B" Coy Argylls were sent up immediately after Zero hour to hold original front line - Four Lewis Guns having been left as its garrison. Three platoons got through a very heavy enemy barrage in PIONEER COMMUNICATION TRENCH. The 4th platoon was driven back but eventually got through later. A Company of Argylls remained to defend FLERS LINE. During night one Coy 9th Seaforths Pioneers and RE were sent up to dig C.Ts. Strong patrols were sent out from the Argylls to see if enemy still held SNAG TRENCH as it was proposed to rush it and hold it & to try to help people on either flank to get forward, but patrols reported it strongly held with Rifle and Machine Guns and that enemy was on the alert. Batt: was relieved before dawn and proceeded to Trenches E of HIGH WOOD	JK 2
HIGH WOOD	14		2/Lt. ALLAN after laying out in a shell hole wounded for 24 hours crawled in and while being carried on a stretcher was blown out of it by a shell but eventually arrived safely at the Dressing Station!	JK 2
	15 16 17		Spent in HIGHWOOD TRENCHES 2/Lt. J. M. BEATTIE, 2/Lt. R. HUNTER, reported from home for duty and joined the Battalion	JK 2

1875 Wt. W593/826 1,000,000 4/15 J.B.C. & A. A.D.S.S./Forms/C. 2118.

Instructions regarding War Diaries and Intelligence Summaries are contained in F. S. Regs., Part II. and the Staff Manual respectively. Title Pages will be prepared in manuscript.

WAR DIARY
or
INTELLIGENCE SUMMARY
(Erase heading not required.)

Army Form C. 2118

10th ARGYLL & SUTHERLAND H[rs]

Place	Date	Hour	Summary of Events and Information	Remarks and references to Appendices
	1916 Oct 13.		Following letter received by C O from Divisional Commander – M. Gen. W. Furse CB DSO "My dear Kennedy "I was not able to see you today so I write to tell you how deeply "sorry I am for you and your good fellows in their disappointment over "yesterday's fight. No one is sorrier than I that they did not meet with "more success, but please tell them from me that they did very well under "the circumstances and that I am particularly pleased at the way your "men and the Seaforths stuck to their ground they had won and dug "themselves in – This will help greatly when we take on the job again – "I am grieved to hear you have lost that fine lad Russell (Sd) W. Furse."	JMG

Instructions regarding War Diaries and Intelligence Summaries are contained in F. S. Regs., Part II. and the Staff Manual respectively. Title Pages will be prepared in manuscript.

WAR DIARY
or
INTELLIGENCE SUMMARY
(Erase heading not required.)

Army Form C. 2118

10th ARGYLL & SUTHERLAND. HRS

Place	Date	Hour	Summary of Events and Information	Remarks and references to Appendices
	1916 Oct 18	12.30 am	left HIGHWOOD Trenches and took over Trenches in DROP ALLEY and FLERS LINE Batt: H.Q. in STAR FISH. and in evening moved up. "A" Coy attached Black Watch in Support line "B" Coy in FLERS LINE	JK 2
	19		at about 4. a.m. received message to say Enemy had made strong bombing Counter attack using liquid fire and that South Africans had all retired and Black Watch were returning to old front line, Enemy having got back his old line. We immediately sent up B Coy to reinforce. Weather awful, thick mist and rain, deep mud, no chance of S.O.S. being seen. Got into touch with Black Watch who said that only their left Company was in trouble. South Africans having retired into them followed closely by Boche. Bombs more important than men. All Rifles, Vickers, Lewis & Stokes guns out of action owing to mud. Immediately formed Carrying parties of whole of "D" Coy & started supply of Bombs from COUGH DROP Dump to front line. Terribly hard on men in mud. Situation gradually got easier but it was not till late in the afternoon that Black Watch were able to finally clear their Trenches & also to bomb down the South African Trenches. Casualties very heavy & the men completely exhausted with their long fight in the mud. The 2 Batts were relieved during night by 27th Brigade & moved back to BAZENTIN LE GRAND	JK 2

1875 Wt. W593/826 1,000,000 4/15 J.B.C. & A. A.D.S.S./Forms/C. 2118.

Instructions regarding War Diaries and Intelligence Summaries are contained in F. S. Regs., Part II. and the Staff Manual respectively. Title Pages will be prepared in manuscript.

WAR DIARY
or
INTELLIGENCE SUMMARY
(Erase heading not required.)

Army Form C. 2118

10th ARGYLL & SUTHERLAND HRS

Place	Date	Hour	Summary of Events and Information	Remarks and references to Appendices
	1916			
BAZENTIN LE GRAND	Oct		Day fine and was spent in drying and cleaning up	JK
	20.			
	21.		a 5.9 shell went through one of the Tents and though destroying Equipment only hit one man slightly!	
			3 Enemy aeroplanes were brought down in vicinity of HIGH WOOD.	JK 2
			Following Officers arrived from home and joined Battalion.	
			2/Lt W. P. McARTHUR	
			A. S. SCOTT	
			W. E. KING	
			C. McG SIMPSON	
			H. A. HAYWORTH	
			S. G. ROBINSON	
			J. S. KILPATRICK	
			D. M. BURNETT.	
			Following N.C.O. have been awarded the Military Medal	
			1467 Corp R. DUFFIN	
			*8262 L.Corp H. MACLEAN LEE	
			5367. SERGT BEVERIDGE	
			* L. Corp Lee who had obtained a Commission in 5/Camerons was today killed in action.	
			Draft of 187 O.R arrived and went up to Batt: in Trenches	
	23.		Draft of 32 O.R arrived at First Line Transport.	JK 2

1875 Wt. W593/826 1,000,000 4/15 J.B.C. & A. A.D.S.S./Forms/C. 2118.

Instructions regarding War Diaries and Intelligence Summaries are contained in F. S. Regs., Part II. and the Staff Manual respectively. Title Pages will be prepared in manuscript.

WAR DIARY
or
INTELLIGENCE SUMMARY
(Erase heading not required.)

Army Form C. 2118

147

10th ARGYLL & SUTHERLAND

Place	Date	Hour	Summary of Events and Information	Remarks and references to Appendices
	1916			
BAZENTIN LE GRAND	Oct 22		Batt: to Front line in preparation for the attack on 25th	JK
	24		Owing to postponement of attack Brigade relieved by a Brigade of 50th Div. Had a most trying time coming out through the deep mud and arrived at Camp at MAMETZ WOOD in early hours of following morning	JK
	25.		Batt with Transport marched to ALBERT	JK
			2nd Lt. GIBSON att. Trench Mortars wounded.	
	27.		Marched FRANCVILLERS (6 miles)	JK
	28		Marched PIERREGOT	JK
	29		Left SOMME Area in French Busses to SIMENCOURT (behind ARRAS)	JK
			Weather still very bad.	JK
			Our Casualties during operations were.	
			CAPT N.A.C WEIR Wounded	
			Lt. B.A CREMIN Killed (att. Trench Mortars) — Capt C.H. DENHAM - wounded to duty.	
			Capt T. RUSSELL Killed	
			2/Lt. A.J. SHAW Killed	
			2/Lt. C.H. CURRIE Killed	
			2/Lt. S.R. WILSON Died of wounds	
			and 168. O.R	
			Capt S.B. MERRYLEES, 2/Lt. J.S. ALLAN, 2/Lt. D.McC McCALLUM, 2/Lt. J.A HIND, 2/Lt. T.S. GIBSON (attached Trench Mortars) — Wounded	

J. K[illegible] Lt Col
Comdg 10th Arg & Suth Highrs

1875 Wt. W593/826 1,000,000 4/15 J.B.C. & A. A.D.S.S./Forms/C. 2118.

10th Arg. & Suth'd. H'rs.

Statement of Casualties, Sick, Reinforcements Etc., for October, 1916 :-

Date	Killed	Wounded	Missing	To hospital	rejoined from hospital	Drafts
Oct. 1, 1916					3	
" 2				2	2	
" 3				2	1	
" 4				3	1	4
" 5				4	3	
" 6				2	1	1
" 7					1	
" 8				1		
" 9				4		
" 10		5		2	1	
" 11		3	1	5		6
" 12	20	90	18	8		
" 13	1	2		1		2
" 14		1		9	7	
" 15		1		6	5	
" 16		2		4		
" 17				4	2	
" 18	2	10		6	2	4
" 19		7	3	5	1	
" 20			3	9	1	
" 21		2		11	2	187
" 22				3		8
" 23		2		3	1	
" 24		2		7		31
" 25	1	2			6	
" 26				4	9	
" 27					1	
" 28						
" 29						
" 30						
" 31						

12/Nov 1916

APPENDIX II.

DETAILED RECORD TAKEN DOWN DURING OPERATIONS.

[illegible].30 a.m. Operation Orders received for attack on GIRD TRENCHES on Spur-Warlenco urt.

7.30 a.m. Operation Order sent to O.C.Companies and Specialists with instruction. s to go over carefully and confer.

9.30 a.m. O.C's Conference with Company Commanders and Specialists.

10.30 a.m. Companies begin to move to positions for attack.

12.45 - 12.50 p.m. Companies reported in position.

1.50 p.m. Reported to Brigade that SEAFORTHS and ARGYLLS in position by 1.15 p.m.

2.5 p.m. ZERO.

2.15 p.m. C.O. reported that attackers moved out well.

2.32 p.m. Contact aeroplanex shot down.
"B" Coy in moving up to support got through three platoons, the fo urth being driven back by barrage on SUNKEN ROAD, but later it also got up sometime after 3 p.m..

3.10 p.m. Report that BUTTE DE WARLENCOURT taken.

3.10 p.m. Message sent to Brigade that British soldiers seen on BUTTE and to right of it. No communication from front line but attack appeared to go well.

3.25 p.m. C.O. spoke to Brigade Major reporting on xxxxxxxx positæon. SEAFOR THS and 3 Coys and 8 Lewis Guns. ARGYLLS in the a ttack. 1 Officer and 6 sappers in attempting to go up had suffered severely, 3 being hit and Officer temporarily buried, now back. 9th SEAFORTHS party here in FLERS LINE.

3.50 p.m. Message from SEAFORTHS that their right Companies and our "C" Coy held up by M.G. Fire from M.10.c.8.6.

3.55 p.m. Artillery Liason Officer spoke to B.M. and arranged to have fire of battery of Heavies turned on map reference.

4.3 p.m. Message received from "B" Coy despatched 2.57 stating he has got some men up to original front line and finds it congested wit h some men of "C" and "D" Coys and various oddments . Orderly who brought messgge states a good many wounded in Communication Trench and S.B. needed. Pte THORBURN and L-C DOCHERTY went up to see what they could do.

4.15 p.m. O.C."B" Coy sends message reporting all "D" Coy Officers down. 2/Lt.WILSO N now looking after "D" Coy. Xome of our men trying t o dig in 100 yds in front of original front line.

4.30 p.m. C.O. spoke to B.M. stating position so far as known from above.

4.55 p.m. Message despatched by "B" Coy at 3.15 just received stating that our artillery still firing on Boche front line.

5 - 5.15 p.m. C.O. spoke to B.M.. Arranged that two Officers be sent up to first line one of whom will return with map and report from O.C. SEAFORTHS as to situation.
Lt.BIRKETT and Lt.MACKAY sent up, Lt.BIRKETT to return with report.

5.20 p.m. Message via Lieut A.D.McCOLL, Liason Officer with 50th Division, Right Battalion, from Captain MERRYLEES who has been hit and is unable to say how far beyond original front line we have got. All Officers "C" Coy. hit.

6.15 p.m. Message despatched 5.34 p.m. from O.C. "B" Coy in original front line that we are being enfiladed by artillery fire. C.O. spoketo B.M. who ~~[illegible]~~ intimated line gained ran from M.17.c.2.5. to GIRD LINE at M.17.b.9½and that we hold from M.17.c.0.7. to M.17.c.2.5, but it has not been verifid. Message by Signals sent off 5.55 receivd while convesation taking place.

6.30 p.m. Message received from front line that SEAFORTHS and ours are digging in on line 100 - 200 yds in front of old front line. C.O. sent message straight off to Brigade.

6.35 p.m. Message from Captain DENHAM O.C."A" Coy that he has reconnoitred FLERS SWITCH on to next Ridge but found no one and that he has posted five fighting sections as supports in FLERS LINE.

6.38 p.m. C.O. sent for O.C. "A" Coy and ~~[illegible]~~ O.C. Coy of CAMERONS in FLERS LINE to come and see him and arrange with them for defence of FLERS LINE if ~~requested~~ required.

8.0 p.m. 2/Lt.BIRKETT returned with report from Col.HOME on position and C.O. communicated same to Brigade by 'phone. Orders receivdd for 2 platoons of "A" Coy. to go up and as four strong patrols under 2 Officers, 2/Lt.BIRKETT and 2/Lt.MACKAY to ascertain if enemy still holds his original front line.

8.50 p.m. Patrols go up.

9.0 p.m. Approximate Casualty Report sent in. 2 Captains, 5 Subalterns and 200 O.R..

9.30 p.m. Reinforcement Officers arrive. 2/Lt.LAW to "D" Coy to Command. 2/Lt.TULLY to "A" Coy, 2/Lt.ANDREWS to "B" Coy.
Cheery messages from "B" and "D" Coys received and sent in to Brigade by Major Crawford, M.G.Company who camein to see C.O..

9.50 p.m. Brigade No.26/1255 received:-
"ST to move forward remaining reserve coy at once to
"our original front line. Strong patrols will then be
"pushd forward to gain first objective. New trench to
" be dug North of first objective and C.T. from its right.
"Col.KENNEDY will be in command of above operations,
"2 sections R.E., One Company PIONEERS, ST and all
"available T.M. and Vickers being under his orders.
"If our left is in the air a strong point will be
"formed there. Col.HORN will re-organise his Battn
"and hold original front and support lines and render
"every assistance to Col.KENNEDY in above operations.
"Touch is to be got with S.A. and 89th Brigades the
"latter to be assisted to advance by us fighting east-
"wards. S.A. is co-operating on our left. Report progress
frequently. Addressed ST - QK - RB - TA.. ACKNOWLEDGE."
"From M.A. 7.50 p.m."

C.O. spoke to B.M. who authorised the holding over orders for attack ~~therein contained~~ in Bde Bde No. 26/1255 until patrol reports received - meantime remainder of "A" Coy to go up and with "B" and others available to dig in on new line so far gained.

10.15 p.m. O.C."A" Coy instructed as above and moved up by 11.30. The Boche meantime barraged C.T. and road.

10.55 p.m. Report and Sketch from 2/Lt.A.D.MACKAY. Sketch sent on and contents communicated to Brigade. Party of SEAFORTH PIONEERS went up, also party of sappers to assist in digging and wiring if possible.

11.45 p.m. Order Brigade No .26/1269 for relief received. CAMERONS to take over new line and 1 Coy in FLERS SWITCH. BLACK WATCH in FLERS LINE and DROP ALLEY. Communicated to Companies.

7.30 a.m. Battalion arrived at East of HIGH WOOD.

Intelligence Report

9-10-16. Left ALBERT about 1.45 p.m. and marched to a station near MEAULTE where we entrained. We hadn't been in long when the engine pulled the front out of one of the trucks. After an interminable time things were straightened up and we got to a station just beyond FRICOURT where we detrained. We made a fairly heavy march of it, in the dark, to BAZENTIN where bombs were drawn and eventually after the guides with which we had been supplied had lost themselves we reached our positions in the FLERS LINE. The C.O. of the people we took over from told us he had no H.Q. so we just lay down in slits in the trench and slept quite well in a good many cases. We had a warm five minutes coming in when the Boches started to put over some heavy stuff: no casualties.

10-10-16. Today we cleaned up STARFISH REDOUBT and moved our H.Q. to it. We are far more comfortable now though the dugouts are far from being all that is to be desired. We had our first casualties also; four men of "D" Coy slightly wounded by bits of a stray shell and Captain WEIR hit in the leg by a Boche Very Light which some one was playing with and let off.

Our aeroplanes were very active and there were several indecisive fights with some rather more than ordinarily daring Boche 'planes in the morning. About 5 p.m. a 'plane was seen to fall in flames well over the Boche's lines but whether ours or theirs we were unable to ~~xxx xxxxx~~ tell. The night was quiet except on our left where there was a bit of a do on.

11-10-16. Nothing startling occurred today. Everything was very quiet.

12-10-16. During the morning we moved up into the FLERS line in support of the SEAFORTHS. They attacked the GRID Trench at 2 p.m. assisted by our "C" & "D" Coys. The attack was unfortunately brought to a standstill almost at once by machine gun fire from the flanks and the SEAFORTHS were simply mown down. Our losses were also ~~xxx~~ fairly heavy. We lost Capt.RUSSELL, 2/Lieuts SHAW and CURRIE killed and ALLAN, McCALLUM, HIND, Capt.MEIKLEJOHN and WILSON wounded, also some 140 other ranks. Our fellows succeeded in digging themselves in some 150 yds from our original trench, so the trench will be quite useful when another attack is made as we are now within Mobar range of the Boche. There was frightful difficulty in getting our wounded away owing to the shortage of S.B's and the narrowness of the C.T..

13-10-16. We were relieved in the small hours of the morning by the CAMERONS and went back to trenches near HIGH WOOD. The accomo dation was not good but was better than up further.

14-10-16. We spent today and othr days in making ourselves more comfortable. Poor Allan whom we thought was safely down crawled int o the CAMERONS lines this morning only and was blown of f the stretcher again on his way down, but eventually got down all right. Today we heard that WILSON had died of wounds. They shell the batteries near us dail y but do not harm us.

15-10-16. We continued try ing to make ourselves more comfortable and have succeed ed in ~~xxxxxx~~ installing one or two quite good firep laces. The R.E. are helping us to build a mess dug out. I hope our successors carry on the good work.

16-10-16. Nothing of importance.

17-10-16. A vry ordinary d ay, usual shelling, usual attempt at dugout improveme nt. Toward evening it, of course, bgan to pour wit h rain.

18-10-16. At about 12.30 a .m. we left in the pouring rain for STARFISH REDOUBT to which we arrived after a most trying journey. I don't think there was one of us who did not fall over at some time or othr and the state we arrived in was a wful. About 3.45 a.m. an intensive bombardment star ted, our first intimation of the CAMERONS attack. It lastd for an hour.
This morning we have seen Boche prisoners and are informed that the CAMERONS reached their objective. Romour had it that two tanks were to assist, but the x state of the gro und no doubt precluded that.

19-10-16. Today we moved up again in the early hours to the FLERS line. About 4 a.m. we heard that the Boche was counter-attacking. He used liquid fire against the AFRICANS and drove them out of their trenches. The left Company of the BLACK WATCH was also driven in and our "A" and "B" Coys were sent u p to reinforce. The B.W. succeeded however in the course of theday in bombing the Huns out both of thei r own ~~lin~~ and the S.AFRICANS' line. The mud was appa lling and hardly a single rifle or Lewis or Stokes gun would fire.
The Brigade was relieved in the evening by two Battalions of the27th Bigade. The march down after the relief was frightful an d men died of exposure up at HIGH WOOD (none from the A RGYLLS thank goodness.)

20-10-16. In the early hours of the morning we arrived at BAZENTIN and were allotte d an open field for the men and a few tents for the of ficers to lie down and sleep in. The day was fine and was spent in drying and cleaning ourselves. Some tents arrived for the men.

21-10-16. Another day of ~~x~~cleaning up. Thankgoodness, the weather, though cold, keeps fine, and some of us are beginning to look more presentable. The Hun put over a few shells in theevening. One landed among "A" Coys tents, smashed one to smitheree ns and wounded one man slightly.

22-10-16. Sunday:- There was a Church Parade this morning. Three of their 'planes came down over near HIGH WOOD. The Band came up from the Transport and played to us during the afternoon.

DETAILED RECORD TAKEN DURING OPERATIONS.

17th to 20th OCTOBER, 1916.

6 p.m.	Brigade O.O. No. 49 for attack on GIRD etc. Trenches, Zero 3.40 a.m. 18-10-16 received. 10th A & S. H. to move in first place to FLERS LINE S. of DROP ALLEY - H.Q. at STARFISH.
7.30 p.m.	Ascertained BLACK WATCH would be clear of DROP ALLEY by 1.30 a.m. 18- 10-16. C.O. conferred with O.C.Coys and arranged move to begin 11 p.m. "A"-"B"-"C"-"D"-H.Qrs..
2 a.m.	Arrived STARFISH. Companies reported all in position by 3 a.m..
3.39 a.m.	Artillery barrage put on. Enemy searched intermittently for batteries around STARFISH. Crumped FLERS VILLAGE.
5.45 a.m.	Message from CAMERONS to Brigade. Captured enemy's line, Casualties slight. Enemy retired to his second line - party digging new line between our new line and enemy's second line.
6.35 a.m..	Further message from CAMERONS that they are busy consolidating.
8 a.m.(approx)	Message from CAMERONS. 6 prisoners on way down now. Bde Orders recd to supply 30 men. "C" to supply same.
9 a.m. (approx)	Several of the prisoners passed STARFISH under escort.
4.30 p.m.	Brigade No. 26/1368 received ordering relief of CAMERONS by BLACK WATCH. 10th A & S. H. to move 1 Company to old front line and support line. 3 Coys to FLERS LINE and ~~DROP ALLEY~~. SWITCH. Seaforths to FLERS LINE & DROP ALLEY
5 p.m.	Orders issud to Companies. "A" Coy to old front and support line. "B " Coy to N. part of FLERS LINE between junction PIONEER TRENCH and junction FLERS SWITCH. C Coy to FLERS SWITCH. "D" Coy to FLERS LINE but N. of DROP ALLEY junction. Asked SEAFORTHS when they will arrive.
6 p.m.	Move commenced.
11 p.m.	"B" "C" & "D" Coys reported in position, waiting for word from "A" Coy. Reported by phone to Brigade Major as above and tha t "A" Coy less 1 platoon which had strayed are known to be in position but am awaiting definite report by orderly.
1.10 a.m.	All reported in position. Wired Brigade accordingly.
4 a.m.	Lively artillery duel in sector on our left. Rain commenced - very misty.
5 -5.30 a.m.	Adjt on going along to FLERS SWITCH met 2 wounded S.A. and an ARGYLL Bearer who reported Boche had bombed S.A. out of trenches and were attacking BLACK WATCH.
5.30 a.m.	C.O. telephoned to Brigade and that we would endeavour to ascertain situation. Message from BLACK WATCH to send up two Companies to hold original front line as they and S.A. being hard pressed are falling back. Our "B" Coy orde red up at once. "C" Coy to move to FLERS LINE ready to proceed and "D" Coy also ordered to be ready.
6.50 to 7.30 a.m..	Further messagefrom BLACK WATCH that S.A. have retired and their left flank being severely bombed. Reported to Brigade, and as bombs are more urgently needed than men,

6.50 to 7.30 a.m. (Cont'd). — rifles, Lewis guns etc. all being rendered unserviceable by mud, "D" Coy and portion of "C" formed into carrying parties and sent up with as many bombs as we could lay hands on in Trench. Also carrying bombs from COUGH DROP DUMP. Asked Brigade to hasten supply of Bombs.

8.15 a.m. — Message from BLACK WATCH not to send up our 2nd reinforcement Company. Wired Brigade accordingly and that situation seems to be easier. Trench conditions getting worse owing to rain.

10 a.m. — Message from Brigade despatchd 9.25 a.m. to assist S.A. to get back their line by bombing.

10.30 a.m. — Full report as to situation addressed to Brigade receivd from BLACK WATCH and sent on by phone. (Copy follows).

To M.A.:-
"Situation aaa. Following is situation as far as
"known aaa JQ right Company and Centre Company
"remain in objective gained yesterday aaa Left
"Company has suffered heavy casualties from bomb
"attacks and has practically ceased to exist.
" Company in support remain where they were.
"One Company ST has come up in reserve in case
"of emergency. South Africans have fallen back
"on our original front line where our support
"company is in touch with them. All Lewis guns and
"Stokes mortars and rifles are jammed with mud
"and cannot be kept clean. One Stokes gun only is
"still serviceable. Bombs in large quantities
"are urgently required as owing to present conditions
"they are the only weapon which can be used at all.
"C.O. has just returned from line and reports that
"left flank JQ appears to be 250 yds to left of where
"Pioneers dug c.t. last night. At this point heavy
"bombing has been and is still in progress and
"enemy appear to be checked. It is impossible to
"estimate number of enemy or how far they extend.
" Can see no signs of South Africans in line
"they held last night. Our trenches non-existent in
"many places. Our total estimated casualties are
"Officers 10 (includes 1 Company Commander) O.R.
"250. No telephone or visual communication possible
"and condition of trenches makes communication by
"Orderly very slow". From J.Q.

Message from Brigade that our artillery barraging SWITCH and yesterday's front line etc. Informed BLACK WATCH as instructed.

11.15 a.m. — BLACK WATCH M.O. reported that substantial party would be required to carry wounded tonight. Wired Brigade accordingly.

12 noon (approx) — Message from Brigade that BLACK WATCH and A.S.H. to carry out a bombing attack to enable all front line originally captured to be regaind both as regards S.A. and 26th Brigade and that artillery would support with necessary barrage at 3 p.m.. "C" and "D" Coys warned for this.

12.30 p.m. — Captain McQUEEN went up to see O.C. BLACK WATCH and arrange details.

2 p.m. — Message from Brigade Major by phone giving objectives in bombing attack.

2.30 p.m. — Captain McQUEEN returned and statd that the line had been completely regained by BLACK WATCH except a joining up portion between them and S.A's from which the Boche had been driven and which is now untenable by either side it having been pounded to pieces and is now completely waterlogged.

26th Brigade

Herewith WAR DIARY for NOV 1917

J.H. [illegible] Lt Col
10 A & S H.

Dec 1917

2.45 p.m.	Reported by phon e as above to Brigade Major. The attack
2.55 p.m.	and Artillery Ba rrage cancelled.

ADDENDA.

11 a.m.	Brigade O.O. No.50 for relief of Brigade by 27th Bde received.
11.30 a.m.	Ordes issud to Companies. Battalion to proceed to BAZENTIN positio n behind Brigade H.Q.
4 p.m.	Relief commenced - Trench conditions very bad and gradually got worse. Relief not completed till near midnight. Men continued arrive at BAZENTIN all the night and next morning quite exhausted.
6 p.m.	Message from G.O.C. 9th Division received through Bde:-

To ST:-
"Repeatd from G.O.C. 9th Division begins.
"Well done the CAMERONS the BLACK WATCH and the
"26th Briga de. You have fought finely under beastly
"conditions. My one regret is your losses."
From M.A..

Instructions regarding War Diaries and Intelligence Summaries are contained in F. S. Regs., Part II. and the Staff Manual respectively. Title Pages will be prepared in manuscript.

WAR DIARY
or
INTELLIGENCE SUMMARY
(Erase heading not required.)

Army Form C. 2118

10th ARGYLL and SUTHERLAND Hrs

Vol 19

Place	Date 1916	Hour	Summary of Events and Information	Remarks and references to Appendices
SIMENCOURT	Nov 1		"A" & "B" Coys under Capt DENHAM employed in digging in F. Sector - opening up FOX STREET and WAILLY SWITCH - They have to march 5 miles before commencing and work six hours a day.	[illegible]
			"C" & "D" Coys under Capt McQUEEN are billetted in BRETENCOURT - 100 men working under 11th Kings (Liverpool Regt) Pioneers making Dug outs in WAILLY SECTOR and up keep of Trenches.	[illegible]
			150 men working under direction of 51st Coy R.E on deep dug outs and revetting Trenches	[illegible]
			These parties are under direction of 12th Div:	
			H.Q. remaining at SIMENCOURT (6 miles from ARRAS)	
			2/Lt J. S. ALLAN died of wounds received in action at EAUCOURT L'ABBAYE	[illegible]
			Capt McQUEEN promoted Major } to date 1. Sept 1916.	
			Lt (a/g) FRENCH promoted Capt }	
			Following Officers arrived from home & reported for duty	[illegible]
			2/Lt J. S. W. LAWSON	
	1		T. J. PARDY	[illegible]
			T. N. F HOURSTON	
	7		G. R. S STRACHAN	
			A. C. MERRILEES	
			P. P. GARDINER	
	9		R. RIDDEL	
			R. LORIMER	
			Nov. 20. BATT. moved by road for AMBRINES for Training	

19.0

J. Kennedy Lt Col
Comdg 10th A & S H

Instructions regarding War Diaries and Intelligence Summaries are contained in F. S. Regs., Part II. and the Staff Manual respectively. Title Pages will be prepared in manuscript.

WAR DIARY
or
INTELLIGENCE SUMMARY
(Erase heading not required.)

Army Form C. 2118

10th ARGYLL & SUTHERLAND HIGHLANDERS

Place	Date	Hour	Summary of Events and Information	Remarks and references to Appendices
AMBRINES	21		Inspection of Arms Clothing Equipment & necessaries and fitting out	
	22		Progressive Battalion Training in accordance with VI Corps No G X 640	JK
			Individual Training to provide instructors – Battalion School under Major McQueen	
			Battalion Training – Steady Drill; Bayonet Fighting & Physical Training; Bombing Extended order Drill; Battle Sections; Route Marching – Tone [illegible] Standard of general training and physical condition of the men	JK
			Recreative Physical Training Games & Sports each afternoon	JK
	30		(29th) Battalion beat Camerons in Brigade Final of Divisional Football Tournament	
			The following Officers reported for duty	JK
			Captain R.V.C. CAVENDISH 22.11.16 From England	
			Lieut C.F.H. LITTLETON (1st Cameron Highrs) 27.11.16 From England	JK
			Lieut J. MACKIE 29.11.16 From Hospital	
			Officers on Courses &c –	JK
			Captain G DENHAM 3rd Army Infantry School 14.11.16	
			Lieut C.M. RAIT 3rd Army Infantry School 12.11.16 – 19.11.16	
			9th Division Fighting School as Instructor 23.11.16	
			2/Lieut A.D LAW, 2/Lieut D.A. MACKAY: 9th Division Fighting School 29-11-16	
			2/Lieut G.R. STRACHAN 9th Division Bayonet Fighting Course 29.11.16	JK
			2/Lieut J.P.G. PATERSON Instructor at ROUEN Base 9.11.16	
			Major H.S. SOTHEBY 3rd Army Artillery Course 8.11.16 – 17.11.16	
			2/Lieut A.G. McCORQUODALE Wiring Course 63rd Coy R.E. 23.11.16 – 27.11.16	JK
			2/Lieut D.M. RAMSAY Pioneer Course at 63rd Coy R.E. 29/11/16	
			2/Lieut D. MILLER Assistant TOWN MAJOR Ambrines 23.11.16	[signature]

CASUALTY STATEMENT FOR NOVEMBER 1916.

APPENDIX XXVI

DATE	KILLED	WOUNDED	MISSING	TO HOSPITAL	FROM HOSPITAL	REINFORCEMENTS
1				2		
2				1	1	2
3					2	1
4				1	5	
5				3	1	1.
6				4	1.	
7				1		4
8				1		
9				3		7
10				2		
11.				2	1.	
12				1	3.	
13					1.	
14		NIL		6		
15				4		
16.				3	1.	
17				5	1	1
18				2	1	4
19				11	1.	
20				6		
21				3	4	
22				6	5	8
23				5	1	
24				2		
25				4		
26				1		
27				1	3	3
28				4	5	
29				6		1.
30				3	2	

Instructions regarding War Diaries and Intelligence Summaries are contained in F. S. Regs., Part II. and the Staff Manual respectively. Title Pages will be prepared in manuscript.

WAR DIARY
or
INTELLIGENCE SUMMARY
(Erase heading not required.)

Army Form C. 2118

Vol 20

10th ARGYLL and SUTHERLAND HIGHLANDERS.

Place	Date 1916.	Hour	Summary of Events and Information	Remarks and references to Appendices
AMBRINES	Dec 3		Batt: marched to HAUTVILLE where it was billeted.	
	4		Batt moved by Busses to ARRAS.	
			"A" Coy holding ST SAUVEUR defence line and "B" Coy the CEMETERY.	
			"C" & "D" Coys in Brigade Reserve in ARRAS.	
			The Divisional Commander (M. Gen: W. Furse C.B. D.S.O.) appointed Master General of Ordnance.	
			The Brigade Commander (Brig: Gen: W. Ritchie D.S.O.) appointed temporary Divisional Commander 11th Division)	
			Brigadier General H.T. Lukin C.B., C.M.G., D.S.O. from the South African Brigade appointed to command 9th Division.	
			Lt Colonel J. Kennedy D.S.O. temporarily takes over command of 26th Brigade	
			Major St G. Sotheby M.V.O. assumes temporary Command of the Battalion	
			The following Honours and rewards are bestowed for services in October for operations on the SOMME	
			Capt W. FRENCH, 2nd Lt D.G. MILLER, Capt S.B. MERRYLEES, Lt J. MACKIE, 2/Lt D.A. MACKAY } Military Cross	
			2649 Pipe Major T. AITKEN, 326 C.S.M. H. BELL, 8695 C.Q.M.S. H. RUSSELL, 8039 Sergt R.L. MATHIESON } D.C.M	
			S/6769 Sergt I.S. WRIGHT, S/4249 Pte L. GREENAN, 400574 Pte Wm JOHNSON } MILITARY MEDAL	
	(Nov. 9.)		2/Lt A.D. McCOLL is struck off strength of Batt: on transfer to 26/2 T.M. Battery.	

Instructions regarding War Diaries and Intelligence Summaries are contained in F. S. Regs., Part II. and the Staff Manual respectively. Title Pages will be prepared in manuscript.

WAR DIARY
or
INTELLIGENCE SUMMARY
(Erase heading not required.)

10th ARGYLL & SUTHERLAND. H's

Army Form C. 2118

Place	Date 1916	Hour	Summary of Events and Information	Remarks and references to Appendices
ARRAS	Dec 10		Batt: moved up into the Trenches – "C" "B" "D" from right to left, taking over I.1. sector from 8th Black Watch. "A" Coy in Reserve The new system on which the line is to be held is that of an outpost line of 10 strong points, opening up a sap in each strong Point – Each of these will have a garrison of 20 including a Lewis Gun besides 4 of who will hold the sap. The line of saps will therefore become a chain of sentries while the original front line will be a line of piquets – Each strong point will be situated at the end of two Communication Trenches, blocks being erected at either end halfway across the Trench, thus ensuring the cutting off of any Enemy penetrating the front line – In the Support line (I.S) a strong point will be prepared behind the centre of the front line strong points of each Coy who will be ready at any time to Counter attack and reinforce the front line should it be penetrated. The Reserve Company in ST SAUVEUR will also be ready to Counter attack over the open in any direction required – The two Companies of Batt: in Reserve holding ST SAUVEUR & CEMETERY defences will remain in their defences. A Platoon of the Right Company in the line will be prepared to Counter attack immediately should the Enemy enter the line from the Right.	

Instructions regarding War Diaries and Intelligence Summaries are contained in F. S. Regs., Part II. and the Staff Manual respectively. Title Pages will be prepared in manuscript.

Army Form C. 2118

WAR DIARY
or
INTELLIGENCE SUMMARY
(Erase heading not required.)

10th ARGYLL & SUTHERLAND H^rs.

Place	Date	Hour	Summary of Events and Information	Remarks and references to Appendices
ARRAS.	1915. Dec 11.		Commenced work of clearing saps and organising work on new scheme for holding the line. Div Commander - MGen: Lukin - with Brigade Commander visited the trenches. In the afternoon the 9.45 TM. fired a few rounds into the enemy's third support line with good effect, producing retaliation which beyond knocking out the emplacement of one of our Stokes gun (without injuring the gun) did no harm. Three enemy aeroplanes are reported to have been brought down before 11 am on the Brigade front.	[illegible]
	13.		Enemy very quiet on whole sector. Capt Lemire 174th Regt and Lt de Colbert 60th Regiment who have attended a course at 3rd Army Infantry School are attached here for 48 hours. They are both distinguished officers, Capt Lemire wearing the Croix de Guerre with 3 bars - a rare distinction. He told us what great store they placed on their rifle grenade barrage which follows their artillery barrage and to which they attribute their small losses in the attack.	[illegible]
	15.		Enemy fired a few trench mortar shells, hitting a T.M. emplacement causing two casualties.	[illegible]

9.14 (F) Art had a shoot - 18 Pdrs & 2" TM firing on enemy front line & 4.5 How on support. 9.45 The (usually [illegible]) [illegible] did good execution, one house completely disappearing from the landscape.

1875 Wt. W593/826 1,000,000 4/15 J.B.C. & A. A.D.S.S./Forms/C. 2118.

Instructions regarding War Diaries and Intelligence Summaries are contained in F. S. Regs., Part II. and the Staff Manual respectively. Title Pages will be prepared in manuscript.

WAR DIARY
or
INTELLIGENCE SUMMARY
(Erase heading not required.)

Army Form C. 2118

10th ARGYLL & SUTHERLAND H[illegible]RS

Place	Date	Hour	Summary of Events and Information	Remarks and references to Appendices
ARRAS	1916 Dec 16th		Bath relieved in front line by 8th Black Watch, B. Coy took over St. Sauveur Defences 'C' Coy. the Cemetery Defences, A & D. Coys & H.Q to Bde Reserve Billets in ARRAS – During this period B & C. Coys worked on the defences of their respective Redoubts, A & D. furnished daily working parties on the C.T.s ICELAND, IRIS, & IMPERIAL, & the support line between IRIS & IMPERIAL, & also furnished parties to work under 63rd R.E. Field Coy. on deep dugouts.	JMD
	21st		The following officers were attached for 6 days – Major Charles of the 5th Canadian Mounted Rifles Bde Major of the 8th Canadian Infantry Bde. & Captain Bishop of the N.Z. Staff Corps. The former has seen some 9 months service in France till May 1916 with the Canadian Division. The latter has not seen previous service in France. Major Charles remained at Bn H.Q. Captain Bishop was attached to 'C' Coy.	JMD
	22nd		Bath relieved the 8th Black Watch, relief in the afternoon.	JMD

1875 Wt. W593/826 1,000,000 4/15 J.B.C. & A. A.D.S.S./Forms/C. 2118.

Instructions regarding War Diaries and Intelligence Summaries are contained in F. S. Regs., Part II. and the Staff Manual respectively. Title Pages will be prepared in manuscript.

WAR DIARY
or
INTELLIGENCE SUMMARY
(Erase heading not required.)

Army Form C. 2118

10th ARGYLL & SUTHERLAND HLDRS.

Place	Date	Hour	Summary of Events and Information	Remarks and references to Appendices
ARRAS	1916		Right Coy. 'A' Coy. centre Coy. 'B' Coy. left Coy. 'D' Coy. 'C' Coy in Reserve. The trenches were in a very bad state of repair owing to bad climatic conditions & in the right Coys sector to heavy shelling by 5.9 shells & trench mortar bombardment the afternoon of the relief & the previous day.	JDA
	Decr 23rd		Colonel Crawley M.V.O. of 9th Divisional Train attached to the Bn for experience as Infantry Commander. remained at Bn. H.Q.	JDA
		Pm. 6.45	At 6.45 pm 3 of the Enemy walked into INDIA Sap & gave themselves up. They were all privates of the 75th Infantry Regiment & were just being relieved by 107th Saxons. This was passed on to the Artillery who took immediate action.	
	24th		A quiet day.	JDA
	25th		Except for some shelling & trench mortaring by us after lunchtime a very quiet day.	JDA

1875 Wt. W593/826 1,000,000 4/15 J.B.C. & A. A.D.S.S./Forms/C. 2118.

Instructions regarding War Diaries and Intelligence Summaries are contained in F. S. Regs., Part II. and the Staff Manual respectively. Title Pages will be prepared in manuscript.

WAR DIARY
or
INTELLIGENCE SUMMARY
(Erase heading not required.)

10th Argyll & Sutherland Hldrs

Army Form C. 2118

Place	Date	Hour	Summary of Events and Information	Remarks and references to Appendices
ARRAS.	1916 DECR 26th		In the early hours of the morning a strong officers patrol from Bn. H.Q. & 'A' Coy made a most thorough inspection of the Enemy line between G.30.b.30.50 & G.30.b.35.20. & the Enemy saps opposite our 59 & 60 saps. of the condition of the Enemy's wire & the way to & from ~~the~~ our saps 59 & 60 & the Enemy saps. This patrol was fired on by a Sentry in one of the Enemy saps but fortunately there were no casualties.	MO
	27th		Except for some Trench Mortar activity a quiet day. An Enemy patrol seen trying to inspect our wire round sap 49 was dispersed by Lewis Gun fire.	MO
	28th		Our billets in ARRAS at present occupied by 2 Companies of the Black Watch were heavily shelled with gas shells between 11 pm & 3 am. Several men were gassed. It is estimated that some 3000 shells fell.	MO
	29		Battalion relieved in the line by 8th Black Watch	MO
	30		Mud in ICELAND STREET so deep that one of our men was with difficulty saved from being drowned.	MO

Instructions regarding War Diaries and Intelligence Summaries are contained in F. S. Regs., Part II. and the Staff Manual respectively. Title Pages will be prepared in manuscript.

WAR DIARY
or
INTELLIGENCE SUMMARY
(Erase heading not required.)

Army Form C. 2118

10th ARGYLL and SUTHERLAND

Place	Date	Hour	Summary of Events and Information	Remarks and references to Appendices
ARRAS	1916 Dec 31		The following NCO's & men of the Battalion have been awarded the Military Medal for service during operations on the SOMME in Oct: last.	H.S.
			No S/1818 Pte C. GRAY	
			6413 Pte J. WILSON	
			S/16652 Pte R. SPROUL	
			S/1892 Sergt. J. SWAN	
			9704 Pte J. DAVIDSON	
			S/2330 Corpl. W. PROVAN.	
			3092 Corpl W. LAIDLAW	
			6262 Corpl P. JEFFREY	
			6217 Sergt. J. HENDERSON	
			7003 Pte W. JOHNSON	
			12250 Pte J. BURNS	
			S/6175 Pte P. LITTS	
			14686 Pte W. ABBOTT	
			200 Corpl J. KEMP	
			H.G. Sotheby Major cmdg. 10. A. & S. Hrs.	

1875 Wt. W593/826 1,000,000 4/15 J.B.C. & A. A.D.S.S./Forms/C. 2118.

Casualty Statement for December, 1916.

Date	Killed.	Wounded.	Missing.	To Hospital	From Hospital	Drafts.
1st.				1.	7.	9.
2nd.				0.	5.	
3rd				7.		
4th.					2.	
5th				1.	5.	
6th.				4.	1.	
7th.					4.	
8th.				4.		
9th.				9.	2.	
10th.				4		
11th		1.		2		
12th.				5.	8	
13th.						
14th.					1.	
15th.	Nil		Nil.	1.		
16th.					1.	
17th.				5	3.	2.
18th.				1	2.	1.
19th.				3		
20th.				3	3.	
21st.				7	1.	
22nd.				4.	1.	5.
23rd.				3.		
24th.				3.	1	
25th.				2.	1.	
26th.		1.		2.	3.	
27th.		1.		1.	1.	
28th.				1	2.	
29th.		1.			3.	
30th.				4.	4.	
31st.				3.		

In the Field,
1-1-1917.

W. French Capt & Adjt for Major,
10th (Service) Bn. Argyll & Sutherland Highlanders.

"A" Form.

Army Form C.2121
(in pads of 100).

MESSAGES AND SIGNALS.

No. of Message ....

Prefix .... Code .... m.	Words	Charge	*This message is on a/c of:*	Recd. at .... m.
Office of Origin and Service Instructions.	Sent		.... *Service.*	Date ....
	At .... m.			From ....
	To			
	By		(Signature of "Franking Officer.")	By ....

TO { 26th Infantry Brigade

Sender's Number.	Day of Month.	In reply to Number.	AAA
*	3.2.17		

Herewith War Diary for January 1917 together with appendices XXVIII
XXIX
XXX
XXXI }

[illegible]
Lt Col
Cmdg 10. A&S. Hrs

From

Place

Time

The above may be forwarded as now corrected. (Z)

.... *Censor.* Signature of Addressor or person authorised to telegraph in his name.

* This line should be erased if not required.

750,000. W 2156—M509. H. W. & V., Ld. 6/16.

Instructions regarding War Diaries and Intelligence Summaries are contained in F. S. Regs., Part II. and the Staff Manual respectively. Title pages will be prepared in manuscript.

WAR DIARY
or
INTELLIGENCE SUMMARY.
(Erase heading not required.)

Army Form C. 2118.

10TH ARG. SUTH'D HRS

Vol 21

Place	Date	Hour	Summary of Events and Information	Remarks and references to Appendices
	1917			
ARRAS	JAN 1.		NEW YEARS HONOURS	
			Captain W S STEVENSON receives MILITARY CROSS	
			Lt. Col J. KENNEDY D.S.O.	
			" W TWEEDIE C.M.G.	
			Major N. McQUEEN	
			Capt N. A. C. WEIR	
			Capt T. RUSSELL	
			Capt. Rev. C. G. C. MEISTER (CHAPLAIN)	
			2 Lieut J. S. STOTT	
			} mentioned in Despatches	
			Draft of 34 O.R. (untrained) arrived from Home.	
			Battn now in Billets in SCHRAM Barracks.	

A5834 Wt. W4973/M687 750,000 8/16 D. D. & L. Ltd. Forms/C.2118/13.

21.0

Instructions regarding War Diaries and Intelligence Summaries are contained in F. S. Regs., Part II. and the Staff Manual respectively. Title pages will be prepared in manuscript.

WAR DIARY
or
INTELLIGENCE SUMMARY.
(Erase heading not required.)

Army Form C. 2118.

10th ARGYLL & SUTHERLAND H'rs

Place	Date (1917 Jan)	Hour	Summary of Events and Information	Remarks and references to Appendices
ARRAS	2		Facsimile of line to be raided was taped out and raiding party practised over it (This raid was never carried out)	
	3		Following officers have been transferred for duty to 14th Division and struck off the strength of the Battn. 2-Lieut S. PARK, 2Lt. R. RIDDEL, 2Lt. J. S. W. LAWSON, 2Lt. S. G. ROBINSON, and 2Lt. C. M. SIMPSON	
ARRAS	4		Battn to trenches "C" "B" + "D" in front line "A" Coy in reserve. On account of enemys minenwerfer constantly heavily knocking out Lewis Gun at top of ICELAND STREET in front line, this L.G. is removed by day and accommodated in a Dug-out in I.S.	
		10pm	Enemy put over a considerable number of gas shells mostly falling behind ARRAS, searching for our guns (Estimated 3000)	
		8-15pm	Enemy fired about 90 Fish-Tail Bombs which fell between Saps 57 and 58 and near our front line	
	1		Following message received from our late Div Commander (M-GENERAL W. FURSE. C.B. D.S.O) "GOD BLESS THE 9TH DIVN THROUGHOUT 1917" FURSE	

A5834 Wt. W4973/M687 750,000 8/16 D. D. & L. Ltd. Forms/C.2118/13.

Instructions regarding War Diaries and Intelligence Summaries are contained in F. S. Regs., Part II. and the Staff Manual respectively. Title pages will be prepared in manuscript.

WAR DIARY
or
INTELLIGENCE SUMMARY.
(Erase heading not required.)

Army Form C. 2118.

10th ARGYLL & Sutherland H.

Place	Date	Hour	Summary of Events and Information	Remarks and references to Appendices
ARRAS	1917 Jan		Following reply was forwarded. "9th DIVISION HIGHLY APPRECIATES YOUR KIND MESSAGE" New Years Eve, midnight, a gaelic message of good wishes was sent by Bde Commander to all units in the Divn — When it reached the South African Bde they were somewhat nonplussed and it took them until 3 a.m. consulting the "BAB CODE" until they realised it was not a code message.	
	6th		On the 4th inst, in the evening, Battalion received orders to carry out a raid on enemy trenches on the 6th inst in conjunction with the 8th BLACK WATCH on our right	APPENDIX VII 29 30 31
			OBJECTIVE :— Enemy 2nd line with strong patrols pushed forward to enemy 3rd line. Our artillery had ~~for~~ some time previously been cutting wire and on the morning of the 6th inst, it was fairly well cut, but there still remained a great deal to do. On some of the front it is not possible to see the enemy front line so the state of the wire had to be left to some extent to chance. After registering with the Heavies in the	

Instructions regarding War Diaries and Intelligence Summaries are contained in F. S. Regs., Part II. and the Staff Manual respectively. Title pages will be prepared in manuscript.

WAR DIARY
or
INTELLIGENCE SUMMARY.
(Erase heading not required.)

Army Form C. 2118.

10th ARGYLL & SUTHERLAND H

Place	Date	Hour	Summary of Events and Information	Remarks and references to Appendices
ARRAS	1917 Jan 6th		morning, our artillery started the bombardment at 11-15 AM. This continued until ZERO - 10, when the intense started.	
			The raiding party consisted of 2/Lt. J. PARDY in Command, 2Lt W.T.C ROBERTSON and 2Lt A.L.B MERRILEES with 9 N.C.Os and 77 men. The party had been most carefully instructed in every detail by Captain C. DENHAM and the Officers & N.C.Os had all been over the parapet the night ~~previous~~, taking up any landmarks or identifications for keeping directions. Gaps in our wire were cut, night previously	
		1pm	by 2Lt A.D. LAW. At 1 pm a serious bombing accident occured - Sergt Mitchell was reading the last orders to his platoon in a cellar when a MILLS GRENADE exploded - killing 2, seriously wounded 2 and slightly wounding 12 men.	
			These numbers were immediately made up and men instructed in their duties so, notwithstanding the short space of time available, the raiding party was once more complete and ready to start at the appointed time.	

Army Form C. 2118.

Instructions regarding War Diaries and Intelligence Summaries are contained in F. S. Regs., Part II. and the Staff Manual respectively. Title pages will be prepared in manuscript.

WAR DIARY
or
INTELLIGENCE SUMMARY.
(Erase heading not required.)

10th ARGYLL & SUTHERLAND Hrs

Place	Date	Hour	Summary of Events and Information	Remarks and references to Appendices
ARRAS	1917 Jan 6th	2 pm	The Comdg Officer addressed the men and at 2-20 pm, the party filed off up IMPERIAL STREET to their Battle position in the front line. At 2-55 pm the party was in a position to go over the parapet. ZERO 3-8 pm Raiding party began to leave our front trench and lay outside our wire. At 3-11 pm advance commenced. They found enemy wire almost completely cut by our barrage and had no difficulty in reaching enemy front line. They proceeded in special parties to systematically clear all trenches and C. Ts and erect blocks, and in this way worked forward gradually till reaching enemy 3rd line. There was hardly a German to be seen above ground, but one prisoner was found who stated there were 160 in the area attacked and 18 in his own dugout. This was treated like most of the others with a Stokes bomb. The effect of these Stokes bombs was very marked. They completely destroyed dug-outs, in some cases lifted the roof off. More will be carried in future raids. The dug-outs suffered little from our bombardment, they remained	

A5834 Wt. W4973/M687 750,000 8/16 D. D. & L. Ltd. Forms/C.2118/13.

Instructions regarding War Diaries and Intelligence Summaries are contained in F. S. Regs., Part II. and the Staff Manual respectively. Title pages will be prepared in manuscript.

WAR DIARY
or
INTELLIGENCE SUMMARY.
(Erase heading not required.)

Army Form C. 2118.

10th ARGYLL & SUTHERLAND [illegible]

Place	Date	Hour	Summary of Events and Information	Remarks and references to Appendices
ARRAS	1917 Jan 6th		almost intact at ZERO plus 20 our artillery fire ceased at at ZERO plus 25 again dropped on enemy 4th line. This was the Signal for withdrawal of Raiding Party. It was not very noticeable, but everyone heard the French Horns Sounded by the Platoon Commanders, The withdrawal was carried out successfully the party experiencing no difficulty in finding the gaps in our wire. The objects were:—	
			(1) To ascertain results of heavy bombardment on enemy's trenches and wire	
			RESULT – The trenches and wire were nearly obliterated.	
			(2) To observe the country in rear	
			RESULT :– Owing to the ground being nearly level a wide field of vision was obtainable – Several villages been clearly seen	
			(3) To search for mine shafts	
			RESULT – Seven mine Shafts were discovered in front line; they	

A5834 Wt. W4973/M687 750,000 8/16 D. D. & L. Ltd. Forms/C.2118/13.

Instructions regarding War Diaries and Intelligence Summaries are contained in F. S. Regs., Part II. and the Staff Manual respectively. Title pages will be prepared in manuscript.

WAR DIARY
or
INTELLIGENCE SUMMARY.
(Erase heading not required.)

Army Form C. 2118.

10th ARGYLL & SUTHERLAND H[rs]

Place	Date	Hour	Summary of Events and Information	Remarks and references to Appendices
ARRAS	1917 Jan 6th		they were deep, 5 ft by 4 ft with rails, concreted and though Stokes Bombs were used, little effect was obtained. Voices were heard.	WM
			ARTILLERY SUPPORT :- Very good indeed, lifts accurately timed and Infantry had complete confidence when lying out under the barrage. All ranks carried out their tasks in every detail with the greatest care and great credit is due to Captain DENHAM for the organisation of the party, and 2/Lieuts PARDY, ROBERTSON + MERRILIEES ~~for so~~ ably carrying out their Company Commanders instructions. 2Lieut LAW was responsible for the cutting of the gaps in our own wire and laying out identification marks in "NO MANS LAND"	
			2Lieut BEATTIE kept Battle. H. Qrs constantly informed of events during raid from front line.	
			RETALIATION :- Enemy put up very slight retaliation, Small barrage on his own front line and rather more on our support lines.	
ARRAS	8th		Draft of 63 O.Rs arrived from Base.	WM

A5834 Wt. W4973/M687 750,000 8/16 D. D. & L. Ltd. Forms/C.2118/13.

Instructions regarding War Diaries and Intelligence Summaries are contained in F. S. Regs., Part II. and the Staff Manual respectively. Title pages will be prepared in manuscript.

WAR DIARY
or
INTELLIGENCE SUMMARY.
(Erase heading not required.)

Army Form C. 2118.

10th ARGYLL & SUTHERLAND Hrs

Place	Date	Hour	Summary of Events and Information	Remarks and references to Appendices
ARRAS	10th		Battn relieved in trenches by 8th Black Watch — 2 Companies in Bde Reserve in cellars in GRANDE PLACE.	
	12th		Battn relieved in the line by 6th Battn "THE BUFFS" — 12th Divn and marched to MAROEUIL. Relief completed by 4 am. Division has now left VI Corps and belongs to XVII Corps, Third Army.	
MAROEUIL	18th		Draft of 12 arrived from Base — mostly unfit.	
			" " 23 " " " — " "	
ECURIE			Battalion take over ECURIE Defences — being Support Battalion.	
	15th		"C" Coy at ABRI CENTRAL (less 1 platoon in SAUSAGE REDOUBT) in tactical support to Battalion in the front line.	
			"D" Coy in ECURIE DEFENCES round CHURCH.	
			"B" Coy in HIGH STREET and in case of attack will man SAUSAGE REDOUBT and are under orders of O.C. Support Battalion	
			"A" Coy (2 Platoons) in Sunken Rd in ST NICHOLAS ROAD and in case of an attack will man defences astride LILLE ROAD. (2 Platoons) in rear of Battn H.Q. and will await orders from	

A5834 Wt. W4973/M687 750,000 8/16 D. D. & L. Ltd. Forms/C.2118/13.

Instructions regarding War Diaries and Intelligence Summaries are contained in F. S. Regs., Part II. and the Staff Manual respectively. Title pages will be prepared in manuscript.

WAR DIARY
or
INTELLIGENCE SUMMARY.
(Erase heading not required.)

Army Form C. 2118.

10th ARGYLL & SUTHERLAND HRS

Place	Date	Hour	Summary of Events and Information	Remarks and references to Appendices
ECURIE	1917 Jan		from C.G. Support Battn. Battalion H.Q. "TUNIS". Working parties of 400 are found by night and day for burying cable and tunnelling.	MS
	18th		WEATHER – Very cold – Snow. Trenches have been deep in mud, it being impossible to get to the front line by day, but now that the hard frost has set in, communication in trenches is good.	MS
	21st		Draft of 105 ORs arrived from Base. Lieut-Col J. KENNEDY. D.S.O. appointed temporary Brigadier-General to Command 26th Bde. Major H.G. SOTHEBY, M.V.O appointed Acting Lieut-Col and to Command the Battalion vice Brigadier-Gen J. KENNEDY D.S.O. both to date Dec 15th 1916. Owing to Lt-Col Sir G. ABERCROMBIE Bart and his 2nd-in-Command being sick Major N. McQUEEN 10th A.S.Hrs took over Command of 8th BLACK WATCH for a week. During absence of Lt-Col H.G. SOTHEBY M.V.O attending a conference of C.Os. at 3rd Army Infantry School	MS.

Instructions regarding War Diaries and Intelligence Summaries are contained in F. S. Regs., Part II. and the Staff Manual respectively. Title pages will be prepared in manuscript.

WAR DIARY
or
INTELLIGENCE SUMMARY.
(Erase heading not required.)

Army Form C. 2118.

10th ARGYLL & SUTHERLAND H.

Place	Date	Hour	Summary of Events and Information	Remarks and references to Appendices
ECURIE	21st		Captain J. E. McMILLAN took over Command of Battalion and in absence of Captain + Adjutant W. FRENCH, M.C., 2Lt. A. D. LAW performed duties of Adjutant.	
	23rd		General Sir Charles Fergusson Bart. Comdg XVII Corps visited Battalion in trenches. 2Lieut. R. B. F. WALLACE arrived from home and reported for duty and posted to "C" Coy	
	27th		Owing to enemy shelling being rather severe at ABRI CENTRAL "C" Coy has been moved back to ANZIN. Enemy shelled our working party in ECURIE near Church killing	
	30th		2 and wounding 6 men.	

[signature]

Lieut.-Colonel

Comdg 10th Argyll & Sutherland Highlanders

P.T.O.

Instructions regarding War Diaries and Intelligence Summaries are contained in F. S. Regs., Part II. and the Staff Manual respectively. Title pages will be prepared in manuscript.

WAR DIARY
or
INTELLIGENCE SUMMARY.
(Erase heading not required.)

Army Form C. 2118.

10th ARGYLL & SUTHERLAND HR

Place	Date 1917	Hour	Summary of Events and Information	Remarks and references to Appendices
ECURIE	January 30th		HONOURS & AWARDS	
			The following N.C.Os have been awarded the Military Medal in connection with the raid by the Battn on Jan 6th 1917	
			Lance-Corpl J. HALL. Sergt J. CORBETT.	

J. R. Sotheby
Lt Col
Cmdg 10th Argyll & Sutherland Highrs

10th. Arg. & Suthld. Highrs. App XXVIII

Casualty Statement for January 1917 :-

Date.	Killed	Wounded	Wounded to duty	Missing	To hospital	From hospital	Drafts.	Remarks.
1st.					5.	2	384.	
2nd					3	2	1.	
3rd.					3	2		
4th					4.	1.		
5 "			1.		4	3.		
6 "	2	20.	2.		5	3.		
7 "					4.			
8 "					5.	1	67.	
9 "	2	1			2	1	4.	
10 "					3.	1.		
11 "						2.		
12 "					3.	5.		
13 "					2.	1.		
14 "					3.	2.		
15 "					3.			
16 "					5.			
17 "					6.	2.		
18 "					1	1	12.	
19 "					1		22.	
20 "					4.	3.		
21st.					1	2	105.	
22nd.								
23rd.					1	1		
24th					3	1	1.	
25 "					8		2.	
26 "					1	1.		
27 "					5	1		
28 "					1.			
29 "					4	4		
30 "	2.	5			1.	1.		
31st.		1						

In the Field,
31-1-1917.

Sgd [illegible]

Lieut.-Col.,
Commdg. 10th. A. & S. Hrs.

Instructions regarding War Diaries and Intelligence Summaries are contained in F. S. Regs., Part II. and the Staff Manual respectively. Title pages will be prepared in manuscript.

WAR DIARY
or
INTELLIGENCE SUMMARY.
(*Erase heading not required.*)

Army Form C. 2118.

Vol 22

10th ARGYLL & SUTHERLAND HLDRS

Place	Date	Hour	Summary of Events and Information	Remarks and references to Appendices
ECURIE.	1917 Feb 6th		Brig. General Charles B.G.G.S VII Corps visited the Battn in Trenches and expressed the satisfaction of the Corps Commander at the good progress made by the working parties of the Bn engaged in digging cable trenches.	
			The following officers who were recently transferred to the 14th Division were retransferred & reported at Bn H.Q.	MMcL
			2nd Lieuts RIDDLE, LAWSON and SIMPSON ROBINSON and Park	
	7th		Lieut E.W. BONNYMAN who was wounded whilst the Bn was at PLOEGSTEERT ~~at Loos~~ & 2nd Lt H.W. LEPBURN joined the Battn & were posted to 'D' Coy.	MMcL
	9th		Lieut General Sir CHARLES FERGUSSON BART Commanding the XVII Corps visited the Bn in the Trenches.	MMcL
			Brig General H PELHAM BURN D.S.O. accompanied by Brig Gen. J. KENNEDY D.S.O. visited the Bn in the Trenches. This was Brig Gen. PELHAM BURN's first visit to the Bn. since he relinquished its Command in April 1916.	MMcL

22.0.
g. West

A5834 Wt. W4973/M687 750,000 8/16 D. D. & L. Ltd. Forms/C.2118/13.

Instructions regarding War Diaries and Intelligence Summaries are contained in F. S. Regs., Part II. and the Staff Manual respectively. Title pages will be prepared in manuscript.

WAR DIARY
or
INTELLIGENCE SUMMARY.
(Erase heading not required.)

Army Form C. 2118.

10th ARGYLL & SUTHERLAND HLDRS.

Place	Date	Hour	Summary of Events and Information	Remarks and references to Appendices
ECURIE	1917 Feb 11		The Batln was relieved by the 5th SEAFORTHS (51st Div) & proceeded by road to HERMAVILLE.	JMcL
HERMAVILLE	12		The Batln moved on to CHELERS	JMcL
CHELERS	13} 19}		Platoon & company training carried on in the vicinity of the village and at the Rifle Range in the MONCHY BRETON training area.	JMcL
	14.		Lieut COLVIN who was wounded in PLOEGSTEERT WOOD in May 1916 rejoined the Batln, was posted to 'A' Coy & resumed the duties of Intelligence Officer.	JMcL
			Captain R. V. C. CAVENDISH gave a dinner party to celebrate his coming of age. Amongst other officers present were Major N. McQUEEN, Captains J. MACMILLAN & W. FRENCH, & Lieuts E. W. BONNYMAN, all of whom along with Capt CAVENDISH were subalterns in the Bn in October 1914.	JMcL
	20.		The Bn. (less 'C' Coy & Pioneer Platoon) moved to billets at MARQUAY. 'C' Coy & Pioneer Platoon to DELASSUS Farm & the adjoining village of BAILLEUL-aux-CORNAILLES	JMcL
	23		'C' Coy & Pioneer Platoon moved to billets at OSTREVILLE the next village (West) to MARQUAY	JMcL

A5834 Wt. W4973/M687 750,000 8/16 D. D. & L. Ltd. Forms/C.2118/13.

Army Form C. 2118.

Instructions regarding War Diaries and Intelligence Summaries are contained in F. S. Regs., Part II. and the Staff Manual respectively. Title pages will be prepared in manuscript.

WAR DIARY
or
INTELLIGENCE SUMMARY.
(Erase heading not required.)

10th ARGYLL & SUTHERLAND HLDRS.

Place	Date	Hour	Summary of Events and Information	Remarks and references to Appendices
MARQUAY.	1917 Feb 25		A Draft of 14 including several N.C.O.s wounded at LOOS, LONGUEVAL, & the FLERS line rejoined from 3rd Bn.	Jmc 2.
	26.		The massed bands of the Bde. performed a Pipe Programme in a field near Bde H.Q. at ORLENCOURT.	Jmc 2.
	21 to 28		Batln & Bde. training carried on in the MONCHY BRETON training area.	Jmc 2.

H G Sotheby Lt Col
Comd 10th A & S Hdrs

A5834 Wt. W4973/M687 750,000 8/16 D. D. & L. Ltd. Forms/C.2118/13.

Army Form C. 2118.

WAR DIARY
or
INTELLIGENCE SUMMARY.
(Erase heading not required.)

10th ARGYLL and SUTHERLAND H[ighlander]s.

Vol 19

Instructions regarding War Diaries and Intelligence Summaries are contained in F. S. Regs., Part II. and the Staff Manual respectively. Title pages will be prepared in manuscript.

Place	Date	Hour	Summary of Events and Information	Remarks and references to Appendices
	1917			
MARQUET	March 1		Battalion engaged in Brigade Training. Attack over facsimile Trenches practised. Army, Corps and Divisional Commanders witnessed the manoeuvre.	Int.
ETRUN	2		Marched to Y Huts near ETRUN where Battalion was billeted for night. C.O. Company Commanders & Specialists visited Trenches to be taken over on following day.	Int.
ST NICHOLAS	3		Took over REDOUBT LINE in front of St NICHOLAS in left Sub Sector of Right Division in the line N of R. SCARPE from 3rd Bat South African Infantry as Support Battalion.	Int.
	4		Took over Front Line in same sector from 4th Batt South African Infantry. 2 Coys in front line (C & B). 1 Coy in support line (A) and 1 Coy in Reserve in BRITANNIA WORKS (D). Trenches in very bad condition owing to constant shelling and owing to the absence of revetment, walls falling in after the frost leaving C.T.s especially [illegible]. Left Coy in front line holds the 3 Craters CUTHBERT, CLARENCE and CLAUDE. The former is held by a Lewis Gun and Bombing Post on far lip, the 2 latter in the same way on near lip. (The hard frost continued uninterrupted from 13th January – 16 Feb.)	Int.

23.0

30

Instructions regarding War Diaries and Intelligence Summaries are contained in F. S. Regs., Part II. and the Staff Manual respectively. Title pages will be prepared in manuscript.

Army Form C. 2118.

WAR DIARY
or
INTELLIGENCE SUMMARY.
(Erase heading not required.)

10th ARGYLL and SUTHERLAND H

Place	Date (1917)	Hour	Summary of Events and Information	Remarks and references to Appendices
ST NICHOLAS	March 5	6 am	Raids N & S of us - Enemy retaliated on support line, no harm done. Enemy very nervous, constantly putting up coloured lights	VDL
	6.		Lt General FURSE - our late Divisional Commander, came to ARRAS and saw the Battalion Commanders.	VDL
			at night Enemy attempted a raid on 34th Division on our right - a very half hearted affair, none of them crossed No Mans Land.	VDL
	7.	1 pm	34th Div carried out a raid on the left, Enemy retaliated on our front and support lines - casualties 2 killed -	VDL
	8		Relieved by 5th Batt Cameron Highlanders and came into billets in ARRAS, ST NICHOLAS & ST CATHERINES. working parties of 550 found daily -	VDL
	10		Tapped Enemy wire which gave us the information that he intended to raid which he did but the Black Watch were prepared and found his tape in No Mans Land. The Enemy were afterwards observed lining out on the tape and on advancing were fired on by Lewis guns. The attack was repulsed before enemy got to our line and the following night 4 dead Germans were found -	VDL

Instructions regarding War Diaries and Intelligence Summaries are contained in F. S. Regs., Part II. and the Staff Manual respectively. Title pages will be prepared in manuscript.

WAR DIARY
or
INTELLIGENCE SUMMARY.
(*Erase heading not required.*)

10th ARGYLL and SUTHERLAND HIGHLANDERS

Army Form C. 2118.

Place	Date	Hour	Summary of Events and Information	Remarks and references to Appendices
	1917			
ARRAS	March 11		Shelled all day with 8 inch – no casualties though other units suffered somewhat severely. The CO of the Tyneside Scot. was killed amongst them –	[illegible]
	12.		Still being shelled – Capt McMILLAN wounded –	[illegible]
		10 pm	Message received to "Stand to" and ready to move – 8 Black Watch patrols had entered enemy front line and found it deserted – It was considered possible that he had retired so we were prepared to follow him – However the night passed peacefully	
	13		Batt: to fr Huts ETRUN	[illegible]
	14		" to HERMAVILLE (less A Coy to TILLOY)	[illegible]
			a certain amount of training was carried out – a party of NCO's being instructed in bayonet fighting under an instructor from the Depot Battalion – Programme for Battalion Sports prepared and this time it was considered more than possible that they would come off but on the 20th orders received to move following morning –	
	20.		very successful Concert at which 2/Lt CLARKSON distinguished himself by creating a song "Where is Allemand tonight"	[illegible]
	21.		Batt to fr Huts ETRUN –	[illegible]

A5834 Wt. W4973/M687 750,000 8/16 D. D. & L. Ltd. Forms/C.2118/13.

Instructions regarding War Diaries and Intelligence Summaries are contained in F. S. Regs., Part II. and the Staff Manual respectively. Title pages will be prepared in manuscript.

WAR DIARY
or
INTELLIGENCE SUMMARY.

(*Erase heading not required.*)

Army Form C. 2118.

Place	Date	Hour	Summary of Events and Information	Remarks and references to Appendices
FIRUN	1916 March			
Y Huts	24		Batt: to HAUTES AVESNES	[illegible]
	27		Batt: to Y Huts	[illegible]
	26		Boxing Competition took place. The following were the Winners:	[illegible]
			MIDDLE WEIGHT 1. Private HARKESS – Transport	
			2. Corporal MURDOCH "D" Coy	
			LIGHT WEIGHT 1. Private DICKENSON "D" Coy	
			2. Sergt STARBUCKLE "A" Coy	
			BANTAM WEIGHT 1 Private FRENCH "C" Coy	
			2. Private GERSON "C" Coy	
	27		Capt P. LYLE reported from home to join the Battalion	[illegible]
	31		Batt took over the line from 7th Seaforth Highlanders from R. SCARPE to Sap 86 – The Brigade Battle Front	[illegible]

[illegible] Lt Col
Comdg. 10. A. & S. Hrs

CASUALTY STATEMENT

FOR MARCH 1917.

[redacted] DATE	KILLED	MISSING	WOUNDED	TO HOSPITAL	DISCHARGED FROM HOSPITAL	DRAFTS
1				13		
2				6		
3				6	3	
4				–		
5			2	3		
6				3	2.	
7	2		1.	1	1.	
8				2		
9			1	2	1	
10				4		
11				6		
12			1			
13			1	1	3	
14				2	2	
15					5	
16				–		
17				1 –	7	
18				4	1	9.
19				–	2	
20				4		
21				.		
22				3		
23				7	1.	
24				5		6.
25						
26				4	4	
27				9		
28				4.	1.	
29				1		
30				1		
31				2		

W. Rinch Captain + Adjt

1/4/17 10th Argyll + Sutherland Hrs

10 AGS H
Vol 20
26/9

April 1917

24.0.

G West

Instructions regarding War Diaries and Intelligence Summaries are contained in F. S. Regs., Part II. and the Staff Manual respectively. Title pages will be prepared in manuscript.

WAR DIARY
or
INTELLIGENCE SUMMARY.
(Erase heading not required.)

10th ARGYLL and SUTHERLAND HRS

Army Form C. 2118.

Place	Date 1917.	Hour	Summary of Events and Information	Remarks and references to Appendices
TRENCHES ST NICHOLAS	April 1.		German aeroplane brought down by Anti Aircraft guns behind our lines	
	2.		Shells falling round Cookhouse and REDOUBT LINE. a few casualties [illegible]	
	4		V. Day	
		6.15. am	LIEVENS GAS shells discharged.	
		6.30. am	Report gas attack was successful –	
		6.30. am	Preliminary Bombardment for Attack commenced which continued all day except between 9 and 11 P.m. – Not very much air activity	
		11.15. Am.	C.O. to Conference at Brigade H.Q.	
			Enemy retaliation slight.	
		4 P.m.	Enemy commenced shelling heavily front line & REDOUBT LINE where he blew in 2 dug outs – and later on OIL FACTORY. Casualties increased so asked leave to withdraw 1 Coy out of the line – they were billeted in ARRAS. Short of any cover in the whole sector – however managed to get most of the men into Batt. H.Q. & OIL FACTORY Dug Outs. 1. L. G. destroyed by shell fire.	
		5 P.m.	Enemy fired gas shells – no effect –	
		9 pm to 11 P.m.	Bombardment ceased for purposes of Patrols.	

Instructions regarding War Diaries and Intelligence Summaries are contained in F. S. Regs., Part II. and the Staff Manual respectively. Title pages will be prepared in manuscript.

WAR DIARY
or
INTELLIGENCE SUMMARY. 10th ARGYLL and SUTHERLAND H'RS

(*Erase heading not required.*)

Army Form C. 2118.

Place	Date	Hour	Summary of Events and Information	Remarks and references to Appendices
	1917			
St. NICHOLAS TRENCHES	April 4		Fighting Patrols sent out with orders to enter Enemy Trenches and bring back if possible a Prisoner.	
			Capt DENHAM went across from Sap 86 with a patrol and on reaching Trench was sniped at from Front line – proceeded along the Front trying to find a point of entry – Worked S to S end of PARROTS BEAK where he got into the throat of PARROTS BEAK – Found front of BEAK smashed in & not held. When trying to enter Front Trench fired at by 12 men. Patrol returned the fire for some little time and eventually withdrew as the time was 10.50 PM another bombardment was due to recommence at 11. PM.	
			The Patrol however gained the information that Enemy wire is badly cut and that we can get in almost anywhere – The ground is full of shell holes and the BEAK not held.	
		W DAY	Work done – Assembly Trenches completed –	
	5	8 am	CHINESE BARRAGE – retaliation slight – about 45 shells chiefly round FEBRUARY AVENUE – very few on assembly Trenches. Very misty, no view	
		10 to 10.30 AM	Bombardment ceased for aerial photography.	

Instructions regarding War Diaries and Intelligence Summaries are contained in F. S. Regs., Part II. and the Staff Manual respectively. Title pages will be prepared in manuscript.

WAR DIARY
or
INTELLIGENCE SUMMARY.
(Erase heading not required.)

Army Form C. 2118.

10th ARGYLL and SUTHERLAND HRS.

Place	Date 1917	Hour	Summary of Events and Information	Remarks and references to Appendices
St. NICHOLAS TRENCHES	April 5	11 pm	Bombardment ceased 11 Pm – 1 Am. for the purposes of Patrolling. Patrol consisting of 2/Lt. GARDINER & 10 O.R. with covering party of 2/Lt. STRAUGHAN and 8 O.R. left our Trenches to enter Enemy Line & bring back Prisoner. at 10.45 Pm. Enemy put down heavy Barrage on our front line & FEBRUARY AVENUE, but parties got out and rushed V.6 Sap. Found it occupied by 4 or 5 men who immediately withdrew into Front line where they with many others opened rapid rifle fire on our party. The enemy was in considerable strength and with rifle firing and bombing made it impossible to enter the Trench. Our men returned the fire but as nothing further could be done withdrew. The moon was full and he must have seen party before starting. Casualties 2/Lt GARDINER wounded 2/Lt. STRAUGHAN wounded to duty. 2 O.R. killed 2 wounded. Our front line is completely destroyed by shelling – the vicinity of Sap 84 being particularly dangerous, several posts having been lost there and the men buried. These posts have now been moved. One Platoon is in a Dug out just behind it and is cut off but will be relieved tonight. Enemy must have some strong dug outs in his Front line as he does not appear to have suffered from the bombardment. Heavy Artillery must be brought to bear on it.	

A5834 Wt. W4973/M687 750,000 8/16 D. D. & L. Ltd. Forms/C.2118/13.

Instructions regarding War Diaries and Intelligence Summaries are contained in F. S. Regs., Part II. and the Staff Manual respectively. Title pages will be prepared in manuscript.

Army Form C. 2118.

WAR DIARY
or
INTELLIGENCE SUMMARY.
(*Erase heading not required.*)

10th ARGYLL and SUTHERLAND HRS

Place	Date	Hour	Summary of Events and Information	Remarks and references to Appendices
St NICHOLAS Trench	1917 apl 6 X day		2/Lt. PATERSON slightly wounded (to duty)	
		1.30 pm	CHINESE BARRAGE. Enemy made no retaliation in particular.	
			Attack postponed 24 hours to Monday.	
			Shell landed outside Mess at mouth of Signals Dug Out, by good fortune only 2 men slightly wounded.	
			At height of Bombardment message received "Training report for ensuing week not required"!! Someone must have forgotten for the moment that a Battle was going on!	
	apl 7 Extra day		Batt relieved in Trenches by ½ Batt: Black Watch & ½ Batt Seaforth Highlanders and billetted in Convent.	
			Quiet day.	
	apl 8 Y day Easter Sunday	10.30 P.M.	Batt: commences moving into Assembly Trenches for the attack. 3 "Moppers up" Platoons A moving at 10.30. P.m. and at 11.30 P.M. remainder of Battalion moves in.	
	apl 9 Z Day	2.45 am	Concentration of GROUP reported complete. No casualties.	
			Assembly Trenches were fired on very slightly from now onwards until Zero.	

Instructions regarding War Diaries and Intelligence Summaries are contained in F. S. Regs., Part II. and the Staff Manual respectively. Title pages will be prepared in manuscript.

WAR DIARY
or
INTELLIGENCE SUMMARY.
(*Erase heading not required.*)

Army Form C. 2118.

10th Argyll & Sutherland Hrs

Place	Date	Hour	Summary of Events and Information	Remarks and references to Appendices
BATTLE OF ARRAS.	1917 Apl 9.	ZERO 5.30 am.	Assault commenced - Our Troops moved off from Assembly Trenches and went over the Parapet -	
			Enemy appears to have detected nothing beforehand - The Bombardment restarted punctually and Enemy put up his S.O.S. (Orange Clusters) in great numbers along the line - Retaliation slight - 4 Tanks moved in the wake of Infantry at Zero - Batt. H.Q. in Battle H.Q. Spring Avenue -	
		6.30. am.	Report received BLACK LINE captured up to time and reorganising for attack on BLUE LINE	
		7.0 am	Orders sent to C & D Coys to move forward by Coys to vicinity of SANITATS GRABEN but if Barrage heavy to remain in first German Line -	
		7.20 am.	Moved Batt. H.Q. to Eastern end of SPRING TRAMWAYS -	
			Message received from B. Coy that Lt. MACKIE was wounded and that he was taking command and moving in support of BLACK WATCH	
			2/Lt. BEATTIE wounded to hosp -	
		7.40 am	Orders sent to C & D Coys that they will get in touch with O.C. BLACK WATCH in event of his requiring further support.	
			Message received from Brigade that 2 guns of T.M.B. are to report to 7th SEAFORTHS to assist in clearing Enemy out of LAURENT BLANGY, and that when village is taken O.C. T.M. Section will report to O.C. A & S. Hrs at SANITATS GRABEN.	

Instructions regarding War Diaries and Intelligence Summaries are contained in F. S. Regs., Part II. and the Staff Manual respectively. Title pages will be prepared in manuscript.

WAR DIARY
or
INTELLIGENCE SUMMARY.
(Erase heading not required.)

Army Form C. 2118.

10th Argyll and Sutherland Hrs

Place	Date	Hour	Summary of Events and Information	Remarks and references to Appendices
BATTLE OF ARRAS	1917 Apl 9	8.5 am.	Message received from "A" Coy "Enemy Trenches unrecognisable, moving on to BLUE LINE in support BLACKWATCH - 61 strong"	
		8.30 am	Message received from "C" Coy "In position SANITATS GRABEN in touch with D Coy and left flank. No casualties"	
		8.35 am.	Message received from "D" Coy that BLACKWATCH have ordered them up to reinforce in BLUE LINE as BLACKWATCH is held up. This was only momentary and BLUE LINE was captured up to time.	
			The wire in front of BLUE LINE was untouched and would have been a formidable menace if it had been completed but the Troops got through it fairly easily.	
			Enemy were seen making off so Lewis Guns were pushed forward on Railway Embankment which caused many Enemy Casualties.	
			The BLUE LINE was found to be a position of great strength, the Dug Outs were concreted, dug into the Embankment and immune from Shellfire. The Enemy must have been panicstricken to have given up such a position which should have held a large force at bay for a long time - a Colonel Commandant of Artillery & 3 artillery officers were captured and a few other prisoners later. A 77 cm gun & team complete were captured by A. Coy, Serg. MACLENNAN alone killing with either rifle or bayonet 15 of the enemy.	

Instructions regarding War Diaries and Intelligence Summaries are contained in F. S. Regs., Part II. and the Staff Manual respectively. Title pages will be prepared in manuscript.

WAR DIARY
or
INTELLIGENCE SUMMARY.
(Erase heading not required.)

10th Argyll & Sutherland Hrs.

Army Form C. 2118.

Place	Date	Hour	Summary of Events and Information	Remarks and references to Appendices
BATTLE OF ARRAS	1917 Apl 9		The Battalion captured about 100 prisoners, they were so demoralized that they gave themselves up voluntarily and in some Dug Outs Ham and eggs were found on the table cooked and which were promptly devoured by our men –	
			It appears they imagined the attack was to take place on the 10th and that when it started it was taken to be only a raid.	
			The PARROTS BEAK which had given us so much trouble for so long was pulverised but a Machine Gun was still firing from it as we advanced – The gun was taken & the team killed –	
		10.30 am.	Moved Batt. HQ to BLUE LINE –	
			As Batt now rather weak 1 Plat. from A Coy, 1 Plat: from B. Coy & whole of C. Coy formed one wave – D. Coy forming 2nd wave –	
			formed composition of force for attack on BROWN LINE with right flank on marshes of R. SCARPE and left flank on ESK TRENCH – 5th CAMERONS moving with complete Battalion, their right being on ESK TRENCH (exclusive) & left on Brigade left flank.	

A5834 Wt. W4973/M687 750,000 8/16 D. D. & L. Ltd. Forms/C.2118/13.

Instructions regarding War Diaries and Intelligence Summaries are contained in F. S. Regs., Part II. and the Staff Manual respectively. Title pages will be prepared in manuscript.

WAR DIARY
or
INTELLIGENCE SUMMARY.
(Erase heading not required.)

Army Form C. 2118.

10th Argyll and Sutherland Highrs

Place	Date	Hour	Summary of Events and Information	Remarks and references to Appendices
BATTLE OF ARRAS	1917 April 9.	12.39 pm	In position on BLUE LINE lying under Barrage – heavy Smoke Barrage –	
		12.43 pm	advanced in line with 5th CAMERONS – occupied OLIVE TRENCH and waited under Barrage until 1.22 pm when attack went forward –	
		1.22 pm	Village of ATHIES captured without opposition and PALMY TRENCH	
		2.40 pm	occupied being the BROWN LINE and 3rd objective at the exact moment as laid down in Programme –	
			Consolidation immediately commenced and two Strong Points erected.	
			D. Coy captured 2 . 77 mm guns in ATHIES village.	
			When the attack on ATHIES commenced the village was in a fairly good state of repair but during the bombardment it was entirely levelled to the ground the walls falling down in front of us as we advanced.	
			The Barrage was very accurate we only having 2 casualties from Smoke Shells – 12th Brigade (4th Division) passed through us on Brown Line at 3.10 pm	
		7.30 pm	A & B Coys in BROWN LINE relieved by 5th Camerons and returned to bivouack in BLUE LINE and started to consolidate from S of ESKER Scarp	

A5834 Wt. W4973/M687 750,000 8/16 D. D. & L. Ltd. Forms/C.2118/13.

Instructions regarding War Diaries and Intelligence Summaries are contained in F. S. Regs., Part II. and the Staff Manual respectively. Title pages will be prepared in manuscript.

WAR DIARY
or
INTELLIGENCE SUMMARY. 10th Argyll & Sutherland Highlrs.

(*Erase heading not required.*)

Army Form C. 2118.

Place	Date	Hour	Summary of Events and Information	Remarks and references to Appendices
BATTLE OF ARRAS.	Apr 9.		NOTES. ASSEMBLY TRENCHES had been dug some days in advance & and do not appear to have attracted as much attention as was expected. Hot meal was served before leaving Billets and rum issued 20 minutes before zero. ARTILLERY – Barrage was excellent – and the wire completely cut excepting that in front of BLUE LINE which enemy fortunately allowed us to go through without much interference. DIRECTION. Was occasionally lost, sometimes by Enemy shell fire on a flank which caused Infantry to change direction. This was corrected afterwards. It was somewhat difficult to find points to march on as Trenches were completely obliterated by our shell fire. BOOTY Battalion captured about 100 Prisoners and 3 Field Guns & 1 Machine Gun with Team complete. also the dachshund belonging to the Colonel Commandant of Artillery. Which has been named ATHIES. and becomes the property of our Brigade Commander. The majority of the Prisoners taken were Bavarians and a few Prussians	

Instructions regarding War Diaries and Intelligence Summaries are contained in F. S. Regs., Part II. and the Staff Manual respectively. Title pages will be prepared in manuscript.

Army Form C. 2118.

WAR DIARY
or
INTELLIGENCE SUMMARY. 10th Argyll & Sutherland Highrs

(Erase heading not required.)

Place	Date	Hour	Summary of Events and Information	Remarks and references to Appendices
BATTLE OF ARRAS.	1917 Apl 10		Quiet night – A & S. Hrs and CAMERONS in BLUE LINE very cold no coats for men but rations came up and rum issued. a few of the men had dug outs. B.H.Q with 12 Brig H.Q in Col Commandant's Dug out in BLUE LINE. Day spent in reorganising and cleaning up. Snowing hard.	
			CASualties on the 9th inst.	
			Off: wounded	
			CAPT DENHAM (since died of wounds)	
			Lt. MACKIE	
			Lt. STRACHAN.	
			Lt. SCOTT	
			Lt. PARK	
			Lt. ROBINSON (to duty)	
			Lt. BEATTIE (to duty)	

Other Ranks / Off

	K.	W.	M.	Off
				–7–
A	2	16	11	
B	5	25	6	
C	2	9	–	
D	7	15	1	
	16	65	18	7

99
7
Total 106

A5834 Wt. W4973/M687 750,000 8/16 D. D. & L. Ltd. Forms/C.2118/13.

Instructions regarding War Diaries and Intelligence Summaries are contained in F. S. Regs., Part II. and the Staff Manual respectively. Title pages will be prepared in manuscript.

WAR DIARY
or
INTELLIGENCE SUMMARY.
(*Erase heading not required.*)

Army Form C. 2118.

10th Argyll & Sutherland Hrs

Place	Date 1917	Hour	Summary of Events and Information	Remarks and references to Appendices
BATTLE OF ARRAS	Apl. 11		Heavy snowstorm – Pioneer Company erected a strong point in front of BLUE LINE and similar strong points were started along the Brigade Sector.	
	12.		C.O received orders to reconnoitre with other C.O.s GREEN LINE and country in front, in view of attacking in the evening.	
	"	2 pm.	Met Brigade Commander at ATHIES where operation orders were issued for attack. Batt: moved off in rear of 5th Camerons for GREEN LINE Support Trenches S of ATHIES – FAMPOUX Road.	
		4 pm	B & D Coys in position in GREEN LINE Support Trench. A & C – in ~~Reserve~~ in ARTILLERY HOLLOW (1000 yds in rear)	
		4.30 pm.	C.O. saw Coy Commanders and explained to them verbally orders for attack. Brig: O.O attached – In event of 27th Brigade & South African Brigade being successful 26th Brigade are ordered to attack with 5th CAMERONS leading and 2 Coys A & S.H. in support. The attack by 27th & S. Af. Brigades failed owing to lack of Artillery preparation – They were repulsed by M.G. fire from CHEMICAL WORKS, CEMETRY and MOUNT PLEASANT WOOD and never got nearer than 400x from our own Line where a German Trench was discovered. Both Brigades had heavy casualties. 26th Brigade consequently were not engaged	app:

A5834 Wt. W4973/M687 750,000 8/16 D. D. & L. Ltd. Forms/C.2118/13.

Army Form C. 2118.

Instructions regarding War Diaries and Intelligence Summaries are contained in F. S. Regs., Part II. and the Staff Manual respectively. Title pages will be prepared in manuscript.

WAR DIARY
or
INTELLIGENCE SUMMARY. 10th Argyll & Sutherland Hrs

(Erase heading not required.)

Place	Date	Hour	Summary of Events and Information	Remarks and references to Appendices
BATTLE OF ARRAS	1917 Apl 12.	7.0 pm	Batt received orders to withdraw from assembly area to trenches S of ATHIES–FAMPOUX Road – Coats collected from BLUE LINE where they had been dumped. C.O. went to Brig H.Q. at L'ABAYETTE for orders –	
		12 midnight	Brigade ordered to take over front line in front of FAMPOUX from R. SCARPE to Southern edge of HYDERABAD REDOUBT in order from S to N. BLACK WATCH A & S. Hrs CAMERONS with SEAFORTHS in support – from a Brigade of 4th Div. On an average 3 guides per Battalion only were furnished who in some instances were unacquainted with the position of the Trenches.	
	13	2 am	Batt moved forward to take over line – found a mixed party, a collection of many units – Immediately started digging as trenches were very shallow. Fortunately enemy artillery inactive.	
		4.30 am	Relief complete – B.H.Q. in GREEN LINE Support Trenches S of Road	
		3 am.	Relief complete reported.	
		12 mn	Batt relieved in front line, it being considered sufficient to hold the line with 2 Batts. Batt: holds GREEN LINE Support N of Trenches –	

A5834 Wt. W4973/M687 750,000 8/16 D. D. & L. Ltd. Forms/C.2118/13.

Instructions regarding War Diaries and Intelligence Summaries are contained in F. S. Regs., Part II. and the Staff Manual respectively. Title pages will be prepared in manuscript.

WAR DIARY
or
INTELLIGENCE SUMMARY.
(Erase heading not required.)

10th Argyll and Sutherland Hrs.

Army Form C. 2118.

Place	Date	Hour	Summary of Events and Information	Remarks and references to Appendices
BATTLE OF ARRAS	1917 Apl 14		Enemy fired Gas shells for 2 hours during night – No casualties. Party of 250 men at night dug front & Support line – Enemy Art: inactive. Enemy shells GREEN LINE incessantly, many shells landing in wire in rear, he probably thinks we have a dug a trench using his wire as a screen.	
	15	5 pm.	Relieved by 6th Black Watch (51st Div).	
		10 pm.	Relief completed. As rear Platoon reached a point 1000x E of L'ABBAYETTE two 5.9 shells fell in their midst killing 2/Lt. HAYWORTH & 6 O.R. & wounding 6 O.R. Batt: returned to billets in ARRAS.	
	16.		Pipers met Batt: & played them to the Huts	
			CASUALTIES DURING OPERATIONS APRIL 9 – 15	

Officers
CAPT. G. P. DENHAM died of wounds
2/Lt. H. A. HAYWORTH Killed
2/Lt. A. SCOTT wounded
2/Lt. C. R. STRACHAN "
2/Lt. C. M. SIMPSON "
2/Lt. S. PARK "
Lt. I. MACKIE "
2/Lt. J. P. G. PATERSON " to duty
2/Lt. J. M. BEATTIE " "
2/Lt. J. H. F. HOURSTON " "
2/Lt. S. G. ROBINSON "

OTHER RANKS

	K	W	M
A Coy	3	30	3
B	7	33	
C	7	20	3
D	10	27	3
	27	110	9
Officers	2	9	
TOTAL	29	119	9

(157)

A5834 Wt. W4973/M687 750,000 8/16 D. D. & L. Ltd. Forms/C.2118/13.

Instructions regarding War Diaries and Intelligence Summaries are contained in F. S. Regs., Part II. and the Staff Manual respectively. Title pages will be prepared in manuscript.

WAR DIARY
or
INTELLIGENCE SUMMARY. 10th Argyll and Sutherland Hrs.

(*Erase heading not required.*)

Army Form C. 2118.

Place	Date	Hour	Summary of Events and Information	Remarks and references to Appendices
	1917 Apl		Congratulatory messages were received from ARMY, CORPS, DIV: and Brigade Com.rs and M. Gen: FURSE late commanding the 9th Division.	app:
	17		Draft 139 O.R. arrived from Base and inspected by G.O.C. on 19th	
Y. Huts.	21		Batt: entrained by "Tactical Train" for BAILLEUL aux CORNAILLES.	
			The distance of 12 miles was covered in 6 hours!!	
BAILLEUL aux CORNAILLES			Weather improved and the men getting rested.	
			Arrangements were made to bring off the Batt: Sports, but as usual as soon as the day was fixed upon, Batt: received orders to proceed	
	25		to Y Huts. Again the tactical train was put in motion but this time without the success which it had attained on 21st. On this occasion this Tactical Train did not reach its objective owing to the R.E having removed the rails. Batt detrained at ACQ & proceeded by route march to Y Huts.	
	27.		Batt having drawn fighting kit moved with Transport to BLUE LINE.	

Army Form C. 2118.

Instructions regarding War Diaries and Intelligence Summaries are contained in F. S. Regs., Part II. and the Staff Manual respectively. Title pages will be prepared in manuscript.

WAR DIARY
or
INTELLIGENCE SUMMARY.
(*Erase heading not required.*)

10th ARGYLL & SUTHERLAND HRS.

Place	Date 1917	Hour	Summary of Events and Information	Remarks and references to Appendices
BATTLE OF ARRAS	April 27th	4pm.	Battn reached BLUE Line. Transport brigaded on hill North of St. NICHOLAS. Orders were received to move to BROWN line about H.9.a.&c. early tomorrow. Ground reconnoitred by C.O. Capt LYLE & Lt. RAIT	
		8–9pm.	Battn moved in single file to new area. Companies were disposed	
	28th	1am.	as follows:- 'A' Coy in KEEN trench, 'B' Coy (less 2 platns) in KEEN, remaining platns in LADLE. 'C' Coy in LADLE, 'D' Coy in LAUREL. Bn H.Q. about H.8.b.7.4. Orderlies &c in trenches & shell holes in vicinity.	
		9pm.	Bn. warned to take over from 112th Bde. in the line. Coy. Commanders & Specialists moved to H.Q. 112th Bde (H.4.d.5.3) to get particulars	
		9.30 pm	Bn moved forward but were met by order from 37th Division that relief was postponed until situation cleared up. Bn therefore returned to previous position	
		11.30pm.	The C.O. & Lt RAIT proceeded to 112th Bde H.Q. & eventually it was arranged to proceed with relief.	
		12mn.	Bn. received fresh order to proceed with relief.	

Instructions regarding War Diaries and Intelligence Summaries are contained in F. S. Regs., Part II. and the Staff Manual respectively. Title pages will be prepared in manuscript.

WAR DIARY
or
INTELLIGENCE SUMMARY. 10th ARGYLL & SUTHERLAND HRS.

(*Erase heading not required.*)

Army Form C. 2118.

Place	Date	Hour	Summary of Events and Information	Remarks and references to Appendices
BATTLE OF ARRAS.	1917 ~~April~~ April 29th		N.E. towards CUTHBERT. When within 20x to 30x of CUTHBERT (probably about H.7.d.80.95.) the patrol observed men in CUTHBERT. & Capt LYLE became suspicious & shouted "are you Seaforths?" Receiving no reply he fired his revolver at them. His patrol were immediately assaulted with a shower of cylindrical STICK Grenades. The patrol withdrew but before reaching CASH, Capt LYLE was severely wounded, the N.C.O. was killed & one man wounded.	
	30th		Report received from CAPT LYLE at the Dressing Stn. that CUTHBERT was strongly held by about 200 men.	
			From information gathered during the day & from Capt LYLE'S patrol report it was made clear that we had never held CUTHBERT but a small trench running out of CASH which was not shown on any maps or air photographs handed over or supplied to the Bn.	
		3.15 am	Enemy barraged our front line	
		4.15 am	Enemy again barraged our front line & attempted to counter-attack our rifle fire & Lewis Gun fire stopped him on his own parapet.	

A5834 Wt. W4973/M687 750,000 8/16 D. D. & L. Ltd. Forms/C.2118/13.

Instructions regarding War Diaries and Intelligence Summaries are contained in F. S. Regs., Part II. and the Staff Manual respectively. Title pages will be prepared in manuscript.

WAR DIARY
or
INTELLIGENCE SUMMARY.
(Erase heading not required.)

Army Form C. 2118.

10th ARGYLL & SUTHERLAND H^RS.

Place	Date	Hour	Summary of Events and Information	Remarks and references to Appendices
BATTLE OF ARRAS	1917 April ~~28~~ 29th	12.55 am.	Bn. reached 112th Bde H.Q. Coy. Commanders took over their Companies and relief proceeded.	
		1.15 am.		
		6 am.	A long and very difficult relief was reported complete.	
			Bn. H.Q. then moved forward from 112th Bde. to old 63rd Bde advanced H.Q. at H.10.d.35.60.	
			Dispositions were then as follows:- B. Coy. 1 platn in CASH, 2 platns in CUBA. 1 Platn in CLASP. D Coy in CLYDE & CHILI. C Coy in HONEY - Machine Guns were disposed as follows:- 2 in CASH, 4 in CUBA, 4 in D Coy sector, 4 in C Coy. sector, 2 in A Coy sector.	
			O.C. 'B' Coy (Capt LYLE) reported that dawn had come before absolute completion of relief & that some elements of 37th Divn were unable to get out. Also that he was convinced that CUTHBERT was occupied by him for a short distance N. of CASH & that COD was occupied by elements of 37th Divn. He was also of opinion that Enemy occupied N. end of CUTHBERT.	
			In order to clear up the situation Capt LYLE took out a patrol after dusk. The patrol proceeded along CASH to a point some 50x from the junction of CASH & CUTHBERT & then left CASH & moved	

Instructions regarding War Diaries and Intelligence Summaries are contained in F. S. Regs., Part II. and the Staff Manual respectively. Title pages will be prepared in manuscript.

WAR DIARY
or
INTELLIGENCE SUMMARY. 10th ARGYLL & SUTHERLAND HRS
(Erase heading not required.)

Army Form C. 2118

Place	Date	Hour	Summary of Events and Information	Remarks and references to Appendices
BATTLE OF ARRAS.	1917 April 30th		It transpired during the day that there was a pocket at the end of the newly discovered trench held by 40 men of all ranks of the 37th & possibly 34th Divns These men were relieved & sent down by us during the morning. They had been there for 9 days & for 48 hours had been without food or water.	
		5 to 5.45 pm.	Combined bombardment by ~~so~~ our Artillery & 26th T.M.B of CUTHBERT COD, and CUPID. The Artillery bombardment was ineffective being 200x to 300x over. The T.M.B. bombardment provoked considerable sniping activity from the Enemy's lines.	
		8.30 pm	Our Artillery bombarded Enemy lines, he retaliated on CLASP, CLYDE, & CHILI with 7.7 cm shells but did no damage.	
		11.40 pm.	'C' Coy relieved 'B' Coy in the front line. One platoon of A. Coy relieved the Pioneer Platoon.	

N. McQueen Major,
for Lieut Col. Commanding,
10th Argyll & Suthd Hdrs.

A5834 Wt. W4973 M687 750,000 8/16 D. D. & L. Ltd. Forms/C.2118/13.

SECRET. Copy No. 5

OPERATION ORDER No. 1 Dated MARCH, 1917,

issued by LT-COL.H.G.SOTHEBY, M.V.O.

Commanding 10th ARGYLL & SUTHERLAND HIGHLANDERS.

Map references :1 Trench Map ARRAS 51.b N.W.3. Scale 1/10,000.
2 Sketch Map marked "A".
3 Sketch Map marked "B".
4 Composite Map 1/5000 issued to Companies

GENERAL IDEA.

1. (a) The XVII Corps is to capture enemy third system of trenches which runs from the SCARPE at FEUCHY through LE POINT DU JOUR - MAISON DE LA COTE - COMMANDANTS HOUSE (BROWN Line on Map)

(b) When this has been done a further advance is to be made South of the POINT DU JOUR to capture enemy 4th line system and the village of FAMPOUX (this objective to be referred to as the GREEN LINE).

(c) The attack up to and including the BROWN LINE will be made by three Divisions in line, the 9th Division on the right, the attack on the GREEN LINE by the Division in Corps Reserve (the 4th Divn.)

(d) The 26th Brigade will be the right Brigade of the 9th Division. On its right (South of the SCARPE) it will have the 45th Brigade (15th Division) and on its left the S.A.Brigade.

26th BRIGADE BOUNDARIES

2. (a) In our own lines:-
Right Boundary - River SCARPE.

Left " a line running Westward from the left of Trench 85 to the North end of FORRESTIER REBOUBT thence MAY AVENUE inclusive and CANDLE FACTORY exclusive to G.16.d.8.9½ thence Westward to cross roads G.16.c.6.9. (exclusive)

(b) During Advance:-
Right Boundary - River SCARPE.

Left Boundary:- ISAR GABEL (inclusive) road junction G.18.b.5.8. (exclusive) Trench Junction H.13.a.0.8 (inclusive) Railway Bridge H.8.c.05.05. (exclusive) road junction H.15.a.4.6. (inclusive)

Centre Line:- The PARROTS BEAK - cross roads at G.18.a.8.1½. - road junction H.13.a.3.3. (all inclusive to right front Battn.) road junction H.13.a.70.38. - thence a line to the Railway Bridge at H.14.a.0.3. (inclusive to left front Battalion)

9th DIVN. OBJECTIVES

3. There are three systems of trenches to be attacked viz:-
(i) FRONT SYSTEM including all trenches as far East as RESERVE LINE which runs North from the East end of ST. LAURENT BLANGY through G.6.d.9.6.
This includes four organized fire trenches.

(ii) The second system which follows the line of the Railway from the SCARPE through BOIS DE LA MAISON BLANCHE apparently organised in two trench lines in the Southern Half and three trench lines in the Northern Half of Brigade area.

(iii) The third system now in progress of development running from ATHIES through LE POINT DU JOUR which consists of two trench lines.

The capture of each of the above systems constitutes a separate phase in the operations and there will therefore be three main objectives namely:-
(1) BLACK LINE.
(2) BLUE " (3) BROWN LINE.

26th BRIGADE. DISPOSITIONS.

4. The 26th Brigade will attack with 2 Battalions in line one Battalion in support and 1 Battalion in reserve as follows:-

Right Battalion	7th Seaforths.
Left "	8th Black Watch.
Support Battalion	10th A & S. Highlanders.
Reserve "	5th Camerons.

The 7th Seaforths and 8th Black Watch will attack on a two Company front each company on a front of two platoons, giving four waves to each Battn. Waves at 100x distance as per sketch which follows:-

10th A & S.H. "A" Coy.

"A" Coy. less 1 Platoon will follow the leading wave of the 8th Black Watch and "mop up" the first three enemy trenches after they have been taken by the 8th BLACK WATCH

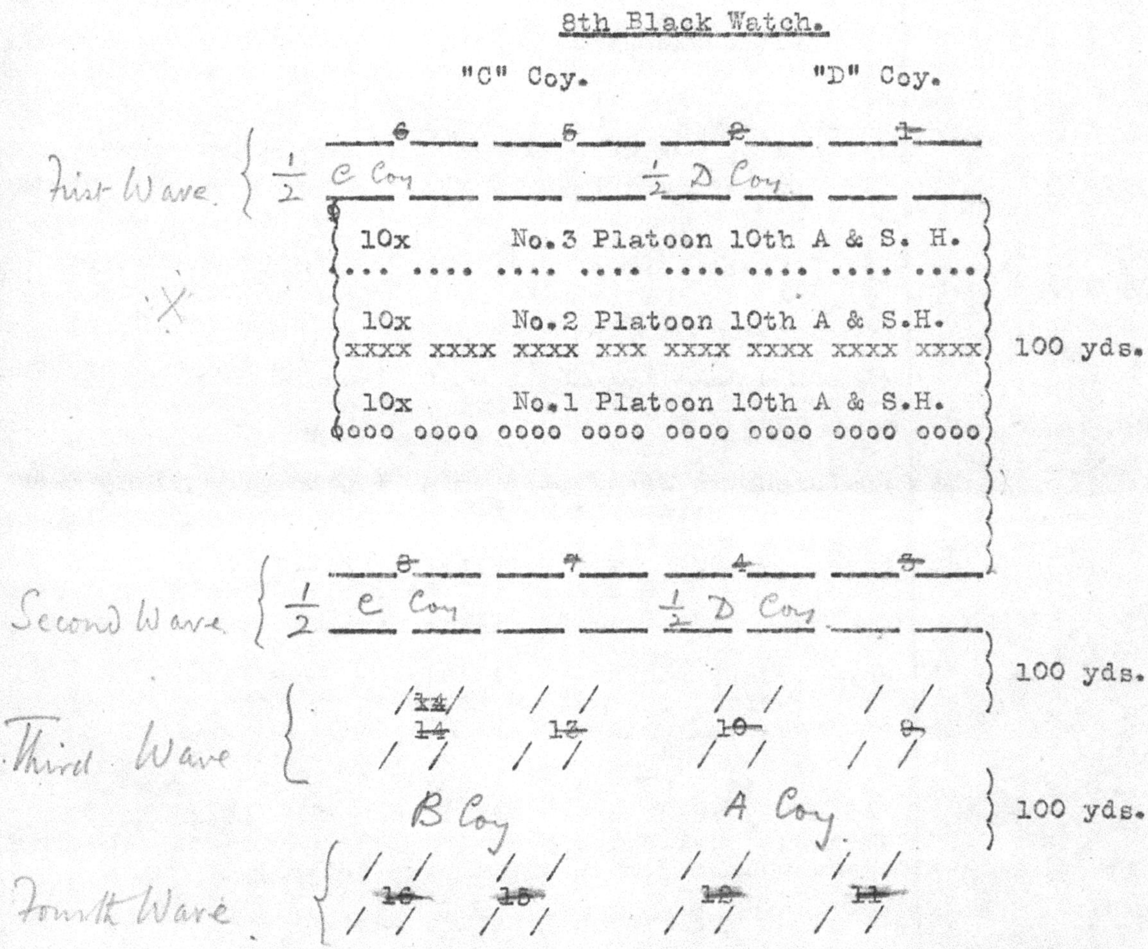

x Note — .... xxxx oooo = 1 Platoon each line from "A" Coy. 10th A & S.H. to act as moppers up for 1st, 2nd and 3rd enemy lines behind 8th Black Watch.

No.3 Platoon to move first and mop up first enemy line.
No.2 " " " second " " " second " "
No.1 " " " third " " " third " "

ASSEMBLY POSITIONS. AND BATTALION HEADQUARTERS.

5. The assembly positions of the Companies will be as shown in the map marked "B" herewith.

Battle Headquarters at FORRESTIER REDOUBT. (dugout No.16 or 17 - G.17.a.7.4½.)

OPERATIONS. 10th A & S.H.

6. It will be noted that during the first two phases of the Divisional Operations the Battalion is in support and if carried out according to orders the Battalion will not, except as to the 3 platoons of "A" who are mopping up for the 8th Black Watch, take any active part in the fighting line.

If however it is not possible to carry out these operations exactly as laid down by Divisional Orders the Battalion will have to be ready at any time to form defensive flanks to the right or left or support the 7th Seaforths in ST. LAURENT BLANGY or the 8th Black Watch in their attack on the BLACK LINE.

For the reasons appearing above it is necessary to burden Battalion Operation Orders with a considerable amount of detail which must be carefully explained to all ranks.

Unless otherwise ordered the Battalion frontage until approaching the BLUE LINE is the same as that of the 8th Black Watch and is bounded by the left Brigade Boundary on the left and the centre line on the right.

after Blue line is taken the Bn will deploy on whole Bde frontage

(On reaching the BLUE LINE) and on deployment therefrom the whole Brigade Frontage becomes the Battalion frontage.

DISTRIBUTION OF COMPANIES.

7. The leading Companies will be "A" Coy. on the left and "B" Coy. on the right. The rear Companies will be C Company on the left and D Company on the right.

MOVES.

8. <u>First phase of the Battle - Advance on BLACK LINE.</u>

Moves at <u>ZERO.</u>

7th Seaforths to BLACK LINE point P - D and various points in rear.

8th Black Watch - D & C Coys to BLACK LINE D to E.
B & A " " SANITATS GRABEN L to O.

10th A & S. H.

"A" Coy. less 1 Platoon immediately after first wave of 8th Black Watch (see para. 4 and sketch) to mop up 1st, 2nd and 3rd enemy lines.

"A" Coy. (less 3 platoons) and "B" Coy. move ~~xxxxxx~~ from Assembly trenches to 3rd line enemy front line system X to Y collect 3 platoons mopping up for 8th Black Watch and complete mopping up if necessary.

<u>NOTE.</u> C & D Coys. and H.Q. stand fast.

<u>Second phase of Battle - Preliminary moves.</u>

<u>ZERO plus 1 hour 30 mins.</u>

7th Seaforths close up on leading Companies.

10th A & S. H.

"A" & "B" Coys. from enemy's third line to close support of "B" & "A" (the rear) Coys. 8th Black Watch in SANITATS GRABEN.

~~10th A & S. H. (contd).~~

ZERO plus 1 hour 45 mins.

7th Seaforths - re-arrangement of Companies.

8th Black Watch "B" & "A" Coys move up through "C" & "D" Coys. on BLACK LINE and form up under barrage.

10th A & S. H.

"A" & "B" Coys. move up to BLACK LINE through "C" & "D" Coys. 8th Black Watch ~~xx xxxxxx~~ (now become rear Coys.) ready to move in close support of "B" & "A" Coys. 8th Black Watch (now leading Coys.)

"C" & "D" Coys. move from Assembly Trenches to SANITATS GRABEN.

The advance on BLUE LINE.

ZERO plus 2 hours 6 mins.

7th Seaforths - "A" Coy. with "B" Coy. in close support advance to attack BLUE LINE (G to H)

8th Black Watch - "B" and "A" Coys. advance to attack BLUE LINE (H to F)

10th A & S. H.

"A" & "B" Coys. move in close support of "B" & "A" Coys. 8th BLACK WATCH in attack on BLUE LINE.

NOTE. In the event of the 8th Black Watch and 7th ~~xxxxxx~~ Seaforths gaining the BLUE LINE the three supporting Coys - viz. "B" Coy 7th Seaforths and "A" & "B" Coys. 10th A & S. H. will halt on the line K.L.M.

"B" COMPANY.

O.C. "B" Coy. will then arrange to reconnoitre ~~for~~ a convenient place in the vicinity of HERVIN Fm. or the road junctions North thereof in which to establish Battalion H.Q. He will send back a message to Battn. H.Q. notifying the position selected by him on receipt of which Battalion H.Q. will move forward. He will at ~~xx~~ the same time notify position to "A" "C" and "D" Coys.

Third phase of Battle - Preliminary moves:-

ZERO ~~PL~~ plus 4 hours.

5th Camerons move in artillery formation from assembly trenches to vicinity of BLUE LINE.

ZERO plus 4 hours 30 mins.

10th A & S. H.

"C" & "D" Coys. move from SANITATS GRABEN to vicinity of BLUE LINE passing to the right of "A" & "B" Coys.

10th A & S. H. **ZERO plus 6 hours 35 mins.**

"A" "B" "C" "D" Coys cross the BLUE LINE and form up close under the barrage and prepare to advance on the BROWN LINE.

10th A & S. H. **ZERO plus ~~6~~ 7 hours ~~46~~ 9 mins.** 7 hours 9 mins

"A" "B" "C" & "D" Coys move forward to attack the BROWN LINE. This advance will commence in artillery formation , "A" "B" & "D" Coys in line, "C" Coy in support behind "A" & "B". As and when any Coy. comes under M.G. or rifle fire they will extend under orders from their Commanders. If necessary the extensions may have to take place when lying out under the barrage.

5th Camerons (4 Coys.) cross the BLUE LINE and move forward in support of 10th A & S. Hdrs..

FORMATIONS. 10th A & S. H. Prior to attack on BROWN LINE.

9. With the exception of the mopping up platoons of "A" Coy., while advancing after 1st wave of 8th Black Watch, all movements by Coys. up to and including deployment in front of BLUE LINE will normally be carried out in Artillery formation as practised in training, but all Commanders of Units must use their discretion as to extensions where in their opinion the necessity arises.

The Attack on the BROWN LINE.

10. FRONTAGES - Left to Right.
"A" Coy. - Point "F" to a point 175x South .
"B" " - From point 175x South of point "F" to Tramway (exclusive) approximately 175x.
"D" Coy. - South of Tramway to a point about 300x South to be determined by O.C. "D" Coy, after personal reconnaissance, according to the nature of the ground.
"C" Coy. (less 2 sections) in rear of ~~"A"~~ "A" & "B" Coys.

"C" Coy will detail two sections to bomb and clear ESK trench and two sections to bomb and clear TEES Trench.

OBJECTIVES.

"A" & "B" Coys. The BROWN LINE from Left Boundary to junction of Trench and road at H.15.a.2.1.

"C" Coy. (less 1 Platoon) When the above objective has been reached "C" Coy. (less 1 Platoon) will hold itself in readiness on receipt of orders from Battn. H.Q. to bomb and clear PALMY Trench from H.15.a.2.1. to H.15.c.3.5.

"D" Coy. The BROWN LINE from H.15.c.3.5. to the River SCARPE.
If "D" Coy. is held up West of the village of ATHIES it will immediately dig in, ask for assistance from supporting Coys. of 5th Camerons and from the 26th T.M.B. and if possible reconnoitre the low ground lying to the South and South-west of the village.

If this eventuality occurs "D" Coy. will send very full details and reports to Bn. H.Q. so as to enable arrangements to be made to bring pressure to bear on the North and in rear of the village at the same time as any further assault is launched by "D" Coy.

ACTION OF THE RESERVE DIVISION.

11. (a). The 4th Division will assemble in the area xxx S.E. of ANZIN lower end of ROCLINCOURT VALLEY - ST. NICHOLAS, its Divisional Headquarters being alongside h the 9th Division Headquarters.

(b). On receipt of the information that the BLUE LINE is in our possession, it will move forward so as to xxx reach the BLUE line at approximately ZERO plus 6 hours 40 minutes, i.e. The hour at which the advance of the 9th Division from the BLUE line to the BROWN line commences.

(c). From the BLUE line the attacking Brigades of the 4th Division will follow up the 9th Division so as to reach the German 3rd system of trenches at ZERO plus 8 hours 40 mins.

(d). They will pass throughx the 9th Division on the BROWN line at ZERO plus 9 hours 40 minutes and proceed to the attack of the German 4th system.

(e). The consolidation of the BROWN line by the tropps of the 9th Division will be continued until they are relieved kxx by troops of the 4th Division, other than those who pass through them to the attack of the GREEN line.

(f). On relief, the 9th Division (less 3 Fd. Coys. R.E. and Pioneer Battalion) will concentrate in the area of ST.NICHOLAS.

POINTS REQUIRING SPECIAL ATTENTION IN THE ATTACK.

12. The village of ST.LAURENT BLANGY has been strongly fortified apparently with a view to flanking any advance made by us to the North of it.

(a) It will receive special attantion during the bombardment. In addition, that portion of the creeping barrage which passes through the village will be preceded at 100 yards distance by a 6" Howitzer barrage. A 4.5" Howitzer barrage will be substituted for the 18 pdr barrage through the village.

(b). Two TANKS will also be employed to assist in its capture.

(c). If it holds out the troops to the North must push past it and endeavour to isolate it.

2. The valley S.W. of the BOIS DE LA MAISON BLANCHE has been filled with wire.

3. The village of ATHIES has a fortified perimeter. It will require to be subjected to a continuous bombardment by Heavy Howitzers from the time the assault is launched. Two TANKSE will be detailed to assist in its capture.

CONSOLIDATION OF OBJECTIVES.

13. (a). The lines to be consolidated will be:-
(1). The BLACK line.
(2). The BLUE line.
(3). The BROWN line.

(b). The work of consolidation will be carried out by the Infantry and must be commenced immediately each line is captured, and be undertaken by the troops who are x detailed to halt on that line.

(c). The consolidation will be carried out on the principle laid down in "Instructions for the Training of Divisions for Offensive Action".

On reaching the objective, an outpost line will immediately be established 100 to 200 yards in front of the line and as close as possible to the final barrage, the Commander of each assaulting Company being responsible for thus protecting his own front.

(d). The outpost line will consist of a line of small posts, 150 to 300 yds apart, each held by a N.C.O., about 6 riflemen and a Lewis gun.

(e). Communication trenches running through the line towards the enemy must be doubled blocked and bombers, both Hand and Rifle, posted at the Block together with a Trench Mortar as soon as it can be got up.

(f). At the same time selected localities in the captured line will be put in a state of defence by converting the captured trench into a fire trench, facing the enemy.

The exact siting of these localities must depend on the reconnaisances of local Commanders and on the number of men available for work, but they must be so designed as to afford each other mutual support.

(g). The section of 64th Fd.Coy. R.E. and 25 men specially detailed for the purpose will assist in the consolidation of the BROWN line by constructing a supporting point in the first line of the German 3rd system.

The exact site of this must be fixed by reconnaisance but will be approximately at H.14.b.7.3. (L'ABBAYETTE). Two guns 26th Machine Gun Company will form part of the garrison of this post.

CONSTRUCTION OF COMMUNICATION TRENCHES ACROSS NO MAN'S LAND.

14. The following Communication trenches will be made across NO MAN'S LAND:-

FEBRUARY AVENUE to be joined, South of the ST.NICHOLAS-ST.LAURENT BLANGY Road, to the German Trench opposite. This will be continued by the main German Tr ench through ST.LAURENT BLANGY, along the main road to H.14.a.0.3. This communication trench will be known as KENNEDY AVENUE and will be the main communication trench for the 26th Brigade.

EMPLOYMENT OF MACHINE GUNS.

15. (a). Machine guns will be employed during the days preceding the assault:-

(1). To prevent the enemy from repairing his wire.
(2). By indirect fire to search communication trenches, lines of approach, Road junctions, etc..

(b). Immediately the BLUE line is captured, O.C. 26th M.G.Coy. will arrange to reconnoitre positions about H.14.a.00.20. from which covering fire can be brought to bear on FEUCHY REDOUBT, during the advance on the BROWN line. One section will be moved up to this position but fire will not be opened until the 10th A & S. H. start to leave the BLUE line.

(c). The 3 Brigade Machine Gun Companies (less 1 section each) will be employed under the orders of the Division for covering fire during the advance to the BLUE line in accordance with a scheme to be issued separately.

On completion of their task, one section of each Coy. will remain in Divisional reserve, the remainder rejoining their Brigades.

Under instructions from Divisional H.Q. 7 guns will be placed under the command of G.O.C. 26th Brigade.

These will be allotted as follows:-

2 guns to O.C. 7th Seaforths and 2 to O.C. 8th Black Watch.

These will be used as mentioned above ~~in~~ in sub-para (b), remaining 3 will be held in reserve.

EMPLOYMENT OF LIGHT T.M's.

16. During advance to BROWN line 6 guns of the 26th T.M.B. will advance with and under the orders of O.C. 5th Camerons to assist in the attack on ATHIES.

LIVENS GAS PROJECTORS.

17. 300 Livens Gas Projectors have been allotted to the Division and will be employed against ST.LAURENT BLANGY.

~~(1). If the wind is favourable, the first discharge from projectors will take place on all Corps fronts simultaneously at ZERO - 48 hours 15 mins. and the second discharge at dusk on "Y" day. The exact time for second discharge will be notified later.~~

Back X

(2). The following precautions will be taken for the protection of our troops:-

(a). "Gas-Alert" precautions will be maintained while the gas bombs are in the trenches.

(b). Bombs will not be discharged over the heads of our troops.

VISUAL SIGNALLING.

18. Divisional Visual Receiving Stations will be established at G.22.c.9.8. viz: Refugee O.P. and G.13.c.4.3. viz: South African O.P. All Battalion and Company Signallers must know the position of these stations.

Brigade Visual Receiving Station will also be established.

(1). As soon as possible after capture of BLACK line, near LECH TRENCH, about G.18.a.6.4.

(2). As soon as possible after capture of BROWN line, on Embankment about H.14.a.O.2

Arrangements are being made for the acknowledgement of all visual messages.

Daylight Signalling lamps will be used as far as possible. The B.A.B. Trench code and the aeroplane code will be used for all visual messages except in exceptional cases.

The following light signals will be used for communication with the artillery:-

Succession of	GREEN lights	-	Open fire.
"	" ~~RED "~~	-	~~Shorten range~~.
"	" WHITE "	-	Lengthen range,

The amount the range will be increased ~~and decreased~~ is 100 yards. Back ⊕

RUNNERS.

The route for runners LECH TRENCH and APRIL AVENUE.

Relay posts will be :-

No.1 Advanced Brigade Station No.1 in No.14 dug-out at top of APRIL AVENUE.

No.2 Linesmen's Station off LECH TRENCH about G.18.a.6.4.

No.3 Advanced Brigade Station No.2 in sunken road at G.18.b.28.32.

When the Brigade H.Q. moves forward a relay post will be formed at Advanced Brigade Station No.3 about H.13.b.central.

If found necessary, further relay posts will be formed at Visual Station on EMBANKMENT at H.14.a.O.2, and midway between Brigade H.Q. and No.3 Advanced Station.

All Signal Offices and Linesmen's Stations will be marked by BLUE & WHITE Signal flag hung outside, in trench.

All Runners relay posts by BOARDS.

(PP)

* The discharge from Projectors will take place 15 minutes before the Artillery Bombardment begins.

If the wind is unfavourable at that time the discharge will take place between the time fixed and Zero - 6 hours at the first opportunity, which will be decided by Corps H.Q.

It is expected that there will be a further 200 LIVENS gas projectors allotted to the Division - They will be placed between MARCH and APRIL Avenues for employment on amongst other places CEMETRY, Battn. H.Q. and Sunken Road ~~at~~ in G.18.b.

(PP)

⊕ The above light-signals are to be used for calling for artillery support, they will not be used during the actual progress of an attack to recall the barrage or accelerate its lift. There will be no signal to "cease fire" or "shorten range"

Each battalion will take into battle the pre-arranged 24 Signallers. This does notx includes men specially detailed for Power Buzzer xx sets. The remainder, except for three, who will form the first reserve, will remain with the battalion Transport. The 3 first Reserve signallers will be attached to Brigade H.Q. and will be under the orders of the Brigade Signal Officer. They will be used for forming the Brigade Visual Receiving Station and to assist the Brigade Linesmen or Operators if necessary. On the Battalion requiring them to replace casualties men to fill their places will be supplied from the Reserve of Signallers left at the Battalion Transport.

Back x

NOTICE BOARDS TO MARK ENEMY TRENCH SYSTEM.

19. In order thatx the troops who follow up the leading Battalions in the attack may recognise what portion of the Battlefield they have reached, Brigade will arrange to send forward with their assaulting battalions, a number of notice boards or canvas screens marked "BLACK LINE", "BLUE LINE" and "BROWN LINE", which will be erected on the various objectives as they are reached.

Number of screens to be issued will be notified later.

PRISONERS OF WAR.

20. ~~The Brigade is responsible for escorting prisoners as far as ST. NICHOLAS, where they will be taken over by special escorts under orders of the A.P.M. Escorts will not exceed 10 per cent of the prisoners taken Attention of all Commanding Officers is called to page 56 S.S.135.~~

Prisoners of war after being disarmed will be passed back through Bn.H.Q. . Escorts will not exceed 10 per cent of prisoners taken.

TRENCH POLICE

21. 10th A & S.H. will be responsible for the control of traffic in and through FORRESTIER REDOUBT. & will detail 2 Regimental Policemen.

Back

"IN" and "OUT" COMMUNICATION TRENCHES.

22. "IN" - FEBRUARY AVENUE. "OUT" - (a) SPRING TRAMWAY as far as its junction with MAY AVENUE at G.17.a.33. thence MAY AVENUE to ST.NICHOLAS. (b). If time permits, MARCH AVENUE East of G.17.5.0. will be opened up and used as the "OUT" trench in place of SPRING TRAMWAY.

MEDICAL.

23. (a) Aid Post G.17.b.4.4. SPRING TRAMWAY.
(b) Advanced Dressing Station - ST.NICHOLAS, G.16.c.4.9.

DUMPS.

24. (a). R.E. Advanced Divisional Dump G.16.d.3.7.
26th Brigade - Head of Spring Tramway ~~for stores to be held in R.E. Dump see sub-appendix Z.~~

(b). S.A.A. & GRENADES:-
Advanced Divisional Dump - BRASSERIE - ST. NICHOLAS.
26th Brigade G.16.d.4.7.

Reserve of S.A.A. WILL BE KEPT AT

FORRESTIER REDOUBT	14,000 rds S.A.A. 375 Grenades.
OIL WORKS	14,000 rds S.A.A. 375 Grenades.
LAUNDRY POST	12,000 rds S.A.A. 60 Grenades.

(c) ~~(d)~~. RESERVE SUPPLIES.
Dumps of Reserve supplies will be placed at:-
CANDLE FACTORY consisting of 8000 rations for 3 days.

×

Contact aeroplanes.

In addition to the above means of Communication contact aeroplanes will be employed to receive signals from Brigade & Battalion H.Q. by means of

(1) Ground Signal panels.

(2) Lamps.

and from attacking Infantry by means of flares. Information thus obtained will be dropped at the Corps Dropping Station at F29.a.3.3. whence it will be transmitted to the Unit concerned.

The Infantry will be prepared to light their flares and will be on the look out for the contact planes at:-

(a) Zero plus 1 hour. i.e. after the BLACK Line is expected to be captured.

(b) Zero plus 3 hours 10 minutes, i.e. after the BLUE line is expected to be captured.

(c) Zero plus 8 hours 10 minutes, i.e. after the BROWN line is expected to be captured.

Note. The flares will be lit when the aeroplane actually calls for them.

(k9)

⊕ These 2 policemen will be posted at the IN and OUT entrances to Bde H.Q. & will ensure that there is no congestion. They must clearly understand that only Runners & Officers & O.R. directly connected with Bde H.Q. & whose duty places them there are to be allowed to pass them.

The Battn will provide the following post on the Brigade line of Battle Stops – 1 Provost Sgt & 2 policemen at G.17 a 35°.42. Who will be responsible for men "SPRING TRAMWAY & all traffic down OLD MAY AVENUE."

This post will be in position by ZERO plus 1 hour & will move & be under the orders of 5th CAMERON HLDRS. They will be furnished with written instructions as to their duties.

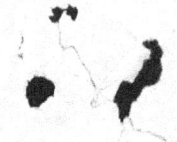

Reserve Supplies are also kept at:-

FORRESTIERS REDOUBT -	400 rations &	400 gals. water.
OIL WORKS -	400 "	400 " "
LAUNDRY POST -	60 "	60 " "

WATER. 25. (a). Forward Water Points:-

G.11.b.6.1.
G.11.d.2.2.
G.17.a.7.4.
G.17.c.4.9.

(b). 1,000 filled Petrol tins at advanced Divisional Dump.

(c). 500 " " " " main Brigade Dump.

Brigades will be responsible that water tanks at forward Water Points, and Petrol tins at Brigade main Dumps, are kept filled.

PUBLIC MONEY. 26. No PUBLIC MONEY will be taken into action. Attention is drawn to G.R.O.2112, dated 31-1-17.

M.G.CARRYING PARTY. 27. 2/Lieut.HEPBURN and 20 O.R. will report on receipt of further orders to O.C. 26th M.G.Coy. as carrying party.

T.M.B. CARRYING PARTY. 28. 2/Lieut.LAWSON and 20 O.R. will report on receipt of further orders to O.C. 26th T.M.Battery as carrying party.

BATTALION DUMPS. 29. 2 Battalion Dumps will be established in original front line. If possible arrangements will be made to move these Dumps forward to the BLUE line when captured.

TANK SIGNALS. 30. The following Disc or light signals used by TANKS must be known to all ranks. From TANK to Infantry

GREEN. = Come on or Wire cut.

RED = Danger or wire uncut.

~~Lt)Colonel,~~
~~Commanding 10th A & S. Highlanders.~~

RED
GREEN } = Wait a bit.

The following signal can be used by Infantry to TANKS

"TANK WANTED" Helmets placed on the end of fixed Bayonets and raised straight above the head.

Lieut-Colonel.
Commanding 10th A & S. Highlanders.

Copies to:
1-4 Coys.
5 B.H.Q.
6 26 Brigade
7 Signal Off.
8 Transport Office.
9 Adjutant
10 File
11 War Diary

SECRET Copy No. 4

26th INFANTRY BRIGADE OPERATION ORDER NO.97.

Reference
1/10,000 Trench Map
Sheet 51.b.N.W. 3 ARRAS, Edition 7.a. 6/4/17.

1\. (a) The enemy opposite the FIFTH ARMY and opposite the right of the THIRD ARMY has fallen back to the HINDENBURG LINE.

(b) The XVII Corps as part of the THIRD ARMY has been ordered to attack on the front between the River SCARPE (exclusive) and the ARRAS - LILLE Road (inclusive) with the object of capturing the German third trench system which runs through ATHIES, LE POINT DU JOUR and MAISON DE LA COTE, and pushing on to the capture of FAMPOUX and the German fourth system as far/as HYDERABAD REDOUBT (inclusive). North

(c) The disposition of the Divisions of the XVII Corps will be:-

3 Divisions in line. 9th Division on the Right.
34th Division in the Centre.
51st Division on the Left.

The 4th Division will be in Reserve.

The 15th Division of the VIth Corps will attack simultaneously on the South of the River SCARPE.

2\. (a) The task of the 9th Division will be to capture the enemy's third system of trenches between River SCARPE and LE POINT DU JOUR, and to establish a line along the Eastern edge of ATHIES to road junction H.15.a.05.05., thence along the road running towards LE POINT DU JOUR as far as H.9.c.45.10, thence along the trench parallel to and 100 yards East of ~~the~~ the ~~xxxx xx xxx~~ above mentioned road.

(b) After the capture of this line the 4th Division will pass through the 9th Division and attack the German fourth system.
The ~~11th~~ 12th Brigade will pass through the 26th Brigade.

3\. When the ~~11th~~ 12th Brigade of the 4th Division has passed through the 26th Brigade, Battalion Commanders and Officers Commanding 26th M.G.Company and 26th T.M.Battery will withdraw their units to their original assembly areas.
No unit of the 26th Brigade will withdraw until actually relieved by a unit of the 4th Division.
It must be impressed on all ranks that the passing through of certain units of the ~~11th~~ 12th Brigade will not necessarily mean that the relief is complete.
Units of 26th Brigade must wait for relieving units of the ~~11th~~ 12th Brigade.

4\. The 26th Brigade will be the Right Brigade of the 9th Division and has been allotted the task of capturing the villages of ST LAURENT BLANGY and ATHIES.
The 45th Brigade will attack on the right of the 26th Brigade as far as the BLUE Line, here the 46th Brigade will take its place.
The S.A.Brigade will attack on the left.

5\. - Right and Left Boundaries in the attack will be:-

26th Inf.Brigade

Right Boundary River SCARPE.

Loft do. ISAR BABEL (inclusivo) road-junction G.18.b.5.8.(exclusive) tronch junction H.13.a.0.8.(exclusive) Railway Bridge H.8.c.05.05 (exclusivo) trench junction H.15.b.3.3.(inclusive).

6. The 26th Brigade will attack with two battalions in line - 8th Black Watch and 7th Seaforth Hrs.
One battalion in support, 10th A.& S.Hrs., and one battalion in reserve, 5th Cameron Hrs..

7. There will be three separate objectives in the attack:-

1st. The capture of the enemy's front system of trenches.

2nd. The capture of the enemy's second system.

3rd. The capture of the enemy's third system and the establishment of the line defined in para. 2.

Each of these lines will be consolidated by the Infantry as soon as it is captured.

8. In accordance with the plan already laid down in 26th Brigade Instructions No.2., the leading battalions viz.- 8th Black Watch and 7th Seaforth Hrs., will capture the first two objectives, and the 10th A.& S.Hrs., supported by the 5th Cameron Hrs. will capture the third objective.

9. The attack will be supported by the 9th Divisional Artillery reinforced by

14th, 23rd and 52nd Army Field Artillery Brigades and

29th and 32nd Field Artillery Brigades of 4th Division.

10. (a) The infantry will advance under a creeping Field Artillery Barrage, the details of which have already been laid down in 26th Brigade Instructions No.2. and 26th Brigade letter No.26/6092.
(b) The advance will also be ~~carried out~~ covered by machine gun fire in accordance with Appendix D., 26th Brigade Instructions No.2.

11. The 26th T.M.Battery will have attached to it for the battle 1 section of a T.M.Battery from the 4th Division.
Their employment has already been laid down in 26th Brigade Instructions No.2.

12. Four TANKS will assist the 26th Brigade in the capture of the second objective and the villages of ST LAURENT BLANGY and ATHIES.
Details as to their employment have already been issued.

13. One section of 64th Field Company R.E. and a ½ company of 9th Seaforth Hrs. (Pioneers) have been allotted to the 26th Brigade to assist in the consolidation of objectives.
The Pioneer Platoons of all four battalions will assist in this task.

14. Contact aeroplanes will fly over our lines at the following hours:-

(a) Zero plus 1 hour i.e. after the first objective is expected to be captured.

(b) Zero plus 3 hours 10 minutes i.e. after the second objective is expected to be captured.

(c) Zero plus 8 hours 10 minutes i.e. after the third objective is expected to be captured.

Infantry in the front line will be prepared to light their flares at the above hours.

15. The date of the attack will be April 9th - Zero hour will be notified later.

16. All units of 26th Brigade, attached section 64th Field Company R.E. and the half company 9th Seaforth Hrs. will each send an officer to Brigade H.Q. daily at 12 noon and 6 p.m., commencing at 6 p.m. on April 7th, to synchronise watches.
The final hour of synchronisation will be notified later.

17. Brigade Battle H.Q. will open in FORRESTIER REDOUBT at 4 p.m. on April 7th.

18. ACKNOWLEDGE.

J. F. Evetts

Captain,
Brigade Major,
26th Infantry Brigade.

Issued at...11 pm....

5.30
8.10
1.40 pm

Copy No.1 8th Black Watch
2 7th Seaforth Hrs.
3 5th Cameron Hrs.
4 10th A.& S.Hrs.
5 26th M.G.Company
6 26th T.M.Battery
7 9th Division "G"
8 9th Division "Q"
9 105th Company A.S.C.
10 27th Brigade
11 S.A.Brigade
12 64th Field Coy.R.E.
13 Town Major, ARRAS
14 45th Brigade
15 9th Seaforth Hrs. (Pioneers)
16 51st Brigade R.F.A.
17 A.D.M.S., 9th Division.
18 197th M.G.Company
19 Major Lumsden, Divisional M.G.Officer.
20 Major Haslam, "Tanks" Officer.
21 2/Lieut. A.L.Evelyn, (5th Cameron Hrs.)
22 26th Brigade Signals
23 26th Bde. Supply Officer.
24 26th Bde. Transport Officer.
25 Staff Captain
26 War diary
27 File.

SECRET Copy No....4....

26TH INFANTRY BRIGADE OPERATION ORDER NO.96.

Reference
1/10,000 Trench Map.
ARRAS - 51.N.W.3.- Edition 7.A. 6/4/17.

1. During the night 8/9th April the 26th Brigade (less half battalions 8th Black Watch and 7th Seaforth Hrs. in the line), assembled in ARRAS on the night 7/8th April, will concentrate in the assembly areas already allotted, and in accordance with the attached table.

2. For the purposes of assembly the Brigade and attached troops will be divided up into groups as follows, and units will march in the order named.

No.1. Group -(½ Bn.8th Black Watch
(and 3 platoons 10th A.& S.Hrs.
((moppers up).
(1 section 26th T.M.Battery
(½ section 26th M.G.Company

No.2. Group -(½ Bn.7th Seaforth Hrs.
(1 Pioneer Platoon 7th Seaforth Hrs.
(1 Section 26th T.M.Battery
(½ Section 26th M.G.Company

No.3. Group -(10th A.& S.Hrs. (less 3 platoons).
(2 Sections 26th M.G.Company (C.group).

No.4. Group -(5th Cameron Hrs.
(1 Section (4th Divn.) T.M.Battery.

No.5. Group -(1 Section 64th Field Company R.E.
(3 Pioneer Platoons.
((8th Black Watch, 5th Camerons Hrs.,
(10th A.& S.Hrs.).
(½ Company 9th Seaforth Hrs.(Pioneers).

3. All units will move from ARRAS completely equipped in every detail.

4. The Officer Commanding the 8th Black Watch, 7th Seaforth Hrs., 10th A.& S.Hrs., 5th Cameron Hrs., and the section 64th Field Company R.E. will be responsible for reporting to Brigade H.Q. that the concentration of groups is complete. This will be sent by runner to FORRESTIER REDOUBT by 3 a.m. on April 9th.

5. (a) The routes to be followed will be as under -

Route 1. Nos. 1 & 2 Groups	(Track from G.22.b.2.7. to bridge at (G.16.d.4.3., thence along towpath to (G.17.c.05.20., thence along track to (G.17.c.06.65..
Route 2. Nos.3, 4 and 5 Groups	(As above to bridge at G.16.d.4.3., (thence along track to FEBRUARY CIRCUS (G.16.d.40.75.

(b) In the event of the bridge at G.16.d.4.3. being destroyed by shell fire the following bridges will be used -

Nos. 1 & 2 Groups	(Bridge No.2. on 1/20,000 map showing bridges (across River SCARPE (issued to all units of (26th Brigade).
Nos. 3, 4 & 5 Groups.	(The lock gate and bridge at G.16.c.95.28 thence (along Northern bank of River SCARPE to route (already detailed.

(c) O.C., 8th Black Watch will arrange to send forward at 8 p.m. on April 8th a post of 1 N.C.O. and 2 men to remain near the bridge at G.16.d.4.3..

The N.C.O. i/c will at once send back a man to ARRAS to report of the bridge is destroyed. This post will rejoin its platoon when No. 1 Group crosses the bridge.

6. The Officers Commanding 8th Black Watch and 7th Seaforth Hrs. will arrange to have the route to No.2. bridge reconnoitred during the day of April 8th.

7. (a) During the march units will keep closed up as much as possible, and the correct distances must be kept, otherwise the timing of the moves of units of the Brigade will be thrown out.

(b) On reaching the trench area all moves where possible will be made over the open.

8. Units of the S.A.Brigade will be moving from 7.15 p.m. on the night 8/9th April along the Eastern edge of the BASIN G.22.a.6.5. to lock bridge at G.16.c.95.28.

9. Starting Point.- Will be at the GASOMETERS G.22.a. 76.60.. An officer and 1 orderly of the Brigade Staff will be at the starting point at 10.25 p.m. on April 8th to direct units.

10. The section of 26th M.G.Company detailed as Brigade Reserve guns, and which will be assembled in FORRESTIER REDOUBT, will take up positions in the sector on the morning of April 8th from which they can bring fire to bear on NO MANSLAND.

This section will be concentrated in dug-outs and shelters already allotted in FORRESTIER REDOUBT, by 4 a.m. on April 9th.

11. The platoon of 7th Seaforth Hrs. forming the garrison of the LAUNDRY POST, will be withdrawn at 8.30 p.m. on the night 8/9th April and will move to the vicinity of the OIL FACTORY prior to assembly.

It will be relieved by the detachment of Lewis Guns, 9th Seaforth Hrs.(Pioneers), allotted to 26th Brigade.

12. Cookers, water carts and mess carts from ARRAS will return to transport lines at ETRUN during the night 8/9th April by the following route -

OCTROI - Road Junction G.15.d.1.2. - DEAD MANS CORNER and main ARRAS - ST POL Road.

13. Reports will be sent to Brigade H.Q., FORRESTIER REDOUBT.

14. ACKNOWLEDGE.

J. F. Evetts -

Captain,
Brigade Major,
26th Infantry Brigade.

Issued at...2 pm.......
P. T. O.

March Table for night 8/9th ~~7/8th~~ April.

Units	From	To	Time at which head of column will pass starting point.	Remarks
No.1 Group ½ Bn.8th Black Watch 3 Platoons 10th A.& S.Hrs. 1 Sec.26th T.M.Battery ½ Sec.26th M.G.Company	ARRAS	Assembly trenches	10.30 p.m.	Route 1.
No.2. Group. ½ Bn.7th Seaforth Hrs. 1 Pioneer platoon, 7th Seaforth Hrs. 1 Sec.26th T.M.Battery ½ Sec.26th M.G.Company	ARRAS	Assembly Trenches	11.20 p.m.	Route 1.
No.3. Group 10th A.& S.Hrs. (less 3 platoons) 2 Sec. 26th M.G.Company (C. Group)	ARRAS	Assembly Trenches	11.55 p.m. Pde 11.30	Route 2.
No.4. Group 5th Cameron Hrs. 1 sec.(4th Div.) T.M.Batty.	ARRAS	REDOUBT LINE and Assembly Trenches	12.50 a.m.	Route 2.
No.5.Group 1 sec. 64th Field Coy.R.E. 3 Pioneer platoons - 8th Black W., 5th Cameron H., 10th A.& S.H.	ARRAS	Trenches & shelters near Battn. Cookhouses & dead ground between them and CANDLE FACTORY.	1.50 a.m.	Route 2.
½ Coy. 9th Seaforth Hrs. (Pioneers)		To shelters & trenches West of OIL FACTORY.		

SECRET.

26th INFANTRY BRIGADE INSTRUCTIONS NO.2. dated 20-3-17.

A P P E N D I X. 'C'.

Plans of Attack on the Villages of ~~ST LAURENT BLANGY~~ & ATHIES.

Reference
Map 1.(issued with 26th Brigade Instructions No.2.) and Trench map ARRAS,51.B. N.W.3. Edition.7.A.

1. It is impossible to lay down any hard and fast plan for the attack on the Village as it is dependant on so many circumstances.
2. The main object is to capture theline OPIUM - OLIVE and to isolate the Village by working round it on the Northern and North Western edges while the barrage remains on the Village for a period of 20 minutes. The greater part of the 2 Battalions which will be employed in the attack,will be used in this outflanking movement. The 2 Right Companies of 10th A.& S.Hrs.which capture OLIVE,will advance through the Village close under the barrage which will move Eastwards through the Village at the end of the 20 minutes mentioned above.
3. In the event of the BLUE line being captured successfully,and also if the 10th A. & S. Hrs. are in sufficient strength to attack ATHIES,the following plan will be adhered to as closely as possible.

4. The 10th A. & S. Hrs. will attack from the line F.G. on a 600 yards front,with the 5th Cameron Hrs. in Artillery formation in close support.
The dividing line between the 2 Right Companies and the 2 Left Companies,10th A.& S.Hrs.,will be ESK and ORE,inclusive to the 2 Right Companies.
The 5th Cameron Hrs,will move behind the 2 Left Coys,of the 10th. A. &. S. Hrs.with ESK and ORE inclusive as their Right boundary and line of direction.
The bulk of the attacking battalions thus being placed to work round the Northern edge of ATHIES.
The attack will be supported by overhead machine gun fire from the Northern ~~edge~~ end of the Railway embankment in H.14,a. on to FEUCHY WORK. It is absolutely essential that FEUCHY WORK be kept continually under fire to enable the attack on ATHIES to succeed.
(NOTE: FEUCHY WORK is a good machine gun target at a range of 1500 yards,and accurate ranging fire can easily be obtained on the Western edges of the Lake in H.20.b.)

5. AT ZERO PLUS 7 HOURS, 32 MINUTES.
The barrage will lift off OPIUM & ONION and the leading wave will occupy the trench.
South of ESK & ORE the barrage will lift to the Western edge of ATHIES,and will stand there for 20 minutes (i.e. ZERO plus 7 hours, 52 minutes.
North of ESK & ORE the barrage will continue to advance 100 yards every 3 minutes for 200 yards,then 100 yards every 4 minutes until 300 yards beyond the BROWN line.
The 2 Left Companies of 10th A. & S.Hrs.closely supported by 5th Cameron Hrs,will occupy the BROWN line.
Meanwhile,the 2 Right Companies of 10th A. & S. Hrs.in occupation of OLIVE will move out as close as possible under the barrage,standing on the Western edge of the Village,and will advance through the Village at ZERO plus 7hours 52 minutes,at which moment the barrage lifts and ~~will~~ advances to a line 300 yards E. of the BROWN line.
Directly the barrage ~~xxxxx~~ starts to advance,bombing attacks by 2 Left Companies 10th.A. & S. Hrs. and 5th Cameron Hrs. will be pushed down ONION & PALMY,and into the Village.

6. <u>The following situations may arise:-</u>

(a). The whole attack is held up on the line OPIUM, OOZE, OLIVE, and <u>the barrage has moved on too quickly for the Infantry advance.</u>

Every effort will at once be made to capture OPIUM & ONYX, and the whole of the 5th Cameron Hrs. (in addition to 2 Left Coys. 10th. A. & S. Hrs.) may be used to gain these objectives. The 2 Right Companies of 10th A. & S. Hrs. still being held up opposite OLIVE, bombing attacks down OPIUM, ONYX, ONION, and into the Village will at once be organised.

(b). The line OPIUM, OOZE, OLIVE is captured but the attach is held up opposite ONYX and the Western edge of the Village, the barrage having moved on as in (a).

The 2 Right Companies of the 10th A. & S. Hrs. will then be in occupation of OLIVE trench providing a certain amount of cover and which is within easy Stokes mortar range of the Village. All available Stokes mortars will be brought up ESK and into OLIVE to bombard the Village and ONYX trench in enfilade, before any attempt is made to work round the Northern edge of the Village. The same procedure as in situation (a) will then be adopted. The 5th Cameron Hrs. assisting 2 Left Companies 10th A. & S. Hrs. to capture ONYX and to bomb down ONION into the Village, in conjunction with a frontal attack by 2 Right Companies 10th. A. & S. Hrs. from OLIVE.

(c) OPIUM & ONYX may be captured without opposition, but OLIVE trench and the Village may still hold out, the barrage having moved forward as in (a) and (b).

The troops in occupation of OPIUM & ONYX will then be in a position to bomb down into the Village, and to work round the Northxxx Eastern edge of it. In this situation, the Stokes mortars available will again be brought up to the vicinity of OOZE and the junction of ONYX & ONION, to assist the bombing attacks, and if possible to bombard OLIVE in enfilade, to enable the attack of the 2 Right Coys. 10th. A. & S. Hrs. to be pushed on.

7. In the event of the 45th Brigade gaining its objective on the Southern Bank, immense help can be given to the attack of the 26th Brigade by direct enfilade Machine gun fire being brought to bear on OPIUM & ONYX from about the Railway Cutting in H.20.c. at a range of under 1500 yards, and where direct observation should be obtained.

8. The Right Company 10th. A. & S. Hrs. will be responsible for securing the bridges at H.21.a.2½.6. and H.21.a.2.8. during the advance through ATHIES.

Copy No.8. H.Q. (C.O.)

10th Bn. ARGYLL & SUTHERLAND HIGHLANDERS.

OPERATION ORDERS FOR THE ATTACK ON ATHIES.

1. The Batt. will be formed up in line on the BLUE LINE prior to attack. The Formation to be adopted will be 4 coys, in Line, A.B.C.D. Coys., reading from left to right.

11. At ZERO & 7hrs 9mins.(12.39.p.m.) the Batt. will move from the BLUE LINE in Artillery Formation under the Creeping Barrage. At ZERO & 7hrs 13mins. (12.43.p.m.) Battalion will advance. Signal being Smoke Barrage. The Battalion will deploy to Waves on coming under Enemy Artillery, or M.G. Fire.

111. Boundaries between the two right Coys and the two left coys, will be as follows, ESK & ORE inclusive to the two right Coys.

IV. The whole of the 5th Camerons will move in rear of the two left Coys. 10th A.& S. Hrs., with ESK & ORE (inclusive) as their right Boundary and line direction.

V. At ZERO and 7hrs 32mins.(1.2.p.m.) the whole of the leading Waves 10th A. & S. Hrs., will occupy the line OPIUM & OOZIE after the Barrage has lifted off it. North of ESK & ORE "A" & "B" Coy will continue to advance under the barrage, up to the BROWN LINE, having dropped "Moppers" in OPIUM & OOZE . These Coys. will be closely supported by the 5th Camerons.

VI. "C" & "D" Coys. 10th A.& S. Hrs.will move out as close as possible under the barrage, standing on the western Side of ATHIES, and will advance through the village at ZERO & 7hrs 52 mins. (1.22 p.m.) at moment the barrage lifts , and will advance to the BROWN LINE pushing forward covering parties.

VII. At ZERO & 7hrs 52 mins.(1.22.p.m.) "B"Coy supported by "A" coy, (less 2 platoons) will at once start Bombing Attacksdown ONION & PALMY into the village. These attacks will coincide with attack by "C" & "D" Coys, which are pushing through the village. 2 platns "A" Coy will advance into the village and form strong points about Road junction H.14.d.8.7. These two platoons will garrison their strong posts and will form Battalion Reserve.

VIII. When the village has been captured the following strong points will at once be made:-

H.14.b.7.3.		By 5th Camerons.	
H.15.c.5.2.	(about)	by "C" Coy	ARGYLLS
H.21.a.2.9.	(about)	by "D" Coy.	do
H.14.d.8.7.	do	by 2 platoons of "A" coy. Argylls as above	

IX. 10th Argyll & Sutherland Highlanders will not vacate ONYZ until the 5th Camerons take over.

X. When line is occupied - 5th Camerons will take over defences as far away South as cross roads (inclusive). 10th A. & S. Hrs., from Cross Roads H.14.b.98.02. (exclusive) to River SCARPE.

XI. In event of 5th Camerons having to assist in attack , the 10th A.& S. Hrs. will attack on right & 5th Camerons on left, dividing line being ESK & ORE inclusive to 5th Camerons.

(Sgd) W. FRENCH. Capt & Adjt.,
10th Argyll & Sutherland Highlanders.

8/4/17.

Headquarters,

9th (Scottish) Division.

8th April, 1917.

Officers, Non-Commissioned Officers and Men of the 9th (Scottish) Division.

In the forthcoming offensive I feel confident that you will not only uphold the glorious traditions of the past but add to the splendid reputation the Division gained on previous historic occasions.

My best wishes are with you.

H. T. Lukin

Major-General,
Commanding 9th (Scottish) Division.

Headquarters
26th Infantry B
O.C.
10th A & S Hrs.
April

I wish you all good luck.

[signature]
Brigadier Gen
Commanding

COPY of FAREWELL MESSAGE FROM:-

LIEUTENANT-COLONEL A.F. MACKENZIE. C.M.G. M.V.O.

This message was read out to the Battalion immediately before the Battalion moved into the Assembly Trenches, for the attack on 9th April 1917.

Lieut-col., MacKenzie having been reported as permantly unfit for General Service through wounds received in action at the Battle of LOOS in 27th September 1915, & consequently has had to regretfully realise the fact that he is not allowed to return to the Front, Desires to bid Farewell to his Old Battalion through Lieut-Col., Sotheby, and in doing so he fully realises that he is unknown to the great Majority of the 10th Argyll & Sutherland Highlanders.

Nevertheless as he Commanded them from 1st September 1914 till wounded & is still shown in Command in the Army Lists; he desires to thank all Ranks for the loyal support he received whilst in Command. The bearing of the Battalion both at Home during the primary training and afterwards in the Trenches and in Action, has always been of the Highest Order; the last occasion he himself saw the Regiment in Action proved to him their worth under heavy losses. He has read with pride the praise bestowed on the 10th Argyll & Sutherland Highlanders by their Divisional & Brigade Commanders.

Lieutenant-Colonel Mackenzie severs his connections with the Battalion(through force of circumstances) with the deepest Regret. He will always watch their Career with deepest interest, knowing that wherever the 10th Argyll & Sutherland Highlanders are employed, they will show the highest Standard of discipline and steadiness under fire, which has always distinguished them.

To all Ranks he Bids Farewell; after a fond connection with Argyll & Sutherland Regiment of 33 years.

(Sgd) A.F. MacKenzie. Lieut-Col.,

Late. COMMANDING 10th A. & S. Highlanders.

Sunny Cottage,

Wheathampstead.

HERTS.

27/3/17.

Copy of MESSAGE from :-

Lieutenant-Colonel W.J.B. Tweedie,

This Message was read outnto the men immediately before the Battalion moved into the Assembly Trenches for the attack on 9th April 1917.

"God Grant that things will go well and that the Battalion will add another Star to its already brilliant Crown."

Sgd. W.J.B. TWEEDIE, Lt-Col.,

30/3/17.

WAR DIARY

Headquarters,

9th (Scottish) Division.

10th April, 1917.

I desire to express to the Officers, Non-Commissioned Officers and men of the Division my very high admiration of the fine courage and decision they exhibited in carrying out the tasks allotted to them in yesterday's battle.

[signature]

Major-General,

Commanding 9th (Scottish) Division.

"A" Form.

MESSAGES AND SIGNALS.

Army Form C.2121
(in pads of 100).
No. of Message

H.Q.
2?TH INFANTRY BDE.

Prefix ...... Code ...... m.	Words	Charge	This message is on a/c of:	Recd. at ...... m.
Office of Origin and Service Instructions.	Sent		...... Service.	Date
	At ...... m.			From
	To			
	By		(Signature of "Franking Officer.")	By

TO: ~~MASTER~~ ~~WHIP~~ ~~HOUNDS~~ TERRIER ~~FIELD~~ ~~FOX.~~

Sender's Number.	Day of Month.	In reply to Number.	AAA
* R.71.	11/4/.		

Reptd from HUNT. aaa. Following from C. in C. last night to be circulated to all ranks. aaa. Begins. aaa. My warmest congratulations on the important success achieved by you yesterday. aaa. The manner in which the operations were prepared and carried out reflects the highest credit on Commanders, Staff and troops. aaa. Please convey to all who were employed my appreciation of the great skill and gallantry shown by them aaa. Ends. aaa.

A, B, C, D Coy 11th Bn
Please note & convey
to all ranks
[illegible]

From MEET.
Place
Time 12.5.pm.

The above may be forwarded as now corrected. ...... Censor.

(Z)
(sd). J.F.Evetts. Captain
Signature of Addressor or person authorised to telegraph in his name.
Brigade Major.

* This line should be erased if not required.

750,000. W 2186—M509. H. W. & V., Ld. 6/16.

N O T I C E.

The following telegram has been received from Major General W.T.FURSE, C.B., D.S.O. -

" 9th Division, FRANCE.
Splendid. Best congratulations to all of you
FURSE."

10th (Service) Bn. Argyll & Sutherland Highlanders.

Statement of Casualties, Sick, Etc. for April, 1917 :-

Date	Killed	Wounded	Missing	admitted to Field Amb.	Rejoined from hospital	Drafts
1st	1	2	-	4	1	-
2nd	2	2	-	5	1	-
3rd	1	3		-	3	
4th	1	5		3	2	
5th	-	2		6	-	
6 "	5	5		-	1	
7	-			1	4	8
8 "	-	1		1	3	
9 "	19	79	12	2	3	
10 "				-	1	
11				1	-	
12 "		3		3	1	
13 "		1		3	2	
14 "	4	11		4	-	
15	3	9	8	2	-	
16				1	-	
17				2	-	135
18 "				9	8	
19 "				6	3	
20				3	2	
21st				3	1	
22nd				-	1	
23rd				2	2	27
24th				2	3	
25				-	1	
26 "				2	1	
27 "				4		
28 "				1		
29 "	1	2		1		
30 "						4

In the Field, 1st May, 1917.

N. McEwen Major, for Lt Col, Commndg. 10th (Service) Bn. Argyll & Sutherland Highlanders.

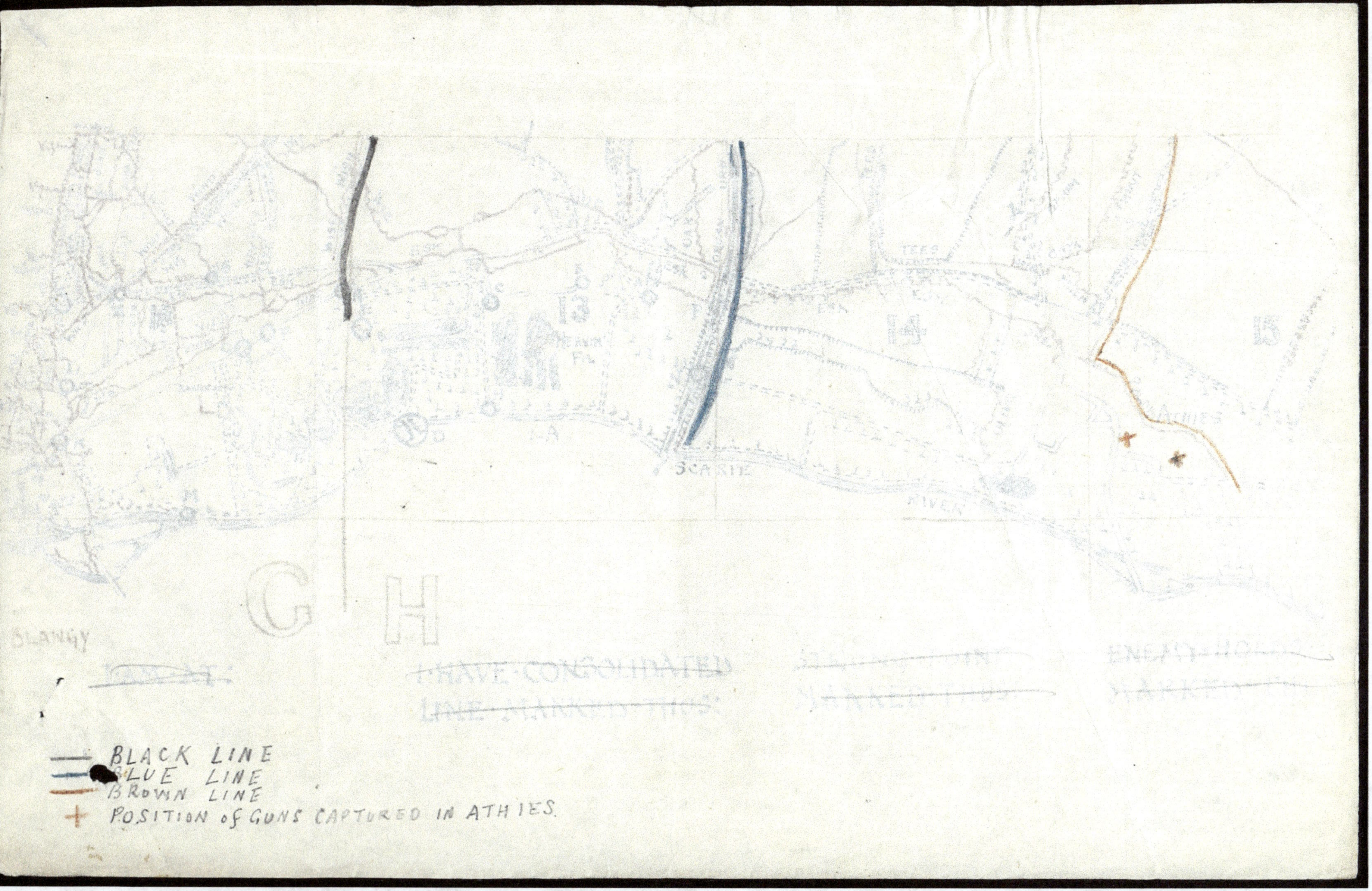
13
14
15
G
H
TEES
ATHIES
SCARPE
RIVER
BLANGY
I HAVE CONSOLIDATED
LINE MARKED THUS
BLACK LINE
BLUE LINE
BROWN LINE
+ POSITION of GUNS CAPTURED IN ATHIES.

Instructions regarding War Diaries and Intelligence Summaries are contained in F. S. Regs., Part II. and the Staff Manual respectively. Title pages will be prepared in manuscript.

WAR DIARY
or
INTELLIGENCE SUMMARY.
(Erase heading not required.)

Army Form C. 2118.

10th ARGYLL & SUTHERLAND HRS

Vol 21

Place	Date	Hour	Summary of Events and Information	Remarks and references to Appendices
BATTLE OF ARRAS	1917. May 1		During night Battalion relieved in front line by 5th CAMERONS who took over as follows. A from our C – C from our D – D from our B – B from our A. At about 10 P.M. CAPT COLVIN was shot through the head by a sniper and died soon afterwards – a most capable officer and a great loss. Batt: moved to area KICK, KEEN, ONYX, LABLE, LILAC in POINT DU JOUR line in H 8 & 9. B.H.Q in LILAC.	
	2.	11.30 am	C.O. & Coy Commanders to Brigadier's Conference. Day spent in completing deficiencies.	
		6 pm.	C.O. saw Coy Commanders and gave them following details for attack for following morning. ZERO. 3.45. a.m. ZERO + 4 min will be first lift – Sign for lift will be smoke barrage, no other smoke will be used till barrage on final objective. "C" Coy Right supporting Coy. "D" " CENTRE " " "A" & "B" Reserve Coys. "C" Coy Duties: To advance in immediate support of 5 CAMERONS in artillery form[n]. On reaching abreast of BUSHES on RAILWAY will wheel to right rushing & holding EMBANKMENT keeping all entries & exits to PLOUVAIN under M.G & L.G. fire.	

Instructions regarding War Diaries and Intelligence Summaries are contained in F. S. Regs., Part II. and the Staff Manual respectively. Title pages will be prepared in manuscript.

WAR DIARY
or
INTELLIGENCE SUMMARY. 10th ARGYLL & SUTHERLAND H^DRS.
(Erase heading not required.)

Army Form C. 2118.

Place	Date	Hour	Summary of Events and Information	Remarks and references to Appendices
BATTLE OF ARRAS	1917. May 2		"D" Coy's orders. to advance in immediate support of 8th BLACK WATCH touching "C" Coy on its right – If attack progressed satisfactorily they would advance to GAVRELLE – PLOUVAIN ROAD and consolidate. but in event of Div. on right (4th DIV) being held up they would wheel to the right and hold EMBANKMENT touching "C" Coy on their left. They were ordered to constantly watch their right during the advance.	
			"A" & "B" Coys to assemble in HOLLY, HAZARD, HAGGARD & LOMBER as near B. HQ as possible – They will move only under orders of C.O.	
			PIONEER PLATOON. to move in artillery formation immediately in rear of "D" Coy and consolidate GAVRELLE – PLOUVAIN ROAD.	
			1 Section 63rd Coy R.E to move immediately in rear of "C" Coy & consolidate GAVRELLE – PLOUVAIN ROAD.	
			B.HQ. SUNKEN ROAD H 11. a. 6.2 & in event of move will go to CHILE (H 12 b. 6. 6)	
			SPECIAL POINTS. RAILWAY EMBANKMENT must be taken & held at all costs. D. Coy will keep slightly to S. ready to assist if required – One round to be kept in chamber – Bayonets not to be fixed before dawn – Contact aeroplanes will call for flares at 6. 15 a.m.	

A5834 Wt. W4973 M687 750,000 8/16 D. D. & L. Ltd. Forms/C.2118/13.

Instructions regarding War Diaries and Intelligence Summaries are contained in F. S. Regs., Part II. and the Staff Manual respectively. Title pages will be prepared in manuscript.

WAR DIARY
or
INTELLIGENCE SUMMARY. 10th ARGYLL & SUTHERLAND HRS.
(*Erase heading not required.*)

Army Form C. 2118.

Place	Date 1917	Hour	Summary of Events and Information	Remarks and references to Appendices
BATTLE OF	May 2	9.30 pm	Batt: moved to assembly positions.	
			Assembly reported complete.	
ARRAS	3.	3.10 am	Enemy bombarded front line – bombardment ceased 3.30. am	
		3.15 am	Our barrage opened.	
		3.45 am ZERO	Orders received from Brigade to move 2 Reserve Coys (A & B) forward by platoons as enemy barrage permitted to CUTHBERT & make good –	
		4.15 am	2 Platoons each Coy to remain in CUTHBERT until relieved by 5th SEAFORTHS. They were then to move forward to GAVRELLE – PLOUVAIN ROAD & consolidate.	
		5.25 am	Reported to Brigade "Coys moving".	
		5.52 am	Telephoned to H.Q. 5th CAMERONS asking situation. They replied they had had heavy casualties and that the attack had failed & we were all back in our original front line consolidating – Enemy aeroplanes flying low over our trenches & firing on our men – Our "A" Coy at that moment passing up CHILI. Asked CAMERONS to halt "A" Coy pending further orders "B" then proceeding up CLYDE to proceed.	
		5.55 am.	Spoke to Brigade informing them of situation & action taken – Received orders B.H.Q. not to move. Brigade ordered 26. M.G. Coy to their front line but to remain sufficiently strong for consolidation.	

A5834 Wt. W4973/M687 750,000 8/16 D. D. & L. Ltd. Forms/C.2118/13.

Instructions regarding War Diaries and Intelligence Summaries are contained in F. S. Regs., Part II. and the Staff Manual respectively. Title pages will be prepared in manuscript.

WAR DIARY
or
INTELLIGENCE SUMMARY. 10th ARGYLL & SUTHERLAND Hrs

(*Erase heading not required.*)

Army Form C. 2118.

Place	Date	Hour	Summary of Events and Information	Remarks and references to Appendices
BATTLE OF ARRAS	1917 May 3	6.30 am	2nd Lt E. MACKINNON came down wounded – unable to give much information as he was wounded early.	
			Message from 5th CAMERONS that our B. Coy are in CUBA & "A" Coy in CHILI. Not much shelling.	
			Told 5th CAMERONS these 2 Coys were at their disposal if required, otherwise to withdraw them.	
		6.45 am	5th CAMERONS said they would like them for a time as position not clear.	
			Message from 2/Lt RAMSAY, PIONEER PLATOON saying he was holding CLASP with mixture of all ranks including a number of D Coy – no officers left. Required bombs & S.A.A. and an officer.	
			Replied sending bombs & S.A.A. but no officer available – and to place himself under orders of O.C. 5th CAMERONS.	
		7.13 am	Informed Brigade of situation.	
		7.30 am	Message from 2/Lt ANDREWS "B" Coy that he was in front line with remainder of 5/7 CAMERONS – only 2 off: left.	
			Also message from 2/Lt PATERSON "A" Coy that he was in CHILI	
		7.55 am	Message from 5 CAMERONS that line was congested & CHILI & CADIZ sh^d be thinned.	
			Replied 2 Plat. A Coy in CHILI may be withdrawn into HAZARD & 2 Plat. B Coy in CHILI to be under his orders – remainder of B Coy in CUBA to withdraw if too congested.	
		8.10 am	Informed Brigade of situation.	

A5834 Wt. W4973/M687 750,000 8/16 D. D. & L. Ltd. Forms/C.2118/13.

Instructions regarding War Diaries and Intelligence Summaries are contained in F. S. Regs., Part II. and the Staff Manual respectively. Title pages will be prepared in manuscript.

WAR DIARY
or
INTELLIGENCE SUMMARY.
(Erase heading not required.)

10th ARGYLL & SUTHERLAND H'RS

Army Form C. 2118.

Place	Date	Hour	Summary of Events and Information	Remarks and references to Appendices
BATTLE OF ARRAS	1917 May 3	8.18 am	Brigade orders to get in touch with 5th CAMERONS and to extricate as many as possible of ARGYLLS who are to be withdrawn to assembly lines.	
		8.20 am	Informed 5th CAMERONS.	
		9 am	2/Lt. PATERSON as ordered arrived B.H.Q with remnants of C & D (about 75 in all) Called Roll & reorganised.	
			Casualties to date D. Lt. A.D. LAW wounded & missing	
			D. 2/Lt. R.G.C. DUNCAN do	
			D 2/Lt. RIDDEL missing.	
			C. 2/Lt. PARDY wounded	
			C 2/Lt. MACKINNON "	
			These being the only officers who were in the attack in C & D.	
		12.45 pm	Several men reported having seen Lt. A.D. LAW with his Coy surrounded E of CUTHBERT and fighting, and Lt. LAW was then wounded.	
			2/Lt. PARDY was brought in shot through both legs - He said attack failed entirely through darkness.	
		12.50 pm	Lt. CALDERWOOD R.E. reported ZERO far too early - impossible to see 5 yds ahead.	
		5.3 pm	Lt. RAMSAY & PIONEER PLATOON relieved in front line	

A5834 Wt. W4973/M687 750,000 8/16 D. D. & L. Ltd. Forms/C.2118/13.

Instructions regarding War Diaries and Intelligence Summaries are contained in F. S. Regs., Part II. and the Staff Manual respectively. Title pages will be prepared in manuscript.

WAR DIARY
or
INTELLIGENCE SUMMARY.
(Erase heading not required.)

Army Form C. 2118.

10th ARGYLL & SUTHERLAND HRS

Place	Date	Hour	Summary of Events and Information	Remarks and references to Appendices
BATTLE OF ARRAS	1917 May 3	7 pm	Message received from Brigade to relieve 5th CAMERONS. C.O. to Brigade to arrange about relief. It was arranged that "A" Coy should hold front line (CUBA &c). "B" Coy in Support – Details of "C" & "D" in HONEY, PIONEER PLATOON near SUNKEN ROAD.	
		12 mn.	2Lt RIDDELL arrived unwounded – He had been lying out in a shell hole all day – He had consolidated the shell hole with some men of the ESSEX REGT and had a Lewis gun with them.	
	4	2.30 am	Relief complete. Dispositions as follows.	
			B. 2 Platoons under 2Lt. LAWSON in CLASP.	
			– 4 L.G. in CLYDE	
			2 Platoons with O.C. Coy in CADIZ.	
			Ready to man CLYDE in event of attack from S.	
			A 2 Platoons & 2 L.G. in CUBA	
			1 " & 2 L.G. & Bombing post in CASH.	
			1 " in CRICHTON.	
			57 men came in from shell holes during the night.	

A5834 Wt. W4973/M687 750,000 8/16 D. D. & L. Ltd. Forms/C.2118/13.

Instructions regarding War Diaries and Intelligence Summaries are contained in F. S. Regs., Part II. and the Staff Manual respectively. Title pages will be prepared in manuscript.

WAR DIARY
or
INTELLIGENCE SUMMARY. 10th ARGYLL & SUTHERLAND HRS

(*Erase heading not required.*)

Army Form C. 2118.

Place	Date	Hour	Summary of Events and Information	Remarks and references to Appendices
BATTLE OF ARRAS	1917 May 4		Fairly quiet on both sides, intermittent Shelling –	
	5.		Orders received to evacuate CASH and CRICHTON as owing to an error in existing maps we were being shelled by our own heavies! A block was established in CASH at junction of CUBA & L.G. with best possible field of fire. These 2 withdrawn platoons to be accommodated in CHILI or CLYDE	
	6.		Lt ROBERTSON arrived from Transport to replace CAPT McKAY	
			CAPT. ARDILL 〃 2nd Lt ANDREWS	
			CAPT BONNYMAN 〃 2nd Lt. RIDDELL	
			Lt. McNEIL	
		12 mn	Relief complete and Batt: now in reserve Trenches –	
	7.	4 am	Very heavy shelling	
		6 pm	Enemy fired 500 4.2 & 5.9 at the batteries behind B. HQ 5 guns were knocked out –	
	9	4 am	Enemy bombarded our front systems for an hour. Trenches have been improved and wire put out on nearly the whole system since Batt has been in the line	

A5834 Wt. W4973/M687 750,000 8/16 D. D. & L. Ltd. Forms/C.2118/13.

Army Form C. 2118.

Instructions regarding War Diaries and Intelligence Summaries are contained in F. S. Regs., Part II. and the Staff Manual respectively. Title pages will be prepared in manuscript.

WAR DIARY
or
INTELLIGENCE SUMMARY.
(Erase heading not required.)

10th ARGYLL & SUTHERLAND H[ighlanders]

Place	Date	Hour	Summary of Events and Information	Remarks and references to Appendices
BATTLE OF ARRAS.	1917 May 10		Battalion relieved in the line by a Batt of W. YORKS (17 Division) Marched to ARRAS and embussed to Y HUTS.	
BAILLEUL aux CORNAILLES	12.		Marched to BAILLEUL aux CORNAILLES.	
			NOTES	
			Owing to there being no officers remaining in "D" Coy and but one in "C" it is not easy to obtain satisfactory accounts of what exactly occurred but By 3. am. all parties were lined out in position and at ZERO 3.45 am the attack was launched in good formation – It was pitch dark and impossible to see 5 yds ahead, consequently it was impossible to pick up any landmarks, however the 2 Companies "C" & "D" held straight on and found themselves a short distance over CUTHBERT and were in the act of swinging when they came under heavy M.G. fire from their front and Railway Embankment – at this time also the enemy who were holding shell holes closed in on both flanks and both Coys suffered severe casualties – Both Coys fought hard and the last thing seen of Lt. LAW was fighting until wounded – He was never seen again – about 75 of the 2 Coys got back into our original front line – The CAMERONS edged somewhat too much to the right and lost direction and the BLACK WATCH on the left perhaps slightly too much to the left – This would account for the 2 Coys Argylls finding themselves alone in front.	

A5834 Wt. W4973/M687 750,000 8/16 D. D. & L. Ltd. Forms/C.2118/13.

Instructions regarding War Diaries and Intelligence Summaries are contained in F. S. Regs., Part II. and the Staff Manual respectively. Title pages will be prepared in manuscript.

WAR DIARY
or
INTELLIGENCE SUMMARY.
(Erase heading not required.)

10th ARGYLL, SUTHERLAND H'drs

Army Form C. 2118.

Place	Date	Hour	Summary of Events and Information	Remarks and references to Appendices
BAILLEUL and CORNAILLES	(1917) May 12		Our right flank was on CASH: 4th Division was on our right and as their front line was 200 yards behind ours it rendered direction still more difficult to keep. 27th Brigade (9th Div) was on our left.	
			Every one was confident of success, the men very fit & fresh and in our opinion we could have gained our objectives if the fatal mistake of fixing Zero 25 minutes before dawn had not been made.	
			The following officers joined from home and reported for duty	
	(30 Apl)		CAPT. R.W.B. ARDILL originally 10th Batt: wounded at LOOS	
			Lt J.T. McNEIL	
			Lt J.E. BURLEIGH	
			Lt W.D. WILLIAMSON	
	14		Brig Gen: KENNEDY D.S.O. (late of commanding this Batt) mentioned in Despatches	
			Capt W.G. CAMPBELL (late of serving with this Batt) mentioned in Despatches	
			Batt. training - 32 reinforcements arrived (all of old wounded men of Batt)	
	16		Weather colder - Musketry at range at MONCHY LE BRETON.	
	(14)		The General ALLENBY (3rd ARMY Commander) visited Brigade and saw the COs	
			CASUALTIES during operations from 28.4.17 to 10.5.17 as under.	
			Off. Capt P.Y. LYLE wounded; Capt R.A. COLVIN Killed; Lieut T.J. PARDY died of wounds; Lieut A.D. LAW wounded & missing; 2/Lt R.G.C. DUNCAN missing; 2/Lt E. McKINNON wounded	
			O.R. K. 19, W. 99, M. 26 Total 144 } Total all ranks: K. W. M.; off. 2 2 2; O.R. 19 99 26	
			TOTAL 21. 101. 28 = 150	

A5834 Wt. W4973/M687 750,000 8/16 D. D. & L. Ltd. Forms/C.2118/13.

Instructions regarding War Diaries and Intelligence Summaries are contained in F. S. Regs., Part II. and the Staff Manual respectively. Title pages will be prepared in manuscript.

WAR DIARY
or
INTELLIGENCE SUMMARY
(*Erase heading not required.*) 10th ARGYLL & SUTHERLAND HRS.

Army Form C. 2118.

Place	Date 1917	Hour	Summary of Events and Information	Remarks and references to Appendices
BAILLEUL AUX CORNAILLES	May 18.		The Battn carried out firing practice, Rifles and Lewis Guns on the Range in the MONCHY - BRETON training area.	
	19.		Inspection of the Battn by the Commanding Officer.	
	21		First days Programme of Brigade "WAPINSHAW" at MONCHY - BRETON Range. Divisional First Line Transport Competition took place at BELLE EPINE. The Battn transport competed - It was exceedingly well turned out but failed to win owing to other units having better horseflesh. A prize was won by 'B' Company Cooker.	
	22.		Brigade "WAPINSHAW" continued - The following prizes were won by the Battn. Open Competitions - 200 yards - application. 2nd prize - No 277124. Pte N. McCORMACK D. Coy. 200 yards - rapid fire. 2nd prize (after a tie) No 2047 Pte J. KIRKWOOD. C Coy. Brigade Championship. 3rd prize - No 43048 L/corpl R FLEMING	

Army Form C. 2118.

Instructions regarding War Diaries and Intelligence Summaries are contained in F. S. Regs., Part II. and the Staff Manual respectively. Title pages will be prepared in manuscript.

WAR DIARY
or
INTELLIGENCE SUMMARY.
(*Erase heading not required.*) 10th ARGYLL & SUTHERLAND HRS.

Place	Date	Hour	Summary of Events and Information	Remarks and references to Appendices
	1917			
BAILLEUL AUX CORNAILLES	May 23		The Battn played 8th the BLACK WATCH at football at AVERDOINGT and beat them by 2 goals to 1.	
	26		Brigade "WAPINSHAW" concluded. The following were won by the Bn: Lewis Gunners. 1st prize Open Compn. (L/c BELL) B. Coy team 2nd prize - Spl. compn. L/c Blaikie (D Coy)	
	27.		The Corps Commander (Sir Charles Fergusson) presented Medal Ribbons to Officers & men of the 26th Brigade, who had been awarded the Military Cross, D.C.M or Military Medal in connection with the Operations in the First Battle of ARRAS. The list of Honours & awards is set out hereafter. Capt Woodburn was unfortunately absent in Hospital, & Sgt. MacLennan at the 3rd Army School. C.S.M. Nicholson died of wounds after his name had been sent in. Several other ranks were unavoidably absent either on leave or in hospital. A detachment consisting of 3 officers + 100 O.R. under Capt. D.A. McKAY. M.C and the Band attended.	

2353 Wt. W2544/1454 700,000 5/15 D. D. & L. A.D.S.S./Forms/C. 2118.

Instructions regarding War Diaries and Intelligence Summaries are contained in F. S. Regs., Part II. and the Staff Manual respectively. Title pages will be prepared in manuscript.

WAR DIARY
or
INTELLIGENCE SUMMARY. 10th ARGYLL & SUTHERLAND HRS.

(*Erase heading not required.*)

Army Form C. 2118.

Place	Date	Hour	Summary of Events and Information	Remarks and references to Appendices
	1917			
BAILLEUL AUX CORNAILLES	May 27.		Major N. McQueen (commanding in the absence of the Colonel on leave) and Capt. E. Bonnyman attended as interested spectators.	
	28		A tactical field exercise was carried out in conjunction with a section of the 26th M. G. Coy & a section of the 26th T. M. Battery. The exercise comprised an outpost scheme and advanced guard passing through at early dawn. The Corps Commander witnessed the final part of the Operations.	
	30		The Battn moved into ARRAS by motor transport.	
	31.		The Battn less the prescribed Officers & personnel moved up to the Railway Embankment at H.13.d.	
			The enjoyment of the summer evenings at BAILLEUL by all ranks was greatly enhanced by the programmes played	

2353 Wt. W2544/1454 700,000 5/15 D. D. & L. A.D.S.S./Forms/C. 2118.

Army Form C. 2118.

Instructions regarding War Diaries and Intelligence Summaries are contained in F. S. Regs., Part II. and the Staff Manual respectively. Title pages will be prepared in manuscript.

WAR DIARY
or
INTELLIGENCE SUMMARY.
(*Erase heading not required.*)

10th ARGYLL & SUTHERLAND HRS

Place	Date	Hour	Summary of Events and Information	Remarks and references to Appendices
			nightly by the Band.	
			The following is a list of Honours and awards published during the month of May.	
			MAJOR N. McQUEEN – Chevalier of the LEGION D'HONNEUR. mentioned in Despatches.	
			CAPTAIN J. WOODBURN. – Military Cross – mentioned in Despatches.	
			2nd Lieut. J.M. BEATTIE – Military Cross.	
			2nd Lieut. T.N.F. HOURSTON – Military Cross.	
			Captain W. MILLERICK – R.A.M.C. — mentioned in despatches.	
			851. C.S.M. J. NICHOLSON – B. Coy } D.C.M.	
			1499 Sergt. A. MACLENNAN. – A. Coy } D.C.M.	
			5629 Sergt. A. McGREGOR. – A. Coy } M.M.	
			14458 Pte A. McFADYEN – C. Coy } M.M.	
			1099 Sgt. J. HAMILTON. – B Coy } M.M.	

2353 Wt. W2544/1454 700,000 5/15 D. D. & L. A.D.S.S./Forms/C. 2118.

Army Form C. 2118.

Instructions regarding War Diaries and Intelligence Summaries are contained in F. S. Regs., Part II. and the Staff Manual respectively. Title pages will be prepared in manuscript.

WAR DIARY
or
INTELLIGENCE SUMMARY.
(Erase heading not required.)

10th ARGYLL & SUTHERLAND H.S

Place	Date	Hour	Summary of Events and Information	Remarks and references to Appendices
			S/2372 Sergt. A. McCAIG – D Coy.	
			S/1756. L/Corpl W. RODGERS. B. Coy	
			3675. Pte A. McKAY. A Coy	
			12455. " J. LANG. A. Coy.	
			S/2619 Sgt. J. THOMSON. C. Coy.	
			619. L/Corpl. J. HAMMOND. D. Coy.	
			9742 Corpl. J. HARVIE. C. Coy	
			9455. Pte W. CAMPBELL. D. Coy.	
			S/4380 L/Corpl W. NEILSON. B. Coy	
			14240. Pte W. ROLLO. D. Coy	

N. McQueen Major
for Lieut-Colonel Commanding
10th Argyll & Sutherland Highlanders.

In the Field. 31/5/17.

2353 Wt. W2541/1454 700,000 5/15 D. D. & L. A.D.S.S./Forms/C. 2118.

10th Argyll and Sutherland Highrs.

Statement of Casualties, Sick, Drafts, etc. for May 1917.

Date	Killed	Wounded	Wounded & Missing	Missing	To hospital	From hospital	Reinforcements
1.	1.	6.			1.	2.	
2		4.				1.	
3.	6.	30.	2.	20.	3.		
4.		1.			3	4.	
5.	4.	24.		6.	6.		1.
6	4.	8			1.		
7.		1.			4.	1.	
8.					2.		
9	2.	3.			3	1	
10.		3.			1	1	
11.					1	4.	
12					3		
13.					2	3.	29.
14.					5		
15.					1		
16.					2.		
17.					3.	4.	
18.					1	1	
19					2.	1	16.
20							
21		1.			2.	3.	
22					2	3.	
23					3		
24					4	1	
25					2	2	
26					7	1	
27					2	3	13.
28						1	
29					4	2	
31					1		
31.					2.		

In the Field
31.5.17

N. McQueen. Major.
Commdg. 10th Arg. & Suth'd. Hrs.

Copy

S E C R E T.

No. R/58. 30th April 1917.

26th Brigade Preliminary Instructions

No.1 for oprtations on May 3rd. 1917.

ACKNOWLEDGE.

Sgd. J.F. Evetts. Capt.,
Brigade Major.
26th Infantry Brigade.

Copies to 1. 8th Black Watch.
2. 7th Seaforth Hrs.
3. 5th Cameron Hrs.
4. 10th A. & S. Hrs.
5. 26th M.G. Company.
6. 26th T.M. Battery.
7. 26th Brigade Signals.
8. Brigade Transport Officer.
9. C.R.A. 9th Division.
10. A.D.M.S. 9th Division.
11. 27th Brigade.
12. 12th Brigade.
13. 64th F.Coy. R.E.
14. 9th Seaforths Hrs. (Pioneers)
15. Staff Captain.
16. Brigade Int. Officer.
17. War Diary.
18. File.

SECRET. (26th Brigade No. R/58. dated 30.4.17.)

PRELIMINARW INSTRUCTIONS No.1 for
OPERATIONS ON MAY 3rd.

Reference 1/10,000 map (attached.) & 1/20,000 ARRAS, trench Map.

1. The XVII th Corps will resume the Offensive on the May 3rd. in conjunction with VIth Corps on the right and XIII Corps on the Left.
2. The objective of the operation of the XVIIth Corps is to secure the line PLOUVAIN - I.2.a.5.8.

Subsequent to this, if the situation admits, the Corps Reserve, (17th Division) will be pushed through to secure a line between BIACHE -FRESNES and to harass the enemy in his retreat.
3. The actual line for the objective of the 9th Division will be:- the RED LINE.

Intermediate Objectives will be the BLUE & BLACK LINES - as shown on the Map. The BLUE & RED LINES on the front of the 9th Division are identical.
4. The 26th Brigade will attack on the right of the 9th Division with with the 12th Brigade (4th Division) on the Right and 27th Brigade on the Left.
5. The Northern & Southern Boundaries for the 26th Brigade and the dividing line between assaulting battalions are shown on the Map.
6. The exact line held by the Germans is uncertain, but he is known to be in the following places:-

ROEUX & the WOOD West of it.
CHATEAU in I.13.d.
STATION & Buildings North of the Railway in I.13.
A Trench 200 yards to 260 yards East of our trenches between CAM & CASH Trenches.
CUPID Trench.
COD Trench.
Shell Holes West of CUTHBERT Trench. CUTHBERT Trench and PLOUVAIN -GAVRELLE Road.

The Trenches on the HAUSA Wood Spur, The PLOUVAIN Defences, WINE Trench and the BIACHE-FRESNES Line are probably held by reserves.

The Enemy Defences are organized in considerable depth, and from prisoners statements, it appears that all small lengths of Trench, shown on Map, will probably be found to be held by detachments, in some cases with Machine Guns.
7. ROEUX, the CHEMICAL WORKS and the buildings North of the Railway will be subjected to continuous Bombardment during the days proceeding the attack. Similarly , the trenches & woods immediately west & south of PLOUVAIN will be systematically bombardment. The Railway Cutting from the ROEUX station Eastwards will be searched by night and day for Machine Guns.

The Wire on GREENLAND HILL, West of PLOUVAIN and on the BIACHE-FRESNES trench line will be cut during the preliminary bombardment.
8. The creeping Barrage will, generally speaking, move forward at a rate of 100 yards every 2 minutes.

There will be pauses on the BLACK & BLUE LINES to admit of troops re-organizing or being passes through for each further advance. The RED LINE on being reached, will be consolidated.
9. One Brigade, 17th Division will be places at the disposal of the 9th Division from Midnight May 2nd/3rd. as a reserve, to be used only in case of emergency. This Brigade will revert to the 17th Division when the latter is ordered forward.

10. It is the intention, should the general situation admit, to undertake a night advance after the Battle of the 3rd. with a view to disorganizing the enemy, capturing his Guns and gaining ground to wards the DROCOURT-QUEANT line.

On the front of this Corps the operations will be carried out by the 17th Division. The division will concentrate forward into the battle area on the 3rd May. One, or portions of two Brigades will be prepared to pass through the front of the 9th Division on the RED Line during the night 3rd/4th.; these troops will assault the PLOUVAIN -FRESNES line with the bayonet; reform and pass on to the GREEN LINE I.10.d.a.4.c.& a. forming a temporary defensive flank along the Railway as they advance. This advance will be carried out without Rifle or Artillery Fire, in order that all those who open fire may be recognised as enemies. Artillery fire during the advance will be restricted to counter-battery work.

The conditions which would make this operation possible, are those which would resultif the enemy is disorganized and wears out, his strength by repeated counter-attacks after we have gained the RED LINE, or even before we reach it.

CANCELLED

II. PLAN OF ATTACK.

1. The attack will be carried out by 5th Cameron Hrs, on the right and by 8th Black Watch on the left - 10th A. & S. Hrs. will be in support - 7th Seaforth Hrs. in Brigade Reserve. The dividing line between assaulting battalions being as shown on the Map. The attack will be carried through to the 2nd & 3rd objectives, which are identical for the 9th Division. There will be a pause on the BLACK LINE.

2. FORMATIONS. - Each battalion will be in 4 waves i.e. A two Company front, each company on a front of 2 platoons.

3. Owing to the nature of the opposition likely to be met with, i.e. M Machine Gun fire and isolated pockets of enemy, echeloned in depth, distances between waves will not be less than 100 yards and waves will be in the following formation:-

Leading wave in extended order covering the whole Brigade Frontage.

Second & Third waves in lines of columns of platoons or sections, as the situation admits.

Fourth wave in extended order, "Mopping Up" all enemy wounded etc, lying in shell holes.

The danger of leaving such enemy must be emphasised.

4. Each battalion will "earmark" one platoon of 3rd wave to be used immediately the objective is gained, as a strong reconnoitring patrol to seize any tactical points of importance, immediately in front of our final objective.

These platoons will carry two days rations and a good supply of Rifle Grenades.

5. One company from 10th A. & S. Hrs. plus 1 section 26th M.G. Coy. plus 2 stokes mortars, will advance immediately in rear of the right flank of 5th Cameron Hrs.

On arrival at the BLUE LINE they will occupy the Railway Embankment facing south from the station to I.9.c.1.1. and will protect the right flank until the 12th Brigade has occupied the RED LINE. In event of the right flank becoming exposed during the advance to the BLUE & BLACK LINES, they will be prepared to operate to that flank and to cover the advance of the Brigade with Rifles & Machine Gun Fire.

6. Pioneer Platoon, 8th Black Watch will be pushed forward when the Black LINE has been gained and will make a strong point about I.2.c.4.0.

Pioneer Platoon, 5th Cameron Hrs, will be pushed forward when the BLUE LINE has been gained and will make a strong point I.8.d.55.

7. Should the attack go through successfully, the 2 leading waves will occupy and consolidate the final objective. & the 2 rear waves will dig a supporting line 200 yards in rear of it.

Every effort will be made to avoid congestion on the final objectives.

9. The remainder of the 10th A. & S. Hrs. will be prepared to move forward to the line of the PLOUVAIN - GAVRELLE Road.

10. After the final objective has been gained, a heavy counter-attack must be expected and it must be impressed on all ranks that effective artillery protection cab only be obtained if the position of the Infantry is clearly defined by the lighting of Flares, when called for by Contact Aeroplanes, (2 artillery boards will be carried by the leading wave of ea Battalion & will,be used to mark the front line & specially the right fla flank) Protection for the men can only be obtained by intensive digging.

12 ACTION OF MACHINE GUNS.

26th Machine Gun Coy. will be disposed as follows:-

2 Guns will advance with, and under orders of O.C. 8th Black Watch.
2 Guns with, and under orders of O.C. 5th Cameron Hrs.
4 Guns will remain in, and hold our original front line while the attack takes place.
4 Guns will remain in Brigade Reserve in HUSSAR Trench.

O.C. 26th M.G. Coy. will arrange the distribution of his Carrying parties.

13. ACTION OF TRENCH MORTARS.
Two Stokes Guns will advance with the 4th assaulting wave on right flank of 8th Black Watch. 2 Guns with flank guard Company of 10th A. & S. highrs.
4 remaining Guns will be held in Brigade reserve with reserve M.G. about HUZZAR trench.

14. ASSEMBLY PRIOR TO ATTACK.
1. Assaulting battalions will be formed up for assembly as follows
2 leading waves in and vicinity of CUBA trench.
3 Rear waves in and vicinity of CLASP trench, the whole to be East of the ROEUX - GAVRELLE Road.
2. 2 Coys. 10th A. & S. Hrs. (including Coy. detailed for right flank guard) will be assemb;ed North of CLYDE, between CHILI & CLASP, in the vicinity of the SUNKEN ROAD, running from 1.7.a.0.0. to 1.7.a.4.3. and in the trench running North from CLYDE at 1.7.c.15.90.
The 4 Machine Guns and 2 Stokes Mortars to operate with the right ~~flank~~ flank guard, will be assembled in CLYDE, between CHILI & CLASP.
3. The assembly will be covered by a screen of Lewis Guns pushed out from the leading waves, 50 yards to 100 yards in front of CUBA trench, and the post in CASH will be manned.
The Screen of Lewis Guns will be withdrawn a quarter of an hour before ZERO.
4. 2 Companies 10th A. & S. Hrs. will be assembled in HOLLY. HAZARD? HAGGARD and LUMBER.
2 Companies 7th Seaforth Hrs. will be assembled in HUDSON? HERON, & LUCIL.
5. The remaining ~~7th Seaforth Hrs~~ 2 Companies 7th Seaforth Hrs, will be assembled in the portions of EFFIE & LAUREL in the Brigade Area.
6. The reserve Machine Guns and trench mortars will be assembled in HUSSAR trench.

~~15.~~
15. POSITION OF H.Q.
Headquarters 8th Black Watch & 5th Cameron Hrs, will be in CHILI ~~tr~~ trench. H.12.b.5.7.
Brigade forward signal station will also be in this trench, and close to H.Q. of assaulting Battalions.
H.Q. 10th A & S. Hrs,) will be in the dugout at H.11.a.6.2.
7th Seaforth Hrs.)
Brigade Battle H.Q. will be in dugout at H.10.d.4.7. Officers Commanding 7th Seaforth Hrs, & 10th A. & S. Hrs. 26th M.G. Coy, and 26th T.M. Battery, will keep in close touch with Brigade H.Q.

16. SIGNALLING COMMUNICATIONS.
1. The following will be telephone stations, and this route will also be the runner route:-
(1) Brigade Headquarters.-H.10.d.4.6.-Station Call-T.B.
(2) Brigade Visual Station & O.P.- H.11.a.2.0.-Station call-T.B.V.
(3) Reserve & Support Battalions ↓ Station call - T.D.
(4) Advanced Brigade Station - H.11.b.5.6. - Station Call - T.B.R.
(5) Linesmen test points - H.6.c.6.1.- Station T.P.
(6) Assaulting Battalions - Station Call - T.C.
Each of these stations except No.2 will be a runner relay station.

There will be a visual station both receiving from, Forward & for sending back at H.12.b.8.5. This will be in telephone communication with No.7 Station, the call will be T.V. There will be, the receiving visual station, at No. 2 station, this station will answer T.V. A long dash ↓ G. two long dashes = R.D. No answer I.M.I.

2/-

2. An advanced battalion station will be established at 1.7.b.1.5. station call P.B. and will be in telephone communication with No.7. xxxxxxx station, it will also be in visual communication with T.V. visual station.
This station will be in charge of Lieut. BARRY, 5th Cameron Hrs., Signalling Officer, who will temporarily be in charge of both 8th Black Watch & 5th Cameron Hrs. Signallers.
The Officer will be responsible for communications back to No 7 station, as long as the Battalions H.Q. are there, and also for carrying forward lines, and establishing the Forward Battalion H.Q. in or near the Black Line, when the situation allows. In front of this advanced H.Q. when established each battalion will be responsible for its own communication to its companies.

3. An ampyfier will be stationed at No.7 station, No. 1 Power Buzzer will be at an advanced battalion signal station in CUBA trench at 1.7.b.1.5. Station call P.B. this power buzzer will remain here.
The second power buzzer will be with the assaulting battalions H.Q. & will move forward when they do so.
No.1 P.B. will not be used after No.2 has gone forward unles definite instructions are received that Amplyfier cannot read No.2 P.B. both P.B. will only work during the odd 5 minutes, viz:-
1 to 5, & 11 to 15, call of amplyfier will be AA.

17. DUMPS & AMMUNITION SUPPLY.
DUMPS (ALREADY ESTABLISHED).

Main Divisional Dump.	-	ST NICHOLAS, G.16.c.7.7.
Advcd. " "	-	POINT DU JOUR, H.3.d.22.
Main Brigade Dump.	-	H.15.d.4.3.
Adve. " "	-	H.11.b. (xxxxxxxxxxxxxxx (HAZARD trench).

Main Brigade Dump contains S.A.A., Hand & Rifle Grenades, Stokes Amm. Ground Flares, Very Lights,(White, red & Green). 350 filled Petrol Tins, and a number of Field Dressings, Very pistols of Both sizes, and Vickers Belts (empty). Sandbags & a small supply of picks & Shovels.
Advanced Brigade Dumpmat present contains a small quantity of S.A.A., tools, red very lights, flares, sandbags & water.
These quantities will be increased and the dump will be situated in HAZARD, and in HOLLOW trench, about H.12.a.1.6.
There is a dump of 40 boxes of Rifle Grenades at H.12.d.85.90. junction of CLYDE & CHILI.
During the advance, the dump will be put forward by carrying parties to the vicinity of the brick works, at 1.7.a.6.9.
After the advance carrying & clearing parties which are at present located round CAM, LAUREL, PAINT & OPIUM trenches will be pushed up to the 4th German System, LUMBER, HAGGARD & HUDSON.
The dump officer 2/Lt. GRIEVE, can at present be found at H.15.d.43. and after the attack commences will be at H.12.a.1.6.

18. WATER & FOOD SUPPLY.
The present system of delivering water and rations is as follows:-
To right Battalion, - by Limberste Battalion H.Q. in H.10.d.
To left Battalion, - by pack Pony to Battalion H.Q. at H.11.c.
Both travel by overland track from H.9.c.42. to h.10.d. central thence North of wirebto H.11.a. central.
If it is necessary to ration the Brigade in the trenches on Z night pack ponies may be taken from H.10.d. central, via., the road H.10.d. H.11.a. thence by track to West end of CLYDE, also by northern track H.11.a. and b. to West end of CHILI trench.
If transport can proceed no further, arrangements will be made to convey rations and water of any Battalion holding the line to the present front line (CUBA TRENCH).
On Y night it is hoped to make an issue of solidified Alcohol for cooking on Z day and also a further issue of chewing gum.

Copy

SECRET. Copy No..4..

26th. BRIGADE OPERATION ORDER No. 111.

Reference, 2.5.17.
1/20,000 ARRAS.
Trench Map. & 1/10,000 map issued to all Units. 26th Brigade

(1)a The XVII Corps will resume the offensive tomorrow May 3rd.
(b) The 9th Division will attack with the 26th Brigade on the right and the 27th Brigade on the left.
The 12th Brigade will be on the right of the 26th Brigade.
(c) The attack will be carried out by the 5th Cameron Hrs. on the right and the 8th Black Watch on the left.
The 10th A. & S. Hrs. will be in support and the 7th Seaforth Hrs. in Brigade Reserve.
Instructions have already been issued as to the employment of Machine Guns & Trench Mortars.

2. Objectives in the attack have already been laid down.

3. 63rd Field Company R.E. and one Company 9th Seaforth Hrs. (Pioneers) will be at the disposal of the G.O.C., 26th Brigade to assist in consolidation.
(a). The Field Coy. R.E. will be assembled at ZERO in its present locality and the Company of the Pioneers in EFFIE and LAUREL with 2 Coys 7th Seaforths.
(b). The Officers Commanding will keep in ~~xxxxx~~ close touch with 26th Brigade H.Q. and their task will be allotted to them as the situation develops and in accordance with verbal instructions already given.

4. 197th Machine Gun Coy., will be at the disposal of the G.O.C., 26th Brigade when the work of covering fire is completed.
The O.C. 197th Machine Gun Coy, will report to the 26th Brigade H.Q. as soon as this is done, with a statement as to the location of his Guns and the number of filled Belts he has in hand.

5. **ARTILLERY BARRAGE & PLAN.**
(a). **18-pounders.** At ZERO hour the barrage will open on the line as shewn in the attached map, and at ZERO plus 4 minutes, commence to Creep East at the rate of 100 yards every 2 minutes, till ZERO plus 24 minutes, when the rate will slow down to 100 yards every 3 minutes till arriving on the final barrage line.
AMMUNITION H.E. If the wind is at all from the West each Gun will fire one smoke shell in each lift.
RATE OF FIRE. 3 rounds per gun per minute; this rate will be maintained till 15 minutes after arriving on the final barrage, when the rate will be slowed down to 1 round per Gun per Minute for a further 15 mins. then rate will slow down to 3 rounds per battery a minute for another 15 minutes, then stop fire; Brigades will be ready to open on their final barrage in case of S.O.S. and engage visible targets.
(b). **4.5" HOWITZERS.** The 4.5" Howitzers will barrage in their Brigade Zones, barraging 200 yards East of the 18-pounders.
RATE OF FIRE. 2 rounds per gun per minute till 15 minutes after reaching the final barrage, and then the same as the 18 pounders.
(c) When the final objective has been gained the 4.5" Howitzers will put down a Smoke Shell barrage, 200 yards East of the 18-pounders protective barrage, to cover the consolidating troops. This barrage will only be put down when the objective is taken and will serve as a signal as well as a screen.
(d) The 52nd Brigade will provide an Artillery Liaison Officer at 26th Brigade H.Q. and an F.O.O. to follow the infantry attack.

6. Contact aeroplanes will fly over the front line at 6.15 a.m. when flares will be lit.

7. ZERO hourx will be at 3.45 a.m. to morrow May 3rd.
The final hour synchr onization will be notified later.

8. Advance Brigade headquarters will open at H.10.d.4.7. at 5.30 p.m. to day May 2nd.

9. AVKNOWLEDGE.

Sgd. J.F. EVETTS. Capt.

Brigade Major.

Issued at 2 p.m. 26th Infantry Brigade.

SECRET.

Ammendment No.1 to 26th Brigade Preliminary Instructions No. 1. for operations on May 3rd 1917.

Under instructions recieved from 9th Division the Copses at 1.8.d.7.1. will be included in the right boundary of the 26th Brigade.

The dividing between 8th Black Watch & 5th Cameron Hrs, will therefore be:-

Trench junction at 1.9.b.15.45.(inclusive to 8th Black Watch) thence a line to 1.8.b.80.11. thence a line to cross roads in 1.7.a. (inclusive to 5th Cameron Hrs.)

Sgd. W. S. Stevenson Captain.
for Brigade Major,
26th Infantry Brigade.

1.5.17.

ACKNOWLEDGE.

SECRET.

Addition No. 1. to 26th Brigade preliminary instructions No. 1. for operations on May 3rd 1917.

BATTLE STOPS.

Two stops will be established, one at the junctions of HECTIC, and HAGGARD, and one at the junction of CHILI and HALKYON.
Each post will consist of a N.C.O not below the rank of Sergeant, and two men.
They will take post half an hour after ZERO, and will be responsible for checking the number of prisoners and wounded which pass the stops. A return showing these numbers will be sent to be Brigade H.Q. every hour.

ACKNOWLEDGE.

2.5.17.

J.F.EVETTS, Capt,
Brigade Major,
26th Infantry Brigade.

SECRET. Copy No.4.

26th Brigade Operation Order No. 112.

Reference. 2.5.17.

1/20,000 ARRAS trenchmap

1. The 26th Brigade will assemble in the areas laid down in the preliminary instructions No. 1. to night May 2/3rd. as follows:-
2. (a).5th Cameron Hrs. to commence at 10 p.m.
(b).10th A. & S. Hrs.(leading Coy) to leave GREEN LINE at 11 p.m
(c).1 sect. 26th M.G. Coy. & 1 sub-sect. 26th T.M.Batt. will report to O.C. "C" Coy. 10th A. & S. H. before assembly under arrangements already made.
(d) 8th Black Watch will commence at 11 p.m.
(e) the sub-sections of the 26th M.G. Coy. & 26th T.M.Batt. (1 sub-section) to advance with 8th Black Watch & 5th Cameron Hrs, will assemble with these Battalions under arrangements to be made between Commanding Officers concerned.
(f) The reserve Machine Guns & Trench Mortars will be assembled in HUSSAR trench, by ZERO hour.
(g) 8th Seaforth Hrs, will commence to leave the BLUE line at 11.30 p.m.
(h) 1 Coy. 9th Seaforth Hrs.(pioneers) will be in position in EFFIE, & LAUREL, by 2 a.m.
(i) 63rd F.Coy. R.E. will be in position in its present bivouac by ZERO hour.
3. Completion of assembly will be reported to Brigade H.Q. by runner
4. ACKNOWLEDGE.

ISSUED at 4 p.m.

Sgd J.F. EVETTS. Capt,
Brigade Major, 26th Infantry Brigade.

MESSAGE FROM BRIGADE.

TO TERRIER.

R.C. 1. 2nd. AAA.

THE FOLLOWING MESSAGE HAS BEEN RECEIVED FROM ARMY AND IS REPEATED FOR INFORMATION OF ALL R RANKS. AAA.

THE FORTHCOMING BATTLE WILL BE THE GREATEST IN WHICH THE BRITISH ARMY HAS PARTAKEN AAA.

FROM MEET.

TIME 10.30. p.m.

(sgd) R. Cavendish, Capt.

Instructions regarding War Diaries and Intelligence Summaries are contained in F. S. Regs., Part II. and the Staff Manual respectively. Title pages will be prepared in manuscript.

Army Form C. 2118.

WAR DIARY
or
INTELLIGENCE SUMMARY.
(Erase heading not required.)

10th Argyll & Sutherland Highlrs

Vol 22

Place	Date	Hour	Summary of Events and Information	Remarks and references to Appendices
LAURENT BLANGY	1917. June 1.		Batt: in Camp "STIRLING CASTLE" in bivouacs in RAILWAY EMBANKMENT BLUE LINE – All bathed – Bathing also in Lakes in Park – Though the Park has been liable to shelling ever since the present position of the line (up to 9 April last) the Trees have suffered very little and the beauty of the Park very little spoilt – It was found that the enemy had thrown up breastworks and formed strong points but they were never held during the advance – Days spent in terracing the slope with wooden bivouacs and it now forms a very receptive comparatively safe Camp. Enemy aeroplane bombing attacks nightly but Batt: did not suffer at all	[illegible]
	5	8 PM	An Attack was carried out by 27th Brigade with the object of capturing Enemy Trenches & organised shell holes forming his front system on a frontage of 2000 yds – The actual front line comprising CHARLIE, CURLY & CUPID Trenches were captured – a pocket of Germans held out in the morning in CURLY, but surrendered later – 2 Off & 60. OR were captured here. The Enemy's losses were severe, 6 Coys being completely shattered	[illegible]

2353 Wt W2544/1454 700,000 5/15 D. D. & L. A.D.S.S./Forms/C. 2118.

26.0

Army Form C. 2118.

Instructions regarding War Diaries and Intelligence Summaries are contained in F. S. Regs., Part II. and the Staff Manual respectively. Title pages will be prepared in manuscript.

WAR DIARY
or
INTELLIGENCE SUMMARY.
(*Erase heading not required.*)

10th Argyll & Sutherland Highrs.

Place	Date	Hour	Summary of Events and Information	Remarks and references to Appendices
	1917			
LAURENT BLANGY	June 5		Our casualties slight – 2 local Counter attacks were made from direction of WHIP. X Roads (I.2.c) but were beaten off with severe losses. Total prisoners captured 6 officers 222 O.R. Enemy placed a heavy Barrage on CHEMICAL WORKS but on the whole front of attack barrage was ragged & eight minutes late in coming down. About 30% of prisoners captured belong to 1918 Class.	J.R.P.
	6		Message received from C in C congratulating Division on success of attack. Batt: relieved 8 Black Watch in support – Enemy heavily shelled Cross Roads on Railway preventing our Coy moving into CRUMP TRENCH. It however chose its own time & got through without casualties – Relief complete 3.30 a.m. – H.Q. in A Coy in CUTTING – C & D in bank –	J.R.P.
	7.	12 Noon.	C.O. visited CRUMP & CRETE Trenches – Everything in good order.	J.R.P.
		5 pm.	Message received that Battle at MESSINES had started 3.10. a.m. & was proceeding very satisfactorily –	

2353 Wt. W2544/1454 700,000 5/15 D. D. & L. A.D.S.S./Forms/C. 2118.

Army Form C. 2118.

WAR DIARY
or
INTELLIGENCE SUMMARY.
(Erase heading not required.)

10th Argyll & Sutherland Highrs.

Instructions regarding War Diaries and Intelligence Summaries are contained in F. S. Regs., Part II. and the Staff Manual respectively. Title pages will be prepared in manuscript.

Place	Date	Hour	Summary of Events and Information	Remarks and references to Appendices
FAMPOUX.	1917 June 7		Attack was from S of R. DOUVE to YPRES-COMINES CANAL – MESSINES captured and outskirts of WYTSCHAETE occupied.	[illegible]
			Message from C in C. received	
			"C in C wishes all ranks to be informed unofficially that he has "most reliable information that the internal situation in Germany is "much more serious than was supposed and that the enemy are much depressed at the failure of the U Boats. He considers it very probable that Peace will be declared before the winter. It is pointed out, however, "that this is unofficial and must be taken for what he considers "its worth"	
	8.		Further message regarding the Battle in the North states 2nd Army have captured OOSTAVERNE line. Enemy counter attacked on 2nd ANZAC Corps but was crushed by artillery fire. Prisoners up to date 4500. & several guns.	[illegible]
		9.10 pm.	Batt: relieved 5 Camerons in front line.	
			A & C Coys in front trench. B & D Coy & 1 Cameron Coy in Support in CRUMP	

2353 Wt. W2544/1454 700,000 5/15 D. D. & L. A.D.S.S./Forms/C. 2118.

Instructions regarding War Diaries and Intelligence Summaries are contained in F. S. Regs., Part II. and the Staff Manual respectively. Title pages will be prepared in manuscript.

WAR DIARY
or
INTELLIGENCE SUMMARY.
(Erase heading not required.)

Army Form C. 2118.

10th Argyll & Sutherland Highlanders

Place	Date	Hour	Summary of Events and Information	Remarks and references to Appendices
	1917			
CHEMICAL WORKS - ROEUX LINE	June 9.		Batt H.Q in CRETE.	
			DISPOSITION of COYS	J.H.?
			The method of holding the line is as follows.	
			A Coy on Right consisting of 6 Posts with Coy H.Q in ROEUX WOOD on R. SCARPE	
			No 1 & 2 Posts are isolated shell holes each garrisoned by 1 N.C.O 4 men & L.Gun with Team.	
			Posts have been consolidated but owing to dampness of ground it is not possible to connect them, rations are taken to them at night.	
			No 3 & 4 & COWIE POSTS are connected by a poor trench and are held as Posts - (COWIE POST being found by "C" Coy)	
			4 Vickers guns posted between No 3 & COWIE POST at 50 yds distance.	
			No 5 & 6. Posts in ROEUX village in CELLARS - These are also cut off except by night.	
			C Coy on Left. 2 Platoons in front line & finds COWIE POST.	
			2 Platoons in CABBAGE Trench - (This is out of our Brigade area & the platoons were afterwards moved into CORONA)	
			B & D Coys. in reserve in CRUMP.	
			Later on a further Post (No 7) was formed between but in rear of No 1 & 2 (4 O.R. L.G. & team) to cover front of posts.	

Instructions regarding War Diaries and Intelligence Summaries are contained in F. S. Regs., Part II. and the Staff Manual respectively. Title pages will be prepared in manuscript.

WAR DIARY
or
INTELLIGENCE SUMMARY.
(Erase heading not required.)

Army Form C. 2118.

10th Argyll & Sutherland Hrs

Place	Date	Hour	Summary of Events and Information	Remarks and references to Appendices
CHEMICAL WORKS - ROEUX LINE	1917 June 9.	1.30 am	C.O. visited all posts after relief was complete. Message received that 2nd Army had reached all its objectives — Prisoners about 9000. Many guns destroyed & captured. 19 mines were successfully blown at zero under Hill 60 which no longer exists — In the latter stages 2 Ersatz Divisions were pushed in from reserve but had no heart for the fighting and surrendered in bunches.	JMA
	10	11 pm	Fighting patrol under Lt. ROBERTSON was sent out to ascertain position of Enemy opposite our posts — Succeeded in locating Enemy in shell holes and small portion of a trench some 150 yds in front of our posts.	JMA
	11.		C.O. accompanied Divisional & Brigade Commanders round front line. The front line is practically cut off after dawn as it is under immediate observation from HAUSA HILL — The Enemy does not yet have realised that our front line is COLOMBA and his barrage usually drops on Support Trench. We are therefore careful to allow no movement in front line during daylight.	JMA

2353 Wt. W2541/1454 700,000 5/15 D. D. & L. A.D.S.S./Forms/C. 2118.

Instructions regarding War Diaries and Intelligence Summaries are contained in F. S. Regs., Part II. and the Staff Manual respectively. Title pages will be prepared in manuscript.

WAR DIARY
or
INTELLIGENCE SUMMARY.
(Erase heading not required.)

10th Argyll & Sutherland Hrs

Army Form C. 2118.

Place	Date	Hour	Summary of Events and Information	Remarks and references to Appendices
	1917.			
CHEMICAL WORKS – ROEUX LINE	June 14		<u>Work done during tour of Trenches.</u> Digging a new front line by connecting COWIE & NO 4 Posts. This Trench is now finished. Six feet in depth & fire stepped – well concealed & not yet observed by Enemy. From this Trench Enemy seen at dawn endeavouring to leave their shell holes which they occupy just in front during the dark in the potato patch. This affords good "Rabbit" shooting and the men thoroughly enjoy sniping him as he bolts from his shell hole. CEYLON Trench cleared and COLOMBA deepened – and shelters erected in trenches. In ROEUX WOOD there still remains the emplacement of a German Naval 9.45 Gun which had been used for firing at ARRAS. The circular emplacement is 25 yds across and the crane still remains which was used for placing the gun in position and bringing up shells on a railway. The shells are 40 inches long very pointed & probably armour piercing ones. The charges are placed in brass cylinders of which several were found. The gun must have only just been evacuated in time.	[illegible]

2353 Wt. W2541/1454 700,000 5/15 D. D. & L. A.D.S.S./Forms/C. 2118.

Instructions regarding War Diaries and Intelligence Summaries are contained in F. S. Regs., Part II. and the Staff Manual respectively. Title pages will be prepared in manuscript.

WAR DIARY
or
INTELLIGENCE SUMMARY. 10th Argyll & Sutherland Highrs

(*Erase heading not required.*)

Army Form C. 2118.

Place	Date	Hour	Summary of Events and Information	Remarks and references to Appendices
CHEMICAL WORKS – ROEUX LINE	1917			
	June		It is supposed that this gun was to fire prussic acid shells into ARRAS.	
	11.		Relieved by a Batt: of EAST LANCASHIRES (4th Div:) relief completed by	JNA
	12.		4. a.m. marched to ARRAS (5 miles) & embussed for BAILLEUL aux CORNAILLES (17 miles) where Batt: goes into rest.	JNA
			Notwithstanding the sector being of a rather dangerous nature our casualties were slight 3 killed & 5 wounded.	
			The following Honours and Awards have recently been conferred on Officers NCOs & men of the Battalion.	
			D.S.O.	
(Kings Birthday Honours)			Major N. McQUEEN	
			LEGION D'HONNEUR. – CROIX DE CHEVALIER.	
			Major N. McQUEEN.	
			MILITARY CROSS.	
(KING'S BIRTHDAY HONOURS)			2nd Lt. A. T. McNAB. (R.F.C)	
			2nd Lt. S. G. ROBINSON.	

Instructions regarding War Diaries and Intelligence Summaries are contained in F. S. Regs., Part II. and the Staff Manual respectively. Title pages will be prepared in manuscript.

WAR DIARY
or
INTELLIGENCE SUMMARY.
(Erase heading not required.)

10th Argyll & Sutherland Highrs

Army Form C. 2118.

Place	Date	Hour	Summary of Events and Information	Remarks and references to Appendices
BAILLEUL aux CORNAILLES	1917 June 13.		D. C. M.	
			8376. Sergt. J. CORBETT. (This is first instance of anyone in this Batt receiving both D.C.M & M.M)	JWA
			4386 L/Corpl N. G. TAYLOR.	
			MILITARY MEDAL.	
			2398. a/C.S.M. C. FRASER.	
			6842. Sergt. W. CUMMINGS.	
			949. Corpl. J. COWAN	
			580. L/Corpl. R. BUTTERWORTH	
			L5820. Pte. G. GRAHAM.	
			MENTIONED in DESPATCHES.	
		KINGS BIRTHDAY HONOURS	Major N. McQUEEN D.S.O.	
			Capt J. WOODBURN. M.C.	
			Capt W. MILLERICK. R.A.M.C.	
			6217 Sergt JOHN HENDERSON	
			8470. L/Corpl RICHARD SCOTT.	

2353 Wt. W2541/1454 700,000 5/15 D. D. & L. A.D.S.S./Forms/C. 2118.

Army Form C. 2118.

WAR DIARY
or
INTELLIGENCE SUMMARY.
(Erase heading not required.)

10th Argyll & Sutherland Hrs

Instructions regarding War Diaries and Intelligence Summaries are contained in F. S. Regs., Part II. and the Staff Manual respectively. Title pages will be prepared in manuscript.

Place	Date	Hour	Summary of Events and Information	Remarks and references to Appendices
	1917			
BAILLEUL aux CORNAILLES	June 13.		Weather - Still very hot - We have now had this fine weather since about 15 April.	[illegible]
			First 2 days devoted to cleaning and scrubbing -	
	16.		Batt: inspected by Brigade Commander (B.Gen: Kennedy)	[illegible]
	17.		Batt commenced Training - (1st week Platoon & Company) Bayonet Fighting, physical drill, Steady drill, handling of arms, musketry, use of Bombs & Rifle grenades, Company in attack, Deployment in artillery formation, building up firing line - fight for superiority of fire, assault, reforming & reorganising to hold line gained, Route march & lectures being the subjects dealt with -	[illegible]
			A Riding class has been arranged for Officers under Lt. DAWNAY Yorkshire Hussars	
	19.		Divisional Commander (Lt Gen: Lukin) visited the Battalion.	[illegible]
	(15)		Major McKuen gave a dinner party to celebrate his receiving the D.S.O. & Legion d'Honneur - amongst others Capt French, Capt Stevenson Capt Cavendish, Capt Sir John Dashwood Bart, Capt Awill were invited, all of whom came out with the Batt to France - These are probably the only original officers of the Battalion now serving in France -	[illegible]

W. W. 1141/1454 700,000 5/15 D. D. & L. A.D.S.S./Forms/C. 2118.

Army Form C. 2118.

Instructions regarding War Diaries and Intelligence Summaries are contained in F. S. Regs., Part II. and the Staff Manual respectively. Title pages will be prepared in manuscript.

WAR DIARY
or
INTELLIGENCE SUMMARY.
(Erase heading not required.)

10th Argyll & Sutherland Hgrs

Place	Date	Hour	Summary of Events and Information	Remarks and references to Appendices
BAILLEUL AUX CORNAILLES	1917 June		Major McQueen then proceeded to England on a month's leave. his private affairs requiring his personal attention.	WS
	21		CO, CAPT WOODBURN & CAPT BONNYMAN proceeded to ETAPLES for 2 days to inspect the Training Camps.	WS
	25.		An exhibition of the Company in the attack was given at 3rd Army School at AUXI LE CHATEAU which several Officers of the Battalion attended.	WS
	23		The following Officers having joined from home are taken on the strength of the Battalion 2/Lt. E. ROSE, 2/Lt. A. YOUNG, 2/Lt. DENTON	WS
			The weather which has been very hot since the middle of April has now become cooler since the thunderstorms. Batt: training daily	WS

J. R. [illegible]
Lt Col.
10th A. & S. H.

2353 Wt. W2544/1454 700,000 5/15 D. D. & L. A.D.S.S./Forms/C. 2118.

"A" Form.

MESSAGES AND SIGNALS.

Army Form C. 2121.

No. of Message............

Prefix........... Code............m. Office of Origin and Service Instructions.	Words / Charge	This message is on a/c of:	Recd. at..........m.
	Sent At..........m. To.......... By..........	..........Service.	Date..........
			From..........
		(Signature of "Franking Officer.")	By..........

TO: 17th Inf Bde

* Sender's Number	Day of Month	In reply to Number	AAA
	1		

Hepworth was drawing for Imme—

V. G. Scobell
Lt Col
10 a.m. 1.10

From

Place

Time 9.30 Pm

The above may be forwarded as now corrected. (Z)

.... *Censor.* Signature of Addressor or person authorised to telegraph in his name.

* This line should be erased if not required.

(A1) O. Ltd., London— W.14042/M.44. 150,000 Pads. 12/15. Form C.2121.

Confidential

26. Brigade

Herewith War Diary

for month of July

[illegible]

Lt Col

[illegible]

1. Aug 1917

WAR DIARY
or
INTELLIGENCE SUMMARY.
(Erase heading not required.)

Instructions regarding War Diaries and Intelligence Summaries are contained in F. S. Regs., Part II. and the Staff Manual respectively. Title pages will be prepared in manuscript.

Vol 23 Army Form C. 2118.

10th Argyll & Sutherland Hrs

Place	Date	Hour	Summary of Events and Information	Remarks and references to Appendices
BAILLEUL AUX CORNAILLES	1917 July 1.		Battalion Sports were brought off successfully – One Event being for the French Children which was amusing.	Vol
	2	7.30 a.m.	Batt: moved by route march to FOSSIEUX via AVERDOINGT–AMBRINES–GIVENCHY LE NOBLE–AVESNES LE CONTE (14 miles) – Only one man fell out and he had been wounded 3 weeks previously –	Vol
FOSSIEUX				
DAINVILLE	6		Batt: moved to DAINVILLE into a new Training area – Just behind the original front line – a mile S of ARRAS – before the Germans retired in February last.	Vol
			R.S.M. BRACKEN of this Batt: has been promoted 2/Lieut and posted to this Batt:–	
	10		The Brigade Sports were brought off with Great Success in brilliant weather – The whole Brigade assembled in the Training area near WAILLY	Vol
	24.		Battalion Revolver Competition – Best Officer Shot – 2/Lt. H. W. HEPBURN (27) Battalion Shot Private J. S. BRADLEY ~~BRADBURY~~ (30) C Coy Best N.C.O or man 1. Private J. S. BRADLEY ~~BRADBURY~~ (30) C Coy 2. L/Cpl G. MARTIN, (29) A Coy 3rd Pte W. McMARTIN (2?) C Coy [equal] Pte MORGAN (2?) D Coy.	Vol

27.0 [?] D.

Instructions regarding War Diaries and Intelligence Summaries are contained in F. S. Regs., Part II. and the Staff Manual respectively. Title pages will be prepared in manuscript.

WAR DIARY
or
INTELLIGENCE SUMMARY.
(Erase heading not required.)

10th ARGYLL & SUTHERLAND HIGHL^rs

Army Form C. 2118.

Place	Date	Hour	Summary of Events and Information	Remarks and references to Appendices
	1917			
DAINVILLE			Batt: has finished training which amongst other subjects has comprised a considerable amount of field training and carrying out of schemes over the original German front line system of trenches. We have been out six weeks which is by a long way the longest rest the Batt: has experienced since arriving in France.	
	July	24	The Corps Commander (Lt General Sir Charles Fergusson) visited the Battalion to wish it goodbye on leaving the XVII Corps under whose orders it has been for seven months and congratulated the Battalion on the good work done by it during this period.	[illegible]
BERTENCOURT		25	Batt: moved in Brigade by route march to BEAUMETZ and from thence to BAPAUME by Tactical Train, marching on to BERTENCOURT billetting there for the night.	[illegible]
RUYAULCOURT		26	Moved to RUYAULCOURT. The whole country is completely devastated, every house having been blown up by the enemy in the retreat last February and most of the trees cut down. Coys chiefly in Tents. H.Q. in Huts. Batt in Divisional Reserve	[illegible]

2353 Wt. W2544/1454 700,000 5/15 D. D. & L. A.D.S.S./Forms/C. 2118.

Instructions regarding War Diaries and Intelligence Summaries are contained in F. S. Regs., Part II. and the Staff Manual respectively. Title pages will be prepared in manuscript.

WAR DIARY

or

INTELLIGENCE SUMMARY.

(Erase heading not required.)

Army Form C. 2118.

10. A & S. Hrs

Place	Date	Hour	Summary of Events and Information	Remarks and references to Appendices
	1917			
RUYAULCOURT	July 28, 29, 30		Batt: Employed during the night digging new Communication Trench between TUFNELL ALLEY and MORTEMARE	[illegible]
	(22)		Major R. NICOL reported from home for duty on being posted to the Batt:	[illegible]

[illegible] Lt Col
Comd. 10. A & S. H.

Instructions regarding War Diaries and Intelligence Summaries are contained in F. S. Regs., Part II. and the Staff Manual respectively. Title pages will be prepared in manuscript.

WAR DIARY
or
INTELLIGENCE SUMMARY.
(*Erase heading not required.*)

Army Form C. 2118.

10th ARGYLL & SUTHERLAND HIGHLrs

Vol 24

Place	Date	Hour	Summary of Events and Information	Remarks and references to Appendices
	1917			
RUYAULCOURT	Aug 1.		Lt Gen: Sir L. WOOLLCOMBE KCB. (IVth Corps Commander) visited the Battalion.	
	2		Batt to Trenches.	
			DESCRIPTION OF FRONT – Our line is sited on the slope of the Spurs which run Northwards into the GRAND RAVINE, with its right resting on the centre of SHROPSHIRE SPUR and its left on the CANAL DU NORD.	
			Between these two boundaries there are two Spurs known as BANBURY HILL and CHEETHAM HILL – The valleys formed between them are known as	
			OXFORD VALLEY – between SHROPSHIRE SPUR and BANBURY HILL	
			HUBERT VALLEY between BANBURY HILL and CHEETHAM HILL.	
			The Spurs emerge from HAVRINCOURT WOOD, under observation of the Enemy from his commanding positions on the Northern side of the GRAND RAVINE, the village of HAVRINCOURT and the FLESQUIERES RIDGE.	
			HAVRINCOURT WOOD, which until felled by the Germans spread over SHROPSHIRE SPUR across the GRAND RAVINE to the village and which covered the greater part of CHEETHAM HILL, now only provides a covered approach to within 1500 yards of our line – The felled portion is covered with a thick low scrub	

2353 Wt. W2544/1454 700,000 5/15 D. D. & L. A.D.S.S./Forms/C. 2118.

Instructions regarding War Diaries and Intelligence Summaries are contained in F. S. Regs., Part II. and the Staff Manual respectively. Title pages will be prepared in manuscript.

WAR DIARY
or
INTELLIGENCE SUMMARY.
(Erase heading not required.)

Army Form C. 2118.

10th ARGYLL & SUTHERLAND HIGHLRS

Place	Date	Hour	Summary of Events and Information	Remarks and references to Appendices
	1917.			
HAVRINCOURT SECTOR.	Aug 2.		which affords cover for small isolated parties.	JMS
			On the extreme left of our line on the Bank of the Canal is a large spoil heap of chalk, excavated from the Canal, known as YORKSHIRE BANK – This is held by us and gives us observation in enfilade along our entire front, it renders it impossible for the enemy to mass for attack by day against any portion of our line. It also affords a covered approach to the left of our line forming as it does a narrow valley with CHEETHAM HILL.	Sh/p
			Our position lends itself to defence and its strength lies in the fact that machine guns can enfilade the valleys from end to end, and that machine guns emplaced on the spurs can be sited so as to enfilade our trenches on adjoining spurs. Thus the protection of each spur is dependent to a large degree on cross fire brought to bear upon it from the spur on either flank.	
			This applies equally to YORKSHIRE BANK.	
			The 26th Brigade is now the Centre Brigade of the Division, the South African Brigade being on the right and the 27th Brigade on the left over the Canal – (The Div: front having sideslipped by one Brigade Northwards since we came into the line)	

Instructions regarding War Diaries and Intelligence Summaries are contained in F. S. Regs., Part II. and the Staff Manual respectively. Title pages will be prepared in manuscript.

WAR DIARY
or
INTELLIGENCE SUMMARY.
(Erase heading not required.)

10th ARGYLL & SUTHERLAND H'L'RS

Army Form C. 2118.

Place	Date	Hour	Summary of Events and Information	Remarks and references to Appendices
	1917			
HAVRINCOURT SECTOR.	Aug:		DESCRIPTION OF DEFENCES. The Trench system consists of an Outpost line, a front line, a Support line (not at present held) and a Reserve line. Behind this again is the Intermediate line in HAVRINCOURT WOOD.	[illegible]
			The OUTPOST LINE is lightly held by a series of Posts - 2 Posts of the right Company consisting of 10 O.R. each - One officer being always on duty in the right Post and in the left Post an Officer visits it continually by day & night. These Posts are relieved every 24 hours by the Front line Company.	
			The men are to be awake the whole night and during the day half the posts are allowed to sleep.	
			A BATTLE PATROL found from the Coy immediately in rear of the Front Company on the right consists of 1 Off & 16 O.R. It will actively patrol the front all night, every two hours withdrawing for a short time to a position somewhere in rear of Outpost line when it becomes the INLYING PIQUET and will be in support in case of attack on the Outpost line.	
			The duties of the Posts are to hold on to the last in case of an Enemy Raid	

2353 Wt. W2544/1454 700,000 5/15 D. D. & L. A.D.S.S./Forms/C. 2118.

Instructions regarding War Diaries and Intelligence Summaries are contained in F. S. Regs., Part II. and the Staff Manual respectively. Title pages will be prepared in manuscript.

WAR DIARY
or
INTELLIGENCE SUMMARY. 10th ARGYLL & SUTHERLAND HIGHLrs.
(*Erase heading not required.*)

Army Form C. 2118.

Place	Date	Hour	Summary of Events and Information	Remarks and references to Appendices
	1917.			
HAVRINCOURT SECTOR	Aug		and only in case of a strong attack will they withdraw into the front line which is 400x in rear.	Jno
			The rear right Company is accommodated in the Reserve line right of HUBERT ALLEY.	
			LEFT SECTION. Position of defences is as follows:-	
			One Platoon in Outpost line at summit of YORKSHIRE BANK in a continuous Trench well wired in front	
			One Platoon in Reserve line on YORKSHIRE BANK	
			two Platoons on CHEETHAM HILL in continuous Trench.	
			a post is found at night near S.E corner at foot of YORKSHIRE BANK	
			The system of holding front line Trench is that of LOCALITIES, 2 of which are in right Company Section & 2 in left Coy Section.	
			A large Mining Dugout is being built in each locality capable of holding at least 50 men.	
			DISTRIBUTION of BATTALIONS in BRIGADE 2 BATTs front line, 1 BATT in Brigade Reserve 1200 yds behind YORKSHIRE BANK & 1 Batt in Div: Reserve in RUYAULCOURT.	

2353 Wt. W2544/1454 700,000 5/15 D. D. & L. A.D.S.S./Forms/C. 2118.

Instructions regarding War Diaries and Intelligence Summaries are contained in F. S. Regs., Part II. and the Staff Manual respectively. Title pages will be prepared in manuscript.

WAR DIARY
or
INTELLIGENCE SUMMARY.
(Erase heading not required.)

10th ARGYLL & SUTHERLAND HIGHL^RS

Army Form C. 2118.

Place	Date	Hour	Summary of Events and Information	Remarks and references to Appendices
	1917			
HAVRINCOURT	Aug:		Batt: has completed a 6 days tour in front line without casualties.	JRS
SECTOR	7.		TRENCHES. in front line have been considerably improved, LOCALITIES constructed and MINING DUGOUTS commenced in front line by the 4 Pioneer Platoons which are now brigaded. WIRE has been put out in front of FRONTLINE and in front of OUTPOST LINE considerable amount of wire has been erected in serpentine formation so as not to indicate too clearly the exact position of Posts. Several new shelters have been built in all Trenches. Up to the time of the Div: taking over the line there was very little shelter at all for the men.	
			INTELLIGENCE Patrols have been out constantly during the night nightly. It is not clear whether the Enemy is not or some part of YORKSHIRE BANK. WIGAN COPSE & DEAN COPSE both in NOMANSLAND are lightly held by night with Machine guns but they give us little trouble. NOMANSLAND owing to active patrolling gradually becoming British and being denied to the Enemy. ETNA & VESUVIUS CRATERS are held by the Enemy with Machine guns.	

2353 Wt. W2544/1454 700,000 5/15 D. D. & L. A.D.S.S./Forms/C. 2118.

Instructions regarding War Diaries and Intelligence Summaries are contained in F. S. Regs., Part II. and the Staff Manual respectively. Title pages will be prepared in manuscript.

WAR DIARY
or
INTELLIGENCE SUMMARY.
(Erase heading not required.)

Army Form C. 2118.

10th ARGYLL & SUTHERLAND HIGHrs

Place	Date 1917	Hour	Summary of Events and Information	Remarks and references to Appendices
HAVRINCOURT SECTOR.	Aug 7		Our Artillery has been active, the village of HAVRINCOURT on the further side of NO MANS LAND being constantly shelled, the heavy, medium & light Trench Mortars continually bestowing attention on the Copses & craters & other points of interest.	[illegible]
			Batt: HQ. situated in a chalk pit near the W. end of HUBERT ALLEY has been improved and new shelters erected for the Specialists. Mess the trench leading from HUBERT ALLEY deepened & duck boarded.	
			Batt moved into Brigade Reserve into a Bank which is completely defiladed some 1000 yds to the N. of front line position & near the CANAL.	
			250 men found nightly for working parties in the Wood. Batt bathed by Platoons in RUYAULCOURT. Batt: HQ. is in a quarry, huts having been built all round the sides. Officers accommodation being still required a new house to hold 30 officers is being erected.	
			The following officers have arrived & reported for duty	
	9		Capt D. O MILLER, M.C formerly with this Batt: 2nd Lt J. F. DUNCANSON, 2nd Lt	[illegible]
	10		A.L. MILLER & 2nd Lt R.C. MacINTYRE from 3rd Reinforcing Battalion.	[illegible]

2353 Wt. W2544/1454 700,000 5/15 D. D. & L. A.D.S.S./Forms/C. 2118.

Instructions regarding War Diaries and Intelligence Summaries are contained in F. S. Regs., Part II. and the Staff Manual respectively. Title pages will be prepared in manuscript.

WAR DIARY
or
INTELLIGENCE SUMMARY.
(Erase heading not required.)

10th ARGYLL & SUTHERLAND HIGHLrs

Army Form C. 2118.

Place	Date	Hour	Summary of Events and Information	Remarks and references to Appendices
HAVRINCOURT SECTOR.	1917 Aug 10		M. Gen: Sir W. FURSE KCB Master General of Ordnance and formerly Commanding the 9th Division visited the Division and saw all officers with whom he had acquainted.	VRS
			The Corps Commander has expressed his appreciation of the work done in the Trenches since the Division took over the Line.	
			Major NICOL has taken over command of D. Coy as a temporary measure from a tour of Trenches.	
	12.		Gen: Sir J. H. G. BYNG KCB. KCMG. MVO. (ARMY COMMANDER) accompanied by Lt. Gen: Sir L. WOOLLCOMBE, KCB. DSO. (CORPS COMMANDER) visited Batt: H.Q.	VRS
	13	7am	Enemy shelled a battery near Batt H.Q. heavily with 4.2 & 5.9 shells for 1½ hrs about 200 shells falling. The guns were however taken out last night so he was merely shelling empty emplacements.	VRS
			Batt: to the Front line taking over from 5th CAMERONS.	
			2/Lt. P. S. DENTON took out a Covering party for a Lewis Gun Detachment and is reported missing.	

Army Form C. 2118.

WAR DIARY
or
INTELLIGENCE SUMMARY.
(*Erase heading not required.*)

Instructions regarding War Diaries and Intelligence Summaries are contained in F. S. Regs., Part II. and the Staff Manual respectively. Title pages will be prepared in manuscript.

10th ARGYLL & SUTHERLAND HRS

Place	Date	Hour	Summary of Events and Information	Remarks and references to Appendices
	1917			
HAVRINCOURT	Aug		During the 6 days tour patrolling was nightly carried out in front of our outpost lines towards WIGAN COPSE and round and on top of YORKSHIRE BANK.	VJJ.
	15		On the 15th Lt. BURLEIGH while reconnoitring on N.E corner discovered a large Quarry and looking over the top observed an Enemy sentry - This would be some 70x in front of our own wire. The question had at length been solved whether Enemy were holding any part of YORKSHIRE BANK. On reporting this to Brigade it was determined to immediately organise a raid, as there appeared considerable possibilities, from the noise of working that was heard, that tunnelling operations were in progress.	
			Trenches have been improved and for the last two days dry weather set in which has enabled us to carry out more work.	
			The wire in front of outpost line has been thickened.	
			Mining Dug Outs are in course of preparation	
			The general attitude of the Enemy has not been offensive it is considered he has very few guns at all on this sector	
		18	The Batt: was relieved by the 5th CAMERONS on night of 18th & Batt: went into Divisional Reserve at RUYAULCOURT.	VJJ

2353 Wt. W2544/1454 700,000 5/15 D. D. & L. A.D.S.S./Forms/C. 2118.

Army Form C. 2118.

WAR DIARY
or
INTELLIGENCE SUMMARY.
(*Erase heading not required.*)

Instructions regarding War Diaries and Intelligence Summaries are contained in F. S. Regs., Part II. and the Staff Manual respectively. Title pages will be prepared in manuscript.

10th ARGYLL & SUTHERLAND HIGHLRS

Place	Date	Hour	Summary of Events and Information	Remarks and references to Appendices
	1917			
HAVRINCOURT	Aug 18		A Raid was organised and carried out successfully on night of 18th.	
			It was divided into 5 Parties.	
			A Party to search Cutting in YORKSHIRE BANK on Northern side for suspected Enemy Dug out or Mining Shaft and to destroy any such works.	
			B Party to move out in rear of A Party and to act as Covering Party on reaching CUTTING.	
			C Party to move out on Southern side of YORKSHIRE BANK until reaching a Bank running N & S when they were to clear the whole slopes of Plateau from Bank Eastwards	
			D Party to raid DEAN COPSE or if it was found to be filled with wire to work round to Sunken Road behind & clear it	App. 1. O.O
			E Party to drop 2 Mobile Ammonal Charges over top of CUTTING at ZERO.	" 2 ART PROG
			A, B & E Parties were found from D Coy. C Party from C Coy. D Party from A Coy.	" 3. Sketch of YORKSHIRE BANK
			MAJOR NICOL appointed O.C. Raiding Parties.	
			OPERATION ORDERS & ARTILLERY PROGRAMME attached	

2353 Wt. W2544/1454 700,000 5/15 D. D. & L. A.D.S.S./Forms/C. 2118.

Instructions regarding War Diaries and Intelligence Summaries are contained in F. S. Regs., Part II. and the Staff Manual respectively. Title pages will be prepared in manuscript.

WAR DIARY
or
INTELLIGENCE SUMMARY.
(Erase heading not required.)

10th ARGYLL & SUTHERLAND HIGHrs

Army Form C. 2118.

Place	Date	Hour	Summary of Events and Information	Remarks and references to Appendices
	1917			
HAVRINCOURT	Aug 18.		A. PARTY – Moved off at scheduled time and entered CUTTING at ZERO – This they found unoccupied, it was thoroughly searched. On advancing along bank they came upon a strong point which was at the entrance to a second CUTTING. The Strong point was completely wired and manned strongly by the Enemy who bombed and used their machine guns on our men. Party bombed and threw 2 Mobile Charges of Ammonal into the Strong point and rushed in to cut the wire – Enemy must have suffered severely as groans were heard and fire slackened – It being impossible to enter 2nd CUTTING, owing to thick wire, party withdrew with wounded on signal from Outpost line for withdrawal – Lt. BURLEIGH showed great gallantry throughout and carried a badly wounded man back to our lines. Had it not been for this he would never have got back. Severe casualties must without doubt have been inflicted on the Enemy and the position of enemy firmly established.	WS
			B PARTY. Acted as covering party to A & withdrew with them.	
			C. PARTY Succeeded in reaching Plateau, which they had received orders to clear, without discovery and wheeled to the left advancing to	

2353 Wt. W2544/1454 700,000 5/15 D. D. & L. A.D.S.S./Forms/C. 2118.

Instructions regarding War Diaries and Intelligence Summaries are contained in F. S. Regs., Part II. and the Staff Manual respectively. Title pages will be prepared in manuscript.

WAR DIARY
or
INTELLIGENCE SUMMARY. 10th ARGYLL & SUTHERLAND Hrs.
(*Erase heading not required.*)

Army Form C. 2118.

Place	Date	Hour	Summary of Events and Information	Remarks and references to Appendices
	1917		C Party (cont'd)	
HAVRINCOURT	Aug 18.		Northern Edge and lot as far as the first terrace about 6 ft lower on to which they dropped – They were then held up for a time by wire running across from W 15b – Thus the party penetrated and then discovered a small crater – 2/Lt. MacDonald the officer i/c Party gave orders to work round this crater and deal with it by rifle fire & bombs and a number of shrieks & groans were heard. 2/Lt. MacDonald then ordered party to move on to limit of objective i.e. Northern Edge of the Bank. On reaching it the enemy counter attacked about 30 strong. Orders for 5 rounds rapid were given & carried out. 2/Lt. MacDonald was not seen again and party fell back to West Corner of Plateau on order to withdraw, the signal at zero+20 having being then given from Support line. They remained however another 10 minutes firing on Enemy. Later on at 1.30.am a search party went out to try & find Lt. MacDonald and again at dawn but unhappily without success.	HR

2353 Wt. W2541/1454 700,000 5/15 D. D. & L. A.D.S.S./Forms/C. 2118.

Instructions regarding War Diaries and Intelligence Summaries are contained in F. S. Regs., Part II. and the Staff Manual respectively. Title pages will be prepared in manuscript.

WAR DIARY
or
INTELLIGENCE SUMMARY.
(Erase heading not required.)

10th ARGYLL & SUTHERLAND HRS

Army Form C. 2118.

Place	Date	Hour	Summary of Events and Information	Remarks and references to Appendices
	1917			
HAVRINCOURT	Aug 18		D. PARTY at ZERO were lying out some 100x in front of our own wire and commenced to advance as far under own Stokes barrage as possible – at ZERO +2 on barrage lifting they rushed in to attack WIGAN COPSE – The Enemy were lying out in shell holes & were promptly killed by our men who proceeded to cut through Enemy wire. By this time 2/Lt. BIRKETT & 4 O.R. were the only ones unwounded & they continued attacking until the time for the recall – They found many German dead which proves the good effect our Stokes barrage produced. 2/Lt. BIRKETT took a prisoner, this man was the only one who stayed at his post, the others ran back & into our gas barrage so we have hopes that none survived – This post was to the N of DEAN COPSE, the Germans in the shell holes fought well until eventually destroyed – Our casualties from Enemy bombs rather severe – 2/Lt. BIRKETT though wounded led his men on and after the raid returned to Coy HQ to write his report before having his wounds dressed –	SJA

Instructions regarding War Diaries and Intelligence Summaries are contained in F. S. Regs., Part II. and the Staff Manual respectively. Title pages will be prepared in manuscript.

Army Form C. 2118.

WAR DIARY
or
INTELLIGENCE SUMMARY.
(Erase heading not required.)

10th ARGYLL & SUTHERLAND H.S

Place	Date	Hour	Summary of Events and Information	Remarks and references to Appendices
	1917.			
HAVRINCOURT	Aug 18		On the morning of the same day one of our snipers while crawling on the [illegible] top of YORKSHIRE BANK killed one German and wounded another at a post just below the bank.	HJL
			Our casualties during the raid were:	
			2nd Lieut G.A. MACDONALD missing believed killed.	
			2nd Lieut E. BIRKETT, wounded and 2/Lt J.E. BURLEIGH & Lt W.D. WILLIAMSON slightly wounded to duty	
			2 O.R. missing believed killed	
			1 O.R. missing believed wounded	
			5 O.R. severely wounded	
			5 O.R. wounded.	
			2. O.R. died of wounds Total 4 off: 15 O.R.	
	22.		Capt E. BONNYMAN while riding fell from his horse by stumbling over wire causing a fracture of the base of his skull.	HJL
	24		Took over Trenches from 5th CAMERON HIGHLANDERS.	HJL
			CAPT J.E. MACMILLAN arrived from home and reported for duty.	HJL
			The following were awarded the Military Medal in connection with the raid	HJL
			Sergeant HOME	
			Private DOCHERTY.	

2353 Wt. W2544/1454 700,000 5/15 D. D. & L. A.D.S.S./Forms/C. 2118.

Instructions regarding War Diaries and Intelligence Summaries are contained in F. S. Regs., Part II. and the Staff Manual respectively. Title pages will be prepared in manuscript.

WAR DIARY
or
INTELLIGENCE SUMMARY.
(Erase heading not required.)

Army Form C. 2118.

10th ARGYLL + SUTHERLAND HRS.

Place	Date	Hour	Summary of Events and Information	Remarks and references to Appendices
	1917.			
HAVRINCOURT.	Augt. 25-30		A quiet tour of duty until the last day except for daylight reconnaissances carried out by us for the purpose of ascertaining whether the wire had been cut at the N.E. and S.E. corners of YORKSHIRE BANK for a projected raid by the 5th CAMERON HIGHLANDERS	MMR.
			We received visits from numerous Officers and O.R. of the 12th Royal Irish Rifles who were to relieve us in the evening of the 30th inst.	MMR.
	30th	p.m. 12.45	The Commanding Officer who chanced to be at Bde. H.Q received instructions from the Brigade Commander who had just returned from a Conference at Divl H.Q to carry out the raid projected by the 5th CAMERONS who had already left for a new area. The objects of the Raid were (a) To clear YORKSHIRE BANK of the enemy. (b) To raid the Quarries at K.32. b. 4.9 with a view to ascertaining whether the enemy was mining, and if so, to destroy his mine shafts and dugouts and inflict loss.	MMR.

2353 Wt. W2541/1454 700,000 5/15 D. D. & L. A.D.S.S./Forms/C. 2118.

Instructions regarding War Diaries and Intelligence Summaries are contained in F. S. Regs., Part II. and the Staff Manual respectively. Title pages will be prepared in manuscript.

WAR DIARY
or
INTELLIGENCE SUMMARY. 10th ARGYLL & SUTHERLAND HRS.
(*Erase heading not required.*)

Army Form C. 2118.

Place	Date	Hour	Summary of Events and Information	Remarks and references to Appendices
	1917 Augt			
HAVRINCOURT	30		(c) To establish 2 strong points about K32.b.40.45. and K.32.b.4.6. These posts to consolidate their positions and remain out until relieved.	
			The orders drawn up by the 5th CAMERONS were handed over and adopted with some modifications – Copy in Appendix.	Mne 2.
			b & c parties were found by 'A' Coy. 'b' party under Lieut ROBERTSON, 'c' party under Sgt. MACGREGOR. 'a' and 'd' parties by 'B' Coy. 'a' party under Sgt. MARCHBANKS. 'd' party under 2nd Lieut ROSE.	
			The arrangements were carried through with the greatest possible despatch all ranks rising to the occasion with splendid energy and keenness, and at 7.55 pm the parties were ready to proceed from the outpost line on YORKSHIRE BANK and the right flank of that line.	
			At zero (8 pm) the smoke barrage came down and all the parties went over. The raid was carried out with great dash and all parties reached their objectives within a few minutes. no opposition was encountered, the Quarries were found to be empty and were really only successive shelves formed at	

2353 Wt. W2541/1454 700,000 5/15 D. D. & L. A.D.S.S./Forms/C. 2118.

Instructions regarding War Diaries and Intelligence Summaries are contained in F. S. Regs., Part II. and the Staff Manual respectively. Title pages will be prepared in manuscript.

WAR DIARY
or
INTELLIGENCE SUMMARY.
(Erase heading not required.)

Army Form C. 2118.

10th ARGYLL & SUTHERLAND HRS.

Place	Date	Hour	Summary of Events and Information	Remarks and references to Appendices
	1917			
HAVRINCOURT.	Augt 30.		different dumping points – A few shelters and posts were found and destroyed, but no mine shafts or deep dugouts. Lieut ROBERTSON and part of his party penetrated as far as the cross roads at the East end of the BANK. The posts required were both captured, consolidated, wired, flanked & grenade reserves formed & handed over intact to the 12th R.I. RIFS on relief about 1am next morning. The right post at K.32 b.4.6. had encounters with the Enemy at a later hour. At 9.15pm 3 men were seen coming down the road from the WILLOWS evidently to occupy the captured post. The post opened fire with L.G. and rifles and killed 2 & wounded one who got away. Half an hour later another man came down the same road evidently to visit the post; he was certainly hit and probably killed. About 1 hour later a party of from 15 to 20 came across from the WILLOWS on the right flank of the post, and extended before they reached the Sunken road. The post opened fire with L.G. & rifles	

2353 Wt. W2544/1454 700,000 5/15 D. D. & L. A.D.S.S./Forms/C. 2118.

Instructions regarding War Diaries and Intelligence Summaries are contained in F. S. Regs., Part II. and the Staff Manual respectively. Title pages will be prepared in manuscript.

WAR DIARY
or
INTELLIGENCE SUMMARY.
(Erase heading not required.)

Army Form C. 2118.

10th ARGYLL + SUTHERLAND HRS.

Place	Date	Hour	Summary of Events and Information	Remarks and references to Appendices
HAVRINCOURT.	1917 Aug 30		Killed between 8 and 10 and the attack broke up, the remainder retired. The Moon was too bright to risk crossing the road to recover any bodies. This post had previously barricaded with concertina wire the road to the WILLOWS. and the road to ETNA.	JMcQ
	31st.		The Relief was completed at 2.10 am. the Sector being handed over to the 12th ROYAL IRISH RIFLES	JMcQ.
			Total casualties of the RAID, 2 Sergeants Wounded. 2 privates Wounded at duty.	JMcQ.
			The Bn. embussed on the METZ - ROYAULCOURT road and reached its new area at CARLTON HILL CAMP, GOMIECOURT at 6 am.	JMcQ.
In the Field 31. 8. 17.			J. McQueen. Major Commanding 10th Argyll + Sutherland Highlanders.	

2353 Wt. W2544/1454 700,000 5/15 D. D. & L. A.D.S.S./Forms/C. 2118.

War Diary. (NO 141)

SECRET.

10TH BATTALION ARGYLL AND SUTHERLAND HIGHLANDERS.
Operation Orders No.112. by LT.-COL.H.G.SOTHEBY.M.V.O.
COMMANDING.

A raid will be carried out on August 18th. 1917.

1; OBJECTS.
(a) To search cutting in YORKSHIRE BANK K.32.b.3.9. for suspected enemy dugout or mining shaft and to destroy any such enemy works.

(b) To search Noethern and Eastern edge of YORKSHIRE BANK for evidence of enemy occupation.

(c) To obtain an indentification.

(d) To kill or capture Germans.

2. INFORMATION.
Patrols report-
(a) Enemy sentry seen on night of 15/16th Aug. in cutting K.32.b.3.9. and signs of enemy work.

(b) Much enemy activity at night on Nothern edge and Eastern edge of bank, and in DEAN COPSE.

(c) That enemy has also been seen along Bank K.32.b.5.6. to K.32.b.4.9.

(d) That the enemy occupy WIGAN COPSE and rifle pits to N. of it.
That there is a machine gun in ETNA CRATER.
That DEAN COPSE and rifle pits in vicinity are occupied.
That the whole of this line of posts is strongly wired from K.26.c.9.4. to K.26.d.8.0. thence to K.32.b.8.7. thence Eastwards along Outpost line.

3. ORGANISATION.

The raid will be carried out by 5 parties, consisting in all of 3 Officers, 9 N.C.Os, 47 men, 1 L.G. team, of 4 and 2 R.E.. detailed as follows:-

A. Party.- 1 Officer, 1 Sergt, 1 Corpl, 10 men and 2 R.E..

B. Party.- 1 Officer, 1 Sergt, 1 Corpl, 8 men and Lewis Gun and 4 Men.

C. Party.- 1 Sergt. and 10 men.

D. Party.- 1 Officer, 2 Sergts, 1 Corpl and 15 men.

E. Party.- 1 Corpl, and 4 Men.

4. INSTRUCTIONS.
A.PARTY.- At Zero minus 3 party will be in position under Bank at K.32.b.1.9. (North end of Outpost Line) and will move forward towards North edge of cutting K.32.b.3.9. where they will remain until Zero when they will rush the Quarry, kill or capture anyone there, blow up all dugouts and deal with Trench Mortar positions - R.E. carrying each 2 mobile ammonal charges. 2 Men of the party will be detailed as carriers for 4 extra mobile ammonal charges.

At Zero plus 20 party will withdraw by same route, entering Outpost Line at point of exit.

P.T.O.

INSTRUCTIONS. (Continued.)

B.Party. At Zero minus 3 party will be in position immediately in rear of A. Party and will form a covering party from K.32.b.5.9. to a point 25 yards Northwards.
TIME OF WITHDRAWAL. - At Zero plus 25 party will withdraw along Northern edge of YORKSHIRE BANK.

C.Party.-

At Zero minus 2 party will be inposition at K.32.b.4.6. and at Zero will move through German Wire following the edge of YORKSHIRE BANK until meeting Bank running North and South when they will incline to the left and clear the whole of the slopes of plateau from Bank Eastwards.
At Zero plus 25 party will withdraw by Sunken Road into HUBERT ALLEY and thence into Reserve Line East of HUBERT ALLEY.
This party will move to assembly position via Front Line and No.4. Locality to YORKSHIRE BANK.

D.Party.- Will assemble in left post line of RIGHT COMPANY.
At Zero minus -10 they will move forward and lie out as far outside our wire as possible and at Zero plus 2 on barrage on DEAN COPSE lifting they will advance and seize DEAN COPSE detailing 1Sergt, and 6 men especially to guard their left flank and deal with any opposition on Sunken Road bearing in mind that C Party will at that time be clearing the plateau on Eastern end of YORKSHIRE BANK.

At Zero plus 20 party will withdraw via SUNKEN ROAD to HUBERT ALLEY thence to RESERVE trench on Eastern side of HUBERT ALLEY.

E.Party.- Will bomb cutting K.32.b.3.9. at Zero and will withdraw immediately into Outpost Line.

5. ZERO Hour will be notified later.

6. ARTILLERY. programme attached.

7. DRESS. Patrol Order (bandolier and P.H.Helmet) Bayonets will be fixed before starting and they must all be dulled. Eachman will carry 2 MILLS Bombs No.5. Torches will be issued. Kilt aprons will not be worn - Officers will carry their own Torches.

8. INDENTIFICATIONS. All ranks will be searched before starting. All N.C.Os and men will carry a slip of paper in their right hand breast pocket, with Number Rank and Name written on it. Identity discs will not be carried. O.C.Companies will be personnally responsible for seeing this done.
All ranks will wear a White "1" band on each arm.

9. BATTLE-CRY. "Glasgow"

P.T.O.

10\. REPORT CENTRES. "A" "B" and "E" parties. Each man will report at "D" Company H.Q.

"C" and "D" parties. Will withdraw to RIGHT RESERVE TRENCH East of HUBERT ALLEY Q.2.a.6.8. and report to officer at corner of HUBERT ALLEY and FRONT LINE.

11\. TELEPHONE. No message concerning the raid will be transmitted at anytime even over Fullerphone.

12\. SYNCHRONISATION OF WATCHES. Watches will be synchronised at 6.pm. on August 17th and again at 6.pm. on August 18th. Signalling Officer will be responsible for having this done.

13\. MEDICAL ARRANGEMENTS. "A" "B" and "E" parties. Casualties will be attended to at forward R.A.P. at "D" Coy H.Q.

"C" and "D" parties. Will be attended to at Battalion R.A.P. route SUNKEN ROAD.

14\. STRETCHER BEARERS. 1.Stretcher will accompany each of the parties "A" "B" "C" "D".

15\. SIGNAL FOR WITHDRAWAL. Zero plus 20. 1 blast on French horn.
Zero plus 25. 2 blasts on French horn.

16\. WITHDRAWAL. The word "RETIRE" is never to be used.

17\. WIRE BREAKERS. will be carried by all ranks.
Wire cutters will be carried by every man.

18\. INLYING PICKET. Under 1 Officer, 15 men will be held in readiness to go out and search for " missing".

19\. NOMINAL ROLLS.
A Roll of all ranks taking part in the operations will be rendered by Companies concerned to Battn H.Qrs; by 6.pm. on the 18th inst.

20\. COMMAND.
LIEUT.J.E.BURLEIGH will command A. party.
LIEUT.W.D.WILLIAMSON do do B. do.
~~Sergt.~~ 2/Lt. G.A. MacDonald do do C. do.
2/LT.E.BIRKETT. do do D. do.
11095 Corpl. MURDOCH. D do do E. do.
2/LT.T.N.F.HOURSTON.,M.C. will control report centre at "D" Company Headquarters.
2/LT.S.G.ROBINSON.,M.C. will control report centre at Q.2.a.6.8.
2/LT.J.S.W.LAWSON. will be in charge of IN LYING PICKET.

21\. PRISONERS. Will be brought to ~~XX~~ "D" Company Hd.Qrs.

22\. Battle H.QRS. "D" Coy, Headququrters YORKSHIRE BANK.

(Sd) N.McQUEEN. MAJOR? for LT. COL,
COMMANDING,
10TH ARGYLL AND SUTHERLAND HIGHLANDERS.

Copy, No. 1. File.
2\. C.O.
3\. Adjt.
4\. "D" Coy.
5\. do
6\. do
7\. "A" Coy.
8\. "B" "
9\. "C" "
10\. Signals.
11\. Brigade.
12\. 26th T.M.B.
13\. Medium. T.M.
14\. War Diary.

9th. Divisional Artillery
Operation Order
No.141. 17/8/17.

1. The 26th Infantry Brigade are raiding the quarry in YORKSHIRE BANK at K.32.b.3.9. Eastern edge of YORKSHIRE BANK and DEAN COPSE at Zero hour on the night 18/19th. At Zero + 25 minutes the raiding parties withdraw to our own lines.

2. ACTION OF ARTILLERY.

Right group. (a) 18-pounders will barrage with shrapnel along a line K.33.a.1.1. to K.27.c.0.4. and on the rifle pits to the East of this line.

Ammunition and rate of fire.
ZERO to ZERO + 1 minute. First half minute 4 rds. of smoke shell per gun second half minute 2 rds. shrapnel per gun.

ZERO + 1 minute to ZERO + 30 minutes.

One round smoke and 2 rds. shrapnel per gun per minute.

4.5" Howitzers. Shell rifle pits in K.26.d., K.27.c. and K.33.a.

Ammunition and rate of fire.

2 rds. per gun per minute, one round gas and one round H.E. per gun per minute.

Left group. (b). 18-pdrs. barrage along a line K.26.d. 0.4. South edge of WIGAN COPSE to K.27.c.0.4.

Ammunition and rate of fire.

ZERO to ZERO + 1 minute. First half minute 4 rds. smoke shell per gun, second half minute 2 rds. shrapnel or H.E. per gun.

ZERO + 1 minute to ZERO + 30 minutes.

One round smoke shell and 2 rounds of H.E. or shrapnel per gun per minute.
A/210 will fire H.E. "B" and C/210 will fire shrapnel.

4.5" Howitzers.

On trench from K.26.d.3.9. to VESUVIUS (The 27th. Infantry Brigade Stokes mortars are shelling the West end of this trench).

Ammunition and rate of fire.

2 rds. per gun per minute, one round of gas and one of H.E. per gun per minute.

(c). 9th. Trench Mortar Brigade.

9.45" Trench Mortar.

ZERO to ZERO 30 minutes.

One gun on BOGGART'S HOLE.
One gun on VESUVIUS.

2" Trench Mortars.

(over) /

2" Trench Mortars.

ZERO to ZERO +1 minute.

One 2" Trench Mortar on each of the following:-

WIGAN COPSE.
DEAN COPSE.
ETNA.

Ammunition.

H.E.

ZERO + 1 minutes to ZERO - 30 minutes.

Trench mortar on DEAN COPSE will cease fire.
Trench mortar on ETNA will cease fire.
Trench mortar on WIGAN COPSE will fire H.E.

3. Gas shell will not be fired by any nature of Ordnance unless the wind is West or South West.

4. Smoke will not be fired unless the wind is West, South West or South.

5. The right group will provide a Liaison Officer with the battalion carrying out the raid.

6. The right group Commander will take direct command of the Field Artillery and Trench Mortars engaged till the operation is completed, in Liaison with the G.O.C., 26th. Infantry Brigade.

7. The right group Commander willx arrange to obtain the time from 26th. Infantry Brigade and synchronise with the left group and 9th. Trench Mortars.

8. The hour of ZERO will be notified later.

9. At 9.15.pm. to-night the 17th., there will be apractice barrage for 1 minute of Field Artillery and Trench Mortars on the targets detailed above. No smoke or gas will be fired the rates of fire will be as above.

ACKNOWLEDGE BY WIRE .

(sgd). L. Rose, Major, R.F.A.,
Brigade Major.
R.A., 9th. Division.

WAR DIARY.

Letters of appreciation to Battalion in connection with Raid on August 18th, 1917.

---

(1). The Corps Commander is very pleased with the work of the two strong patrols of the 7th. Seaforth Highlanders and 10th. Argyll and Sutherland Highlanders. It has gone a long way towards clearing up the situation in the neighbourhood of YORKSHIRE BANK.

(Sgd). H. De PREE, Bg-General,
21/8/17. General Staff, IV Corps.

---

(2). The G.O.C. wishes you to convey to all concerned his congratulations on the manner in which the 7th. Seaforth Hlrs., and 10th. Arg. and Suth. Hlrs., carried out their respective operations on the 18th. August.

(Sgd). P. STEWART, Lt.-Col.,
General Staff, 9th. Division.

---

(3). The Brigade Commander conveyed his congratulations to the Battalion, on the successful carrying out of the raid.

---

(4). The Commanding Officer wishes to express to all ranks taking part in the raid on the enemy's lines on the 18th. August, his high appreciation of the manner in which it was organised, and the gallantry with which it was carried out.

By skilful leading and bold following, under difficult conditions, information of the greatest importance was obtained, and severe casualties inflicted upon the enemy.

The Commanding Officer wishes also, to thank the Company Officers who so ably organised the several parties, or carried out the duties allotted to them, without which cooperation, the enterprise could not have met with the success it did.

The enemy, by this time, doubtless has reason to regret finding itself in a sector opposite to the 10th. Argyll and Sutherland Highlanders.

Rec'd Aug 18th 1917

App. Ref. WAR DIARY.

10TH. ARGYLL AND SUTH. HIGHRS.,

OPERATION ORDER No. 116, of the 30th. August, 1917.

By Major N. McQUEEN, D.S.O., Commdg.,

A Raid will be carried out this evening.

1. OBJECTIVE.

(1). To clear YORKSHIRE BANK of the enemy.
(2); To raid QUARRIES at K.32.b.4.9., with a view to destroying dugouts, capturing and inflicting loss on the enemy.
(3). To establish posts on N. E. Edge of YORKSHIRE BANK.

2. STRENGTH OF FORCES.

Total:- 2 Officers, and 71 O.R. plus 3 Lewis Guns and 2 R.E., divided into parties, as follows:-

A Party:- One Sergt., 10 O.R. and 1 Lewis Gun, to advance along YORKSHIRE BANK to edge of QUARRIES. (2). dislodge enemy posts, if established, and bomb QUARRIES with explosives, if necessary.

B Party:- 1 Officer, 35 O.R. 1 Lewis Gun, and 1 R.E., divided as follows:-
(1). 10 O.R. and 1 Lewis Gun will hold cliff at N.E. edge of YORKSHIRE BANK, while
(2). 1 Officer, 20 O.R. and 1 R.E., will sweep down N.E. slope of of BANK into QUARRY and proceed with destruction of dugouts. 5 OR. will proceed to establish a post. These 5 O.R. will carry 1 Pick, 1 Shovel and Concertina Wire. These 5 men will be reinforced by (1), on withdrawal.

C Party:- 1 Sergt. 10 O.R. and 1 Lewis Gun, to capture or kill enemy post at K.32.b.5.5. on SUNKEN ROAD, and establish post on SUNKEN ROAD at S.E. Corner of YORKSHIRE BANK; Lewis Gun to take up position connecting RAVINE and ETNA roads. This Party will carry Picks and Shovels and Concertina Wire and will dig in and consolidate at once.

D Party:- 1 Officer, 15 O.R. and 1 R.E. assault party for QUARRIES.

3. ZERO.- Zero hour will be at 8 pm.

4. TIMING.-

A and B at Zero leave OUTPOST LINE - A from LEFT, B from RIGHT of Line - A to cease dropping explosives at ZERO PLUS 4 minutes.

C will move forward from K.32.b.3.6. just below RIGHT Flank OUTPOST LINE at Zero.

At / :over:

App. Ref. WAR DIARY.

Sheet 2: Operation Order No. 116. dated 30.8.17.

4. TIMING.-
(contd).

At Zero, D will leave PATH immediately below LEFT FLANK of OUTPOST LINE, and at Zero PLUS 5 minutes, will rush QUARRIES and execute objective.

5. WITHDRAWAL.-

(30)

D Party will withdraw at Zero PLUS30 minutes.
A and B less 5 O.R. forming post on S.E. Corner of BANK will withdraw at Zero PLUS 30 minutes.
10 O.R. and 1 Lewis Gun, from B (1). will reinforce post at S. E. Corner.

6. DRESS.-

Patrol Order; Bandolier and P.H. Helmet. Each Man will carry 2 No. 5. BOmbs. Kilt Aprons will not be worn.

7. DATE.-

30th. AUGUST, 1917.

8. IDENTIFICATIONS.-

All ranks will be searched before starting. Identity Discs will not be carried. All N.C.Os. and Men will carry a slip of paper, in the Right hand breast pocket with number rank and name written on it. O.C. "A" and "D" Coys., will be personally responsible for carrying this out.

9. RALLYING POINT.-

All ranks, other than those garrisoning posts will report at H.Qrs. in YORKSHIRE BANK, where roll will be called.

10. MEDICAL ARRANGEMENTS.-

Medical Officer will establish forward Aid Post at H.Qrs., in YORKSHIRE BANK. He will be responsible that sufficient stretcher-bearers are there.
Second Aid Post will be at Support Battalion.

11. PRISONERS.-

Prisoners will be brought to Battle H.Qrs., in YORKSHIRE BANK.
Advanced Battalion Headqrs., at Coy., H.Qrs., in YORKSHIRE BANK.

12. WITHDRAWAL CRY.- PAISLEY. -- WAR CRY-- ARGYLLS!

13. WITHDRAWAL SIGNAL.- A succession of Very Lights fired from RIGHT Company Front.

14. "MISSING". -

"C" Company will provide a Party to be ready to search in NO MAN'S LAND, for any ranks who are missing.

Issued at ....H...pm.

(Sgd). J.B. MACMILLAN, Capt., for Adjt., 10TH. ARG. AND SUTH. HRS.

Recd 30th Aug 1917.

SQUARE K

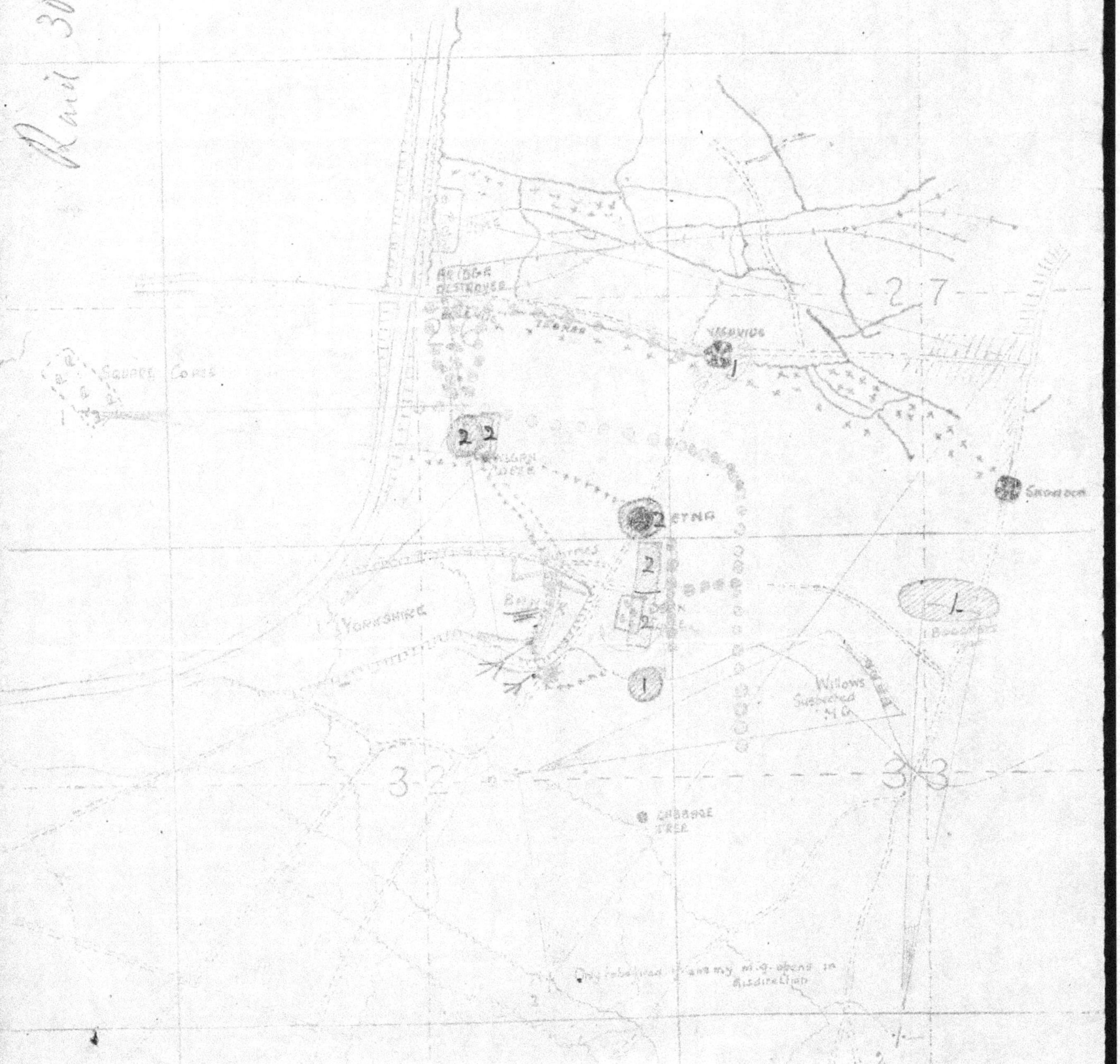

2" Mortars
Stokes
Heavy
Machine guns positions

Nos. denote number guns on each target.

Issued with TTC.
Operation Order No
Secret. 135

Army Form C. 2118.

Instructions regarding War Diaries and Intelligence Summaries are contained in F. S. Regs., Part II. and the Staff Manual respectively. Title pages will be prepared in manuscript.

WAR DIARY
or
INTELLIGENCE SUMMARY. 10th ARGYLL & SUTHERLAND HIGHLANDERS.
(Erase heading not required.)

Vol 25

Place	Date	Hour	Summary of Events and Information	Remarks and references to Appendices
	1917			
GOMIECOURT.	Sept 1		At CARLTON HILL camp in the GOMIECOURT area, the Battn under canvas. After the usual period for rest and refitting the Battn started training for future Offensive operations on lines adapted to meet the new tactics of the Enemy in the Northern War Zone.	
			Particular attention was devoted to the use of Gas appliances, to fire direction and fire control, to rapid wiring, and to Command of their sections by section commanders.	
			Afternoon addresses were given by the Officer Commanding and Major R. J. Nicol to subaltern officers & N.C.O.s respectively.	
			On the 6th a successful Field Firing exercise was carried out by Companies in accordance with a scheme drawn up by Major NICOL.	
			Battn tactical exercises were carried out on typed orders with plans attached on the 7th and 10th Sept, and a Brigade exercise in conjunction with 8th The Black Watch on the 11th Sept.	
			A Brigade Drumhead Service was held on the outskirts of the Camp on the 8th Sept. after which the G.O.C. Brigade presented 9th Divl	

29.0

2353 Wt. W2544/1454 700,000 5/15 D. D. & L. A.D.S.S./Forms/C. 2118.

Army Form C. 2118.

WAR DIARY
or
INTELLIGENCE SUMMARY. 10th ARGYLL & SUTHERLAND HIGHLANDERS.

Instructions regarding War Diaries and Intelligence Summaries are contained in F. S. Regs., Part II. and the Staff Manual respectively. Title pages will be prepared in manuscript.

(*Erase heading not required.*)

Place	Date	Hour	Summary of Events and Information	Remarks and references to Appendices
COMIECOURT			parchment testimonials for gallantry in the field to the following O.R.	VIK
			8016 Sgt. J. EADIE.	
			9446 " A. HOME.	
			15011. Pte J. W. JOLLY.	
			S/1428 Sgt. E. SHENAN.	
			7419 " W. SMITH	
			644. Corpl S. SMITH.	
			39. Sgt. D. J. BUCHANAN	
			5708 " J. FLEMING.	
			S/2190. L/Corpl J. COOK	
			9655. Pte A. DALGLEISH.	
			15532 Corpl R. CAMPBELL	
			14206. L/Corpl D. GILFILLAN.	
			A number of the above being in Hospital or in England their parchments were given to the Commanding Officer for safe keeping until they could be traced.	MMcD

2353 Wt. W2544/1454 700,000 5/15 D. D. & L. A.D.S.S./Forms/C. 2118.

Army Form C. 2118.

Instructions regarding War Diaries and Intelligence Summaries are contained in F. S. Regs., Part II. and the Staff Manual respectively. Title pages will be prepared in manuscript.

WAR DIARY
or
INTELLIGENCE SUMMARY. 10th ARGYLL & SUTHERLAND HIGHLANDERS

(Erase heading not required.)

Place	Date	Hour	Summary of Events and Information	Remarks and references to Appendices
	1917. Sept.		Letters of appreciation of the Raid carried out on the 30th Augt were received from the Divl & Army Commanders, they were published in Bn. R. O. & copies are attached.	MMc2
			6 leaves per day to AMIENS were granted to the Bn & taken full advantage of. Priority was given to any O.R. who had taken part in recent raids and fares of raiders were disbursed by the P.R.I.	
			An excellent concert was got up on the evening of the 6th by Padre JOHNSTONE from the 27th F.A. & the Batln, the Padre supplying the audience with free cigarettes.	
			A wet canteen was run in Camp and much appreciated.	
			A football competition was organised and resulted in a win for 'B'.	
			The Band played nightly in Camp between 5 and 6 pm.	
			After the first few days the weather was magnificent and the troops were in great fettle.	
	9th		The C.O. second in Command Adjutant and O.C. 'D' Coy visited the South African Bde Sports & renewed acquaintance with many old friends.	

Instructions regarding War Diaries and Intelligence Summaries are contained in F. S. Regs., Part II. and the Staff Manual respectively. Title pages will be prepared in manuscript.

WAR DIARY
or
INTELLIGENCE SUMMARY. 10th ARGYLL & SUTHERLAND HIGHLANDERS

(Erase heading not required.)

Army Form C. 2118.

Place	Date	Hour	Summary of Events and Information	Remarks and references to Appendices
	1917 Sept 10th		Transport Competition for money prizes from Divl Canteen funds. Major NICOL judged.	[illegible]
			1 Subaltern officer from each Coy & the Signalling Officer visited the 8th/10th GORDONS of the 15th Division near ARRAS to hear accounts of the fighting near YPRES.	[illegible]
WATOU (Belgium)	13th		Marched to BAPAUME and entrained at noon for GODEDERSVELDE which was reached at 4am the following morning. Breakfasted in the Village Street and then marched to a Camp in the WATOU area.	[illegible]
POPERINGHE	15th		Marched through POPERINGHE to a field at the S.E corner and established a Camp there.	[illegible]
	16th		Sunday – a day of rest. Various officers visited V Corps H.Q to inspect a model map in relief of the ground to be taken by the Divn.	[illegible]
TORONTO CAMP	17th		Marched to TORONTO Camp near BRANDHOEK. Small parties from H.Q and Companies went up the line for the day to reconnoitre.	[illegible]
			Division now belongs to 5th Corps (5th ARMY)	

Army Form C. 2118.

Instructions regarding War Diaries and Intelligence Summaries are contained in F. S. Regs., Part II. and the Staff Manual respectively. Title pages will be prepared in manuscript.

WAR DIARY
or
INTELLIGENCE SUMMARY.
(Erase heading not required.)

10th Argyll & Sutherland Hrs

Place	Date	Hour	Summary of Events and Information	Remarks and references to Appendices
TORONTO CAMP	1917 Sept 18.		Batt: drew fighting kit preparatory to going into action. Further parties went up to reconnoitre tracks & positions that Coys would occupy.	MK
YPRES.	19.	6. pm	G.O.C. 9th Division visited Batt: to wish them good luck and Batt moved at 6.30. pm to YPRES SOUTH AREA (about 1½ miles W of YPRES) and bivouacked until 3. AM. when it moved into	MK
	20		the line via MENIN GATE. H.Q. & C & D & Pioneer Platoon into RAILWAY WOOD. B. Coy into Trenches quite near & just E of CAMBRIDGE ROAD A. Coy into PILL BOXES & Trenches just E of MILL COT. 170 men engaged as Stretcher bearers under 28 Field Ambulance and numerous other parties were found as carriers guards etc. In the end only the Lewis Gunners and 50 men remained at disposal of Battalion. Batt: were in position by 4.30 am without casualties.	MK
		5.40 am	ZERO. attack commenced. 27th Brigade on right, South African Brigade on left. 2nd ANZAC DIVISION on right & 55th DIVISION on left of Division.	MK

2353 Wt. W2544/1454 700,000 5/15 D. D. & L. A.D.S.S./Forms/C. 2118.

Army Form C. 2118.

WAR DIARY
or
INTELLIGENCE SUMMARY. 10th Argyll & Sutherland Highlanders
(Erase heading not required.)

Instructions regarding War Diaries and Intelligence Summaries are contained in F. S. Regs., Part II. and the Staff Manual respectively. Title pages will be prepared in manuscript.

Place	Date	Hour	Summary of Events and Information	Remarks and references to Appendices
YPRES Battle.	1917 Sept 20.	7am	Prisoners commenced to arrive and reports seemed to show that the attack had been successful.	[illegible]
		1.30pm.	Orders received to call in all employed men and be ready to move at short notice to the assistance of South African Brigade who were being counterattacked on their left flank – Batt: strength available to move about 300. O.R. 7th Seaforths moved up to support of South African Brigade and at 4pm	[illegible]
		4pm.	Batt informed it would not be required, and continued to find working parties, Stretcher bearers, Guards &c until whole Batt: was employed except Lewis Gunners & Signallers of H.Q.	[illegible]
		6.30 pm	Brigade Office moved from RAILWAY WOOD and went back to BRANDHOEK AREA – Batt: then coming under orders of Division in event of emergency. In the attack today all objectives were gained and many counterattacks completely repulsed with considerable loss to the enemy. Our casualties reported slight –	[illegible]
	21.	10pm.	After a quiet day Batt ordered to move back to BRANDHOEK AREA which was reached at 4 am. without loss.	[illegible]

Instructions regarding War Diaries and Intelligence Summaries are contained in F. S. Regs., Part II. and the Staff Manual respectively. Title pages will be prepared in manuscript.

WAR DIARY
or
INTELLIGENCE SUMMARY. 10th ARGYLL & SUTHERLAND H.

(Erase heading not required.)

Army Form C. 2118.

Place	Date	Hour	Summary of Events and Information	Remarks and references to Appendices
	1917.			
BRANDHOEK AREA	Sept. 21		Casualties during these 2 days 1 killed 17 wounded	WA
			The Dug out which Batt. H.Q. used in RAILWAY WOOD is a large system of tunnelling in our original front line with many passages & rooms all named and lit by electric light. It is very deep and safe from shelling but most unhealthy, the floors and passages being under water.	
		9 am.	Batt. embussed at TORONTO CAMP and proceeded to WINNEZEELE AREA.	WA
	22 23 24 25		At rest in Good billets.	
	26	6.45 am	Batt. left Camp proceeding by route march to WINNEZEELE (3 miles) & there embussed for TORONTO CAMP.	WA
YPRES.		5.40 pm	Orders received Batt. moved to YPRES SOUTH AREA in 5th Corps Reserve. Co. together with Co. of 8th Black Watch reported to G.O.C. 3rd Division for instructions in YPRES RAMPARTS.	WA
		8pm	Both C.O.s received orders to move Batts. to RAILWAY WOOD immediately. Move completed by 12.30 A.M. Coys disposed as before in old trench. Situation obscure it being reported that Enemy had broken through – The report proved to be entirely without foundation and front line was perfectly intact	WA

2353 Wt. W2544/1454 700,000 5/15 D. D. & L. A.D.S.S./Forms/C. 2118.

Instructions regarding War Diaries and Intelligence Summaries are contained in F. S. Regs., Part II. and the Staff Manual respectively. Title pages will be prepared in manuscript.

WAR DIARY
or
INTELLIGENCE SUMMARY.
(Erase heading not required.)

Army Form C. 2118.

10th ARGYLL & SUTHERLAND H.RS.

Place	Date	Hour	Summary of Events and Information	Remarks and references to Appendices
	1917			
YPRES.	Sept 26		Came under orders of 9th Brigade (3rd Division) Brig. Gen: POTTER.	[illegible]
		3 PM.	Co. visited SQUARE FARM (HQ. 8th Brigade) and reconnoitred the line.	
	27	6.30 pm	The Heavies were turned on to Hill 40 in preparation for attack following night by with the result that enemy put down a heavy barrage on our front line probably thinking we were about to attack. 9th Brigade had some 200 casualties in consequence. Our S.O.S. was shown when an intense bombardment started on enemy's line until 7.15 PM. – Owing to casualties in the 9th Brigade the attack intended to take place tomorrow was postponed.	[illegible]
		8 PM.	Orders received for Batt: to move back into YPRES SOUTH AREA bivouacked for night and entrained following morning from	[illegible]
ERINGHEM	28		VLAMERTINGHE to a new area detraining at ERINGHEM 3 miles S.W of BERGUES and 8 miles from DUNKIRK. Marched to Billets (2 miles) where Batt is most comfortable in farms – best billets we have ever had. – Men very fit. We sustained only 1 casualty (wounded) during tour in line.	

2353 Wt. W2541/1454 700,000 5/15 D. D. & L. A.D.S.S./Forms/C. 2118.

Instructions regarding War Diaries and Intelligence Summaries are contained in F. S. Regs., Part II. and the Staff Manual respectively. Title pages will be prepared in manuscript.

WAR DIARY
or
INTELLIGENCE SUMMARY.
(*Erase heading not required.*)

Army Form C. 2118.

10th ARGYLL & SUTHERLAND H'rs

Place	Date	Hour	Summary of Events and Information	Remarks and references to Appendices
ERINGHEM	1917 Sept: 30.		Following is an extract from Wireless news 27 Sept 1917.	
			"Yesterday after a severe struggle lasting throughout the greater part of the day, English & Scottish Batts drove enemy from his position and accomplished the task allotted to them of securing the flank of our principal attack – In their advance our troops relieved two Coys of ARGYLL & SUTHERLAND HIGHLANDERS who had held out with great gallantry during the night in a forward position in which they had been isolated by the enemy's attack yesterday morning"	
			This refers to the 2nd Battalion –	
			The Division has now left the 5th Corps 3rd Army and has joined the 18th Corps (Lt Gen: MAXSE) 3rd Army –	
			After the Battle of 20th inst: Congratulations on work done by the Division were received by Army, Corps & Divisional Commanders.	
			The following decorations have recently been awarded in connection with reconnaissance raids on YORKSHIRE BANK in the HAVRINCOURT SECTOR last month.	
			M.C. { 2Lt JAMES EMIL BURLEIGH / Lt WILLIAM THOMAS GRAY ROBERTSON }	
			Bar to M.M. 5629 Sergt NORMAN McGREGOR	
			M.M. 9448 Sergt ALEXANDER HOME	
			M.M. 423 Pte JAMES DOCHERTY	

App. Ref. WAR DIARY.
Letters of appreciation.

10TH. ARGYLL AND SUTHERLAND HIGHLANDERS.

- -

26th. Inf. Bde.

X.S:3 777/10. 5th. Septr., 1917.

The attached remarks by the Army Commander are forwarded with reference to the occupation of enemy posts about YORKSHIRE BANK on August 30th.

(Sgd).H.J. SIMSON.
Major.
General Staff.
9th. (Scottish) Division.

....

G. O. C. 4th. A.C.

A very satisfactory operation. – Major McQueen's enterprise in carrying it out at such short notice is most commendable.

(Sgd). J. BYNG.
General.
4th. September, 1917.

....

Extract from Routine Orders, No. 381, dated 1.9.17.

The Commanding Officer has received the following letter of appreciation from Major Gen. H. T. LUKIN, C.B., C.M.G., D.S.O., of Raid carried out on 30.8.17.

"Please accept my best thanks for the prompt "manner in which you made arrangements for the "successful raid on YORKSHIRE BANK, this afternoon.

"I should be glad if you will convey to the "Officers and Men, who took part in the raid, my "appreciation of their good work".

30th. August, 1917.

....

26/9

WAR DIARY
or
INTELLIGENCE SUMMARY.
(Erase heading not required.)

Army Form C. 2118.

Instructions regarding War Diaries and Intelligence Summaries are contained in F. S. Regs., Part II. and the Staff Manual respectively. Title pages will be prepared in manuscript.

10. ARGYLL & SUTHERLAND HRS.

Vol 26

Place	Date	Hour	Summary of Events and Information	Remarks and references to Appendices
	1917			
ERINGHEM.	Oct 1		CO inspected the last 2 drafts – good stamp of men, [illegible] served abroad before	[illegible]
	2		Company officers detailed to go in to the next battle proceeded to 18th Corps School on a 3 days Course – where Corps Commander (Lt Gen. MAXSE) delivered a lecture at which CO & Senior Officers were present	[illegible]
	3.		CO attended Conference at Brigade HQ where plans of future operations were discussed. Major NICOL & Capt. HEPBURN laid out tapes on facsimile ground that Brigade will attack over. –	
	5		Batt practised laying out on tapes –	[illegible]
	6		Brigade day – Practised the attack – Brigade Conference to settle details of the Battle –	[illegible]
	7		Still raining hard – This is the 4th day of the change of weather. Transport moved by Route March to new area –	[illegible]
			L/Cpl A. FERGUSSON granted a Commission and posted to this Battn. Cavalry Brigade went through on their way to the Front. –	[illegible]
			Officers taking part in next operations reconnoitred the front	

30.0

12

Instructions regarding War Diaries and Intelligence Summaries are contained in F. S. Regs., Part II. and the Staff Manual respectively. Title pages will be prepared in manuscript.

WAR DIARY
or
INTELLIGENCE SUMMARY.
(Erase heading not required.)

10th ARGYLL & SUTHERLAND H^rs

Army Form C. 2118.

Place	Date	Hour	Summary of Events and Information	Remarks and references to Appendices
	1917 Oct 8	4. a.m.	Batt: marched to ESQUEBECQUE and entrained for SIEGE CAMP a large camp 1 mile from FLAMERTINGHE behind YPRES	MS
	9.	10 a.m.	Brigade Conference	MS
	(5)		Lieut G. CASSIE rejoined Batt – he was wounded at LONGUEVAL –	MS
	10	10 a.m.	Batt moved 2 miles to REIGERSBURG Camp and bivouacked – Drew fighting Kit and 2 days rations	MS
		6.30 P.m.	and at 6.30 P.m. moved via CANAL BANK and MOUSE TRAP TRACK to St. JULIEN – POELCAPELLE Road where guides from 8th WORCESTER BATT of 48 Division were met – Batt spent night in Shell holes at SPRINGFIELD HQ in Pillbox at SPRINGFIELD – a few minutes afterwards Enemy shelled St. JULIEN Road but Batt had just got clear.	
	11.		After several days of rain Weather cleared and hopes were entertained that it might be fine for the attack but this was not to be. Brigade Conference at ARTILLERY HOUSE at 2. P.m. and at 5 P.m. C.O saw Coy Commanders and issued final instructions for the attack.	MS
		9 P.m.	Batt filed off for the assembly positions. "A" & "B" by Y Route leading to CEMETERY at BURNS HOUSES and "C" & "D" by Z route to COUNTY X ROADS.	

2353 Wt. W2544/1454 700,000 5/15 D. D. & L. A.D.S.S./Forms/C. 2118.

3 71

Army Form C. 2118.

Instructions regarding War Diaries and Intelligence Summaries are contained in F. S. Regs., Part II. and the Staff Manual respectively. Title pages will be prepared in manuscript.

WAR DIARY
or
INTELLIGENCE SUMMARY. 10th ARGYLL & SUTHERLAND HIGHrs
(*Erase heading not required.*)

Place	Date	Hour	Summary of Events and Information	Remarks and references to Appendices
	1917			
PASCHENDALE RIDGE BATTLE	OCT 12		The taping party lost their way in the darkness and were not available for guiding Coys on to their lines.	JOP
			The routes were very clearly indicated there being a duck walk the whole way and lamps cleverly arranged by Major Woolner R.E. It took about 2 hours reaching assembly positions and lines were fairly well picked up but the shell holes filled with water which overflowed gave one the appearance of a vast lake. By 3 a.m. Batt was in position laying ready for the attack. Enemy shelled fairly heavily all the way along the Duck Walks and during the night just behind assembly positions but no casualties were sustained. From about 1 a.m. for 3 hours heavy barrage of gas shells fell over the whole of the back area but owing to a fall of wind and rain the mustard gas had little effect fortunately.	
		5.25 am	ZERO. Attack commenced. Left of Batt: was on LEKKERBOTERBEEK in touch with 55th Brigade 18th Division and the right in touch with 8th Black Watch of our Brigade.	app.1 app.2

2353 Wt. W2544/1454 700,000 5/15 D. D. & L. A.D.S.S./Forms/C. 2118.

3

Instructions regarding War Diaries and Intelligence Summaries are contained in F. S. Regs., Part II. and the Staff Manual respectively. Title pages will be prepared in manuscript.

WAR DIARY
or
INTELLIGENCE SUMMARY.
(Erase heading not required.)

10th ARGYLL & SUTHERLAND H'rs

Army Form C. 2118.

Place	Date	Hour	Summary of Events and Information	Remarks and references to Appendices
PASCHENDAELE RIDGE BATTLE	1917. Oct 12		The attack was made on a double company front each Coy on a two Platoon front in 4 waves on the 3 Platoon system (4th Platoon becoming Coy H.Q and forming a reserve Platoon) All in snake formation The Division attacked with (55th Div) 18th Div on left and (3rd Rifle Brigade) New Zealand Div. on Right. 26th Brigade with 8th Black Watch on right and 10th ARGYLL on left with 7th Seaforth on right & 5th Camerons on left in support attacked. 27th Brigade being in support and South African Brigade in Reserve. A & B Coys the leading assaulting Coys moved forward at ZERO but found great difficulty in crossing over the wet ground, and did not get quite close enough up behind the barrage when it lifted. The 2 right Coys A & C kept direction but B & D inclined rather too much to the left, one platoon of B crossing the LEKKERBOTERBEEK without recognising it owing to the wet ground looking so much alike and found itself in the 18th Div. area. The remaining 2 platoons of this Coy advanced with the LEKKERBOTERBEEK on their left and gained	MB

4.5

Instructions regarding War Diaries and Intelligence Summaries are contained in F. S. Regs., Part II. and the Staff Manual respectively. Title pages will be prepared in manuscript.

WAR DIARY
or
INTELLIGENCE SUMMARY.
(Erase heading not required.)

Army Form C. 2118.

10th ARGYLL & SUTHERLAND HIGH[rs]

Place	Date	Hour	Summary of Events and Information	Remarks and references to Appendices
	1917.			
PASCHENDALE RIDGE BATTLE.	Oct 12		touch with 18th Div: on the North side of the Stream. A & C Coys discovered a Pill Box 250x in front of BURNS HOUSES in a little Copse which was not marked on the map. They were there held up by machine gun fire and sniping and for a time were unable to advance but with 5th CAMERONS & elements of 11th Royal Scots & 6th K.O.S.B a rush was made on the Pill Box which was captured. The enemy showed a white flag but still continued to fire so the occupants were all killed, some 40 in front and another 20 attempting to escape from the rear. The enemy had 4 Machine Guns in this Pill Box. On the capture of this Pillbox A & C. Coys moved forward 150 yards and started consolidating shell holes. There was constant Machine Gun fire from BEER HOUSES and a considerable amount of sniping from the left and in front. The Platoon of B. Coy which crossed the Stream advanced on 18th Div: front for some 80 yards but were held up by Machine Gun fire at BEER HOUSES. They bombed a strong point and opened rifle fire on OXFORD HOUSES from which enemy were retiring – about 40 Germans were killed here.	

2353 Wt. W2544/1454 700,000 5/15 D. D. & L. A.D.S.S./Forms/C. 2118.

6

Instructions regarding War Diaries and Intelligence Summaries are contained in F. S. Regs., Part II. and the Staff Manual respectively. Title pages will be prepared in manuscript.

WAR DIARY
or
INTELLIGENCE SUMMARY. 10th ARGYLL & SUTHERLAND HIGHrs

(*Erase heading not required.*)

Army Form C. 2118.

Place	Date	Hour	Summary of Events and Information	Remarks and references to Appendices
	1917			
PASCHENDALE RIDGE BATTLE	Oct 12		D. Coy which was unable to make much progress formed a defensive flank on the left and gained touch with the 18th Div; which made no appreciable advance. This then was the line held by the Battalion during the rest of the day and handed over the following night to the relieving Battalion. As soon as it was found that no further progress could be made the Battalion was reorganised and the whole line consolidated. The 2 right Battalions, the BLACK WATCH and SEAFORTHS made better progress as it was on higher ground and consequently drier while our line of attack took us along the bed of the River, the whole of which was nothing but a quagmire. Some of the men remaining embedded in the mud and were shot down while others wounded fell into the shell holes and were drowned. The Enemy seemed to leave their organised shell holes & retired into the Pill Boxes when the Bombardment started which accounted for so many being found in them.	

2353 Wt. W2544/1454 700,000 5/15 D. D. & L. A.D.S.S./Forms/C. 2118.

7

Instructions regarding War Diaries and Intelligence Summaries are contained in F. S. Regs., Part II. and the Staff Manual respectively. Title pages will be prepared in manuscript.

WAR DIARY
or
INTELLIGENCE SUMMARY. 10th ARGYLL & SUTHERLAND H'rs

(*Erase heading not required.*)

Army Form C. 2118.

Place	Date	Hour	Summary of Events and Information	Remarks and references to Appendices
PASCHENDALE RIDGE BATTLE.	1917 Octr		BARRAGE was thin and did not come down quite punctually. The 12 minutes allowed for the first lift was not sufficient in this case owing to the state of the ground to allow the infantry to get under it in time but under normal conditions it should be ample. The Bombardment did not appear to dwell on the strong points with the result that they were not knocked out and we suffered most of our losses from Machine Gun fire. The hostile Barrage was very moderate & did not hurt us much.	MM
			DIRECTION. as always the most difficult question. The night was dark, water was everywhere and in trying to skirt round shell holes direction must necessarily be lost and the smallest amount once lost is very difficult to get adjusted on a wide front. Batt frontage 800 yards.	
			RIFLES. were all covered with a sandbag which were not removed until Zero. For this reason a good amount of firing was done with the Rifle but they soon got caked with mud. also the Lewis Guns.	

8

Instructions regarding War Diaries and Intelligence Summaries are contained in F. S. Regs., Part II. and the Staff Manual respectively. Title pages will be prepared in manuscript.

WAR DIARY
or
INTELLIGENCE SUMMARY.
(Erase heading not required.)

10th ARGYLL & SUTHERLAND H'rs

Army Form C. 2118.

Place	Date	Hour	Summary of Events and Information	Remarks and references to Appendices
	1917			
PASCHENDAELE RIDGE BATTLE	Oct 12		The men, though 10 out of the 12 officers going over had become casualties early in the attack & 40 N.C.O., fought splendidly never giving up any ground once gained and consolidated their positions. It was a section leader's battle, the men forming themselves into small groups under a leader. The men attacked without great coats to save weight but their coats were brought up to them during the afternoon. The 2 days rations carried on each man were sufficient and the sterilizing tablets carried by every one enabled the water in the shell holes to be purified & used. Although when they had consolidated the line everyone was physically exhausted and drenched in mud & water yet the troops were always cheerful. Dogs were taken in as message bearers but did not prove a success as in our case the men with them became casualties and the dogs went away. – In one case two dogs coming back had a fight on their own account in a shell hole!	WS

9

Instructions regarding War Diaries and Intelligence Summaries are contained in F. S. Regs., Part II. and the Staff Manual respectively. Title pages will be prepared in manuscript.

WAR DIARY
or
INTELLIGENCE SUMMARY.
(Erase heading not required.)

10th ARGYLL & SUTHERLAND Hdrs

Army Form C. 2118.

Place	Date	Hour	Summary of Events and Information	Remarks and references to Appendices
PASCHENDALE RIDGE BATTLE.	1917 Oct 12.		2/Lt. RIDDEL the senior officer of the 2 remaining (the other being 2/Lt. MACINTYRE) reorganised the Batt: as a Coy: and brought it out the following night.	WA
		11am	Batt H.Q. moved to BURNS HOUSE where there was considerable congestion - H.Q. of 11 Royal Scots & 5 Camerons being also there. It was turned into a dressing station - BURNS HOUSE is a Pill Box about 20 ft square in which were accumulated over 40 persons sleep was snatched standing up during the night - All wounded were brought in during the day but owing to the lack of Stretcher Bearers they had to wait until the morning -	
	13.		Raining very hard all day and at 8.30 P.M. relief commenced by 4th South AFRICAN BATT. Relief complete by about 11. P.M. and Batt moved back by ALBERTA TRACK to ADMIRALS ROAD by duck board track (4 miles) where Batt Cookers gave the men tea. Reached IRISH CAMP a further 800 yards where Major McQUEEN had made all arrangements providing the men with hot soup & clean socks and Tents.	

2353 Wt. W2541/1454 700,000 5/15 D. D. & L. A.D.S.S./Forms/C. 2118.

10 -

Instructions regarding War Diaries and Intelligence Summaries are contained in F. S. Regs., Part II. and the Staff Manual respectively. Title pages will be prepared in manuscript.

WAR DIARY
or
INTELLIGENCE SUMMARY.
(Erase heading not required.)

Army Form C. 2118.

10th ARGYLL & SUTHERLAND HRS.

Place	Date	Hour	Summary of Events and Information	Remarks and references to Appendices
YPRES.	1917 Oct 14.	10 am	Batt marched back via CANAL BANK to SIEGE CAMP when the Gothas came over dropping bombs quite near but missing our part of the Camp.	WA
			Remainder of the day spent cleaning up & refitting	
			Our Casualties were Killed: Lieut J. E. BURLEIGH. M.C.	
			Lieut R.W. DAVIDSON	
			2/Lieut A.L. MILLAR.	
			2/Lieut J. GIBSON	
			2/Lieut I. F. DUNCANSON.	
			Wounded Capt R.W.B. ARDILL	
			2/Lt. H. W. HEPBURN	
			Capt T. S. GIBSON M.C.	
			2/Lt. A. YOUNG	
			Lieut J. P. G. PATERSON	
			Lieut G. CASSIE	
			Total Casualties	
			K. 56.	
			W. 154	
			M. 23	
			W & M. 5	
			W & duty 2	
			240	

2353 Wt. ~~W3111~~/1454 700,000 5/15 D. D. & L. A.D.S.S./Forms/C. 2118.

Instructions regarding War Diaries and Intelligence Summaries are contained in F. S. Regs., Part II. and the Staff Manual respectively. Title pages will be prepared in manuscript.

WAR DIARY
or
INTELLIGENCE SUMMARY. 10th ARGYLL & SUTHERLAND Hrs

(Erase heading not required.)

Army Form C. 2118.

Place	Date	Hour	Summary of Events and Information	Remarks and references to Appendices
	1917			
YPRES.	Oct		The next few days working parties employed carrying ammunition	MS
(Siege Camp).	14		to the front line.	
	18		The following officers joined Batt for duty & taken on strength	MS
			Lieut COLIN CAMPBELL	
			2/Lieut JAMES SMITH THOMPSON RUSSELL	
			2/Lieut MORTON MUNGO MUIR.	
			2/Lieut JAMES BOUGH MORRISON.	
			2/Lieut KENNETH IAN GEORGE MATHESON.	
			2/Lieut GEORGE CECIL NASH.	
			2/Lieut THOMAS EDWARD TRINDER.	
			Lieut J. J. CLARKSON rejoined from being Adj: 17th Corps Depot and appd. 2nd in Command B Coy.	
	19	1?	Major McQUEEN D.S.O proceeded to England on 6 months duty	MS
	(16 Sept)		Capt: D A. POWELL RAMC appointed medical officer vice Capt N. MILLERICK RAMC who proceeded home on completion of contract.	
	21.		Better weather at last — Gen. Sir H. GOUGH. (5th ARMY Commander) attended Brigade Presbyterian Service today	

2353 Wt. W2541/1454 700,000 5/15 D. D. & L. A.D.S.S./Forms/C. 2118.

187

Instructions regarding War Diaries and Intelligence Summaries are contained in F. S. Regs., Part II. and the Staff Manual respectively. Title pages will be prepared in manuscript.

WAR DIARY
or
INTELLIGENCE SUMMARY.
(Erase heading not required.)

10th ARGYLL & SUTHERLAND Hrs

Army Form C. 2118.

Place	Date	Hour	Summary of Events and Information	Remarks and references to Appendices
	1917 Oct 22	am 6.30	Battn moved by march route to SCHOOL HOUSE (WATOU AREA) behind POPERINGHE (10 miles).	MS
	23	am 9	To WORMHOUDT (12 miles)	MS
	24	am 8.5	To TETEGHEM (9½ miles).	
	25		To COUDEKERQUE-BRANCHE (5 miles) – Black Watch at MALO-LES-BAINS SEAFORTHS at FORT des DUNES & Camerons at ZUYDCOOTE – These 3 battns forming part of the Coast Defences under the French and encamped on the seafront – COUDEKERQUE is a suburb of DUNKIRK outside the PORT LOUIS. Excellent billets and the men very comfortable and enjoying being on the sea. Major SCOTT & Major NIELSON of the 93rd are both on the Corps Staff. Battn now belongs to the 4th (COAST) ARMY) 15th CORPS. Enemy bombing raids nightly – up to now no damage to the Battalion.	
	(5)		Capt McMILLAN appointed Adjutant vice Capt FRENCH promoted Major & 2nd in Command 8th Black Watch	MS
	(19)		Major NICOL appointed 2nd in Command vice Major McQUEEN to England on 6 months duty	MS

2353 Wt. W2544/1454 700,000 5/15 D. D. & L. A.D.S.S./Forms/C. 2118.

13

Instructions regarding War Diaries and Intelligence Summaries are contained in F. S. Regs., Part II. and the Staff Manual respectively. Title pages will be prepared in manuscript.

WAR DIARY
or
INTELLIGENCE SUMMARY. 10th ARGYLL & SUTHERLAND H.Rs.

(*Erase heading not required.*)

Army Form C. 2118.

Place	Date	Hour	Summary of Events and Information	Remarks and references to Appendices
	1917.			
COUDEKERQUE (DUNKIRK)	Oct.		The following is a copy of a letter from the Divisional Commander to G.O.C. 26 (Highland) Brigade, who wishes it made known to all ranks:- "The Army Commander and the Corps Commander have requested me to "convey to you their high appreciation of the splendid gallantry and "endurance shown by all ranks of the 26th (Highland) Brigade during "the operations which took place on the 12th inst:- I should be "glad if you would make known to the Brigade how much I personally "appreciate its fine work" -	[illegible]
	28	5 am	Received orders to move at midday for Trenches at NIEUPORT les BAINS.	[illegible]
NIEUPORT LES BAINS.			Embussed at 2.15 pm to OOST DUNKIRK and moved into Trenches at 9.30 pm relief complete by 2.30 am. Took over from 21st K.R.R.C 41st Division. There being only accommodation for 350, the details remained with Transport at MIDDLESEX CAMP. Batt: took over left sub sector in the line on YSER CANAL with their left flank on the Sea by South Jetty. D Coy on left in 2 Posts and B Coy on right with one Post left of STATION the other being on the Embankment (right of Station).	

14

Instructions regarding War Diaries and Intelligence Summaries are contained in F. S. Regs., Part II. and the Staff Manual respectively. Title pages will be prepared in manuscript.

WAR DIARY
or
INTELLIGENCE SUMMARY.
(*Erase heading not required.*)

10th ARGYLL & SUTHERLAND HRS

Army Form C. 2118.

Place	Date	Hour	Summary of Events and Information	Remarks and references to Appendices
NIEUPORT LES BAINS	1917 Oct		A & C Coys in support near REGINA. The System of communication is by Tunnels and covered ways - There are 2 main Tunnels named BRISTOL and BEDFORD starting at junction of a Tunnel running the complete length of the houses of NIEUPORT LES BAINS through the Cellars and branching off to front line. There are 3 Covered ways (Communication Trenches) named BATH AVENUE running along the sea shore, BATH LANE running up the Centre and BLIGHTY AVENUE on the right - These 3 C.Ts although well hidden are not safe and are sometimes blown in by the Enemy but the Tunnels which have been constructed during the last 2 months by the Australian Tunnelling Coy are safe from shell fire - There are also several Cross Trenches connecting through the Tunnels & C.T.s - The rooms in the Tunnels are well furnished from the houses, before they were badly shelled, and everything is lit by Electric Light. On the left the front line is about 150x from the YSER CANAL while on the right there is a distance of about 300x.	1/A

15

Instructions regarding War Diaries and Intelligence Summaries are contained in F. S. Regs., Part II. and the Staff Manual respectively. Title pages will be prepared in manuscript.

WAR DIARY
or
INTELLIGENCE SUMMARY.
(Erase heading not required.)

10th ARGYLL & SUTHERLAND HLRS

Army Form C. 2118.

Place	Date	Hour	Summary of Events and Information	Remarks and references to Appendices
NIEUPORT LES BAINS	1917 Oct		The left front Coy always lives in the trenches, the right front Coy mans 2 posts at night, the right support Coy mans and stands to in BATH SUPPORT and the left support Coy stands to in BLIGHTY ALLEY (these 2 support Coys counter attack over the open in case of an attack) From observation posts OSTEND can be seen and all observers are ordered to report immediately if any German ships leave that harbour. One Platoon of the left support Coy is in BATH AVENUE and is in readiness for attack from the sea. Beside the 9 Lewis guns with the Coys there are 4 more at Batt. H.Q. in reserve. Batt frontage about 800x when it touches 8th Black Watch on right. The whole sector is held by 2 Batts in the line and 2 in reserve. The German front line is our original front line in the LOMBARDZYDE Sector which was lost in June last.	WD
	30.		Enemy heavily shelled the vicinity of REBINA where are the 2 support Coys firing some 250 5.9s from 8.30 am until 1.30 pm. One Platoon of C was buried but was dug out in an hour without a casualty. As the Dug Outs there are [illegible] sufficiently strong the 2 Coys were moved this evening into the Cellars	

(A7092). Wt. W12839/M1293 750,000. 1/17. D. D. & L., Ltd. Forms/C.2118/14.

Army Form C. 2118.

Instructions regarding War Diaries and Intelligence Summaries are contained in F. S. Regs., Part II. and the Staff Manual respectively. Title pages will be prepared in manuscript.

WAR DIARY
or
INTELLIGENCE SUMMARY. 10th ARGYLL & SUTHERLAND H[illegible]

(Erase heading not required.)

Place	Date	Hour	Summary of Events and Information	Remarks and references to Appendices
NIEUPORT les BAINS.	1917 Oct. 31.		Enemy artillery active all day shelling REGINA (which is now unoccupied) the Embankment and gun positions. The Division now belongs to V Corps 4th ARMY. [illegible] Lt Col Cmdg. 10. A. & S. Hrs	[illegible]

(A7092). Wt. W12839/M1293. 750,000. 1/17. D. D. & L., Ltd. Forms/C.2118 14.

Army Form C. 2118.

WAR DIARY
or
INTELLIGENCE SUMMARY. 10th ARGYLL & SUTHERLAND HRS

(Erase heading not required.)

Instructions regarding War Diaries and Intelligence Summaries are contained in F. S. Regs., Part II. and the Staff Manual respectively. Title pages will be prepared in manuscript.

Vol 27

Place	Date	Hour	Summary of Events and Information	Remarks and references to Appendices
NIEUPORT BAINS	Nov		Enemy consistently shelled fairly actively during the tour of duty in the line but Batt: did not suffer.	[illegible]
	3.		Relieved by 5th CAMERONS and came out to MIDDLESEX CAMP at OOST DUNKIRK. – Half Battalion daily employed tunnelling or carrying.	[illegible]
	6		3 shells nightly fall in Camp but without effect The following Officers arrived & are posted to Battalion. 2/Lt. D. A. DAVIDSON W. THOMSON J.R.T. MACCLOY D. DUNN J. DALGLEISH J. MATTHEWS. J.W.J. YOUNG. T.A. GILCHRIST.	
			2nd Lieuts M. M. MUIR and J. B. MORRISON } promoted Lieuts 1.7.17	[illegible]

81.0.

A7092). Wt. W12839/M1293 750,000. 1/17. D. D & L., Ltd. Forms/C2118/14.

Army Form C. 2118.

Instructions regarding War Diaries and Intelligence Summaries are contained in F. S. Regs., Part II. and the Staff Manual respectively. Title pages will be prepared in manuscript.

WAR DIARY
or
INTELLIGENCE SUMMARY.
(*Erase heading not required.*)

10th ARGYLL & SUTHERLAND H[ighlanders]

Place	Date	Hour	Summary of Events and Information	Remarks and references to Appendices
OOST DUNKIRK	1917 Nov		2/Lt. J. A. AGNEW-WALLACE reported for duty and posted to C. Coy.	[initials]
			The following decorations have been awarded to the Battalion in connection with the battle of Oct 12:-	
			Capt & Adjt. J. E. Macmillan — Military Cross	
			2/Lt. R. C. Macintyre — "	
			2/Lt. R. Riddel — "	
			No. 391 Coy Sergt. Major D. Thomson — D.C.M.	
			2108 Sergt. W. S. McLachlan — D.C.M.	
			No. S/2472 Sergt. M. McCaig — Military Medal (Bar to)	
			S/2116 Sergt. J. Dunsmore — Military Medal	
			14602 Pte. W. Waters — "	
			8739 Pte. J. Rushford — "	
			S/9417 Pte. D. M. Johnstone — "	
			14206 L/Cpl. D. Gillfillan — "	
			17474 L/Cpl. J. Dickie — "	
			16716 Sergt. J. Connelly — "	
			1865 L/Cpl. T. Richardson — "	
			S/6694 Sergt. D. McIntyre — "	
			9274 Pte. D. McQuarrie — "	
			S/1739 Cpl. A. Bell — "	
			2073 L/Cpl. A. McWilliams — "	
			S/3363 Pte. J. Fleming; S/40001 Cpl. W. Foy; 9846 Pte. H. McTaggart — Military Medal	[initials]

A7092). Wt. W12839/M1293 750,000. 1/17. D. D & L., Ltd. Forms/C2118/14.

3

Instructions regarding War Diaries and Intelligence Summaries are contained in F. S. Regs., Part II. and the Staff Manual respectively. Title pages will be prepared in manuscript.

WAR DIARY
or
INTELLIGENCE SUMMARY. 10th ARGYLL & SUTHERLAND Hdrs
(Erase heading not required.)

Army Form C. 2118.

Place	Date	Hour	Summary of Events and Information	Remarks and references to Appendices
COXYDE BAINS	1917 Nov 8		Brigade relieved in the line by South African Brigade and took up position in Coast defence –	[illegible]
			Batt moved back 800 yds to WILTSHIRE CAMP at COXYDE BAINS Camp in the Sand dunes –	
			The following days were devoted to training in the Dunes & Musketry Ranges were built and the Batt put through a Short Course	[illegible]
	16.		The Commandant of the Batt: of the French Army came to reconnoitre the position of the Battalion	[illegible]
	17		Division relieved in the Sector by the French who have also taken over the Sector hitherto held by the 42 Division on our right	[illegible]
		12.30 pm.	Batt moved via ADINKER to TETINGHEM (18 miles)	
	18		To WORMHOUDT (9 miles) – A considerable number of men fell out after a very trying march on previous day – Those who fell out were chiefly men arriving with the late drafts, who through the bad training at home with which the Army abroad has to contend with, were quite untrained in Marching.	[illegible]

(A7092). Wt. W12839/M1293. 750,000. 1/17. D. D. & L., Ltd. Forms/C.2118/14.

Army Form C. 2118.

Instructions regarding War Diaries and Intelligence Summaries are contained in F. S. Regs., Part II. and the Staff Manual respectively. Title pages will be prepared in manuscript.

WAR DIARY
or
INTELLIGENCE SUMMARY.
(Erase heading not required.)

10. ARGYLL & SUTHERLAND H[illegible]

Place	Date	Hour	Summary of Events and Information	Remarks and references to Appendices
	1917. Nov. 19.		To. WEMAERS–CAPPEL (6 miles)	[illegible]
	20		To HEURINGHE (14 miles	
	21		To ASSINGHEM (7 miles	
	22		To CRECKY (20 miles)	
			After the first two days when the bad marchers of the lately joined drafts were eliminated the Batt: marched very well, only 7 falling out in the last 4 days, notwithstanding the last day's march being 20 miles.	[illegible]
CRECKY.			The billets are very bad indeed, Companys very scattered, some being as far as 2 miles away. The area could never have been reconnoitred or it would never have been selected for a battalion area. The men being accommodated! in many cases in nothing better than pig sties.	
			After the first days march the horses & mules of the Transport began to sicken and by the third day no less than 8 had died and 20 had to be left behind as sick. It has not yet been decided whether this has been caused by	

(A7092). Wt. W12839/M1293. 750,000. 1/17. D. D. & L., Ltd. Forms/C.2118/14.

WAR DIARY
or
INTELLIGENCE SUMMARY.
(Erase heading not required.)

Army Form C. 2118.

Instructions regarding War Diaries and Intelligence Summaries are contained in F. S. Regs., Part II. and the Staff Manual respectively. Title pages will be prepared in manuscript.

10th ARGYLL & SUTHERLAND H[illegible]

Place	Date	Hour	Summary of Events and Information	Remarks and references to Appendices
CRECKY.	1917 Nov		Sand cholic, Influenza or results of gas shelling –	[illegible]
	23.		Day given up to cleaning up.	
	24.		Work under Company arrangements.	
			Col. Sergt. McKENZIE promoted to a Commission and posted to 14th Battalion.	[illegible]
	26		Recently joined drafts inspected by G.O.C. 26th Brigade	[illegible]
			Division now belongs to X Corps III army	
	30.		Orders received for Brigade to move to PERONNE	[illegible]

[illegible] Lt Col
10. A. & S. Hrs.

Instructions regarding War Diaries and Intelligence Summaries are contained in F. S. Regs., Part II. and the Staff Manual respectively. Title pages will be prepared in manuscript.

WAR DIARY
or
INTELLIGENCE SUMMARY.
(Erase heading not required.)

Army Form C. 2118.

10th ARGYLL & SUTHERLAND HIGHRS

Vol 28

Place	Date	Hour	Summary of Events and Information	Remarks and references to Appendices
	1917 Dec. 1		Batt moved by route march to LE MARAIS where it encamped prior to entraining	[illegible]
	2		Batt entrained for PERONNE	
PERONNE	3		Arrived PERONNE billetted in town	[illegible]
	4		Moved by route march to HEUDICOURT (10 miles) – During the break through by the Enemy on 30 Nov he reached this village but was quickly ejected.	[illegible]
			Wintry weather commenced on 1st Dec since which there has been sharp frosts nightly –	
	5		5 men accidentally wounded by one man foolishly fingering a German bomb.	[illegible]
		6pm	Batt moved to GOUZEAUCOURT WOOD (2 miles) Brigade taking over from 1st Guards Brigade – 2nd Grenadier Guards Batt in Reserve –	[illegible]
			200 Details under Lt McNeill remaining at AIZECOURT LE BAS	[illegible]
	7		Company Commanders visited the sector of the line to be taken over.	
	8		Batt took over left sector of left Brigade in line – The Front being held by 3 Brigades in line – Each Brigade has 2 Batts in front line & 2 in Reserve. The line taken over is part of that which Enemy broke through & he advanced as far as HEUDICOURT when the Guards counter attacked, retaking as far as	

32.D.

(A7092). Wt. W12839/M1293. 750,000. 1/17. D. D. & L., Ltd. Forms/C.2118/14.

Instructions regarding War Diaries and Intelligence Summaries are contained in F. S. Regs., Part II. and the Staff Manual respectively. Title pages will be prepared in manuscript.

WAR DIARY
or
INTELLIGENCE SUMMARY.
(Erase heading not required.)

10th ARGYLL & SUTHERLAND HRS

Army Form C. 2118.

Place	Date	Hour	Summary of Events and Information	Remarks and references to Appendices
GOUZEAUCOURT	1917. DEC		the original reserve line this side of CONNELIEU – This is the line now held by the Division.	[illegible]
			The Trenches were in a good state as long as the frost continued but on 8th Dec the thaw set in which [the trenches] in places were deep in mud and owing to there being no revetment the walls fell in –	
			An enormous amount of salvage was found which included the entire wardrobe of Brigade & Divisional Commanders and their Staff, an Ordnance Store, Motor Cars, Steam rollers and a large amount of Ammunition Bombs &c besides guns which had been lost in the retreat but recovered by the Guards in their Counter attack – a large store of enemy machine guns which had also been taken in the Counter attack were recovered.	
			The line about 1000 yds long is held by 3 Coys in line & one in Support and one Company from the reserve Battalion occupying GUARDS TRENCH which is held as a line of resistance – The Support Company to be used as a Counter attack Company.	
			The enemy does not appear to hold the woods in front of CONNELIEU by day but by night he holds them strongly with Machine guns which impedes wiring considerably.	

(A7092). Wt. W12839/M1293. 750,000. 1/17. D. D. & L., Ltd. Forms/C.2118/14.

3

Instructions regarding War Diaries and Intelligence Summaries are contained in F. S. Regs., Part II. and the Staff Manual respectively. Title pages will be prepared in manuscript.

WAR DIARY
or
INTELLIGENCE SUMMARY. 10th ARGYLL & SUTHERLAND H'rs

(*Erase heading not required.*)

Army Form C. 2118.

Place	Date	Hour	Summary of Events and Information	Remarks and references to Appendices
	1917			
GOUZEAUCOURT	Dec. 11		Patrol under Capt GIBSON explored GIN AVENUE (Sap) but after penetrating about 60 yards enemy opened such rapid machine gun fire that patrol had to withdraw – a German revolver and German Officer's Trench bundle were discovered by 2/Lt. NASH in NOMANS LAND.	JP
			A reconnaissance was made by C Coy on left and discovered enemy working party digging a new Trench and wiring it connecting GIN AVENUE to FIFTEEN ALLEY – This Trench is about 150 yards from our front line but cannot be seen owing to the wire. Neither side has observation.	
			The Batt. took over a further 100 yds on the left from 61st Division establishing a bombing block at FIFTEEN AVENUE.	
			A considerable amount of work was done in improving the state of the Trenches and a C.T. started by the Pioneer Platoon connecting FLAG RAVINE to Front line –	
			Batt H.Q moved into some old Brigade H.Q. on Railway under the bank which are far safer. –	
		6pm	Batt. relieved by 5th CAMERONS and moved back to GOUZEAUCOURT Wood into Trenches – H.Q shelled 5 times during following day & night with 8" shells landing a few feet off H.Q which is but an Elephant Shelter & gives no cover. No casualties however.	

(A7092). Wt. W12839/M1293. 750,000. 1/17. D. D. & L., Ltd. Forms/C.2118/14.

Instructions regarding War Diaries and Intelligence Summaries are contained in F. S. Regs., Part II. and the Staff Manual respectively. Title pages will be prepared in manuscript.

WAR DIARY or INTELLIGENCE SUMMARY. 10th ARGYLL & SUTHERLAND HIGHRS

(Erase heading not required.)

Army Form C. 2118.

Place	Date	Hour	Summary of Events and Information	Remarks and references to Appendices
GOUZEAUCOURT	1917 Dec 14	4. am	Report from prisoners that Enemy intended attacking in force at 6.30 am but nothing happened. Everyone stands to every morning 5.30 am – 7.30 am	[illegible]
			Weather cold and raw with slight frosts at night – Fortunately up to date very few cases of Trench feet.	[illegible]
			Batt to Trenches.	
	15	3.20 pm	Enemy put down heavy bombardment on Railway where Batt HQ were situated – 7 Casualties amongst the servants, Runners & Cooks. Enemy by the shelling today showed his S.O.S. Lines. At night Gas shells were sent over.	[illegible]
			During the bombardment message received Enemy expected to attack in the early morning. Attack however did not develop.	[illegible]
	17.		Batt relieved in Line by 5 Camerons and came into Huts on FINS ROAD.	
	21		A/Lt. Colonel H.G. SOTHEBY M.V.O. appointed Temp Lt Col and to command the Batt: vice Lt Col MacKENZIE CMG M.V.O. to command 3/ Seaforth Hrs to date 1 Dec 1917. T/Major N. McQUEEN D.S.O. appointed 2nd in command of the Battalion.	[illegible]

Instructions regarding War Diaries and Intelligence Summaries are contained in F. S. Regs., Part II. and the Staff Manual respectively. Title pages will be prepared in manuscript.

Army Form C. 2118.

WAR DIARY
or
INTELLIGENCE SUMMARY.
(*Erase heading not required.*)

10th ARGYLL & SUTHERLAND HRS

Place	Date	Hour	Summary of Events and Information	Remarks and references to Appendices
GOUZEAUCOURT	1917 Dec 21		Capt EWING M.C. The Black Watch took over temporary Command of the Battalion.	HHL
			Batt moved into trenches Front line night 21/22 Dec. in relief of 5th Camerons.	
	22		Quiet day. 4 O.R. wounded during night of 21/22 while coming up with rations	VB
	23		Quiet day.	VB
	24		At 1 am were alarmed of possible impending German attack, beyond a certain amount of shelling nothing more happened. 1 OR killed, 2Lt D.A. DAVIDSON and Lt & Q.M. R. McCutcheon wounded.	VB
	25		Quiet day; relieved by 5th Camerons and went back to Support Trenches	VB
	26		Quiet day.	VB
	27		Quiet day.	VB
	28		Enemy shelled Batteries behind our position. Killed Sgt Gordon Sig Sgt and a linesman. Certain amount of shelling during night. 2 OR wounded.	VB
	29		Enemy shelled same position as previous day intermittently killed 1 OR wounded 2 OR. Relieved 5th Camerons in front line night 29/30 Dec.	VB
	30		6.35 am Enemy opened heavy bombardment of our trenches, also behind attacked C Coy commanded by Capt BONNYMAN also right of D Coy commanded by Lt Campbell the enemy succeeded in entering our front line at two points but were immediately ejected loosing about 20 killed. Our casualties fairly heavy in C Coy & D Coy Lt CLARKSON killed 20 OR killed 2Lt MATHEWS and 18 O.R. wounded	VB

A7092). Wt. W12839/M1293 750,000. 1/17. D, D & L., Ltd, Forms/C2118/14.

Instructions regarding War Diaries and Intelligence Summaries are contained in F. S. Regs., Part II. and the Staff Manual respectively. Title pages will be prepared in manuscript.

WAR DIARY
or
INTELLIGENCE SUMMARY.
(Erase heading not required.)

Army Form C. 2118.

Place	Date 1917	Hour	Summary of Events and Information	Remarks and references to Appendices
GOUZEAUCOURT	Dec 30		(Continued) Died of wounds 1 O.R. MISSING believed killed SIX O.R.	
			The whole day continued more or less disturbed especially in the Division on our left where intermittent heavy artillery Barrages were put down by enemy. Night 30/31 Dec Quiet; everyone available employed on repairing our damaged line.	B.
	31	4am	Gas shell bombardment of line close behind Bn H.Q. gas more or less considerable at Bn H.Q.	
			Some artillery activity on our left (63rd Divn) which ~~[illegible]~~ was accompanied by S.O.S. being sent up several times. Our left Coy "stood to" in consequence but were able to stand down after short time as the front on our left quietened down.	B.

J.H.S. Ewing Maj
Cmdg 10th A.&S. Hdrs

(A7092). Wt. W12839/M1293. 750,000. 1/17. D. D. & L., Ltd. Forms/C.2118/14.

app 1

COPY.
S E C R E T.

26TH.(HIGHLAND) BRIGADE OPERATION ORDER No.149.

Ref.Maps SPRIET 1/10.000.
WESTROUSEBEKE 1/10.000.
ZONNEBEKE - 28 N.E. 1/10.000.

11/10/17.

1. The 26th. (Highland) Brigade will attack on Z day, with the 3rd. New Zealand (Rifle) Brigade on the right, and the 55th. Brigade on the left, in accordance with 26th.(Highland) Brigade Instructions No. 3 already issued.

A map shewing objectives and boundary lines has already been issued with this instruction.

This map and Instruction should be amended so that the dotted PURPLE line BECOMES the dotted YELLOW line, and the PURPLE line, the dotted BLUE line.

Amended copies of this map are issued to Units of 26th. Brigade.

2.(a).Two battalions of 27th. Brigade will pass through the 26th. Brigade after the capture of the dotted BLUE line, and will advance to the capture of the dotted PURPLE line.

(b).After these 2 battalions have crossed the dotted BLUE line, command of the front will pass to G.O.C. 27th. Infantry Brigade.

3. MACHINE GUNS.-

2 Machine guns 26th. M.G.Company will be detailed to accompany each assaulting battalion, and will move to definite points already arranged with a view to defending the objectives captured. The 8 guns which will be in ~~xxxxxxxxxx~~ position in the front line tonight 11/12th, during the assembly, will remain there in Brigade reserve.

Officer Commanding 26th. M.G.Company will notify Brigade H.Q., where he establishes his H.Qrs., and will send two Orderlies to remain at Brigade H.Q., during the battle.

The D.M.G.O. is arranging for a machine gun barrage to precede the Field Artillery barrage. The following guns will be available.-

16 guns - 197th. M.G.Company.
8 guns - 28th. M.G.Company.

The 16 guns of the 197th. M.G.Company will take up positions in squares D.2.a.b. and d. to cover the advance as far as the second objective.

The 8 guns of the 28th.M.G. Company will form up in rear of the 26th. Brigade and will move to squares V.27.a. and D.3.a; immediately in rear of the Brigade, and will take up positions to cover the advance to the 3rd. objective.

4. EMPLOYMENT OF R.E. AND PIONEERS.

Four parties, each consisting of a N.C.O. and 2 Sappers, will be attached to the 26th. Brigade for the purpose of assisting in the bridging of the stream crossing the front of the advance.

Two parties will accompany 7th. Seaforth Hrs., and two will will accompany the 5th. Cameron Highrs., in the attack. Each of these battalions will detail 6 men to act as carriers for the R.E. parties.

The N.C.O's., in charge of these parties should report at H.Q. 7th. Seaforth Hrs., and 5th. Cameron Hrs., today to make arrangements as to assembly.

5. The Brigade Signal Officer will arrange for a system of Runner relay posts forward of Brigade H.Qrs., to Battalion H.Qrs.,

6.
/ over:

6. CONTACT AEROPLANES.

The 7th. Squadron R.F.C. will detail -
(a). Contact machine to fly over the objectives at -

Zero plus 2 hours 30 minutes.
Zero plus 4 hours 30 minutes.
Zero plus 7 hours and when ordered by Corps H.Q.

Infantry will be ready to light REDflares at these hours, but will not do so unless called for by Klaxon horn or by the ~~xxxxxxxxx~~ dropping of WHITE lights.

Each contact aeroplane will be marked with two BLACK rectangular flags (2ft. by 1ft. 3ins.) attached to and projecting from the lower planes, on each side of the fusilage.

(b). Counter-attack machine.
An aeroplane will be up continuously during daylight from Zero onwards, whose mission will be to detect the approach of hostile counter-attacks.

Whenever the patrol observes hostile parties of 100 or over moving to counter attack, it will drop a smoke bomb over that portion of the front to which the enemy is moving.

The smoke bomb will burst about 100 feet below the machine into a white parachute flare which descends slowly, leaving a long trail of brown smoke about 1 ft. broad behind it.

7. LIAISON.
(a). 8th. Black Watch will detail a special party to meet a similar party of the New Zealand Divn., at junction of roads V.28.c.8.2.

7th. Seaforth Hrs., will detail a liaison party to meet a party of New Zealand Divn., at V.28.d.7.7.

10th.A.and.S.Hrs., will detail a liaison party to meet a party of 18th. Divn., at V.21.c.9.2.

(b). Major KNOX, R.W. Kent Regiment - attached 26th. Brigade H.Qrs., - will act as liaison officer between 26th. Brigade H.Qrs., and 9th. Division H.Q.

In addition, 2 Officers of the Brigade will act as liaison officers with 3rd New Zealand Brigade and 55th. Brigade (18th. Divn.). These Officers have been detailed.

8. Positions of Headquarters at Zero.-

9th. Divn. Adv. H.Qrs.)	-	CANAL BANK.
26th. Brigade Adv.H.Q.)	-	ARTILLERY HOUSE, ST. JULIEN (where it will remain).
27th. Brigade Adv.H.Q.)		
3rd.N.Z.(Rifle) Bde. Adv.H.Q.	-	GALLIPOLI.
55th.Brigade Adv.H.Q.	-	VARNA FARM(C.4.a.5.1).

9.ARTILLERY.-
Full particulars and barrage tables will be issued separately.

10.
/over:

10. Arrangements as to synchronisation of watches have already been made.

11. Zero hour will be notified later.

12. ACKNOWLEDGE.

Issued at 2pm.

(Sgd). J. F. EVETTS.Captain.
Brigade Major.
26th. (Highland) Brigade.

Copy No. 1	8th. Black Watch.		
2	7th., Seaforth Hrs.		
3	5th. Cameron Hrs.		
4	10th. A. and. S. Hrs.		
5	26th. M.G. Company.		
6	26th. T.M. Battery.		
7	26th. Bde. Sig. Officer.	)	
8	9th. Division 'G'.	)	
9	64th. Fd. Coy. R.E.	)	Maps
10	C.R.A. 9th. Division.	)	
11	27th. Brigade.	)	not
12	S.A. Brigade.	)	
13	55th. Brigade.(18th.Divn.	)	issued
14	3rd. N.Z. (Rifle) Bde.	)	
15	Staff Captain.	)	to.
16	War Diary.	)	
17	File.	)	
18	Major Knox.	)	

....

COPY.
S E C R E T.

app 2

26TH.(HIGHLAND) BRIGADE OPERATION ORDER No.149.

Ref.Maps SPRIET 1/10.000. 11/10/17.
WESTROUSEBEKE 1/10.000.
ZONNEBEKE - 28 N.E. 1/10.000.

1. The 26th. (Highland) Brigade will attack on Z day, with the 3rd. New Zealand (Rifle) Brigade on the right, and the 55th. Brigade on the left, in accordance with 26th.(Highland) Brigade Instructions No. 3 already issued.

A map shewing objectives and boundary lines has already been issued with this instruction.

This map and Instruction should be amended so that the dotted PURPLE line BECOMES the dotted YELLOW line, and the PURPLE line, the dotted BLUE line.

Amended copies of this map are issued to Units of 26th. Brigade.

2.(a).Two battalions of 27th. Brigade will pass through the 26th. Brigade after the capture of the dotted BLUE line, and will advance to the capture of the dotted PURPLE line.

(b).After these 2 battalions have crossed the dotted BLUE line, command of the front will pass to G.O.C. 27th. Infantry Brigade.

3. MACHINE GUNS.-

2 Machine guns 26th. M.G.Company will be detailed to accompany each assaulting battalion, and will move to definite points already arranged with a view to defending the objectives captured. The 8 guns which will be in ~~xxxxxxxxxx~~ position in the front line tonight 11/12th. during the assembly, will remain there in Brigade reserve.

Officer Commanding 26th. M.G.Company will notify Brigade H.Q., where he establishes his H.Qrs., and will send two Orderlies to remain at Brigade H.Q., during the battle.

The D.M.G.O. is arranging for a machine gun barrage to precede the Field Artillery barrage. The following guns will be available.-

16 guns - 197th. M.G.Company.
8 guns - 28th. M.G.Company.

The 16 guns of the 197th. M.G.Company will take up positions in squares D.2.a.b. and d. to cover the advance as far as the second objective.

The 8 guns of the 28th.M.G. Company will form up in rear of the 28th. Brigade and will move to squares V.27.c. and D.3.a; immediately in rear of the Brigade, and will take up positions to cover the advance to the 3rd. objective.

4. EMPLOYMENT OF R.E. AND PIONEERS.

Four parties, each consisting of a N.C.O. and 2 Sappers, will be attached to the 26th. Brigade for the purpose of assisting in the bridging of the stream crossing the front of the advance.

Two parties will accompany 7th. Seaforth Hrs., and two will will accompany the 5th. Cameron Highrs., in the attack. Each of these battalions will detail 6 men to act as carriers for the R.E. parties.

The N.C.O's., in charge of these parties should report at H.Q. 7th. Seaforth Hrs., and 5th. Cameron Hrs., today to make arrangements as to assembly.

5. The Brigade Signal Officer will arrange for a system of Runner relay posts forward of Brigade H.Qrs., to Battalion H.Qrs.,

6.
/ over:

6. CONTACT AEROPLANES.

The 7th. squadron R.F.C. will detail -
(a). Contact machine to fly over the objectives at -

Zero plus 2 hours 30 minutes.
Zero plus 4 hours 30 minutes.
Zero plus 7 hours and when ordered by Corps H.Q.

Infantry will be ready to light REDflares at these hours, but will not do so unless called for by Klaxon horn or by the dropping of WHITE lights.

Each contact aeroplane will be marked with two BLACK rectangular flags (2ft. by 1ft. 3ins.) attached to and projecting from the lower planes, on each side of the fusilage.

(b). Counter-attack machine.
An aeroplane will be up continuously during daylight from Zero onwards, whose mission will be to detect the approach of hostile counter-attacks.

Whenever the patrol observes hostile parties of 100 or over moving to counter attack, it will drop a smoke bomb over that portion of the front to which the enemy is moving.

The smoke bomb will burst about 100 feet below the machine into a white parachute flare which descends slowly, leaving a long trail of brown smoke about 1 ft. broad behind it.

7. LIAISON.
(a). 8th. Black Watch will detail a special party to meet a similar party of the New Zealand Divn., at junction of roads V.28.c.8.2.

7th. Seaforth Hrs., will detail a liaison party to meet a party of New Zealand D ivn., at V.28.d.7.7.

10th.A.and.S.Hrs., will detail a liaison party to meet a party of 18th. Divn., at V.21.c.9.2.

(b). Major KNOX, R.W. Kent Regiment - attached 26th. Brigade H.Qrs., - will act as liaison officer between 26th. Brigade H.Qrs., and 9th. Division H.Q.

In addition, 2 Officers of the Brigade will act as liaison officers with 3rd New Zealand Brigade and 55th. Brigade (18th. Divn.). These Officers have been detailed.

8. Positions of Headquarters at Zero.-

9th. Divn. Adv. H.Qrs.	-	CANAL BANK.
26th. Brigade Adv.H.Q. / 27th. Brigade Adv.H.Q.	-	ARTILLERY HOUSE, ST. JULIEN (where it will remain).
3rd.N.Z.(Rifle) Bde. Adv.H.Q.	-	GALLIPOLI.
55th.Brigade Adv.H.Q.	-	VARNA FARM(C.4.a.5.1).

9.ARTILLERY.-
Full particulars and barrage tables will be issued separately.

10.
/over:

10. Arrangements as to synchronisation of watches have already been made.

11. Zero hour will be notified later.

12. ACKNOWLEDGE.

Issued at 2pm.

(Sgd). J. F. EVETTS.Captain.
Brigade Major.
26th. (Highland) Brigade.

Copy No. 1	8th. Black Watch.		
2	7th.,Seaforth Hrs.		
3	5th. Cameron Hrs.		
4	10th.A.and.S.Hrs.		
5	26th. M.G.Company.		
6	26th. T.M.Battery.		
7	26th. Bde. Sig. Officer.	)	
8	9th. Division 'G'.	)	
9	64th. Fd. Coy. R.E.	)	Maps
10	C.R.A. 9th. Division.	)	
11	27th. Brigade.	)	not
12	S.A. Brigade.	)	
13	55th. Brigade.(18th.Divn.	)	issued
14	3rd. N.Z. (Rifle) Bde.	)	
15	Staff Captain.	)	to.
16	War Diary.	)	
17	File.	)	
18	Major Knox.	)	

....

App 3

COPY.

S E C R E T. 26TH. (HIGHLAND) BRIGADE.

Narrative of Operations on October 11th., 12th., and 13th., East of ST. JULIEN.

---

1. During the night 10th./11th. the Brigade relieved the 144th. Brigade, 48th. Division, and after relief battalions were disposed as follows.-

7th. Seaforth Hrs., Right Subsector, 5th. Cameron Hrs., Left Subsector, with 10th. Arg. and Suth. Hrs. in support in trenches and shelters, in the vicinity of SPRINGFIELD (C.12.c). and 8th. Black Watch in reserve in old German trenches - CANOPUS TRENCH and CALIFORNIA DRIVE (C.17.).

Advd. Brigade H.Q. was established at ARTILLERY HOUSE, ST. JULIEN, with rear H.Q. in the CANAL BANK.

2. The assembly was carried out during the night 11/12. Oct. under adverse circumstances, as the enemy barraged the assembly area with both H.E. and gas shells, and several of the taping parties became casualties.

However all four battalions were formed up, though not very accurately, before zero.

3. The Attack.

(a). From various accounts the attack seems to have started well, though the start of the barrage was very ragged, but direction was lost almost immediately owing to the wide frontage, and the extremely bad ground - and the 8th. Black Watch and 10th. A.and.S.Hrs. as far as can be ascertained, spread out to right and left in fan formation - to give an accurate account it seems best to take first of all the doings of the right battalions - viz. the 8th. Black Watch and 7th. Seaforth Hrs., and then the doings of the left battalions - viz. the 10th. A.and S.Hrs., and 5th. Cameron Hrs.

(b). A. Coy., the right assaulting Coy., 8th. Black Watch met with serious opposition from positions East of ADLER FARM. This was dealt with by Lewis guns and rifle fire, and a few prisoners were taken. The enemy appear to have been in the open lined up behind a sort of hedge and not in the farm or any strong point. The enemy shelling was heavy, and this Coy., came under heavy machine gun fire from both flanks at close range. As it advanced good progress was made until the Company objective was reached, when a halt was made and a line of shell holes consolidated, as far as the state of the ground would permit. 6 or 8 enemy machine guns were encountered and, put out of action, but were unable to be brought back owing to the heavy state of the ground.

B. Coy., the right rear Coy., on passing through A. Coy., appearto have reached SOURCE TRENCH and a point about V.28.C.8.0. East of WALLEMOLEN where there was a Pillbox (unmarked on the map), which was captured, and where O.C. B. Coy., was killed.

Apparently some New Zealand troops and 12th. Royal Scots became mixed up on the right of B. Coy., but about half an hour later these troops began to retire. B. Coy., was extricated later from its position.

About 5pm. in the afternoon a small and apparently unorganised counter attack was made by the enemy on our extreme right and was driven off by rifle and Lewis gun fire.

2/Lieut. A. L. Milroy, who was then commanding B. Coy., sent back 4 messages and reports to Battalion H.Q. as to the situation. None of the runners ever got through with these messages and none of Battalion H.Q. runners managed to get through to him.

The /

Sheet 2.

The left assaulting Coys. suffered casualties from our own barrage and apparently lost direction altogether and went too far to the left. Opposition was encountered when they reached trench V.27.c.5.5. - V.26.c.8.0., and C. Coy., was held up by snipers and machine guns, but managed to advance by section rushed a further 100 yards, where they consolidated a line of shell holes forming a line V.27.c.10.2. - V.27.c.3.8.

A Pillbox at D.3.a.5.8. had been razed to the ground by our shell fire and was not held by the enemy. Many enemy dead were lying round it.

D. Coy., having gone too far to the left, came up on the left of C. Coy. and suffered casualties from severe rifle and machine gun fire from the direction of OXFORD HOUSES.

Lt. A. S. Harper in command of the Coy. attempted to take with one section and Coy. H.Q. a Pillbox at V.26.b.8.1. from which the Coy., was being enfiladed by heavy machine gun fire. All this party became casualties except the C.S.M., Lieut. Harper being killed.

The Pillbox is reported to have contained over 100 men, who had obviously taken cover there from our barrage. The 6th. K.O.S.B. and 10th. A.and.S.Hrs., who had been checked by heavy machine gun fire from left, came up, and the enemy 'bolted', some 60 of them, and were mostly accounted for by Lewis gun fire. Over 40 were killed in and around the Pillbox and about 40 prisoners were taken. When OXFORD HOUSES were taken D. Coy., reorganised and consolidated, on a line from OXFORD HOUSES to V.27.c.Central, with C. Coy., on their right and 5th. Cameron Hrs. on their left.

According to reports received from 7th. Seaforth Hrs., who were to have passed through 8th. Black Watch on the yellow Dotted line, the barrage came down two minutes too early, and was patchy and thin, giving the men no definite line to go on.

Owing to the fact that the 8th. Black Watch lost direction at the beginning of their advance, the leading Companies of 7th. Seaforth Hrs., moved forward with nothing in front of them, and on the left were behind the barrage by about two minutes. It was owing to this that the left Coys. were checked for some 30 minutes by enemy in organised shell holes, soon after the advance commenced. The 12th. Royal Scots moved forward with the 7th. Seaforth Hrs. and filled up gaps in their line. There was slight resistance at INCH HOUSE from which the enemy soon retired, but in several places small parties of enemy in shell holes checked our advance until taken in flank. Two Sergts. in one case who had themselves been wounded, charged a party of nine enemy in a shell hole and killed them all.

The 7th. Seaforth Hrs. started in touch with 5th. Cameron Hrs. on their left, but the latter inclined to the left almost at once and a large gap of some 400 yards was formed.

The farthest point known to have been reached by the 7th. Seaforth Hrs. was in WALLEMOLEN where Lieut., Stuart captured a Pillbox containing 3 Officers and 4 men, and was himself killed by a German Officer.

A mixed force of 7th. Seaforth Hrs., 8th. Black Watch and 12th. Royal Scots eventually found themselves in WALLEMOLEN but as they came under both heavy frontal, and enfilade fire and had lost their barrage, they were forced to withdraw.

A line was then consolidated on the line CEMETARY - INCH HOUSE until the situation was cleared up.

Remainder of the battalion was at this time held up by machine gun and rifle fire from their left front and consolidated from INCH HOUSE to a point V.27.c.4.6. At 8.10am. H.Q. 7th. Seaforth

Seaforth Hrs. moved forward to INCH HOUSE, and it was from there that a party of Highlanders was seen advancing on VAT COTTAGES.

At 2.15am. orders were received from Brigade Headquarters by O.C. 7th. Seaforth Hrs. to take command of all parties of 8th. Black Watch; 12th, Royal Scots and 9h. Scottish Rifles in the subsector, and to endeavour to make good the line SOURCE TRENCH - BERKS HOUSE, as the New Zealanders were attacking again at 3pm. on our right. This attack was however cancelled, and a series of posts was established, tough gained on right and left, and preparations made for counter attack.

(c). A. and B. Coys., the leading assaulting Coys., 10th. A. and.S.Hrs., moved forward at zero but found great difficulty in crossing over the wet ground, and did not get quite close enough up behind the barrage when it lifted. As far as can be ascertained the two right Companies A. and C., kept direction, but B. and D. Coys., inclined too much to the left one platoon of B. Coy., crossed the LEKKERBOTEBEEK without recognising it andfound itself in the 18th. Division area. The remaining two platoons of this Coy. advanced with the LEKKERBOTEBEEK on their left and gained touch with the 18th. Division on the North side of the stream.

A. and C. Coys., discovered a Pillbox, 250 yards in front of BURNS HOUSE situated at V.26.b.7.1. in a little copse. This Pillbox is not marked on the map.

They were then held up by machine gun fire and sniping and for a time were unable to advance, but with the 5th. Cameron Hrs., and elements of the 11th. Royal S cots and 6th. K.O.S.B. a rush was made, on the Pillbox which was captured.

The enemy showed a white flag but still continued to fire, and so the occupants were all killed, some 40 in front, and another 20 attempting to escape from the rear. The enemy had 4 machine guns in this Pillbox. On the capture of the Pillbox A. and C. Coys., moved forward 150 yards and started to consolidate shell holes. There was constant machine gun fire from BEEK HOUSES, (which may possibly have been mistaken to have come from MEUNIER HOUSE), and a considerable amount of sniping from the left, and in front. The platoon of B. Coy., which crossed the stream, advanced on the 18th. Division front for some 80 yards, but were held up by machine gun fire at BEEK HOUSES. This platoon was not in touch with the 18th. Division. There is some doubt as to what happened to one platoon of this Coy., as the Officers and senior N.C.Os. having become casualties, there is no one who can give reliable information, but it is possible it went right on by itself.

The general opinion on the left is that the barrage was accurate and that there were few 'shorts', but it was thin and did not come down punctuallyn at zero, and does not appear to have dwelt on strong points as previously arranged.

The Officer Commanding 10th.A.and.S .Hrs., reports an interesting incident, namely that Red cross parties of, the enemy were seen dumping ammunition in shell holes.

The 5th. Cameron Hrs., who attacked in rear of 10th. A.and.S.Hrs. appear to have started well except that direction was soon lost owing to the state of the ground and the large front. This battalion was badly enfiladed by machine gun fire ~~where~~ /

fire from BEEK HOUSE and MEUNIER HOUSE, and in addition, was held up at BURNS HOUSE by the same Pillbox in the copse at V.26.b.7.1. which held up 10th.A.and.S.Hrs. Several attempts were made to take this by parties of 5th. Cameron Hrs., especially to outflank it from the left, which was impossible owing to the swamp on that flank. As has already been described, this Pillbox was taken by a party composed of 10th.A.and.S.Hrs., 5th. Cameron Hrs., 11th. Royal Scots, and 6th. K.O.S.B.

The O.C. 5th. Cameron Hrs., reports that when the enemy came out of the Pillbox they were led by an Officer, who shot a Corporal of the 10th.A.and.S.Hrs., who was the first man up. This Officer was immediately shot by one of our men and the whole of the garrison with the exception of four men who were taken prisoners, were killed.

Shortly after this O.C. 5th. Cameron Hrs., went forward to find out the situation and found that some men of his battalion and the 10th.A.and.S.Hrs., were as far forward as the battalions on the right, so, he gave orders to consolidate and to get into touch, which they succeeded in doing. On the left the 5th. CAMERON Hrs., were in touch with the 18th. Division in their old front line.

On the morning of the 13th. a Sergeant of the 27th. Machine gun Company, reconnoitred the Pillboxes in front of the Pillbox at V.26.b.7.1. about 200 yards in front of BURNS HOUSES and found them unoccupied. Thereupon the C.O. of the 11th. Royal Scots, who was in charge of that sector, put a small party into each Pillbox, he was also able to get into touch with some men of the 5th. Cameron Hrs., and the 10th.A.and.S.Hrs., who were in Pillboxes in OXFORD HOUSES at V.26.b.25.40.

4. Machine guns - At zero, 26th. Machine Gun Company was disposed as follows.-

Guns holding the line in following positions.-

2 at D.3.a.6.2.
2 at D.3.a.5.4.
2 at V.26.a.4.7.
2 at V.26.a.9.1.

2 guns with each battalion.

Company H.Q. at HUBNER FARM.

The four guns with 5th. Cameron Hrs., and 10th.A.and.S.Hrs. moved into positions about about 7am. on 12th.

2 at V.26.d.5.9.
2 at V.26.d.9.9.

but they were unable to give the Infantry much help owing to the slope of the ground, so dug in and consolidated.

Small parties of the enemy were seen and shot at.

One of the guns at V.26.d.5.9. was put out of action by a direct hit from a shell.

On the right 2 guns with 7th. Seaforth Hrs., pushed up to about V.27.d.3.6..

On the Officer in command of these guns seeing that the Infantry on the left were held up, he got his guns into action and opened covering fire in the direction of the Pillbox at V.26.b.8.1. Several small parties of the enemy were engaged with effect, but the guns had to cease fire owing to running out of ammunition, but a sufficient supply was maintained later. These guns were then withdrawn to about V.27.d.7.6. where the Infantry were

/

were consolidating. The 2 guns with 8th. Black Watch got forward to a position on the flank about D.3.b.4.4.

The Officer in charge of them then went forward to reconnoitre the exact position of our infantry and found and reported to O.C. 7th. Seaforth Hrs., who ordered him to place his guns in position about V.27.d.1.2. in front of INCH HOUSE and to consolidate. Two excellent gun positions were chosen which entirely covered the right flank.

Several small reconnoitring parties of the enemy were engaged about dusk, with good effect, on the 12th.

5. The front of the Brigade was reorganised during the night 12/13th. in accordance with Brigade Operation Order No. 180.

On His Majesty's Service.

CONFIDENTIAL

D.A.G.

(War Diaries)

Base

9TH DIVISION
26TH MACHINE GUN COY.

26TH MACHINE GUN COY.

FEB 1916-DEC 1917

26 M G Coy

Vol 1 2 3

Feb 1916 – Dec 1917

I

Instructions regarding War Diaries and Intelligence Summaries are contained in F. S. Regs., Part II, and the Staff Manual respectively. Title Pages will be prepared in manuscript.

WAR DIARY

~~INTELLIGENCE SUMMARY~~

(Erase heading not required).

Army Form C. 2118.

Place	Date	Hour	Summary of Events and Information	Remarks and references to Appendices
	1/2/16		Captain S Crawford 3rd Batt Black Watch took over command of the 26th Infantry Brigade Machine Gun Company, from Capt M G Millar.	
			The following Officers are Section Commanders	
			No 1 Section 2nd Lieut Duffus; " " 2nd Lieut Ramage } 8th Black Watch	
			No 2 Section 2nd Lieut Munro; " " 2nd Lieut Mackenzie } 7th Seaforths	
			No 3 Section Lieut Hilditch; " " 2nd Lieut Woodward } 8th Gordons	
			No 4 Section Lieut Black; " " 2nd Lieut Milne } 5th Camerons	

BSD - B. M351/22/11. 12/15. 5000.

2

Instructions regarding War Diaries and Intelligence Summaries are contained in F. S. Regs., Part II, and the Staff Manual respectively. Title Pages will be prepared in manuscript.

WAR DIARY

or

INTELLIGENCE SUMMARY

(Erase heading not required).

Army Form C. 2118.

Place	Date	Hour	Summary of Events and Information	Remarks and references to Appendices
Ploegsteert	1/2/16 – 3/2/16		Company in reserve	
	5/2/16		Nos 1 & 3 Sections went into Subsidiary line	
	6/2/16		Nos 2 & 4 do also	
	"		" 1 & 3 took over from 24th Brigade Machine Gun Company Trenches	
	"		" 103 – 127 in firing line	
	7/2/16		" 1.2.3.4 Sections in Trenches	
	8/2/16		" do do do do	
	9/2/16		" do do do do	
	10/2/16		Indirect fire by Sections no ~~2~~ – ~~4~~. No 4 Section fired ~~f~~ from U 15 C 2 3 on	
	"		Trois Tilleuls Farm U 17 C 1.2 no 2 fired ~~f~~ from U 14 B 10.0 neighbourhood of AU	
	"		CHASSEUR CABARET U 16 B 2 3½	
	11/2/16		Nos 1.2.3.4 Section in Trenches	
	12/2/16		" 2 – 4 " Came out to Transport lines and nos 1 & 3 went into Subsidiary lines.	
	13/2/16		Nos 2 – 4 Sect in rest billets	
			" 1 3 " in Subsidiary lines	
	14/2/16		No 3 Section fired 2000 rounds indirect fire ~~indirect fire~~ from neighbourhood Gunners Farm.	
	15/2/16		Nos 1 – 3 Sections came out to transport lines; nos 2 – 4 as reliefs went into Subsidiary lines	

BSD - B. M351,22/11. 12/15. 5000.

3

Instructions regarding War Diaries and Intelligence Summaries are contained in F. S. Regs., Part II, and the Staff Manual respectively. Title Pages will be prepared in manuscript.

WAR DIARY

~~or~~

~~INTELLIGENCE SUMMARY~~

(Erase heading not required).

Army Form C. 2118.

Place	Date Feb	Hour	Summary of Events and Information	Remarks and references to Appendices
	16th		Nos 1–3 Sections in rest billets	
	"		" 2–4 do in Subsidiary lines	
	17th		Indirect Fire in conjunction with 27th Brigade Machine Gun Company on targets ~~at~~ in neighbourhood of LA BASSE VILLE firing particularly on U 17 d 0 8 and the left of the Sugar Refinery U 17 b 40	
	18th		No 1, 2, 3, 4 Sections relieved 27th Brigade Machine Gun Company in the firing line	
	19th		No 4 Section fired indirect from MOATED FARM ~~on~~ at target at LES TROIS TILLEULS between 9 & 9.30 am which some nine men were reported to leave each morning at this hour bound for the Trenches. A group of men were seen to have been scattered by this fire, and later in the day a flag was hung out, which appeared to bear a red cross	
	"		No. 2 Section fired at working parties at various times during the night	
	21st		" 4 " fired ~~at~~ on a working party at end of Avenue U 15 a 38	
	22nd		All Sections engaged and dispersed working parties throughout the earlier part of the night	
	24		27th Brigade Machine Gun Company relieved 26th Infantry Brigade Machine Gun Company. Nos 2 & 4 Sections went into Subsidiary lines for 6 days No 1–3 Sections came out to Transport lines	
	"		The 27th Brigade Machine Gun Company were very late in relieving	

4

Army Form C. 2118.

Instructions regarding War Diaries and Intelligence Summaries are contained in F. S. Regs., Part II, and the Staff Manual respectively. Title Pages will be prepared in manuscript.

WAR DIARY
or
INTELLIGENCE SUMMARY
(Erase heading not required).

Place	Date	Hour	Summary of Events and Information	Remarks and references to Appendices
	Feby 24		A new system of relief started 2 Sections remained 6 days in Subsidiary line thus giving the Sections in rest sufficient time to refit and continue training	
	25		GRANDE HAIE FARM U 23 A 5.7 was fired on by no 4 Section from the Subsidiary line. Indirect fire used	
			2nd Lieut S O Cowper arrived for duty and was taken on the strength of the Coy	
	26		500 Rounds were fired between 4 and 6 pm on the following targets by indirect fire Working party near GRANDE HAIE FARM U 23 A 3.6, French Railway and tracks U 30 A 0.7 and north REFINERY U 17 D 3.7, neighbourhood of HALTE U 17 C 8.0, Bridges U 29 B 6.3, PONTOON BRIDGE C 5 A 3.3, French Railway C 5 C 2.9 These targets were fired on during the night as well. This firing took place from the Subsidiary line at Lancashire Cottage.	
	27		Nothing to report	
	28		Indirect fire from Gunners Farm at Road through FRELINGHIEN 250 rounds were fired between 3.30pm & 5pm.	
	29		Nothing to report	
	March 1st		26th Brigade Machine Gun Company relieved 27th Brigade Machine Gun Company. Nos 1 – 3 from Transport lines nos 3 – 4 from Subsidiary lines	

Instructions regarding War Diaries and Intelligence Summaries are contained in F. S. Regs., Part II, and the Staff Manual respectively. Title Pages will be prepared in manuscript.

5

WAR DIARY
or
INTELLIGENCE SUMMARY
(Erase heading not required).

Army Form C. 2118.

Place	Date	Hour	Summary of Events and Information	Remarks and references to Appendices
	March			
	2/3/16		Private D Ferguson no 6555, killed by Gun Shot (S1)	
	3/3/16		Indirect fire was brought to bear between 7.15 pm and 8-30 pm from W 27 A 3 2 on the following points, where Railway Trench, Railway track, and road meet W 3 C 6 4 also on WHITE FARM C 5 A 6 2. Target A was first engaged. The Shooting here must have caused the enemy considerable annoyance, his artillery opened fire and several H.E Shells of larger size than usual, burst about 100 Yards from the Gun position. The order cease fire was given to encourage the hostile Artillery to think that the Gun had been silenced by his fire. After a lapse of 15 minutes target A was again engaged, which caused the Hun Artillery to retaliate with renewed vigour. Later our Artillery opened fire on the enemy, which distracted the attention of the hostile Battery from the machine Gun on to the S.E Corner of PLOEGSTEERT WOOD	
			II Shooting on target. B. did not draw any retaliation	
	4/3/16		Information was received from O/C 8th Black Watch that our Artillery were to Strafe the Hun front line trench, between U 22 A 3 0 and U 22 C 3.7 our machine Gun was to fire on U 22 A 7.3. If Hun Artillery retaliated the Gun was to continue firing until the German Battery was silenced by a Canadian Battery standing by for this purpose	

BSD - B. M351.22/11. 12/15. 5000.

6

Army Form C. 2118.

Instructions regarding War Diaries and Intelligence Summaries are contained in F. S. Regs., Part II, and the Staff Manual respectively. Title Pages will be prepared in manuscript.

WAR DIARY
or
~~INTELLIGENCE SUMMARY~~
(Erase heading not required).

Place	Date	Hour	Summary of Events and Information	Remarks and references to Appendices
	March 4th		The Machine Gun opened fire on junction on C.T. (U22 A 7 3) at 9.35 pm. The Hun Artillery did not retaliate. The Gun ceased fire at 9.40 pm. 2nd Lieut K. J. Mackenzie went to WISQUES	
	5th		Our Gun in Trench 122 silenced a Hun Machine Gun at U 21 B 7.9 which had been very troublesome. Our Gun was fired from the Canadian Concrete emplacement in Trench 122 and succeeded in altogether silencing the Gun of the enemy. The same night another enemy Gun was silenced opposite Trench 124 in a similar manner.	
	6th		No 4 Section fired at working party at U 33 A 9.3 and dispersed it. The same place was fired on between 5-pm and 6-pm the same night. About 700 rounds were fired altogether. Our Gun fired from MOATED FARM	
	7th		The 27th Brigade Machine Gun Company relieved the 26th Brigade Machine Gun Company. Nos 1 & 3 Sections went into Subsidiary line. Nos 2 & 4 Sections came to Transport lines	
	8th		Nothing to report	
	9th		Nothing to report	
	10th		Nothing to report	

7

Instructions regarding War Diaries and Intelligence Summaries are contained in F. S. Regs., Part II, and the Staff Manual respectively. Title Pages will be prepared in manuscript.

WAR DIARY
or
INTELLIGENCE SUMMARY
(Erase heading not required).

Army Form C. 2118.

Place	Date	Hour	Summary of Events and Information	Remarks and references to Appendices
	March 11th		Indirect fire was used on the following targets on the night of the 10th at the times stated 530pm Shed (Billet) in the vicinity U 22 d 83 6pm Dump also work reported near U 22 c. The Gun again fired at 7pm and 9pm on same places. Between 630pm and 830pm various targets were fired on Cross Roads (Transport heard here) U 28 b 9½ Loophole Farm U 22 d 23, Strong point U 28 b 56. Pontoon Bridge C 5 a 33. White Farm C 5 a 26. Ammunition expended 4000 rounds	
	12th		The following targets were engaged on the night of the 11th between 6pm and 730pm from U 26 c 87. A U 22 d 83 Shed, Billet B " c 87 Dump " c 77 Work reported " c 88 do road from U 22 c 7 6½ to U 22 d 09 also searched. Ammunition expended 1000 rounds	
	13th		The 26th Infantry Brigade Machine Gun Company relieved 27th Brigade Machine Gun Company at 730 am in the line.	
	14th		About 7 O'clock on the night of the 13th inst our left Gun in T 127 fired on a German Gun which was sweeping trenches 126-127 from a point about U 15 a 3½ 8. A belt was fired and the enemy ceased fire for the night	

BSD - B. M351/22/11. 12/15. 5000.

8

Army Form C. 2118.

WAR DIARY
or
INTELLIGENCE SUMMARY

(Erase heading not required).

Instructions regarding War Diaries and Intelligence Summaries are contained in F. S. Regs., Part II, and the Staff Manual respectively. Title Pages will be prepared in manuscript.

Place	Date	Hour	Summary of Events and Information	Remarks and references to Appendices
	March 15th		Nothing to report	
	16		The following Targets were engaged on the night of the 14/3/16 between 6 30 pm and 10 pm from U 27 a 3.2 A Dump at U 23 A 9 3 work was reported at this point	
			B X roads at trench Rlwy at U 28.B 9½ 7½	
			C Trench Rlwy and road running from U 28 B 9½-7½ to U 23 C 6 4 on the same night the Gun at MOATED FARM fired on U 22 B 5 5½ and U 23 A 8[illegible] as a relief was reported to be in progress.	
	17		The following targets were engaged last night and early this morning from U 26 D 9 9½	
			A U 22 C 8 7 Dump	
			B U " D 2 3 Loophole Farm	
			C U 23 a 9 3 Dump	
			D U " C 6 4 Trench Rlw track road	
			E U 22 D 2.3 Shed Billet	
			F from U 23 C 6 4 to U 23 D 23 Track leading to Billet and C.T	

BSD - B. M351/22/11. 12/15. 5000.

9

Army Form C. 2118.

WAR DIARY
or
~~INTELLIGENCE SUMMARY~~

(Erase heading not required).

Instructions regarding War Diaries and Intelligence Summaries are contained in F. S. Regs., Part II, and the Staff Manual respectively. Title Pages will be prepared in manuscript.

Place	Date	Hour	Summary of Events and Information	Remarks and references to Appendices
	March 17th		Target A. was engaged every half hour between 7pm and 10 pm and between 4-AM and 5-30 AM in the morning. Target B was engaged at 8 pm Targets C.D.E.F. were engaged every hour between 7-pm and 10-pm also between 4.0 AM and 5-30 AM. The Hun replied with machine Gun fire doing some very wild traversing. In the morning between 7-30 AM & 8.0 AM the enemy retaliated on and about LANCASHIRE. SUPPORT FARM with Artillery fire. An enemy Aeroplane was fired at this morning An enemy working party was fired on and dispersed by our Gun in Trench 106 Between 6.30 pm and 8-0 pm one of our Guns firing from U 15 C 7½.1¼ Searched from U 17 D 2½ 1¼ to U 17 D 7.4. A German Gun was located about U 15 A 4½ 8. firing during the day The Gun in Trench 127 was removed at "Stand to" in the evening and laid on the spot where the German Gun had fired, it however remained silent during the night. Our Gun however swept the enemys Wire opposite	

BSD - B. M351/22/11. 12/15 5000.

10

Instructions regarding War Diaries and Intelligence Summaries are contained in F. S. Regs., Part II, and the Staff Manual respectively. Title Pages will be prepared in manuscript.

WAR DIARY
or
INTELLIGENCE SUMMARY
(Erase heading not required).

Army Form C. 2118.

Place	Date	Hour	Summary of Events and Information	Remarks and references to Appendices
	March 18th		On the evening of the 16/3/16 between 6-30 pm and 8-30 pm the Gun at MOATED FARM fire 1000 rounds on U17 b 8.5 acting in Concert with two of the Guns of No 2 Section. The Gun in T 126 firing from about U15 a ½ 3 fired 750 rounds on the Railway just South West of FME DE LA CROIX about U11 a 9.7½ The Gun from T 126 fired 250 rounds on the same Target from a position about U15 A 5 1. In concert with above No 2 Sections Guns (2) fired from U15 b 5.5½ and U15 c 7½ 1¼ on Targets at U18 a 9 8 & 18 a 7½ 7 respectively. The enemy retaliated fiercely with 15 pounders light Howitzers and Shrapnel about 8.15 pm no damage was done. On 17/3/16 at 8 20 am a working party was reported on the road just South of GRANDE HAIE FARM direction given as 1° right of FARM (bearing from OP ST IVES) U23 A 9 6½ was fired on accordingly. The observer reported that he believed one man to have been hit. At 9.35 am a man was carried away on a Stretcher. At 9.58 am another burst was fired on the party which had restarted work, but no casualties were reported, although the bullets fell all around them. On the night of 17th & 18th inst No 2112 Cpl A Smith and No 6505 Pte G Henderson were wounded (by Rifle Grenade)	
	19th		The 26th Brigade Machine Gun Company were relieved by 27th Brigade Machine Gun Company at 7.45 am. No 1–3 Sections came to Transport lines No 2. 4 Sections went into Subsidiary lines. All indirect fire cancelled by Divisional order	
	20th 21st 22nd 23rd 24th		Nothing to report	

11

Instructions regarding War Diaries and Intelligence Summaries are contained in F. S. Regs., Part II, and the Staff Manual respectively. Title Pages will be prepared in manuscript.

WAR DIARY
or
INTELLIGENCE SUMMARY
(Erase heading not required).

Army Form C. 2118.

Place	Date	Hour	Summary of Events and Information	Remarks and references to Appendices
	March 25th		The 26th Brigade Machine Gun Company relieved the 27th Brigade Machine Gun Company at 6 30 am No 1-3 Sections went up from Transport lines No 2-4 Sections from Subsidiary line	
			Two Guns of No 4 Section returned to Transport lines to make place for 2 Guns of 27th Brigade who remained in the line to cooperate with the raid by the 10th Argyll and Sutherland Highlanders These were to march up again on the 26th when the Guns of the 27th Brigade Machine Gun Company were to be withdrawn	
	26th		Relief by two Guns of No 4 Section which had been withdrawn cancelled till further orders	
			Argyll raid failed	
	27th		The two Guns relieved at 5 30 am. Everything quiet in our own part, with exception of a few rounds 7.7 am when mine went up at St Eloi	
	28		Nothing particular to report No 2 Section fired at intervals on the enemy parapet throughout the night	
	29		No 3 Section expended 1750 rounds on O23a.4.3 firing from Gloucester Fort They ~~were~~ in telephone communication with the look out post at LONDON FM which had reported much movement at that place The fire obviously much embarrassed the enemy who retaliated vigorously on the neighbourhood of LANCS SUPPORT FARM. Owing to ~~the~~ casualties caused to Work Party this Gun had to stop firing No 2 Section traversed enemy parapet through the night	

BSD - B. M351/22/11. 12/15. 5000.

12

Instructions regarding War Diaries and Intelligence Summaries are contained in F. S. Regs., Part II, and the Staff Manual respectively. Title Pages will be prepared in manuscript.

WAR DIARY

or

INTELLIGENCE SUMMARY

(Erase heading not required).

Army Form C. 2118.

Place	Date	Hour	Summary of Events and Information	Remarks and references to Appendices
	March 30th		In the early evening enemy machine Guns displayed some activity opposite No 3 Section the two front line Guns were accordingly moved from their Battle emplacement and succeeded in keeping down fire of enemy Guns. No 4 Section fired on enemy Parapet in the early part of the evening.	
	31st		From 2pm to 5pm enemy shelled MOATED FARM and DEAD HORSE CORNER with 15 and 21 cm Shells. At dead Horse Corner one of the men attached from Battalion was wounded by a Shell Splinter. L/c Howie Gun in T 119 moved to WESTMINSTER AVENUE	
	April 1st		Notification transfer of Gun in T 119 to emplacement in WESTMINSTER AVENUE sent to 27th Brigade Machine Gun Company	
	2nd		26th Brigade Machine Gun Company relieved by 27th Brigade Machine Gun Company in front line trenches. Nos. 1-3 Sections going to Subsidiary line No 2-4 Sections return to transport lines	
	3rd		27th Brigade Machine Gun Company notify they will not occupy WESTMINSTER AVENUE.	
	4		Nothing to report. 24 men per Battalion to undergo course instruction	
	5		2nd Lieut P.B. Duffus and Lt H Hilditch relieve 2nd Lieut S.A. Cowper and 2nd Lieut B.R. Woodward in Subsidiary line. Ammunition brought from WESTMINSTER AVENUE to Subsidiary line	

BSD - B. M351/22/11. 12/15. 5000.

13

Instructions regarding War Diaries and Intelligence Summaries are contained in F. S. Regs., Part II, and the Staff Manual respectively. Title Pages will be prepared in manuscript.

Army Form C. 2118.

WAR DIARY
or
~~INTELLIGENCE SUMMARY~~
(Erase heading not required).

Place	Date	Hour	Summary of Events and Information	Remarks and references to Appendices
	April 6th		Inspection by Lt Colonel Marshall of men in reserve. Instructions concerning kit issued.	
	7th		Course of instruction ends (Started on 4th)	
	8th		26th Brigade Machine Gun Company relieves 27th Brigade Machine Gun Company in front line trenches	
	9th		MOATED FARM Gun fired indirect on the following points traffic having been heard there between 8-30pm and 11.0 pm. AU CHASSEUR CABARET U17 A 42 Cross roads U17 A 92 8 Level Crossing LA BASSEVILLE HALTE 750 rounds were fired	
	10th		Nothing to report	
	11th		Nothing to report	
	12		During the night a belt was fired from the Canadian Concrete Emplacement on to work in progress behind the German line opposite Trench 121	

BSD - B. M351/22/11. 12/15. 5000.

14

Instructions regarding War Diaries and Intelligence Summaries are contained in F. S. Regs., Part II, and the Staff Manual respectively. Title Pages will be prepared in manuscript.

WAR DIARY
or
INTELLIGENCE SUMMARY
(Erase heading not required).

Army Form C. 2118.

Place	Date	Hour	Summary of Events and Information	Remarks and references to Appendices
	April 13th		MOATED FARM Gun fired twice during the morning at 8 15 AM and at 8 55 AM. The first target was a working party at U6 b66 2 men fell the remainder escaped into a trench. The second target was a group of 4 men at U23 a 5½ 0 they were scattered by the first burst, but looked like resuming their conversation shortly afterwards a second burst was fired which decided them, and they disappeared. The GLOUCESTER FORT Gun also fired at 8.45 AM men were reported to be moving in groups along the HALTE - PONT ROUGE ROAD. Indirect fire was brought to bear on U29 B27 between 9.0 AM and 10.0 AM from GLOUCESTER FORT the enemy retaliated with about 20 7.7 cms in the Neighbourhood.	
	14th		The 27th Brigade Machine Gun Company relieved the 26th Brigade Machine Gun Company in the front line. Two Guns of the 26th Brigade were detailed to remain up one for LONE HOUSE AVENUE the other for FORT BOYD. Strictest Secrecy was to be observed by men occupying these emplacements as they were under observation and intended as a surprise in case of attack	
	15th		At 9.30 a telegraph arrived from the 26th & 27th Brigade Machine Gun Company giving an imaginary situation. The enemy were supposed to hold our front line between SEAFORTH FARM and BELCLIERS Cottages and to have gained a footing in two places further South.	

BSD - B. M351/22/11. 12/15. 5000.

15

Army Form C. 2118.

Instructions regarding War Diaries and Intelligence Summaries are contained in F. S. Regs., Part II, and the Staff Manual respectively. Title Pages will be prepared in manuscript.

WAR DIARY
or
INTELLIGENCE SUMMARY
(Erase heading not required).

Place	Date	Hour	Summary of Events and Information	Remarks and references to Appendices
	April 15th		15 minutes later news was received that the road from 84 FARM to about TOUQUET BERTH was heavily Barraged. By 10-10 AM the sections were under way No I to be under orders of the 26th Brigade Machine Gun Company No 3 (less two teams) under the 27th Brigade Machine Gun Company. No I reached positions in the Subsidiary line by 12.10 pm. No 3 by 12.20 pm. The arrangements made proved effective	
			Arrived from England: Corpl G W Hobber No 12831	
			Pte H Bailey " 15882	
			" R Beardmore " 21750	
			" C Frebor " 12450	
			" E Gardner " 15729	
			" A Holt " 12468	
			" G L Tinker " 15619	
			G Williams " 12112	
			The general physique of this draft is (poor)	
	16		Nothing to report. Course of instruction (4 days) started 3 men Ltn Battalion	
	17		Nothing to report	
	18		Nothing to report	
	19		Nothing to report Course of instruction finished	

BSD - B. M351,22/11. 12/15. 5000.

Army Form C. 2118.

Instructions regarding War Diaries and Intelligence Summaries are contained in F. S. Regs., Part II, and the Staff Manual respectively. Title Pages will be prepared in manuscript.

WAR DIARY

or

~~INTELLIGENCE SUMMARY~~

(Erase heading not required).

Place	Date	Hour	Summary of Events and Information	Remarks and references to Appendices
	April 20th		26th Brigade Machine Gun Company relieved the 27th Brigade Machine Gun Company in front line No 1–3 Sections from Trenchline 2–4 Section from Subsidiary line	
			Inspection of new draft by A D M.S 9th Scottish Division	
	21		Men for class report at READING FORT These are untrained men who will be with us for a month (5 men per Battalion)	
	22		Emplacement at Burnt out Farm was shelled this morning and the loophole blocked. The concrete was uncovered. A working party opposite T 109 was fired at but the work could not be stopped, presumably it was going on inside the trench	
	23		Between 3 30 pm and 8-30 pm indirect fire was brought to bear on U 22 a 5½.2 (a gap in the trench) by no 3 Section no result was reported No 2 Section used indirect fire against Gap in C.T U 23 a 17½, U 17 C 9½ 4, U 17 D 25 } no result reported	
	24		No. 3 Section again fired from former position at U 22 A 5½ 2 between 5 pm and 6 30 pm No 4 Section fired on enemys parapet opposite T. 124	

17

Instructions regarding War Diaries and Intelligence Summaries are contained in F. S. Regs., Part II, and the Staff Manual respectively. Title Pages will be prepared in manuscript.

WAR DIARY
or
INTELLIGENCE SUMMARY
(Erase heading not required).

Army Form C. 2118.

Place	Date	Hour	Summary of Events and Information	Remarks and references to Appendices
	April 25th		No 3 Section fired between 4 30 pm and 7 00 pm on the following points	
			Gap in CT at U 22 A 5 ½ 2	
			PONT ROUGE U 29 B 2 7	
			LOOK HOLE FM U 22 D 3 4	
			C T at U 17 c 1 0 U 17 C 5 8	
			from U 26 B 9 ½ 0 also at 7 30 pm	
			on DEULEMONT V 2 4 D 0 4 from Gap in front line	
			Total S A A expended 950 rounds	
	26th		27th Brigade machine Gun Company relieved 26th Brigade machine Gun Company in front line.	
	27th		Gas alarm at 1 00 AM this morning. Company Stood to for about ¾ of an hour then ordered by Brigade to Stand down	
	28th		nothing to report	
	29th		nothing to report	
	30th		Gas alarm at 1-0 AM this morning Company "Stood to" At 2-AM message from Brigade that all was quiet on Divisional front. Company Stood down at 2-15 am	
			C.H.M. Crawford Capt	
			O/c 26th Infantry Brigade machine Gun Company	

BSD - B. M351/22/11. 12/15. 5000.

26th Brigade Machine Gun Company

To

D A G

3rd Echelon

Base

Herewith original copies of War diary for this month (May)

S. H. W. Crawford Capt

31/5/16

O/C 26th Brigade Machine Gun Company

26th Infantry Brigade Machine Gun Company

Instructions regarding War Diaries and Intelligence Summaries are contained in F. S. Regs., Part II, and the Staff Manual respectively. Title Pages will be prepared in manuscript.

18 **WAR DIARY** or **INTELLIGENCE SUMMARY**

(Erase heading not required).

Army Form C. 2118.

Place	Date	Hour	Summary of Events and Information	Remarks and references to Appendices
	1/5/16		Nothing to report	
	2/5/16		26th Brigade Machine Gun Company relieved 27th Brigade Machine Gun Company in the front line	
	3/5/16		On the night of the 2nd and 3rd inst No IV SECTION co-operating with the 8th Battalion the Buffs fired at U.9.c.5.1 Company Headquarters } the U 9. d 7 5 Battalion " }	
			Gun position was U.15. a ½ . 3½ . No IV SECTION also fired on enemys support trench running from U.15 a. 8. 4½ to U 9 c. 7 3½ The gun was situated at U 15 a 5 1¼ Enemy retaliated with four 77 mm shells all of which fell short of our front line	
	4/5/16		One Gun of No 2 SECTION fired on Level crossing at U 17 d 0 8 and on junction of Roads at U 17 d. 3 7. The Gun position was U 15 c. 3. 1½.	
			Enemy retaliated with 77 mm shells but did no damage. No IV SECTION fired on gap in enemys wire at U 15 b 2 7	
			The following men having reported for duty are taken on the strength of the Company from this date. No 9787 Pte Castles W. No 9880 " Baker C. No 9678 " Whetton H No 9578 " Chamberlain E	

Instructions regarding War Diaries and Intelligence Summaries are contained in F. S. Regs., Part II, and the Staff Manual respectively. Title Pages will be prepared in manuscript.

26th Infantry Brigade machine Gun Company

19

WAR DIARY
or
INTELLIGENCE SUMMARY
(Erase heading not required).

Army Form C. 2118.

Place	Date	Hour	Summary of Events and Information	Remarks and references to Appendices
	4/5/16		The general standard of these men is much higher than with previous reinforcements	
	5/5/16		No 2 SECTION fired at LEVEL CROSSING At U.11.d 5½.0 also at U.17.d.2.5 BUILDINGS and on "Grande Hais farm" V 23.b.0.7 Total number of rounds expended 350 The Gun position was U 15 c.3 1½	
			There was a Gas alarm at 9-15 pm, men in Camp "Stood to" a message was received from the Brigade stating all was quiet on Divisional front and also on the front of the Division on our right The order to "Stand down" was given at 2 15 AM The alarm appeared to come from some distance to the South	
	6/5/16		One Gun of No 2 SECTION fired from Gun position U15.c.3½.1½ at U17.a.2.7 LEVEL CROSSING. 100 rounds were fired	
			The Company move from its line at B.8.a 2 10. to new lines at T20.a.9.2 in relief of 8th Battalion the Gordon Highlanders. Our late lines at B.8.a.2 10. were taken over by the 2nd South African Battalion	

BSD - B. M351/22/11. 12/15. 5000.

26th Infantry Brigade Machine Gun Company

Army Form C. 2118.

Instructions regarding War Diaries and Intelligence Summaries are contained in F. S. Regs., Part II, and the Staff Manual respectively. Title Pages will be prepared in manuscript.

20/

WAR DIARY
or
~~INTELLIGENCE SUMMARY~~

(Erase heading not required).

Place	Date	Hour	Summary of Events and Information	Remarks and references to Appendices
	7/5/16		27th Brigade Machine Gun Company relieved the 26th Brigade Machine Gun Company in the front line trenches	
	8/5/16		Nothing to report	
	9/5/16		Enemy Shelled TOUQUET BERTHE and CALVAIRE in the morning. In the former place a Shell Splinter entering through loop hole put one Gun out of action by piercing barrel casing, knocking off foresight and damaging muzzle attachment. In the latter place the Officer in occupation was forced to leave his billet and take to his dug out by three hits	
	10		Nothing to report from line. Transport Billet shelled with 6" gun about 6-pm	
	11		Nothing to report	
	12		During morning transport billet was again shelled, a waggon of the 24th Division was hit. Our own transport Animals were cleared out immediately and we had no casualties. In the course of the Afternoon the Camp was moved to B10 b33	
	13		At 6-30 pm on the 13th inst the enemy began an intensive bombardment of our line extending from PIQUET HOUSE locality to the left of T120, this lasted till 7-40 PM but was recommenced with renewed vigour between 7-50-PM and 8-45 PM. A German raiding party attempted to enter our trenches in the neighbourhood of HAMPSHIRE T only one or two entered our trench, these were dealt with by the infantry, some nine others were shot on the parapet by Lt Henry 11th Royal Scots and one man. The Germans made back to their trenches as fast as possible aided by our rifle fire. During the Bombardment our casualties were one killed two wounded	

BSD - B. M351.22/11. 12/15. 5000.

26th Infantry Brigade machine Gun Company

Army Form C. 2118.

Instructions regarding War Diaries and Intelligence Summaries are contained in F. S. Regs., Part II, and the Staff Manual respectively. Title Pages will be prepared in manuscript.

21

WAR DIARY
or
~~INTELLIGENCE SUMMARY~~

(Erase heading not required).

Place	Date	Hour	Summary of Events and Information	Remarks and references to Appendices
	14th		In the evening at 8.30 PM the Gun in T 127 fired at a working party at AVENUE END and dispersed them	
	15th		Nothing to report	
	16th		" " "	
	17th		Gas alarms	
	18th		Nothing to report	
	19th		The 27th Brigade machine Gun Company relieved the 26th Brigade machine Gun Company in front line trenches. Nos 2 & 1 teams of no 4 Section proceeded to transport lines, the remainder to Subsidiary line and supports	
	20th		Nothing to report	
	21st		" " "	
	22nd		" " "	
	23rd		" " "	
	24th		" " "	
	25th		The 26th Brigade machine Gun Company relieved the 27th Brigade machine Gun Company in front line trenches. Six offrs & 50 men of the 122nd machine Gun Company attached for instruction. Indirect fire by no SECTION from moated farm on LA BASSEVILLE HALT and PETIT HAIE FM between 9-30 PM and midnight. No 3 SECTION fired indirect from U26 b 9&1 between 5 PM and 8 PM on X road PONT ROUGE & U29 b 2Y TROIS TILLEULS U17 C12 & GRANDE HAIE FM U23 A 78	

BSD - B. M351/22/11. 12/15. 5000.

26th Infantry Brigade Machine Gun Company

Army Form C. 2118.

Instructions regarding War Diaries and Intelligence Summaries are contained in F. S. Regs., Part II, and the Staff Manual respectively. Title Pages will be prepared in manuscript.

WAR DIARY
or
~~INTELLIGENCE SUMMARY~~

22

(Erase heading not required).

Place	Date May	Hour	Summary of Events and Information	Remarks and references to Appendices
	26th		No 3. Section fired from the same place between 6 PM & 8 PM: Loophole Fm U22 d24; Trois Tilleuls U17 c12; X Rd Pont Rouge U29 b27 and	
			from U27 b80 between 7 pm and 8.00 pm: Basseville Warneton Rd U17 c80 - U18a 08; Huts Dug-outs Tracks U18a 24; Farm Wicarte U18 c 20; Deulemont Warneton Rd at U24 c0H; Two Hedges at U24 c80 U29 b8	
			During the day this same indefatigable section combed out various groups of trees behind the Hun line at the request of O/C 7th Seaforth Highlanders in search of Sniper	
	27th		Nothing to report	
	28th		The 26th Brigade Machine Gun Company was relieved in the front line trenches by the 122nd Brigade Machine Gun Company. One man per team and an officer per two sections were left in the line as instructors. The 26th Brigade Machine Gun Company in the turn relieved the 27th Brigade Machine Gun Coy in the Subsidiary line	
	29th		Nothing to report	

26th Infantry Brigade Machine Gun Coy

23

Army Form C. 2118.

IX 26 MG Coy Vol 4

WAR DIARY

~~INTELLIGENCE SUMMARY~~

(Erase heading not required).

Instructions regarding War Diaries and Intelligence Summaries are contained in F. S. Regs., Part II, and the Staff Manual respectively. Title Pages will be prepared in manuscript.

Place	Date	Hour	Summary of Events and Information	Remarks and references to Appendices
	May 30th		The 28th Brigade Machine Gun Company was relieved in the Subsidiary line by the 4th Motor Machine Gun battery. The two Guns of No 3 SECTION at CALVAIRE were relieved very late indeed, owing to the reliefs which should have been provided from the 28th Brigade Machine Gun Company not turning up. They did not leave until 11.45 AM instead of 6 AM as the relief was timed. Three teams stayed in a man per team was detailed to act as instructor in each case	
	31st		Remaining teams and men of the 28th Brigade Machine Gun Company were withdrawn from the line. The company marched out from billets by Section at 200 yards interval and halted at PONT D'Achilles, formed column of route and billeted for the night at 36A 24a	

26th Brigade Machine Gun Company

To/ D.A.G.

3rd Echelon

Herewith original copies of the War Diary of this Company for June 1916

S. Crawford Capt

30/6/16

O/c 26th Brigade Machine Gun Company

26th Infantry Brigade Machine Gun Company

24

Army Form C. 2118.

26 MG Coy
Vol 5

IX

WAR DIARY
or
~~INTELLIGENCE SUMMARY~~

(Erase heading not required).

Instructions regarding War Diaries and Intelligence Summaries are contained in F. S. Regs., Part II, and the Staff Manual respectively. Title Pages will be prepared in manuscript.

Place	Date	Hour	Summary of Events and Information	Remarks and references to Appendices
	1/6/16		The company paraded ready to move off at 5-15 PM. It marched from (36A 24a LA CRECHE billeting area) to DOULIEU when it arrived at 6-45 PM. Headquarters were at 36 a F30 c52.	June
	2/6/16		at "DOULIEU"	
	3/6/16		DOULIEU to MORBECQUE via VIEUX BERQUIN and LA MOTTE. The Brigade was inspected about 700 Yards after VIEUX BERQUIN by the Second Army Commander. The march commenced for BLEU F19 B73 at 3-50 PM and ended at 7-45 PM. No men fell out	
	4/6/16		MORBECQUE to LIETTRE VIA STEENBECQUE (Starting place for Brigade) BOESEGHEM – AIRE – WITTERNESSE. March started at 3-30 PM and ended at 7-45 PM. No men fell out	
	5/6/16		Checking equipment. Inspection. Examination of ground in training area	
	6/6/16		Gun mounting. Immediate action. Overhauling Belts	
	7/6/16		No I LINGHEM range for tap traversing, ranging fire, field firing. Nos 2 3 & 4 Sects Ammunition lines and taking up positions	
	8/6/16		No 2 LINGHEM range. Nos 1, 3 & 4 SECTIONS practised coming into action and overhead fire	
	9/6/16		No 3 SECTION LINGHEM RANGE. Nos 1, 2 & 4 SECTIONS Co-operated with Battalions practising phases of the attack – advance in Artillery formation and in extended order, Indirect overhead and direct overhead	

26th Brigade Machine Gun Company

25

Army Form C. 2118.

Instructions regarding War Diaries and Intelligence Summaries are contained in F. S. Regs., Part II, and the Staff Manual respectively. Title Pages will be prepared in manuscript.

WAR DIARY
or
INTELLIGENCE SUMMARY
(Erase heading not required).

Place	Date	Hour	Summary of Events and Information	Remarks and references to Appendices
	10/6/16		A scheme was carried out under Brigade arrangements. Nos 1 & 2 Sections formed the rear guard of a force. They had 12 Sharpshooters attached and were commanded by Lt Black. Nos 2 & 4 Sections commanded by Lieut Aldrich formed the advance guard of a pursuing force they also had 12 Sharpshooters attached. Reference Hazebrook 5 A Western rear guard was retiring along CUHEM ERNY COYECQUES road it cleared CUHEM moving in direction of ERNY at 9-30 AM. Eastern advance guard reached CUHEM at 10 AM. Western rear guard took up a position at ERNY each Section having two guns pushed forward to CUHEM side of the valley and two on the higher side near COYECQUES. Each Section had 2 Sharpshooters attached for its local protection. Pushed forward on either flank were two parties of 4 Sharpshooters commanding on the left flank the sunken CUHEM - ENQUIN road and on the right the BOMY Wood. The advanced Guns had orders to retire through those on the COYECQUES side of the valley, drop over the crest and proceed to the right to occupy some scattered trees. The Guns on the COYECQUES side of the valley had order to hold on till the enemy reached ERNY and then retire covered by the Guns which had retired before them. Limbers were on the COYECQUES side of the crest. All Guns used pack mules. The Eastern advance guard reached CUHEM and pushed forward their Sharpshooters and Scouts. Two Guns were despatched to the left flank to come through the wood, two to the right to use the sunken road. The remaining four advanced across the open, all arrived unseen by the left pair of advanced Guns — They were however located by the Guns in support who found the limbers, small knots of men and officers, excellent targets, despite the considerable range. The advanced Guns on the left retired unlocated when the enemy reached effective range. In his remarks after the fight the umpire pointed out that the methods of advance attempted by the Eastern advance guard were too slow, and that some Guns should have been brought into action	

BSD - B. M351/22/11. 12/15 5000.

Instructions regarding War Diaries and Intelligence Summaries are contained in F. S. Regs., Part II, and the Staff Manual respectively. Title Pages will be prepared in manuscript.

26th Brigade Machine Gun Company

26/

WAR DIARY

or

~~INTELLIGENCE SUMMARY~~

(Erase heading not required).

Army Form C. 2118.

Place	Date	Hour	Summary of Events and Information	Remarks and references to Appendices
	10/6/16		immediately on the crest along Cuhem to cover the advance of the remaining Guns and men. The action fought by the advance guard would have held up the main body more than a hour. The rear guard had occupied a position with great advantages in concealed approach to positions and an easy line of retreat. It would have been better to have one section pushed forward in the case of the rear guard and one occupying the heights. This would have rendered the command easier	
	11/6/16		Brigade training. The Brigade attacked a trench system marked out by flags, starting from trenches similarly marked out. A Section cooperated on either flank of the two leading Battalions, two guns going with the third, two with the fourth wave. The Section in Support sent two Guns to either flank, the right subsection being given as its objective the consolidation of cross roads some 1500 yards in front. The Section in reserve used overhead indirect fire to support the infantry and was ready to move to any spot required. Dumps had been organised in forward trenches near the spot where the pioneers were to dig the communication trenches to join up the old trenches and the enemy front line. These were under a corporal and were given before hand fixed places to move to on receipt of an order to advance	
	12/6/16		Brigade training. The Brigade advanced in Artillery formation on the edge of a wood. The objective of the leading Battalion was to capture and Consolidate enemy line in front of wood of the supports to clear wood and capture line in rear of wood. One Section was pushed forward on either flank to cover the advance from commanding ground on right and left. As the Battalions passed there Guns came out of action and advanced with them	

Instructions regarding War Diaries and Intelligence Summaries are contained in F. S. Regs., Part II, and the Staff Manual respectively. Title Pages will be prepared in manuscript.

24

26th Brigade Machine Gun Company WAR DIARY or INTELLIGENCE SUMMARY

(Erase heading not required).

Army Form C. 2118.

Place	Date	Hour	Summary of Events and Information	Remarks and references to Appendices
	12/6/16		Each Section had a carrying party of 20 men. During the advance a gap occurred between the two leading Battalions. The left Section immediately filled this with two Guns. The gap was however seen from in rear and one of the Sections in reserve sent up to fill it. When the front of the wood was captured and consolidation was in progress two limbers were sent forward with S.A.A. On returning from this day the Brigade was warned for entrainment	
	13/6/16		Packing and preparing to leave Billets	
	14/6/16		Standing by ready to move. One Battalion moves this night	
	15/6/16		The Transport paraded at 5 AM and moved to BERGUETTE. The Company moved off at 6 AM and marched there. The train started at 10.10 AM. About 6 pm the company arrived at LONGEAU and disentrained by 6.30 PM. It then marched to SAINT SAUVEUR where it arrived about 9 pm	
	16/6/16		Company rests. Officer Commanding and Second in Command go by to visit the trenches. Remaining officers proceed to Roman Camp to view replica trenches. In the afternoon these were explained to the men.	
	17/6/16		Lt Hilditch and 2nd Lt Mackenzie visit trenches. The Officer Commanding met Brigadier	
	18/6/16		2nd Lt Cowper and 2nd Lt Milnes visit trenches. Church parades for all the Company	
	19/6/16		2nd Lts Duffus and Wilson visited trenches. Company paraded carrying Guns, Tripods, and Ammunition, and marched to No 1 training area, where a short tactical exercise was carried out	

BSD - B. M351/22/11. 12/15 5000.

Instructions regarding War Diaries and Intelligence Summaries are contained in F. S. Regs., Part II, and the Staff Manual respectively. Title Pages will be prepared in manuscript.

Army Form C. 2118.

28

26th Brigade Machine Gun Company WAR DIARY ~~or INTELLIGENCE SUMMARY~~

(Erase heading not required).

Place.	Date	Hour	Summary of Events and Information	Remarks and references to Appendices
	20/6/16		The company went for a route march of 9 miles in Battle Order. Carrying parties, Sharpshooters Officers in Charge Carrying parties paraded under Captain Crawford for instruction in their duties 2nd Lt A. C. E. Snell and 2nd Lt C. A. Webster visited the trenches	
	21/6/16		The whole company together with carrying parties, sharpshooters, and transport, paraded under Captain Crawford at 9-15 AM and marched to No I area where the attack was practised in full, observing the orders laid down in Appendix A attached +	+ This Appendix will be forwarded next month with comments on the working of arrangements in action.
	22/6/16		The scheme was repeated and worked very satisfactorily	
	23/6/16		The company moved at 4-15 pm from SAINT SAUVEUR to LONGPRÉ	
	24/6/16		At LONGPRÉ	
	25/6/16		Transport started for CORBIE at 9-30 AM by road. The remainder of the Company paraded at 11-15 AM marched to Ailly and entrained for CORBIE They reached their new billet at 3-35 PM., The Transport arrived there very shortly afterwards	
	26/6/16		At CORBIE	
	27/6/16		The Company paraded at 9 PM and marched to WELCOME WOOD in rear of 8th BLACK WATCH and 5th CAMERON HIGHLANDERS. Enthusiasm in CORBIE	

BSD - B. M351/22/11. 12/15. 5000.

28th Brigade Machine 29 Gun Company

Army Form C. 2118.

Instructions regarding War Diaries and Intelligence Summaries are contained in F. S. Regs., Part II, and the Staff Manual respectively. Title Pages will be prepared in manuscript.

WAR DIARY
or
~~INTELLIGENCE SUMMARY~~

(Erase heading not required).

Place	Date	Hour	Summary of Events and Information	Remarks and references to Appendices
	28/6/16		Move from WELCOME WOOD postponed 48 hours	
	29/6/16		Inspections and practice in wood fighting. Arrival of Vickers Gun to replace old Maxim. This rendered unnecessary the reserve of 3 Maxim Gunners which had been formed especially for this Gun. These men accordingly returned to their Sections.	
	30		Inspections etc. Immediate action. The company paraded at 9-15 pm and marched to Celestin Wood.	

BSD - B. M351/22/11. 12/15. 5000.

26th Bde.
9th Division.

WAR DIARY

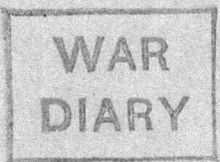

26th MACHINE GUN COMPANY.

JULY 1916

Operations on the Somme .

Attached:- Report on Operations 5th to 19th.

30

Instructions regarding War Diaries and Intelligence Summaries are contained in F. S. Regs., Part II, and the Staff Manual respectively. Title Pages will be prepared in manuscript.

WAR DIARY ~~or~~ INTELLIGENCE SUMMARY

(Erase heading not required).

1st Brigade machine Gun Company

Army Form C. 2118.

9 July

26 MG Coy

Vol 6

Place	1916 Date	Hour	Summary of Events and Information	Remarks and references to Appendices
	July 1st		This morning at 7 30 AM (apparently for we were not informed at what hour zero fell) the 18th and 30th Division of our Corps attacked and met seemingly with slight opposition. By the end of the day the had apparently occupied all the objectives set them, the Chief of which was MONTAUBAN. The Germans appear to have continued to occupy a very small part of the Village. On the left MAMETZ was Captured, and after an attempt of the Germans to recover DANZIG ALLEY had been frustrated it was Consolidated. The Company paraded at 8.30 and marched along X road to GROVE TOWN where it bivouacked.	S.C.
	2nd		At GROVETOWN. German counter attack on the BRICQUETERIE and the east face of the MONTAUBAN Salient was repulsed without difficulty, though consolidation in this latter place had made little or no progress. FRICOURT was attacked without bombardment by the 17th Division which then pressed on and took SHELTER WOOD and BOTTOM WOOD	S.C.
	3rd		At GROVETOWN. About 1 AM the Germans are said to have counter attacked in force the position of the French on our right. The date of above mentioned operation by 17th Division is not actually known by us. This day news came that 15th Corps have captured BIRCH TREE WOOD and SHELTER WOOD also RAILWAY ALLEY also BOTTOM WOOD taking 1100 prisoners. FRENCH reported to have captured FLAUCOURT	S.C.
	4th		News received that 27th Infantry Brigade had captured BERNAFAY WOOD and TRENCH running from N.W. corner of wood to S.28 A 08 during the night taking 3 German Field Guns and 5 machine Guns.	S.C.

Instructions regarding War Diaries and Intelligence Summaries are contained in F. S. Regs., Part II, and the Staff Manual respectively. Title Pages will be prepared in manuscript.

Army Form C. 2118.

WAR DIARY or INTELLIGENCE SUMMARY

7th Brigade Machine Gun Company

(Erase heading not required).

Place	1916 Date	Hour	Summary of Events and Information	Remarks and references to Appendices
	July 4th		The FRENCH colonial Corps on the left bank of the SOMME was reported to have occupied FEULLERES, BOUSCOURT and CHADTER WOOD thence to point 97. The FRENCH were also holding FLAUCOURT and ASSEVILLERS and had pushed forward a troop of cavalry to reconnoitre towards BIACHES and BARLAUX as they could find no enemy. The 26th Infantry Brigade moved up to BILLON VALLEY TRIGGER VALLEY and COPSE VALLEY No 1 SECTION had orders to report to 26th Brigade Machine Gun Company in COPSE VALLEY by 8 PM, so left under 2nd Lt P.B. Duffus The carrying party accompanied the Section and was commanded by 2nd Lt Mackenzie 8th Black Watch. The remaining Sections had their carrying parties paraded along with transport and Headquarters at 8.30 and marched off. The Officers were 2nd Lieut Mackenzie no 2 SECTION and 2nd Lieut Gauldie (8th Black Watch) as his carrying officer Lt Hilditch no 3 SECTION and 2nd Lieut Jones 5th Cameron Highlanders as his carrying Officer. 2nd Lt Webster no 4 SECTION and 2nd Lieut Brown 5th Cameron Highlanders as carrying Officer. 2nd Lieut J. Milne O.C. dump and ammunition lines the CSM Working under him. The whole was commanded by Capt S Crawford The following Officers were left at GROVETOWN { Lieut J A Black Second in Command 2nd " S A Cowper Transport Officer 2nd " K B Wilson Officer of no 2 SECTION 2nd " A C E Scott " " " 3 " The Wagons were left up in TRIGGER VALLEY the Animals returned back to GROVETOWN for the night	S C

Instructions regarding War Diaries and Intelligence Summaries are contained in F. S. Regs., Part II, and the Staff Manual respectively. Title Pages will be prepared in manuscript.

Army Form C. 2118.

WAR DIARY or INTELLIGENCE SUMMARY

26th Brigade Machine Gun Company

(Erase heading not required).

Place	Date 1916	Hour	Summary of Events and Information	Remarks and references to Appendices
	5th July		The 26th Brigade Machine Gun Company took over positions held by 21st Brigade Machine Gun Company in GLATZ REDOUBT at 5 PM. Lieut Aldrich with 4 Guns, 20 Carriers under 2nd Lieut Jones 5th Cameron Highlanders and 5 Sharp shooters, took over these positions	S.C.
	6th July		The O.C. 26th Brigade Machine Gun Company considered that the Gun positions formerly held by 21st Brigade Machine Gun Company not satisfactory reported same to Brigade Head Quarters. These Guns were removed to positions which commanded a better field of fire. 2nd Lieut. J. McInnes and 2nd Lieut K. J. Mackenzie of the Company were sent at 2 AM to inspect positions for Guns to cover the advance of the troops on the attack of LONGUEVAL	S.C.
	7th July		The O.C of the Company visited the proposed positions for Guns to cover the Infantry attack. The positions were situated about 200 Yards in front of MONTAUBAN. S 22 C 8 2 and had been used by the ENEMY for the light Artillery	S.C.
	8th July		The Company left TRIGGER VALLEY at 2.30 PM and arrived at TALUS BOISE at 3.45 PM. 2nd Lieut P.B. Duffus and 2nd Lieut C.A. Webster were sent with 8 Guns to relieve the 27th Brigade Machine Gun Company. 5 Guns were posted in MONTAUBAN 2 Guns S 24 b 2½ 1½. 3 in line S 24 b 5½ 4 – S 27 b 9.4½ 2 in S 28. a 3 0½ and 1 in BERNAFAY S 22 d 9.1. Casualties Sergt C.W. Taylor Killed and Pte W. Castles Wounded both of No 4 SECTION	S.C.

33

Instructions regarding War Diaries and Intelligence Summaries are contained in F. S. Regs., Part II, and the Staff Manual respectively. Title Pages will be prepared in manuscript.

WAR DIARY ~~or~~ INTELLIGENCE SUMMARY

9th Brigade Machine Gun Company

(Erase heading not required).

Army Form C. 2118.

Place	Date 1916	Hour	Summary of Events and Information	Remarks and references to Appendices
	9th July		Remainder of Company moved from TALUKS BOISE during the afternoon and took up positions in SILESIA AVENUE (late enemy first line) Lieut Hilditch was relieved by 28th Brigade Machine Gun Company and under orders from O.C. took up positions with 2nd Lieut Mackenzie at 3.30 AM in front of MONTAUBAN (S 22c 8 2) These Guns were to cover the advance of our troops on the assault of LONGUEVAL They remained in these positions until 3 AM on the morning of the 10th when the were recalled to Company HEADQUARTERS Lieut Hilditch was detailed to leave 2 Guns in BERNAFAY WOOD S 22 D 9 1 Casualties Pte R Pelbeam Killed Pte J W Barclay wounded The Gun at S 22 d 9 1 was put out of action by Shell Splinters and was replaced by one of the reserve Guns from SILESIA AVENUE.	S.C.
	10th July		6 Guns returned to SILESIA AVENUE 2 of No 3 SECTION + 4 of No 3 SECTION Casualties Privates W McFetridge J Glennie and Private Rennie were wounded	S.C.
	11th July		Lce Corp J Shaw was killed Pte F Smith was Wounded	S.C.
	12th July		2nd Lieut T Milne relieved Lieut Hilditch with two teams from reserve	S.C.

BSD - B. M351/22/11. 12/15. 5000.

34

Instructions regarding War Diaries and Intelligence Summaries are contained in F. S. Regs., Part II, and the Staff Manual respectively. Title Pages will be prepared in manuscript.

Army Form C. 2118.

WAR DIARY
26th Brigade Machine ~~or~~ Gun Company
~~INTELLIGENCE SUMMARY~~
(Erase heading not required).

Place	Date 1916	Hour	Summary of Events and Information	Remarks and references to Appendices
	13th July		Heavy bombardment of LONGUEVAL. On being relieved in the position held by them No I SECTION under 2nd Lieut P B Duffus proceeded to MONTAUBAN ALLEY. Lieut Hilditch and two teams joined the remaining two teams situated at S22 d.9.1 No 4 SECTION joined No 2 SECTION in Reserve in SILESIA AVENUE A3 d 1.0 and then came under 2nd Lt Y Milne, who had been relieved by Lieut Hilditch. The Company was thus distributed as follows MONTAUBAN ALLEY 2 Sections Nos 1 and 3 8 Guns SILESIA TRENCH 2 " Nos 2 and 4 8 Guns	S.C
	14th July		The situation at the moment of attack appears to have been as follows During the days preceeding the attack, the troops on the left after seizing CATERPILLAR WOOD, MALBOROUGH COPSE, CONTALMAISON, had passed through MAMETZ WOOD, which was now entirely in our hands. While this fighting was in progress on the left, TRONES WOOD had changed hands several times, and on the morning of 14th inst was practically entirely in the enemys hands. The attack on the German 2nd line had thus to be accompanied by an attack by the 18th Division on this wood. The 9th Division attacked the enemys second line between S14 d 7.8 on the right and S16 b 6.5 on the left. On the left of the 9th Division the 3rd Division was also attacking. The 26th Brigade attacked on the right, the 27th Brigade on the left, the boundary between Brigades being line S22 d 2.5 – S.14 a 9.3. The South African Brigade being in reserve. The leading Battalions of the Brigade were the 8th Black Watch on the right and the 10th Argyll & Sutherland Highlanders on the left. The boundary between these two Battalions was the BERNAFAY WOOD LONGUEVAL ROAD (exclusive to right Battalion) The 7th Seaforth Highlanders were in Support, with orders to follow the 10th A & S Highlanders. The heads of the two leading Battalions were to cross the BERNAFAY MONTAUBAN ROAD, 3 hours before zero, and deploy on their markers	S.C.

35

Instructions regarding War Diaries and Intelligence Summaries are contained in F. S. Regs., Part II, and the Staff Manual respectively. Title Pages will be prepared in manuscript.

WAR DIARY

26th Brigade Machine Gun Company

or

INTELLIGENCE SUMMARY

(Erase heading not required).

Army Form C. 2118.

Place	Date 1916	Hour	Summary of Events and Information	Remarks and references to Appendices
14th	July		in front of MONTAUBAN ALLEY. The two Sections of this Company (28th Bdge & 9 Coy in MONTAUBAN ALLEY, were ordered to follow in rear of the Battalion in Support	
			Objectives were assigned as follows 8th Black Watch — First: VILLAGE on E Side of BERNAFAY LONGUEVAL ROAD up to enemy Support line. Strong points S 14 d 3 9, S 14 b 8.1	
			S18.c.8 9½ SECOND: E of above road up to CLARGES STREET to S.18 C 8 9	
			THIRD: Bounded by PRINCES & BUCHANAN St	
			10th A & S H. Strong points S 17 b 1.4, S 17 a 6 2 — FIRST: VILLAGE on W Side of BERNAFAY LONGUEVAL ROAD up to Enemy Support line	S.C.
			SECOND: up to CLARGES St West of above road	
			7th Seaforth Hrs Strong points WATERLOT FARM: Enemy System of Works from LONGUEVAL to WATERLOT latter inclusive.	

BSD - B. M351/22/11. 12/15. 5000.

Army Form C. 2118.

Instructions regarding War Diaries and Intelligence Summaries are contained in F. S. Regs., Part II, and the Staff Manual respectively. Title Pages will be prepared in manuscript.

WAR DIARY or INTELLIGENCE SUMMARY

26th Brigade Machine Gun Company

(Erase heading not required).

Place	Date 1916	Hour	Summary of Events and Information	Remarks and references to Appendices
14th	July		Under cover of our Artillery bombardment, the infantry were to advance and assault the hostile trenches, zero being at 3.25 AM. The defences fell practically immediately, with the exception of the N.W. Corner of the Village. At 3.35 AM Nos 1 & 3 Machine Gun Sections left MONTAUBAN ALLEY, in rear of 7th Seaforth Hrs. No 1 moving by teams in file with (carriers) at 50 yards interval for the first 500 hundred yards, and afterwards extending to about 5 paces, and No 3 advancing all the while in extended order. These Sections reached LONGUEVAL at about 4.30 AM. No 1 SECTION reached the Village with casualties and brought Guns into action as follows.	
			1 Gun S17a 9.4. Supporting A & S Hrs	
			1 Gun S17b 4.4 } 1 Gun S17b 8.5 } 1 Gun S17b 10.5 } Supporting BLACK WATCH	S. C.
			Of these Guns, that at S.17 b 5.5 found suitable targets in small parties of the enemy retiring from various houses, while the Gun S17 b 8.5. inflicted a considerable number of casualties on other Groups of the enemy who had been dislodged from the VILLAGE and driven towards DELVILLE WOOD. The above positions were occupied by this SECTION practically without change until relieved by No 4 on the 16th inst. No 3 SECTION on the right on reaching LONGUEVAL assumed positions around S17 D 4.5 where they remained in position most of the day. From this position good targets were obtained, two Guns firing straight down on a Section of 7.7 C.M. which were causing considerable damage firing from S. edge DELVILLE WOOD. The fire of the Guns was kept down by our Guns until they moved more to the right. At about 4.20 PM when the 7th Seaforth and	

BSD - B. M351/22/11. 12/15. 5000.

37

Instructions regarding War Diaries and Intelligence Summaries are contained in F. S. Regs., Part II, and the Staff Manual respectively. Title Pages will be prepared in manuscript.

Army Form C. 2118.

WAR DIARY ~~or~~ INTELLIGENCE SUMMARY

26th Brigade Machine Gun Company

(Erase heading not required).

Place	Date	Hour	Summary of Events and Information	Remarks and references to Appendices
14th	July		and 5th Cameron Highlanders entered SOUTHERN corner of DELVILLE WOOD the enemy retiring in direction of WATERLOT FARM kept exposing themselves and affording good targets at an extra Shallow piece of about S.18. C 6 5 Many casualties were inflicted on the enemy at this point Another of no 3 SECTION'S guns laid on a doorway at WATERLOT FM. succeeding in putting many of the enemy out of action At about 4 pm no 2 SECTION came up and assumed position at the following points Two Guns under Sergt MITCHELL in strong point at S18 C 2 9, firing along the Southern edge of DELVILLE WOOD 1 Gun at S 17 d.14 in reserve 1 " " S 17 d.46 firing along N of SUNKEN ROAD Casualties 2nd Lt K.F. Mackenzie Killed Ptes Buchanan and D Smith Wounded attached men 13 Wounded 2 Killed	S.C.
15th	July		During this period ~~the~~ fighting round the N.W. corner of the VILLAGE which still remained in the enemys hand was practically continuous. The South African Brigade were also engaged in clearing DELVILLE WOOD No1 SECTION remained as before One Gun of No2 SECTION which was in reserve at S17 d 1.4 moved forward to S.18 C 4.7. to fire due EAST The other Guns of this Section maintained the positions 2nd Lt Webster took charge of this SECTION at 3 - PM The Guns of no 3 SECTION were moved to the following positions 1 Gun in C.T running from LONGUEVAL TRONES WOOD at S.18. C.4.5 1 Gun at S 17 d 5.5 firing in front to trench running EAST OF VILLAGE 1 Gun at S 17 d 6 4 firing N.E. & S.E. ~~this gun~~ could cover any retirement or advance on WATERLOT FM with overhead fire 1 Gun in reserve at S.17 a 8.3. this gun had been moved down the previous evening to cover any attack which might be made from	S.C

38

Army Form C. 2118.

Instructions regarding War Diaries and Intelligence Summaries are contained in F. S. Regs., Part II, and the Staff Manual respectively. Title Pages will be prepared in manuscript.

WAR DIARY
25th Brigade Machine Gun Company
INTELLIGENCE SUMMARY

(Erase heading not required).

Place	Date 1916	Hour	Summary of Events and Information	Remarks and references to Appendices
	15th July		the EAST, but had been moved back to the above position because of heavy shelling directed on the gun itself. DELVILLE WOOD was defended by the 25th Brigade Machine Gun Company as follows	
			1 Gun at S 11 a 5.7 2 Guns at S 18 b 9.7	S.C.
			2 Guns " S 12 c 5.9 2 " " S 18 b 6.3	
			1 Gun " S 12 c 7.6 1 Gun " S 18 b 7.1	
			1 " " S 12 d 6.4	
			2 Guns " S 12 d 6.a	

39

Army Form C. 2118.

Instructions regarding War Diaries and Intelligence Summaries are contained in F. S. Regs., Part II, and the Staff Manual respectively. Title Pages will be prepared in manuscript.

WAR DIARY or INTELLIGENCE SUMMARY

26th Brigade Machine Gun Company

(Erase heading not required).

Place	Date 1916	Hour	Summary of Events and Information	Remarks and references to Appendices
16th	July		No 4 Section was ordered to move off in support of the 1st South African Brigade 2nd Lieut J Milne reported to O.C 1st South African Battalion at 9 AM. Two of his guns were put into position at S.17 b 8.5½ to support 4th South African Battalion, two guns remained in reserve in dug out at S.17 b 7.3. No action by these guns is reported. At about 7 PM they proceeded to relieve no 1 SECTION in its positions. On relief they proceeded back to reserve in MONTAUBAN. One Gun of No 2 SECTION in position at S.18 c.3.9 was blown up by the enemy's Shell fire, this Gun was returned to Ordnance and was replaced by Gun of no. 3 SECTION taken from S.18.c.4.5	S.C.
17th	July		Nos 1 and 2 Guns of No 4 SECTION were withdrawn to S.17 d 7.8 to allow of bombardment of N of LONGUEVAL by our Artillery. In this position they apparently remained until after the counter attack on the afternoon of the 18th inst. In the course of the afternoon, the enemy having been reported to be digging himself in along road S.17 a 4.2 – S.10 b. 3.5, the Gun of no 3 SECTION at S.17 d 6.4. was moved to S.17 a. 8.3 and fired some 800 rounds indirect in short bursts. At 11 PM No 4 Gun of No 4 SECTION under Sergt Davidson perceived a party of the enemy about fifteen strong close on them, the Gun opened raked fire. The enemy who succeeded in reaching to within 15 yards of the Gun was driven off after having thrown about 100 Bombs.	S.C.
18th	July		Early in the morning the N.W end of the VILLAGE OF LONGUEVAL was captured from the enemy. Two Guns were moved North to assist in the consolidation of the newly won Terrain. 1 Gun from No 2 SECTION moved from S.17 d 4.6 to S.17 b 2.9 to cover consolidation being carried out by Gordons and Kings Own Battalions in front of the VILLAGE. One Gun of no 3 SECTION was moved from S.17 a 8.3 to S.11 d 4.2.	S.C.

BSD - B. M351,22/11 12/15 5000.

40

Instructions regarding War Diaries and Intelligence Summaries are contained in F. S. Regs., Part II, and the Staff Manual respectively. Title Pages will be prepared in manuscript.

WAR DIARY
or
INTELLIGENCE SUMMARY

26th Brigade Machine Gun Company

(Erase heading not required).

Army Form C. 2118.

Place	Date	Hour	Summary of Events and Information	Remarks and references to Appendices
18th	July		The position of the Guns of this Company at about 8 AM on this morning was as follows NO I SECTION all 4 Guns in [illegible] at MONTAUBAN No 2 do 1 Gun at S 17 b 2.9 1 Gun " S 18 c 3.9 1 Gun " S 18 c 4.7 No 3 SECTION 1 Gun at S 17 b 7.5 to which point an Officer (name unknown) had moved it from the Strong point at S 18 c 3.9 without notifying or consulting the Machine Gun Officer 1 Guns at S 11 d 4 2 1 Gun " S 17 d 4 5 1 Gun " S 17 d 4 7. NO 4 SECTION 1 Gun at S 17 a 9.4. 1 Gun " S 17 b 4 4 2 Guns " S 17 d 7.8 These last two Guns not having been moved since the bombardment of the enemy in the N of the Village on the morning of the 19th inst	S.C.

BSD - B. M351.22/11. 12/15. 5000.

Instructions regarding War Diaries and Intelligence Summaries are contained in F. S. Regs., Part II, and the Staff Manual respectively. Title Pages will be prepared in manuscript.

41

WAR DIARY

[illegible]th Brigade Machine Gun Company

INTELLIGENCE SUMMARY

(Erase heading not required).

Army Form C. 2118.

Place	Date	Hour	Summary of Events and Information	Remarks and references to Appendices
18th	July		At about 8 AM the enemy began a systematic bombardment of our position concentrating particularly on DELVILLE WOOD. This bombardment he maintained throughout the day. The Guns of no 2 Section report he was particularly reckless and that the Sharpshooters attached to the Gun at S 18 c 3 9 succeeded in bringing down a number of single men. At about 3 - PM the bombardment lifted so as to form a barrage in rear of the village, and the enemy infantry was seen to advance from the direction of FLERS on DELVILLE WOOD and the N of the Village of LONGUEVAL and from GINCHY on the S and S.E. edge of DELVILLE WOOD. On the N. the Guns at S 17 b 2 9 and S 11 d 4 2 saw the enemy as soon as he topped the ridge in front and opened fire at about 800 yards ~~[illegible]~~ as he advanced. At this point he appears to have advanced by groups of from 25 - 30 men at 30 - 50 yards distance. He thus afforded a good target and considerable damage was inflicted on him in spite of the fact that the smoke of shells rendered observation difficult. The Gun at S 11 d 4 2 maintained a steady traversing fire in short bursts, the Gun at S 17 b 2 9 firing bursts of 50. The enemy advance seems to have been hung momentarily by this fire, but shortly afterwards got under weigh again. By this time the infantry supporting the right gun had retired. The Gun however was laid on a place where the sparseness of the crops rendered the enemy's movements more easily observed. At first tap traversing was used but after 100 rounds it was apparent that this method was not developing sufficient volume of fire to check the considerable number of the	S.C.

BSD - B. M351/22/11. 12/15. 5000.

Instructions regarding War Diaries and Intelligence Summaries are contained in F. S. Regs., Part II, and the Staff Manual respectively. Title Pages will be prepared in manuscript.

WAR DIARY
26th Brigade Machine Gun Company
or
INTELLIGENCE SUMMARY
(Erase heading not required).

Army Form C. 2118.

Place	Date	Hour	Summary of Events and Information	Remarks and references to Appendices
18th	July		enemy advancing, and 33 belts were fired using loose traversing fire with excellent results. This Gun continued to check the enemys advance towards DELVILLE WOOD, until a party of the enemy had all but cut off its retreat by crawling down a Gully on its left. By this time the Gun on the left had been ordered to retire, it had only one belt box left. On leaving its first position it passed down the W of the village of LONGUEVAL and finally took up position at S.17 d 6.7 only Sergt Airey and one man being still in action. The right Gun retired Southwards and after narrowly escaping capture at about S.17 b 6.7 finally came into action again at S 17 d 7.9 only Sergt Richmond and one man being left. On these Guns retiring the enemy pressed on into the village. Before the attack the Gun at S 17. a 9 4 under Sergt Davidson had been subjected to heavy shelling which destroyed 13 belt boxes and the spare parts. It had jammed slightly and was being cleaned when a shell killed the man who was cleaning it and destroyed the feed block, and had been sent back to the reserve, whilst the team commander and men retired to S 17 d 7.8. About 3.30 PM the Gun of No 3 SECTION at S 14 b 7.3 was buried under falling brick work, the shelling and the enemy attack preventing its extraction. As the attack was in progress from the N.E. the Guns at S 18 c 3.9 and S.18. c 4.7 sighted the enemy advancing from GINCHY on the S.E. edge of DELVILLE WOOD. The enemy is reported to have advanced in extended order at this point. The guns using a slow swing traverse, believe that they were able to prevent any of the enemy from crossing their front. No enemy approached these Guns in the course of their counter attack. The enemy entered the EAST edge of the wood however and pushed in through it converging on the strong point at S 14 b 4.4.	

Army Form C. 2118.

Instructions regarding War Diaries and Intelligence Summaries are contained in F. S. Regs., Part II, and the Staff Manual respectively. Title Pages will be prepared in manuscript.

WAR DIARY

43

76th Brigade Machine Gun Company

INTELLIGENCE SUMMARY

(Erase heading not required).

Place	Date 1916	Hour	Summary of Events and Information	Remarks and references to Appendices
	18th July		[illegible] The enemy were in possession of the barricade at S 14 b 4.6 and was advancing from the direction of the Church and houses on its right. The Gun accordingly retired to S 14 d.7.9. after firing several bursts. This Gun however moved forward again with the first of the infantry and occupied its old position. On coming into action it observed about 30 of the enemy sheltered behind the barricade. It emptied a belt into the barricade, which appeared not to be bullet proof as the enemy immediately ceased to hold it. The Gun was then moved back a few yards to fire down the road EAST NORTH EAST from its position. At this period the Sharpshooter attached was very useful in keeping down the fire of the enemys snipers in the vicinity of the Church, of whom he was able to kill or wound several. As our Infantry advanced through the S W corner of DELVILLE WOOD, the enemy began retiring in small parties across the road covered by our Gun and suffered considerable number of casualties from the firing of this Gun which expended over 800 rounds. At 4.30 PM No 1 SECTION which was in reserve at MONTAUBAN received orders to reinforce this Section, after passing through a very heavy barrage took up position as follows under command of O.C. Company. S 17 c 7.9 S 14 d 2.4 S 17 b 5.5 S 14 D 8.8	

BSD - B. M351/22/11. 12/15. 5000.

44

Instructions regarding War Diaries and Intelligence Summaries are contained in F. S. Regs., Part II, and the Staff Manual respectively. Title Pages will be prepared in manuscript.

WAR DIARY or INTELLIGENCE SUMMARY

26th Brigade Machine Gun Company

(Erase heading not required).

Army Form C. 2118.

Place	Date	Hour	Summary of Events and Information	Remarks and references to Appendices
18th	July		At this moment 2nd Lt Snell arrived to replace Lt Fielditch who had been wounded whilst visiting his Gun at S 11 d 4 2, this officer had been previously wounded on the 14th inst. While the Infantry was attacking on the S W corner of DELVILLE WOOD 2nd Lieut J Milne, leaving 1 Gun at S 17 d 7 8, led another to support this movement. He gained a point about S 18 a 2 4, but was forced to retire, on the Infantry withdrawing. While this action in progress the Gun an team with the exception of 1 man were all wiped out by a shell 2nd Lt J Milne receiving a severe wound in the eye. Shortly after the Gun of No 4 SECTION, had re-established itself at S 17 b 4 4, Sergeant Richmonds Gun pushed forward to S 17 b 7 4. Here the Gun did much to keep down the enemys sniping activity from the direction of the Churchyard, and put out of action several small groups of men. On the evening of the 18th the Guns were thus disposed of as follows	S.K.

No 1 SECTION	No 2 SECTION	No 3 SECTION	No 4 SECTION
As above	1 Gun S 18 c 3 9	1 Gun S 17 b 7.4.	1 Gun S 17 d 7 8
	1 " S 18 c 4 7	1 " S 17 b 4.5.	1 " S 17 b 4.4.
	1 " S 17 d 6.7	1 " S 17 d 4 7	
	1 " out of action	1 " out of action	2 " out of action

S.K.

Place	Date	Hour	Summary of Events and Information	Remarks and references to Appendices
19th	July		2nd Lieut K B Wilson took over No. 2 SECTION. 10 30 PM Company drawn out of LONGUEVAL	

45

WAR DIARY

26th Brigade Machine Gun Company

or

INTELLIGENCE SUMMARY

(Erase heading not required).

Army Form C. 2118.

Instructions regarding War Diaries and Intelligence Summaries are contained in F. S. Regs., Part II, and the Staff Manual respectively. Title Pages will be prepared in manuscript.

Place	Date 1916	Hour	Summary of Events and Information	Remarks and references to Appendices
20th	July		Company moves to SAND PIT VALLEY	S.C.
21st	"		at SAND PIT VALLEY	S.C.
22nd	"		at SAND PIT VALLEY	S.C.
23rd	"		Company moves off for MERICOURT L'ABBE to entrain. The train moved off very late at 1 30 AM	S.C.
24th	"		Arrived at HANGEST SUR SOMME. Marched to VILLERS SUR AILLY	S.C.
25th	"		Paraded ready to move off at 4.30 AM and marched to LONDPRE LES CORPS SAINTES. Entrained and started for BRYAS at 7.41 AM. On arrival at BRYAS disentrained and marched to BRUAY	S.C.
26th	"		At BRUAY. Inspection for deficiencies in fighting kit	S.C.
27th	"		at BRUAY	S.C.
28th	"		Moved off marching with Brigade Starting at 9 30 AM CAMBLAIN L'ABBE Reached CAMBLAIN L'ABBE at about 1 30 PM	S.C.
29th	"		at CAMBLAIN L'ABBE Received draft of 12 men	S.C.
30th	"		at CAMBLAIN L'ABBE Received draft of 28 " and two officers 2nd Lieut B.E. Hughes and 2nd Lieut D.W. Adams. 2nd Lieut D G MUNRO reported for duty from 7th SEAFORTH HLRS and is taken on the strength of the Company	S.C.

S. Crawford Capt
1.8.16 O.C. 26' Bde M. G. Coy

BSD - B. M351/22/11. 12/15 5000.

26th Bde M.G.C. War Diary - 5.7.16. - 19.7.16

5-7-16. The 26th Bde.M.G.Coy. took over gun positions held by 21st Bde.M.G.Coy. in GLATZ REDOUBT at 5 p.m. Lieut. HILDITCH with 4 guns, 20 carriers under 2/Lt.JONES, 5th Camerons, and 5 sharpshooters, took over these positions.

6-7-16. The O.C.,26th Bde.M.G.Coy. considered that the gun positions formerly held by 21st Bde.M.G.Coy. were not satisfactory, reported same to Bde.H.Q. These guns were moved to positions which commanded a better field of fire. 2/Lt T.MILNE and 2/Lt.K.F.MACKENZIE of this Company were sent at 2a.m. to inspect positions for guns to cover the advance for troops on the attack of LONGUEVAL.

7-7-16. The O.C.Coy. visited the proposed positions for guns to cover the Infantry attack. These positions were situated about 200 yards in front of MONTAUBAN (S.22.c.8.2.) and had been used by the enemy for their light artillery.

8-7-16. The Company left TRIGGER VALLEY at 2.30 p.m. and arrived at TALUS BOISE 3.45 p.m. 2/Lt.P.DUFFERS and 2/LT.C.A.WELSH were sent with 8 guns to relieve the 27th Bde. M.G.Coy. 5 guns were posted in MONTAUBAN; 2 guns S.27.b.2½.1½.3 in line S.27.b.5½.4.-S.27.b.9.4½., 2 at S.28.a.3.0½. and 1 gun in BERNAFAY WOOD, S.22.d.9.1. Casualties Sgt.A.W.TAYLOR(Killed) and Pte.W.CASTLES (Wounded), both of No.4.Section.

9.7-16. Remainder of Compnay moved from TALUS BOISE during the afternoon and took up positions in SILESIA AVENUE (late enemy's first line) Lt.HILDITCH was relieved by the 28th Bde.M.G.Coy. and under orders from O.C.took up positions with 2/Lt.MACKENZIE at 3-30 a.m. in front of MONTAUBAN (S.22.c.8.2.). These guns were to cover the advance of our troops on the assault of LONGUEVAL. They remained in these positions until 3 a.m.on the morning of the 10th, when they were recalled to Company H.Q. Lt.HILDITCH was detailed to leave two guns in BERNAFAY WOOD. (S.22.d.9.1.) Casualties - Pte.R.PILBEAN was killed and Pte.J.W. BARCLAY was wounded. The gun at S.22.d.9.1. was put out of action by shell splinters and was replaced by one of the reserve guns from SILESIA AVENUE.

10-7-16. 6 guns returned to SILESIA AVENUE (2 of No.3 Section and 4 of No.2) Casualties Ptes.W.McFETERIDGE, J.GLENNIE and PTE. RENNIE were wounded.

11-7-16. L/Cpl. J.SHAW was killed and Pte. F.SMITH was wounded.

12-7-16. 2/Lt.T.MILNE relieved Lt.HILDITCH with two teams from the reserve.

13-7-16. Heavy bombardment of LONGUEVAL. On being relieved in the position held by them, No.1 Section under 2/Lt.P.DUFFERS proceeded to MONTAUBAN ALLEY. Lt.HILDITCH and two teams joined his remaining two teams situated at S.22.d.9.1.No.4 Section joined No.2 Section in reserve in SILESIA AVENUE A.3.d.10.and then came under 2/Lt.T.MILNE who had been relieved by Lt.HILDITCH. The Company was thus distributed as follows :-

MONTAUBAN ALLEY.	2 Sections	Nos.1 and 3.	8 Guns.
SILESIA TRENCH.	2 "	Nos.2 and 4.	8 "

14-7-16. The situation at the moment of attack appears to have been as follows. During the days preceeding the attack the troops on the left, after seizing CATAPILLAR WOOD, MALBOROUGH COPSE CONTALMAISON, had pressed on through MAMETZ WOOD, which was now

entirely/

entirely in our hands. While this fighting was in progress on the left, TRONES WOOD had changed hands several times and on the morning of the 14th inst. was practically entirely in the enemy's hands. The attack on the German second line had thus to be accompanied by an attack by the 18th Division on this wood. The 9th Division attacked the enemy's second line between S.17.d.7.8. on the right and S.16.b.6.5. on the left. On the left of the 9th Division the 3rd Division was also attacking. The 26th Brigade attacked on the right, the 27th Brigade on the left, the boundary between Brigades being line S.22.d.2.5.-S.17.a.9.3. The South African Brigade being in reserve. The leading battalions of the Brigade were the 8th Black Watch on the right and the 10th A.& S. Highlanders on the left. The boundary between these two Battalions was the BERNAFAY WOOD-LONGUEVAL ROAD (Exclusive to right Battn) The 7th Seaforth Hrs. were in support, with orders to follow the 10th A.& S.Hrs. The heads of the two leading battalions were to cross the BERNAFAY-MONTAUBAN Road 3 hours before zero, and deploy on their markers in front of MONTAUBAN ALLEY. By ½ hour before zero the 7th Seaforth Hrs. were to form up in MONTAUBAN ALLEY. The two Sections of this Company (26th Bde.M.G.Coy) in MONTAUBAN ALLEY were ordered to follow in rear of this battalion in support. Objectives were assigned as follows:-

<u>8th Black Watch.</u> Strong Points. S.17.d.3.9. S.17.b.8.1. S.18.c.2.9½.	<u>First.</u>	Village on E.side of BERNAFAY-LONGUEVAL ROAD up to enemy support line
	<u>Second.</u>	E.of above road up to CLARGES STREET to S.18.c.2.9.
	<u>Third.</u>	Bounded by PRINCES & BUCHANAN Streets.
<u>10th A.&S.Hrs.</u> Strong Points. S.17.b.1.4. S.17.a.6.2.	<u>First.</u>	Village on W.side of BERNAFAY -LONGUEVAL Road up to enemy support line.
	<u>Second.</u>	Up to CLARGES STREET west of above road.
<u>7th Seaforth Hrs.</u> Strong Points. WATERLOT FARM.		Enemy system of works from LONGUEVAL to WATERLOT, latter inclusive.

Under cove of our artillery bombardment the infantry were to advance and assault the hostile trenches, zero being at 3.25 a.m. The defences fell practically immediately, with the exception of the N.W.corner of the Village. At 3.25 a.m. Nos.1 & 3 M.G.Sections left MONTAUBAN ALLEY in rear of the 7th Seaforths No.1 moving by teams in file (with carriers) at 50 yds.interval for the first five hundred yards, and afterwards extending to about 5 paces, and No.3 advancing all the while in extended order. These sections reached LONGUEVAL at about 4.30 a.m. No.1 Section reached the village without casualties and brought its guns into action as follows:-

1 gun S.17.a.9.4. supporting A.& S.Hrs.
1 gun S.17.b.4.4.)
1 gun S.17.b.8.5.) supporting Black Watch.
1 gun S.17.b.10.5.)

Of these guns that at S.17.b.4.4. found suitable targets in small parties of the enemy retiring from various houses, while the gun at S.17.b.8.5. inflicted a considerable number of casualties on other groups of the enemy who had been dislodged from the village and driven towards DELVILLE WOOD. The above positions were occupied by this section practically without change until relieved by No. 4 on the 16th inst. No.3 Section on

the/

the right on reaching LONGUEVAL assumed positions around S.17.d.4.5. where they remained in position most of the day. From this position good targets were obtained; two guns firing straight away on a section of 7.7cm. which were causing considerable damage firing from S. edge of DELVILLE WOOD, the fire of these guns was kept down by our guns until they moved more to the right. At about 4.20 p.m. when the 7th Seaforths and 5th Camerons entered Southern corner of DELVILLE WOOD, the enemy retiring in the direction of WATERLOT FARM, kept exposing themselves and affording good targets at an extra shallow piece of the trench about S.18.c.6.5. Many casualties were inflicted on the enemy at this point. Another of No.3 Section's guns laid on a doorway at WATERLOT FARM, succeeded in putting many of the enemy out of action. At No.2 Section came up and assumed positions at the following points:-

2 guns under Sgt.MITCHELL in strong point at S.18.c.3.9. firing along the Southern edge of DELVILLE WOOD.
1 gun at S.17.d.1.4. in reserve.
1 gun at S.17.d.4.5. firing along North of Sunken Road.

Casualties. 2/Lt.K.F.MACKENZIE (Killed).
" Pte.BUCHANAN W. (Wounded)
" Pte.SMITH D. (")
" to attached men 13 wounded, 2 killed.

15-7-16. During this period fighting round the N.W.corner of the village, which still remained in the enemy's hands was practically continuous. The South African Brigade were also engaged in clearing DELVILLE WOOD. No.1 Section remained as before. One gun of No.2 Section, which was in reserve at S.17.d.1.4.moved forward to S.18.c.4.7. to fire due east.The other guns of this Section maintained their positions.2/Lt. WEBSTER took charge of this Section at 3 p.m. The guns of No. 2 Section were moved to the following positions:- 1 gun in C.T.Running from LONGUEVAL-TRONES WOOD at S.18.c.4.5. 1 gun at S.17.d.4.5. firing in front to trench running east of Village. 1 gun at S.17.d.6.4. firing N.E. and S.E. this gun could cover any retirement or advance on WATERLOT FARM with overhead fire. 1 gun in reserve at S.17.d.3.6.this gun had been moved down the previous evening to cover any attack which might be made from the east but had been moved back to the above position because of heavy shelling directed on the gun itself. DELVILLE WOOD was defended as follows by the 28th Brigade M.G.Company:-

1 Gun at S.11.d.5.7.	2 Guns at S.12.d.6.0.
2 Guns at S.12.c.5.9.	2 " at S.18.b.9.7.
1 " at S.12.c.7.6.	2 " at S.18.b.9.3.
1 Gun at S.12.d.6.4.	1 Gun at S.18.b.7.1.

16-7-16. No.4 Section was ordered to move off in support of the 1st South African Brigade. 2/Lt.T.MILNE reported to O.C., 1st South African Battalion at 9 a.m.

Two of the guns were put into position at S.17.b.8.5½. to support 4th South African Battalion, two guns remained in reserve in dug-out at S.17.b.7½.4. No action by these guns is reported. At about 7 p.m. they proceeded to relieve No.1 Section in its position On relief they proceeded back to reserve in MONTAUBAN.

One gun of No.2 Section in position at S.18.c.3.9.was blown up by enemy's shell fire. This gun was returned to Ordnance and was replaced by gun of No.3 Section taken from S.18.c.4.5.

17-7-16. Nos. 1 and 2 guns of No.4 Section were withdrawn to S.17.d.7.5. to allow of bombardment of LONGUEVAL by our artillery. In this position they apparently remained until

after/

after the counter attack on the afternoon of the 18th inst.

In the course of the afternoon, the enemy having been reported to be digging himself along road S.17.a.4.2.- S.10.b.3.5., the gun of No.3 Section at S.17.d.6.4. was moved to S.17.a.8.3. and fired some 800 rounds indirect in short bursts. At 11 p.m. No.4 gun of No.4 Section, under Sgt.DAVIDSON perceived a party of the enemy about fifteen strong close on them, the gun opened rapid fire. The enemy, who succeeded in reaching to within 15 yards of the gun, was driven off,after having thrown about 100 bombs.

18-7-16. Early in the morning the N.W.end of the village of LONGUEVAL was captured from the enemy. Two guns were moved North to assist in the consolidation of the newly won Terrain. 1 gun from No.2 Section moved from S.17.d.3.6 to S.17.b.2.9. to cover consolidation being carried out by Gordons and Kings Own battalions in front of the village. One gun of No.3 Section was moved from S.17.a.8.3. to S.11.d.4.2.

The position of the guns of this Company ar about 8 a.m. on this morning were as follows :-

No.1 Section all 4 guns in reserve at MONTAUBAN.
No.2 " 1 gun out of action.
1 gun at S.17.b.2.9.
1 " " S.18.c.3.9.
1 " " S.18.c.4.7.
No.3 " 1 " " S.17.b.7.3. to which point an officer (name unknown) had moved it from the strong point at S.18.c.3.9. without notifying or consulting the M.G.Officer.
1 gun at S.11.d.4.2.
1 " " S.17.d.4.5.
1 " " S.17.d.4.7.
No.4 Section 1 " " S.17.a.9.4.
1 " " S.17.b.4.4.
2guns " S.17.d.7.8. these last two guns not having been moved since the bombardment of the enemy in the N. of the village on the morning of the 17th inst.

At about 8 a.m. the enemy began a systematic bombardment of our positions, concentrating particularly on DELVILLE WOOD. This bombardment he maintained throughout the day. The guns of No.2 Section report that during the bombardment he was particularly reckless, and that the Sharpshooter attached to the gun at S.18.c.3.9. succeeded in bringing down a number of single men. At about 3 p.m. the bombardment lifted, so as to form a barrage in rear of the village and the enemy infantry was seen to advance from the direction of FLERS on DELVILLE WOOD and the N. of the village of LONGUEVAL and from GUINCHY on the S. and S.E.edge of DELVILLE WOOD. On the N. the guns at S.17.b.2.9.and S.11.d.4.2. saw the enemy as soon as he topped the ridge in front and opened fire at about 800 yds. on him as he advanced. At this point he appears to have advanced by groups of from 25-30 men at 30-50 yds. distance. He thus afforded a good target and considerable damage was inflicted on him, in spite of the fact that the smoke of shells rendered observation difficult. The gun at S.11.d.4.2. maintained a steady traversing fire in short bursts, the gun at S.17.b.2.9. firing bursts of 50.

The enemy's advance seems to have been momentarily hung up under this fire, but shortly afterwards got under weigh again. By this time the infantry supporting the right gun had retired. The gun was, however, laid on a place where the spareness of the crops rendered the enemy's movements more easily observed. At first tap traversing was used, but after 100 rounds it was apparent that this method was not developing sufficient volume of fire to check the considerable number of the enemy advancing, and 3½ belts were fired, using loose traversing fire, with excellent results. This gun continued to check the enemy's advance towards DELVILLE WOOD until a party of the enemy had all but cut off its retiral by creeping down a gully on its left. By this time the gun on the left had been ordered to retire,it

had/

had only one belt box left. On leaving its first position, it passed down the W. of the village of LONGUEVAL and finally took up position at S.17.d.6.7. only Sgt.AIREY and one man being still in action. The right gun retired Southwards, and after narrowly escaping capture at about S.17.b.6.7. finally came into action again at S.17.d.7.9. only Sgt.RICHMOND and one man being left. On these guns retiring the enemy pressed on into the village. Before the attack the gun at S.17.a.9.4., under Sgt.DAVIDSON, had been subjected to heavy shelling, which destroyed 13 belt boxes and the spare parts. It had jammed slightly and was being repaired, when a shell killed the man who was cleaning it and destroyed the feed block and had been sent back to the reserve whilst the team commander and men retired to S.17.d.7.8.

About 3.30 p.m. the gun of No.3 Section at S.17.b.7.,3. was buried under falling brick work, the shelling and the enemy attack preventing its extraction. As the attack was in progress from the N.E. the guns at S.18.c.3.9. and S.18.c.4.7. sighted the enemy advancing from GINCHY on the S.E. edge of DELVILLE WOOD. The enemy is reported to have advanced in extended order at this point. These guns, using a slow swing traverse, believe that they were able to prevent any of the enemy from crossing their front. No enemy approached these guns in the course of their counter attack. The enemy entered the East edge of the Wood however and pushed on through it, converging on the strong point at S.17.b.4.4. Here the garrison had left the gun, and on the barrage lifting, it was found that the emplacement and the tripod had been knocked out. The enemy were in possession of the barricade at S.17.b.4&6. and was advancing from the direction of the church and houses on its right. The gun accordingly retired to S.17.d.7.9. after firing several bursts. This gun, however, moved forward again with the first of the infantry, and occupied its old position. On coming into action it observed about 30 of the enemy sheltered behind the barricade. It emptied a belt into the barricade which appeared not to be bullet proof, as the enemy immediately ceased to attempt to hold it. The gun was then moved back a few yards to fire down the road running East, North East from its position. At this period the Sharpshooter attached was very useful in keeping down the fire of enemy's snipers in the vicinity of the church of whom he was able to kill or wound several. As our infantry advanced through the S.W. corner of DELVILLE WOOD the enemy began retiring in small parties across the road, covered by our gun, and suffered considerable number of casualties from the firing of this gun which expended over 800 rounds. At about 4.30 p.m. No.1 Section, which was in reserve at MONTAUBAN, received orders to reinforce this section after passing through a very heavy barrage, took up positions as follows under the command of O.C. Company :-

S.17.c.7.9.
S.17.d.2.7.
S.17.b.5.5.
S.17.d.8.5.

At this moment 2/Lt.SNELL arrived to replace Lt. HILDITCH who had been wounded whilst visiting his gun at S.11.d.4.2., this officer had been previously wounded on the 14th inst.

While the infantry was counter attacking on the S.W. corner of DELVILLE WOOD, 2/Lt.MILNE, leaving one gun at S.17.d.7.8. led another to support this movement. He gained a point about S.18.a.2.4. but was forced to retire on the infantry withdrawing. With this situation in progress, the gun and team with the exception of one man were all wiped out by a shell. 2/Lt.T.MILNE receiving a severe wound in the eye. Shortly after the gun of No.4 Section had re-established itself at S.17.b.4.4. Sgt.RICHMOND'S gun pushed forward to S.17.b.4.4. Here the gun did much to keep down the enemy's sniping activity from the direction of the churchyard and put out of action several

small/

small groups of men.

On the evening of the 18th the guns were thus disposed as follows :-

No.1 Section.	No.2 Section.	No.3 Section.	No.4 Section.
(as above)	1. S.18.c.3.9.	1. S.17.b.7.4.	1. S.17.d.7.6.
	1. S.18.c.4.7.	1. S.17.d.4.5.	1. S.17.b.4.4.
	1. S.17.d.6.7.	1. S.17.d.4.7.	
	(1 out of action)	(1 out of action)	(2out of action)

19-7-16. The Company were relieved at 10.30 p.m.

(Signed) Sydney Crawford, Captain,

O.C., 28th Brigade M.G.Company.

Notes from recent Operations.

It cannot be too strongly impressed upon the Infantry that parties detailed to escort or support Machine Guns should not retire unless the machine gun retires. Two instances occurred on the 18th July where the resistance offered by a machine gun was unduly stunted by the retirement of the supporting infantry.

Parties escorting individual guns should be under the team Commander's orders.

It was proved that the back-bone of any resistance to the enemy is the Vickers gun by reason of it being capable of a sustained resistance when suitably supported. May it be suggested that now battalions have eight Lewis guns some of these could be employed in minor action, e.g., gun sniping and pushing forward into positions which it is not intended to occupy for purpose of consolidation.

That in no training is use and fitting of a condenser sufficiently emphasised.

As many bombs as possible should be carried by gunners, and the supply maintained.

It would be advisable to have all Vickers gunners trained in the use of the German Machine Gun.

That a large reinforcement should be available if possible and kept at the beginning of an action with the M.G.Commander, so that he would be enabled to keep sections as nearly as possible up to strength.

It was found that the belt filling machine need not be brought up with the gun into action as hand filling was found to cope with all requirements.

The steel belt box was found unsuitable as the lid was difficult to open and the sides wore heavily against the nose of the bullet and the base of the cartridge. Perhaps a rib along the sides of the box might serve to keep the sides more rigid.

The carriers attached to each section proved beyond a doubt the necessity of employing men from Battalions for the purpose of carrying ammunition and filling belts. In not one instance did the guns go short of ammunition.

Sharpshooters attached to the gun sections were very useful in keeping down the enemy's snipers.

(sd) Sidney Crawford, Captain,
O.C.26th Brigade M.G.Company.

31/7/16.

26th. Infantry Brigade

Herewith Original Copy of War Diary for the month of June 1917.

C.H. Rigby Capt.
Commanding 26th Machine Gun Coy.

30/6/17

Instructions regarding War Diaries and Intelligence Summaries are contained in F. S. Regs., Part II. and the Staff Manual respectively. Title pages will be prepared in manuscript.

26th Infantry Brigade

46

WAR DIARY or ~~INTELLIGENCE~~ SUMMARY.

(Erase heading not required.)

Machine Gun Company

Army Form C. 2118.

Vol 7

Place	Date 1916	Hour	Summary of Events and Information	Remarks and references to Appendices
	1/8/16		The Company was inspected by the G.O.C 37th Division	S.C.
	2/8/16		Tactical training. 3 Officers reconnoitre roads to CARENCY, ABBAIN SAINT NAZAIRE BERTHONVAL	S.C.
	3/8/16		Conference of Machine Gun Company Commanders and Officers who were engaged in the recent fighting. At 27th Brigade Machine Gun Companys Headquarters	S.C.
	4/8/16		Training Practising [illegible]	S.C.
	5/8/16		Training Consolidation	S.C.
	6/8/16		Baths Training	S.C.
	7/8/16		Tactical exercise half Company against the other half. Clearing BOIS DE-LA-HAIE 2nd Lieut S.A Cooper commanded WEST force Lieut J.A Black the EAST force. Class for NCOs. Subject recent operations etc	S.C.
	8/8/16		R.E. class of 1 Lance Corporal and 5 Men commences under 2nd Lieut S.A Cooper. SECTIONS work in conjunction with their Battalions. Class for NCOs subject indirect etc	S.C.
	9/8/16		SECTIONS work in conjunction with their Battalions. Class for NCOs [illegible] indirect [illegible] maps	S.C.
	10/8/16		SECTION Officers visit the trenches at BERTHONVAL. Company doing drill mechanism etc reconnaissance of ground. Transport Officer goes up with Ration Carts of 63rd Brigade Machine Gun Company	S.C.

T2134. Wt. W708—776. 500000. 4/15. Sir J. C. & S.

Instructions regarding War Diaries and Intelligence Summaries are contained in F. S. Regs., Part II. and the Staff Manual respectively. Title pages will be prepared in manuscript.

47

WAR DIARY
26th Infantry Brigade Machine Gun Company

~~INTELLIGENCE SUMMARY.~~

(Erase heading not required.)

Army Form C. 2118.

Place	Date 1916	Hour	Summary of Events and Information	Remarks and references to Appendices
	11/8/16		Company training 9AM — 12.30 PM 2 PM — 3.30 PM preparing for trenches 8. PM Company less two teams of No1 SECTION parade under Commanding Officer to proceed to the trenches, to relieve 63rd Brigade Machine Gun Company SECTIONS took over as follows No 2 SECTION: COLISEUM No 3 SECTION: Z 1, Z 2, SNARGATE STREET F.2., BROAD STREET F.1 No 4 SECTION: Z 3., Z 4., ALHAMBRA No I SECTION less two teams In Company reserve at	S.C.
	12/8/16		Settling down, Checking Stores, deciding work to be done 2-30 PM Shelling of two rear Guns of front group	S.C

Instructions regarding War Diaries and Intelligence Summaries are contained in F. S. Regs., Part II. and the Staff Manual respectively. Title pages will be prepared in manuscript.

Army Form C. 2118.

26th Infantry Brigade 48 WAR DIARY or INTELLIGENCE SUMMARY. Machine Gun Company

(Erase heading not required.)

Place	Date 1916	Hour	Summary of Events and Information	Remarks and references to Appendices
	13/8/16	2 AM	Slight Shelling round positions of NOS 3 & 4 SECTIONS 1-30 PM - 1 40 PM Shelling of ZOUAVE VALLEY. Work started on altering pattern and positions of alternative emplacements. Clearing trench blocked by Shelling. Indirect fire was brought to bear on ROAD JUNCTIONS S 10 c 2.1 from S 19. b 6.5½. 750 rounds were fired	S.C.
	14/8/16		Indirect fire on S 9 d 6½ 3 — S 10 c ½ 5.	S.C.
	15/8/16		Indirect fire between 12 30 AM and 1.30 AM. One Gun firing from S 19 b 6 7½ another from S 19 b 6 5½. The first gun searched road from S 9 d 6½ 3 to S 10 c ½ 5. The second gun fired on road junction S 10 c 2 1 Ammunition expended 1250 rounds. Guns moved from Z 3. 4 COLISEUM to take up positions at the QUARRY and 74th Street. An advanced position for SMARGET STREET Gun chosen and occupied	S.C.
	16/8/16		Lieut J.A. Black relieved Captain S Crawford at CABARET ROUGE	S.C.
	17/8/16		One Gun of 27th Brigade Machine Gun Company relieved by Gun of NO 1 SECTION under Corporal Hock at end of ERSATZ ALLEY. Ammunition Store built for Gun in QUARRY. Splinter proofs constructed at 21, 22, 24 put in hand. Site for Gun in the CHORD chosen	S.C.
	18/8/16		Work at Chord emplacement started	S.C.
	19/8/16		Working at new emplacements	S.C.

49

Instructions regarding War Diaries and Intelligence Summaries are contained in F. S. Regs., Part II. and the Staff Manual respectively. Title pages will be prepared in manuscript.

WAR DIARY

26th Infantry Brigade ~~or~~ Machine Gun Company

~~INTELLIGENCE~~ SUMMARY.

(*Erase heading not required.*)

Army Form C. 2118.

Place	Date	Hour	Summary of Events and Information	Remarks and references to Appendices
	20/8/16		500 rounds fired from CHORD at enemy working parties in front at dawn Emplace at COLISEUM improved. That on the CHORD continued. Alternative Emplacement at QUARRY commenced. Emplacement at HARTONG BOYEAU commenced	S.C.
	21/8/16		Shelter constructed at CHORD GUN. Dug out commenced at GRANBY AVENUE Emplacements at HARTONG improved and Gun put in. 7th STREET Emplacement improved Trench to proposed new QUARRY emplacement completed.	S.C.
	22/8/16		Nothing to report	S.C.
	23/8/16		26th Brigade Machine Gun Company relieved by 25th Brigade Machine Gun Company Proceed to CAMBLAIN L'ABBE thence by Bus to FREVILLERS	S.C.
	24/8/16		Rest and reconnoitring training area	S.C.
	25/8/16		Practice over training area where replica trenches have been constructed	S.C.
	26/8/16		do do do do	S.C.
	27/8/16		do do do do with Brigade by day and night	S.C.
	28/8/16		do do do do with Brigade by day and night	S.C.
	29/8/16		do do do do by day	S.C.
	30/8/16		do do do do	S.C.

Instructions regarding War Diaries and Intelligence Summaries are contained in F. S. Regs., Part II. and the Staff Manual respectively. Title pages will be prepared in manuscript.

50

WAR DIARY or ~~INTELLIGENCE SUMMARY.~~

26th Infantry Brigade Machine Gun Company

(Erase heading not required.)

Army Form C. 2118.

Place	Date	Hour	Summary of Events and Information	Remarks and references to Appendices
	31/8/16		Inspected by Corps Commander. Practice with Brigade by day and night.	S.C.

S. Crawford Capt.
O.C. 26 Bde M.G. Coy
1-9-16

T2134. Wt. W708—776. 500000. 4/15. Sir J. C. & S.

26th Brigade Machine Gun Company

51

VOL 8

Army Form C. 2118.

WAR DIARY

or

INTELLIGENCE SUMMARY.

(Erase heading not required.)

Instructions regarding War Diaries and Intelligence Summaries are contained in F. S. Regs., Part II. and the Staff Manual respectively. Title pages will be prepared in manuscript.

Place	Date	Hour	Summary of Events and Information	Remarks and references to Appendices
	1/9/16		Training and practicing	S.C
	2/9/16		Company moved from FREVILLERS at 1.30 PM into Divisional Reserve Area at CAMBLAIN L'ABBE.	S.C
	3/9/16		26th Brigade Machine Gun Company relieve 28th Brigade Machine Gun Company in BERTHONVAL SECTOR	S.C
	4/9/16		Gun at CHORD (No1 SECTION) fired one belt at 5AM today. Sounds of mining heard at HARTUNG. Construction of Ammunition reserve and overhauling ammunition	S.C
	5/9/16		Sounds of mining during previous night as before; since proved to have been our own work. Gun at CHORD fired on enemy wire at 5.30 where movement was seen. QUARRY Gun also fired on enemys parapet. Gun position all strengthened. New Shelter at Z.1. made, that at Z2 Strengthened. 6 men go out on patrol	S.C
	6/9/16		CHORD gun fired on gap in enemys wire where enemy was heard working in mist. Improvement of emplacements, trench at GRANBY drained, all trench stores overhauled. Indirect fire positions put in trench 6 men go out on patrol	S.C

T2134. Wt. W708-776. 500000. 4/15. Sir J. C. & S.

26th Brigade Machine 52 Gun Company

WAR DIARY
or
INTELLIGENCE SUMMARY.
(Erase heading not required.)

Army Form C. 2118.

Instructions regarding War Diaries and Intelligence Summaries are contained in F. S. Regs., Part II. and the Staff Manual respectively. Title pages will be prepared in manuscript.

Place	Date	Hour	Summary of Events and Information	Remarks and references to Appendices
	7/9/16		Some trench mortar activity. At 5 AM 6 of the enemy were seen running from sap to sap opposite the CHORD. They were fired on result not known. All emplacements constructed. Communication trench to COLISEUM and ALHAMBRA improved. 6 men of No 2 and 3 SECTION go out on patrol. Indirect fire between 11 PM and midnight on SUNKEN ROAD and DUG OUTS at S 16 central. 1000 rounds were expended. 6 men of Nos 2 and 3 SECTIONS go on patrol. 2nd Lt TORRENS from CAMIERS reports attached for instruction.	S.C.
	8/9/16		Clearing DUG OUT at Z.1, building recess at Z.2. Sandbagging emplacements. Clearing COLISEUM trenches. Indirect fire was brought to bear on CROSS ROADS at S 10c 7.5 and S 10c 8.5. and on trench railways between these two points from 7 PM to 8 PM. CHORD gun fired 250 rounds at enemy working party at 11 PM. Recesses at HARTUNG continued. QUARRY emplacements and alternate QUARRY emplacements concealed. 3 men of No 2 and 3 SECTIONS go on patrol.	S.C.
	9/9/16		Indirect fire was brought to bear on CROSS ROADS S 10a 0.5.25. from S 19?b 6.9. from 11 to 12 AM No of rounds expended 750. Improvements to QUARRY emplacement, Continuation of dumps at ERSATZ and INTERNATIONAL. COLISEUM trench cleared	S.C.

26th Brigade Machine Gun Company

Instructions regarding War Diaries and Intelligence Summaries are contained in F. S. Regs., Part II. and the Staff Manual respectively. Title pages will be prepared in manuscript.

WAR DIARY or INTELLIGENCE SUMMARY.

(Erase heading not required.)

Army Form C. 2118.

Place	Date	Hour	Summary of Events and Information	Remarks and references to Appendices
	10/9/16		Artillery and trench Mortars were active on both sides at 10 — 10.30 PM Recesses for material at BROWNS BURROWS constructed, General improvement of emplacement in front line, clearing trench in COLISEUM	S.C.
	11/9/16		2 Guns of No 1 SECTION changed round with 2 Guns of No 3 SECTION in ALHAMBRA and Z. 1 and 2 positions. Gun from BROAD STREET moved to SOMBARD. One Gun from reserve in CAMBLAIN L'ABBE moved to CAVALIER. Both these last in relief of 180th MACHINE GUN COMPANY. Range cards made	S.C.
	12/9/16		Nothing to report. Recesses for bombs and belt boxes commenced at all emplacements	S.C.
	13/9/16		Gun at CAVALIER fired one belt at BROADMARSH CRATER. Recesses for bombs and belt boxes completed at all emplacements. Checking Dumps. Shelter at QUARRY erected. 2/Lt B.E. Hughes rejoins. Raid by SOUTH AFRICAN BRIGADE on left causes a certain amount of shelling of ZOUAVE VALLEY by field artillery and trench mortars	S.C.
	14/9/16		Day fairly quiet. At 10.7 PM. in support to a raid at that hour by 8th Black Watch and 5th Cameron Highlanders one Gun fired from S.21 d.55.80 along faces of CRATERS 35, 17, 9, 7, and 3. First three minutes rapid, then slowing down to a belt per 5 minutes; at 10.30 PM when party withdrew rapid fire again for 3 minutes	S.C.

26th Brigade Machine 54 Gun Company

WAR DIARY
or
INTELLIGENCE SUMMARY.
(Erase heading not required.)

Army Form C. 2118.

Instructions regarding War Diaries and Intelligence Summaries are contained in F. S. Regs., Part II. and the Staff Manual respectively. Title pages will be prepared in manuscript.

Place	Date	Hour	Summary of Events and Information	Remarks and references to Appendices
	14/9/16		At the same time 2 Guns fired from X 24 d 6 2 on same targets indirect. Ammunition expended 2800 rounds. Enemy retaliation was nowhere strong. Result of raid one prisoner 101st Reserve SAXON REGIMENT, 34 dead at least were counted. Rain shelter at QUARRY completed. Firing platform for Gun at left of COLISEUM rebuilt. Work continued on shaft of new dug out in disused part of GRANBY. 2nd LT Torrens leaves for CAMIERS.	S.C.
	15/9/16		Day quiet. Improvement of recesses for belt boxes, recesses for Vermorel Sprayer and Solution completed	S.C.
	16/9/16		Early morning a small mine was exploded on our left and enemy put down Barrage on usual places. Quiet. Work on minor improvements to dug outs and emplacements	S.C.
	17/9/16		Small bombing attack by LONDON IRISH provoked little retaliation though red lights were sent up. Our aircraft were active during the night 16th – 17th	S.C.
	18/9/16		Indirect fire from S 19 b 6.9 on sunken road and suspected DUG-OUTS S.16 CENTRAL 2000 rounds fired. Overhauling Stores.	S.C.
	19th		27th Brigade Machine Gun Company relieved 26th Brigade Machine Gun Company the latter returning to transport line at CAMBLAIN L'ABBE	S.C.

26th Brigade Machine 55 Gun Company

Army Form C. 2118.

WAR DIARY
or
INTELLIGENCE SUMMARY.
(Erase heading not required.)

Instructions regarding War Diaries and Intelligence Summaries are contained in F. S. Regs., Part II. and the Staff Manual respectively. Title pages will be prepared in manuscript.

Place	Date	Hour	Summary of Events and Information	Remarks and references to Appendices
	20/9/16		Training round billets, over hauling Guns	S.C.
	21/9/16		Packing up	S.C.
	22/9/16		Marched to CHELERS from CAMBLAIN L'ABBE	S.C.
	23/9/16		Marched from CHELER to SARS-LES-BOIS. Settling down. Cleaning Guns	S.C.
	24/9/16		Training in Vicinity of billets. Church parades	S.C.
	25/9/16		References Map 51c. Training scheme involving defence of a large wooded front. Guns of all Sections had to be placed to defend S' edge of BOIS DE FAIE on ROBERMONT to consolidate ground gained by an attack Southwards. Tendency was to get too far forward in Wood and dig patten emplacement instead of slits	S.C.
	26/9/16		Scheme set by Brigade. Our troops hold MAGNICOURT - SARS LES BOIS - DENIER - Bois de FAIE - BLAVINCOURT. Enemy holding HOUVIN - HOUVIGNEUL - BERLIN COURT - LIENCOURT. 26th Infantry Brigade to hold the line from SARS-LES-BOIS exclusive to road junction I 26 a 10.2 inclusive. Line to be held by Vickers Guns with Infantry in Support. On 26th each position to be selected by 10 AM, digging to be commenced by 10 by 2PM Infantry are to be informed that they may withdraw	S.C.

T2134. Wt. W708-776. 500000. 4/15. Sir J. C. & S.

56

26th Brigade Machine Gun Company

WAR DIARY
or
INTELLIGENCE SUMMARY.
(Erase heading not required.)

Army Form C. 2118.

Instructions regarding War Diaries and Intelligence Summaries are contained in F. S. Regs., Part II. and the Staff Manual respectively. Title pages will be prepared in manuscript.

Place	Date	Hour	Summary of Events and Information	Remarks and references to Appendices
	26/9/16		Guns were placed as follows No 2 SECTION two at I 26 a. 46 firing E } two at I 26 a 26 firing W } both with forward positions commanding more directly flanks. No 4 SECTION two guns at I 25 b 39. firing to Cover front of DENIER, Capable also of being moved to left to fire E. Two guns I 19 d 79 (Copse not marked in map) firing South, with alternative positions at little to left and in rear to enfilade edge of Bois de FAIE No 3 Section 2 Guns I 19 c 74. firing E along front of Wood 2 Guns I 19 c 78 firing across more or less open ground through Centre of Village No 1 SECTION 2 Guns I 19 a 1.3 firing across front of DENIER 2 Guns 4 24 b 26 firing across front of DENIER 4.30 PM Section officers to arrange for defence of a Village Nos 1 – 2 MARINCOURT Nos 3 – 4 SARS LES BOIS. tendency of position was to establish a line of guns round fringe The better method appeared to protect fringe by flanking fire and only employ within village itself Guns placed fairly far back to form strong points or to isolate portions of the Village	S.C.
	27/9/16		On the next day these positions were improved. Positions for LEWIS Guns were selected The principle of selecting an alternate position forward to which the Gun could push forward in case of targets offering themselves beneath the enemy barrage was laid down.	S.C.

T2134. Wt. W708–776. 500000. 4/15. Sir J. C. & S.

26th Brigade Machine Gun Company

59

WAR DIARY
or
INTELLIGENCE SUMMARY.

(*Erase heading not required.*)

Army Form C. 2118.

Instructions regarding War Diaries and Intelligence Summaries are contained in F. S. Regs., Part II. and the Staff Manual respectively. Title pages will be prepared in manuscript.

Place	Date	Hour	Summary of Events and Information	Remarks and references to Appendices
	27/9/16		Slits allowing 6 feet per man in length, 4 feet deep, 2 feet wide were advocated the gun being lifted on to the parapet ~~[illegible]~~ It was recommended that they should be ~~strutted apart~~ whenever possible.	S.C.
	28/9/16		Scheme under Brigade arrangements West force had attacked and gained high ground Wood H.8.d H.13.a.46. DENIER and LIENCOURT on night of 27th inst GIVENCHY le NOBLE LIGNEREUIL whole of BOIS-de-FAYE BLAVINCOURT and GD. RULLECOURT remaining in possession of EAST force. One company of WESTERN FORCE supported by 12 Vickers Guns was detailed to reconnoitre BOIS-de-FAYE and if possible to push forward and consolidate on a line running N & S through cross roads I 27 a.8.3. 40 Sharpshooters and 4 Vickers Guns were detailed to hold the WEST of wood at all costs. W. FORCE (2 Guns came into position about I 19 d 88 2 Guns at I 25 a 21 to cover advance with flanking fire.	S.C.
			Men on either flank of infantry advance were sporrans to back to assist these guns No 1 gave overhead fire from I 19 c 74 and vicinity to cover advancing infantry afterwards coming out of action and following with reserve platoon to take up positions on line I 26 b 21 – I 26 c 29 to fire out of wood and, by alternative positions, to form line across wood in case of troops consolidating objective being driven in, the flank of this	

58

26th Brigade Machine Gun Company

WAR DIARY
or
INTELLIGENCE SUMMARY.
(Erase heading not required.)

Army Form C. 2118.

Instructions regarding War Diaries and Intelligence Summaries are contained in F. S. Regs., Part II. and the Staff Manual respectively. Title pages will be prepared in manuscript.

Place	Date	Hour	Summary of Events and Information	Remarks and references to Appendices
	28/9/16		Line was protected by ~~the two subsections of~~ no 3 above mentioned. S.C. No 4 Section followed the infantry Support Platoon with orders to garrison Strong points of consolidation. No 2 Section came into action as follows: One Gun I 19 d 9 9. One Gun I 25 a 9 7 this was captured without its firing. One Gun I 25 d 4 8. One Gun in reserve in rear of BOIS-de-FAYE. Infantry gained objectives, filed into WEST end of Wood instead of assaulting as was necessary.	S.C.
			Scheme for defences of villages prepared 26th inst. discussed by Brigade Major.	
			Advance Guard Scheme	
	29/9/16		Being wet, Mechanism in the morning. In afternoon Advance Guard towards DENIER. One Section with Advance Guard, 3 Sections with Main Guard. The Advance Guard cleared DENIER, but were against a Strong enemy position in WEST end of BOIS-de-FAYE. Main Guard deployed Sections coming into action flanks to cover advance of Infantry. Chief object of practice: Use of pack ponies and writing of messages, and the impressing of the necessity of Speed of motion essential above all for Advance Guards.	S.C.
	30/9/16		Morning. One Section co-operates with each battalion in training.	S.C.
			Afternoon nos 1-2 Sections to range. No 3+4 Sections practising, Coming into action, and running an Ammunition line as a drill.	

26th Machine Gun Company

VOL 9

Army Form C. 2118.

WAR DIARY
or
INTELLIGENCE SUMMARY.

(*Erase heading not required.*)

Instructions regarding War Diaries and Intelligence Summaries are contained in F. S. Regs., Part II. and the Staff Manual respectively. Title pages will be prepared in manuscript.

Place	Date	Hour	Summary of Events and Information	Remarks and references to Appendices
	1st Oct		Morning one Section Cooperates with each Battalion in training. Afternoon inspection of Kit. Evening theoretical tactics for N C Os	
	2nd Oct		Sections training in conjunction with Battalion. Theoretical tactics for NCOs	
	3rd "		Overhauling belts and Spare parts	
	4th "		Filling in trenches, and preparing to move	
	5th "		Company paraded at 8-15 AM and marched to MEZERULLES arriving at 1.45 PM	
	6th "		Transport paraded at 8-30 AM joining Brigade transport at 9-5 AM en route for TALMAS Remainder of the Company paraded at 10 AM Inspection of Smoke helmets, equipment etc, carrying on with squad drill till 12 noon.	
	7th "		Paraded at 9.45 AM to embus for FRANVILLERS Arriving at 6.30 PM 10 Carriers and 5 Sharpshooters per Battalion report under 1 full rank and 1 2nd Lieut	
	8th "		Paraded at 2.45 PM and marched to ALBERT 200 Yards distance between Units 100 Yards between Sections	
	9th "		Lieut S A Cowper and 2nd Lieut Webster proceeded to BAZENTIN-LE-GRAND by Motor Bus at 8-30 AM. Lieut Cowper visits positions to be occupied	J.M.C.

T2134. Wt. W708-776. 500000. 4/15. Sir J. C. & S.

26th Machine 60 Gun Company

Instructions regarding War Diaries and Intelligence Summaries are contained in F. S. Regs., Part II. and the Staff Manual respectively. Title pages will be prepared in manuscript.

WAR DIARY
or
INTELLIGENCE SUMMARY.
(Erase heading not required.)

Army Form C. 2118.

Place	Date	Hour	Summary of Events and Information	Remarks and references to Appendices
	9th Oct		2nd Lieut C A Webster gets what information he can re line for Brigade HQrs returning to X 29 c 66 at 5 PM. Company paraded at 11·15 AM and marched from ALBERT to 3 25 d via BECOURT, FRICOURT and MAMETZ, leading the Brigade transport. Nos 2 – 4 Sections remain at ALBERT parading at 1·45 PM the same day and marched to MOULIN VIVIER Station where they entrained at 3-PM. They detrained at X 29 c. 66 where they met their limbers. 2nd Lieut Webster takes them to BAZENTIN-LE-GRAND where they were met by guides. 2nd Lieut Websters guides lost their bearing and he only reaches his Headquarters at the COUGH DROP M 35 a 9 4 at 1.AM where he put his Guns in reserve trenches. No 4 Carrying party then returned to transport lines. Lieut Cowpers guides likewise lost their way, he finally got two Guns into position at M 17 d 6½. ½ and M 17 d 8½. 1 by 6 AM 10/10/16. His remaining two Guns stayed at M 35 a 9 5. No 2 Carrying party remained throughout the day at this spot.	
	10th		Commanding Officer goes round to inspect positions of Guns etc. 2nd Lieut Websters Guns were placed in consultation with Brigade at M 29 d 3 6 and M 28 d 8 2, M 29 a 9 7 and M 29 b 0 4. Lieut Cowpers remaining two Guns were sent up to occupy positions M 17 d 6 3 and M 17 d 3½ 2½	[initials]

T2134. Wt. W708-776. 500000. 4/15. Sir J. C. & S.

26th Machine Gun 61 Company

WAR DIARY
or
INTELLIGENCE SUMMARY.
(Erase heading not required.)

Army Form C. 2118.

Instructions regarding War Diaries and Intelligence Summaries are contained in F. S. Regs., Part II. and the Staff Manual respectively. Title pages will be prepared in manuscript.

Place	Date	Hour	Summary of Events and Information	Remarks and references to Appendices
	10th Oct		The Brigade first extended from M17 d 1.0 to M17 c 9.1, the Support line running along SUNKEN ROAD from M17 d 6.0 to QUARRY at M23 a 9.2 Transport moved from S25 d to S19 d. No 1 Carrying party takes up rations with it and no 2 returning to transport. Pack mules were used between transport and HIGH WOOD. During the night position at M23 a 5.8 was joined up to front line trench about M17 d 0.1	
	11th		Nos 1 - 3 Sections and all Carriers moved from S19 d to S10 a 5.5, Headquarters moving to S15 a 9.5 During the day from 7 AM to 5 PM enemy trenches were bombarded. At 1.20 PM and 3.15 PM Chinese Attacks were carried out, the Artillery barraging BUTTE-DE-WARLENCOURT to M18 c 3.6. The Brigade was about to attack, its right being a line running M18 a 1.3 - M23 b 8.9 and its left being a line M17 b 1.7 — M23 a 8.8 The 1st SOUTH AFRICAN BDE was to attack on the left a BRIGADE of the 30th DIVISION cooperating on the right. These objectives were assigned. (1) Line between M17 d 0.6 and M17 d 9.4. (2) "Grid" line between M17 b 1.5 and M18 c 0.9 (3) "Grid" Support line on same frontage. Two Companys of the 7th SEAFORTH HIGHLANDERS were to attack and Consolidate the first objective, Waiting for the troops on the right to come up in line, about 18 minutes were allowed for this, the barrage in front of this line continuing till 0 + 23.	J.M.

T2134. Wt. W708-776. 500000. 4/15. Sir J. C. & S.

26th Machine 62 Gun Company

WAR DIARY
or
INTELLIGENCE SUMMARY.
(Erase heading not required.)

Army Form C. 2118.

Instructions regarding War Diaries and Intelligence Summaries are contained in F. S. Regs., Part II. and the Staff Manual respectively. Title pages will be prepared in manuscript.

Place	Date	Hour	Summary of Events and Information	Remarks and references to Appendices
	11th Oct		The remaining two companies were then to pass over them and take the Second and third Objectives Supported by two Companies of the 10th ARGYLL & S. HLRs. The third objective was to be held by two strong points each of two Vickers Guns and an Officer, so placed as to command the two main reentrants on the front, — Cooperation from right and left being arranged for with the two flanking BRIGADES. One Lewis Gun and a battle section were to hold a place between the two points at about M17 b 6 5. On the establishment of this line the Infantry were to withdraw to the Support line (Second objective). Four Guns were to be established in the first objective, the original front and Support lines being garrisoned each by a pair of Guns. Difficulty was experienced in settling positions of assembly the existing trenches being scarcely sufficient to accomodate the attacking Infantry. No 2 Section was directed to assemble in the front line and to advance and consolidate the third objective forming a fifth wave entirely of machine Guns and Carriers. If the objective was not reached they were to dig in as far forward as possible. No 4 Section was to assemble in the QUARRY about M 23 a 9 2 and to consolidate the first objective advancing when the third objective had been reached. No 1 Section was to assemble in the FLERS LINE about M 29 b 2 3 and to send two Guns to the original front and two to the Support line	AM

T2134. Wt. W708—776. 500000. 4/15. Sir J. C. & S.

26th 63 Machine Gun Company

Instructions regarding War Diaries and Intelligence Summaries are contained in F. S. Regs., Part II. and the Staff Manual respectively. Title pages will be prepared in manuscript.

WAR DIARY
or
INTELLIGENCE SUMMARY.
(*Erase heading not required.*)

Army Form C. 2118.

Place	Date	Hour	Summary of Events and Information	Remarks and references to Appendices
	11th Oct		No 3 Section was to remain in reserve in the FLERS LINE in rear of No 1. Three carriers were to advance with each Gun. A dump for S.A.A was formed in the QUARRY at M23 a.92 and rations and Water would be brought to that Spot daily.	
			The above preparations and dispositions were completed by dawn 12-10-16	
	12th "		2nd Lt D W Adam was sent up to take over one Subsection of No 2. Place of assembly for No 1 was changed to FLERS SWITCH. Reports were to be sent to COUGH DROP. ZERO was at 2.5 PM	
			left their trenches the Infantry were met by very strong enfilade machine Gun fire from the left. all attempts to advance proving fruitless. No 2 Section did not advance but came into Action in the original front line. No 4 Section coming up brought its Guns into Action in front and Support. No 1 placed its Guns in Similar positions	
			During this period great difficulty was experienced owing to none of the Section Officers forwarding any report. It was only late at night that any report at all came through though the Battalion stated that only two teams were left. In the course of the night two strong patrols pushed forward and the infantry dug themselves in in two places some 50 – 100 yards in advance of the original front line. In the course of the day 2nd Lt D W Adam was wounded the casualties in other ranks amounting to 14 Wounded 2 Killed.	J.M.L.

26th Machine Gun 64 Company

Instructions regarding War Diaries and Intelligence Summaries are contained in F. S. Regs., Part II. and the Staff Manual respectively. Title pages will be prepared in manuscript.

WAR DIARY
or
INTELLIGENCE SUMMARY.
(Erase heading not required.)

Army Form C. 2118.

Place	Date	Hour	Summary of Events and Information	Remarks and references to Appendices
	13th Oct		This day the Guns in positions were found to be situated as follows, front line 4 {M17 a 7.1 M17 d 4 3 / M17 a 6.2 M17 d 2 4} action and one damaged but capable of firing. Support 3 Guns at about M 23 b 1.9. M 23 a 9.75 M 23 a 8.8.	
			" 2 Guns at about M 23 b 1.6 – M 23 a 9.55	
			one Gun of No 1 Section had been lost.	
			It was decided to relieve Guns in front System. No 3 Section accordingly relieved four front line Guns, being instructed to place one Gun in the left forward position, to fire right as soon as light permitted. The remaining Section were drawn back No 2 to FLERS LINE where it occupied defensive positions. Nos 1–4 Sections to DROP ALLEY about M 35 a 9.7.	
			No 2 Section was reinforced by 4 privates and 1 NCO	
			No 4 " " " " 4 "	
			Lieut J A Black proceeded to GRANTHAM. Lieut Coupar was withdrawn to take his place 2nd Lt KB Wilson taking Command of No 2 Section.	
	14th "		Positions of Guns remained unchanged throughout these days	
	15th "		Emplacements were improved and recesses cut to receive belt boxes spare parts etc	
	16th "		Four Guns 2 of No 4 Section and 2 Guns of No 1 Section in the FLERS SWITCH were changed to the following positions in order to carry out indirect fire. M 29 b ½ 4 M 29 a 5.5 3 M 29 a 4 5 M 29 a 35.25	

T2134. Wt. W708–776. 500000. 4/15. Sir J. C. & S.

26th Machine 65 Gun Company

WAR DIARY
or
INTELLIGENCE SUMMARY.
(Erase heading not required.)

Army Form C. 2118.

Instructions regarding War Diaries and Intelligence Summaries are contained in F. S. Regs., Part II. and the Staff Manual respectively. Title pages will be prepared in manuscript.

Place	Date	Hour	Summary of Events and Information	Remarks and references to Appendices
	16th Oct		These Guns fired on the area M11c27 to M17a25. M11d87 to M17b85. Damage done can only be judged by the enemy Artillery retaliation on FLERS TRENCH in the evening and the next day which was considerable. The Guns in the front line maintained the positions. No 3 Section in front line fired several hundred rounds with the idea of preventing enemy wiring parties which were reported to be working at about M17d55 this had to cease owing to our own burial parties going out	
	17th		In the front line positions remained the same preparations being made for the attack to take place the following morning and the Guns in reserve (FLERS LINE) continued to carry out indirect fire on same area as previous day and must have caused great discomfort to the enemy as it produced further retaliation on the FLERS LINE	
			The Brigade was about to attack on the 18th inst ZERO being 3.40 AM	
			Objective 9th Division Hostile line M18c25 to M17c03. Frontage of attack for 26th Brigade. Between the sunken road running from M17d70 to M18c25 inclusive and a line running from the bending tree in the Quarry just north of the cross roads at M23a9.4. to a lone tree about M17a9.0 that is a North and South line 50 yards west of the dividing line between M17.c and M17.d.	
				J.M.

66

Instructions regarding War Diaries and Intelligence Summaries are contained in F. S. Regs., Part II. and the Staff Manual respectively. Title pages will be prepared in manuscript.

26th Machine Gun Company WAR DIARY ~~or INTELLIGENCE SUMMARY.~~

(Erase heading not required.)

Army Form C. 2118.

Place	Date	Hour	Summary of Events and Information	Remarks and references to Appendices
	17th Oct		Disposition 26th Machine Gun Company. One Section to advance with 4th Wave of 5th Cameron Hrs. One Section to hold original front line and Support lines. 2 Section in Brigade reserve. Preliminary dispositions 26th Machine Gun Company 2 Sections front and Support line one Section FLERS SWITCH one Section FLERS LINE. Tasks Machine Gun Company (a) four Guns to work in pairs (one officer to each pair) from positions about the Strong points para 7 (1)(F) and 17 d 5 6 and the new trench in para 7 (1)(D). "B" One Section to hold original line "C" Two Sections in Brigade reserve	
	18th Oct		At 1 AM No 1 Section went forward from the FLERS LINE and took up positions in the Support preparatory to the Attack. At 3 40 AM the Attack took place and no 3 Section in front line followed the 4th Wave of Infantry and on reaching enemy front line (Objective) took up the following 3 positions (One Gun having been blown up in the advance) M17 d 4 6 and M17 a 9 5. No 1 Section at the Same time moving up from the Support and taking up positions vacated by no 3 Section. 2nd Lt A C E Snell was badly wounded Shortly after the advance	

T2134. Wt. W708–776. 500000. 4/15. Sir J. C. & S.

26th Machine Gun 67 Company

Army Form C. 2118.

Instructions regarding War Diaries and Intelligence Summaries are contained in F. S. Regs., Part II. and the Staff Manual respectively. Title pages will be prepared in manuscript.

WAR DIARY
or
INTELLIGENCE SUMMARY.
(Erase heading not required.)

Place	Date	Hour	Summary of Events and Information	Remarks and references to Appendices
	18th Oct		and 2nd Lieut R E Hughes took over Command. The two Guns at M17 d 4 6 and M17 d 5 7 were both covering our left as the enemy counter attack was effected from this quarter, the Gun at M17 d 9 5 covered our right. During enemy bombing attacks all three Guns were active and succeeded in dispersing many bombing parties, and continued to hold the ground gained by the attack Nos 2 – 4 Section were in FLERS SWITCH and FLERS LINE.	
	19th "		at 2.30 AM No 3 Section in the front line was relieved by No 1 from the Support under 2nd Lieut C J Wright who took one gun up with him making in all 4 Guns in the front line, this was placed in position at M 18 C 1 4 which fired (¼) quarter left and practically enfiladed enemy second line. No 4 Section brought up 1 Gun from FLERS LINE and took over No 1 Section positions in our original front line now support. During the day many small targets presented themselves and all the front line guns claimed many victims. 2nd Lieut C J Wright was killed in the afternoon. In the evening the Company was relieved by the 27th Machine Gun Company and the Company went back to MAMETZ – WOOD about S20 C 1.4.	AM

26th Machine Gun Company 68

Army Form C. 2118.

WAR DIARY
or
INTELLIGENCE SUMMARY.
(*Erase heading not required.*)

Instructions regarding War Diaries and Intelligence Summaries are contained in F. S. Regs., Part II. and the Staff Manual respectively. Title pages will be prepared in manuscript.

Place	Date	Hour	Summary of Events and Information	Remarks and references to Appendices
	20th Oct		In reserve at S 20 C 1.4. Cleaning and overhauling Guns etc, inspection of new clothing	
	21st Oct		In reserve. S 20 C 1.4 issuing kit and equipment deficiencies	
	22nd "		In reserve at S 20 C 1.4 preparing to go into the line reorganisation of Sections etc	
	23rd "		The Company moved from S 20 C.1.4. at 12 noon to relieve 27th Machine Gun Company in the right Sector of the line. Relief was completed about midnight owing to the bad state of the trenches 2nd Lt B E Hughes and 2nd Lt E Eberlin relieved the Guns in the front line and took up the following positions M17 a 1.7. M17 a 4.6. M17 a 9.5 and M 18 c.1.4. No 4 Section under 2nd Lt C A Webster took up the original positions in the support line (our old front line) Nos 1 and 2 Sections were in reserve at FLERS LINE and FLERS SWITCH under 2nd Lt W Chalmers	
	24th Oct		During the day Nos 3 - 4 Sections in front line improved emplacements and trenches In the Afternoon the Gun at 18 C 1 4 was blown up	
	25th Oct		The Company was relieved by the 149th Machine Gun Company. Relief completed by 12 noon the Company moved back to ALBERT by train at 3 PM	AMc

T2134. Wt. W708–776. 500000. 4/15. Sir J. C. & S.

69

Army Form C. 2118.

Instructions regarding War Diaries and Intelligence Summaries are contained in F. S. Regs., Part II. and the Staff Manual respectively. Title pages will be prepared in manuscript.

26th Machine Gun Company WAR DIARY ~~or INTELLIGENCE SUMMARY.~~

(*Erase heading not required.*)

Place	Date	Hour	Summary of Events and Information	Remarks and references to Appendices
	26th Oct		Company in billets at ALBERT the day was spent cleaning etc and reorganising.	
	27th Oct		8-30 AM Started for FRANVILLERS arriving in billets there at 12 30 PM	
	28th Oct		marched from FRANVILLERS at 10 AM to PIERREGOT arriving at about 1 30 PM billet there for the night	
	29th Oct		Company embussed at about 12 noon for GOUY-EN-ARTOIS arriving in billets at 4 30 PM.	
	30th Oct		at GOUY EN-ARTOIS Settling down	
	31st Oct		at GOUY EN ARTOIS Overhauling and cleaning guns etc.	
				A.B.C.

T2134. Wt. W708-776. 500000. 4/15. Sir J. C. & S.

26th Machine Gun Company 70

Instructions regarding War Diaries and Intelligence Summaries are contained in F. S. Regs., Part II. and the Staff Manual respectively. Title pages will be prepared in manuscript.

WAR DIARY
or
INTELLIGENCE SUMMARY.
(Erase heading not required.)

Army Form C. 2118.

Place	Date	Hour	Summary of Events and Information	Remarks and references to Appendices
			During the time the Company was in the line the COUGH DROP about 35a 95.15 was used as an advanced dump 2nd Lt MacLean of the 5th CAMERONS being in charge. Rations were brought up as far as this point on limbers and from here the Section carrying parties took them to the various Sections. 12000 Rounds SAA and belt boxes which were salved were sent here where they were cleaned up and sent back to the line as required. The COUGH DROP was in telephonic communication with Company Headquarters at BAZENTIN-LE GRAND about S 15a 8.4. The transport lines were at MAMETZ WOOD S19a 9.9.	
			Total Casualties during the operations Killed Officers 1 Wounded 3 other ranks Killed 4 Wounded 25 Missing 1	
			S. H. Cooper Lt A/Adj for O.C. 26th Machine Gun Company	

T.2134. Wt. W708-776. 500000. 4/15. Sir J. C. & S.

26th Machine 71 26 Gun Company

Army Form C. 2118.

Instructions regarding War Diaries and Intelligence Summaries are contained in F. S. Regs., Part II. and the Staff Manual respectively. Title pages will be prepared in manuscript.

WAR DIARY
or
~~INTELLIGENCE SUMMARY.~~
(Erase heading not required.)

Vol 10

Place	Date	Hour	Summary of Events and Information	Remarks and references to Appendices
	1/11/16		Company in billets at GOUY-EN-ARTOIS Physical training NCOs instruction in duties etc. Inspection of Kit	S.C.
	2/11/16		Physical training 7-30 AM – 8 AM. Thorough cleaning of all Guns and Small Arms. Interior economy	S.C.
	3/11/16		7-30 AM – 8 AM Physical exercise. Reorganising Sections and posting new men. Inspection of Guns and equipment	S.C.
	4/11/16		Physical training & NCOs instructional class. Overhauling Ammunition and belts Cleaning limbers	S.C.
	5/11/16		Church parade.	S.C.
	6/11/16		Early morning parade as usual. Wet. Elementary class of instruction formed. All Sections carried out indoor instruction in Map reading Compass Indirect fire, Interior economy, Care and Cleaning of Guns.	S.C.
	7/11/16		Physical exercise 7-30 – 8 AM and instructional Class for NCOs Wet. Sections carried out indoor training in Mechanism Spare parts and repairs. Stoppages.	S.C.
	8/11/16		NCOs instructional class and Physical exercise	S.C.

72

Army Form C. 2118.

Instructions regarding War Diaries and Intelligence Summaries are contained in F. S. Regs., Part II. and the Staff Manual respectively. Title pages will be prepared in manuscript.

WAR DIARY 26th Machine Gun Company

or

~~INTELLIGENCE SUMMARY.~~

(Erase heading not required.)

Place	Date	Hour	Summary of Events and Information	Remarks and references to Appendices
	8/11/16		Indoor training. Mechanism Immediate Action Lecture to Officers and NCOs by Medical Officer on first Aid. Baths	Wet S.C.
	9/11/16		Physical training NCOs instructional Class. Small tactical Scheme carried out by two Sections. Study of ground, use of cover, etc. One Section range grouping practice. One Section Squad drill, map reading, points on indirect fire	S.C.
	10/11/16		NCOs class and physical training. Tactical Scheme carried out by two Section, remaining two Sections range, Gun drill, belt repairing and filling. Two Officers and two NCOs attend course of instruction on new Box respirator at Divisional Gas School at BERNEVILLE	S.C.
	11/11/16		Physical training & NCOs class. Tactical Scheme including types of emplacements, use of cover, method of advance. Two Sections Range practice and Squad drill.	S.C.
	12/11/16		Instructional Class for NCOs. Physical exercises. Instruction in packing of limbers	S.C.

T2134. Wt. W708-776. 500000. 4/15. Sir J. C. & S.

26th Machine Gun Company 73

Instructions regarding War Diaries and Intelligence Summaries are contained in F. S. Regs., Part II. and the Staff Manual respectively. Title pages will be prepared in manuscript.

WAR DIARY

or

~~INTELLIGENCE SUMMARY.~~

(Erase heading not required.)

Army Form C. 2118.

Place	Date	Hour	Summary of Events and Information	Remarks and references to Appendices
	13/11/16		NCOs Class and Physical training. Squad drill, Range practice	S.C
	14/11/16		Company route march with transport	S.C.
	15/11/16		Early morning parades as usual. Practice in the Attack, Squad drill, Revolver practice. Instructional Squads fire grouping practice. Instruction to all Officers by Brigade Major in tactical handling of Machine Guns in Attack, on ground used by Sections in tactical Schemes	S.C.
	16/11/16		Physical drill and NCOs instructional class. Short route march by two Sections including reconnaissance of Ground. Revolver practice Squad drill belt filling	S.C
	17/11/16		Early morning exercise and N.C.Os class. Two Sections route march reconnaissance of ground for tactical scheme. Revolver practice Squad drill Spare parts and repairs, Map reading, All officers tactical exercises under Brigade Major	S.C
	18/11/16		Physical training N.COs Class. Revolver practice, Gun drill, belt filling Squad drill, interior economy	S.C

T2134. Wt. W708-776. 500000. 4/15. Sir J. C. & S.

26th Machine Gun Company 74

Army Form C. 2118.

Instructions regarding War Diaries and Intelligence Summaries are contained in F. S. Regs., Part II. and the Staff Manual respectively. Title pages will be prepared in manuscript.

WAR DIARY

or

~~INTELLIGENCE SUMMARY.~~

(*Erase heading not required.*)

Place	Date	Hour	Summary of Events and Information	Remarks and references to Appendices
	19/11/16		Packing limbers ready to move. Church parade	S.C.
	20/11/16		Company paraded at 9 AM and marched to MAIZIÈRES arriving there About 12-45 PM where they billeted for the night	S.C.
	21/11/16		Moved from MAIZIÈRES at 10 AM to rest billets at IZEL-LES-HAMEAU arriving in billets at 12 noon.	S.C.
	22/11/16		Physical training and N.C.Os instructional Class. Gun drill Mechanism etc Section Officers go out with Commanding Officer. Reconnaissance of ground for tactical scheme.	S.C.
	23/11/16		Physical drill N.C.Os class. Short route march and tactical Scheme	S.C.
	24/11/16		do do do One Section Skirmishing with Guns on ground about I 7. C. One Section range. Gas instruction in use of new Box respirator remaining two Sections	S.C.
	25/11/16		Physical exercise. Class for N.C.Os Wet. Sections indoor. Mechanism Stoppages etc.	S.C.
	26/11/16		Church Parades.	S.C.
	27/11/16		Box respirator drill. Tactical scheme. Attack and defense. Cleaning Guns Narratives to all Officers by Commanding Officer	S.C.

T2134. Wt. W708-776. 500000. 4/15. Sir J. C. & S.

26th Machine Gun Company 75

WAR DIARY
or
~~INTELLIGENCE~~ SUMMARY.
(*Erase heading not required.*)

Army Form C. 2118.

Instructions regarding War Diaries and Intelligence Summaries are contained in F. S. Regs., Part II. and the Staff Manual respectively. Title pages will be prepared in manuscript.

Place	Date	Hour	Summary of Events and Information	Remarks and references to Appendices
	28/11/16		Box resperator Drill Tactical Scheme "Attack on Village" Cleaning Guns Officers and N.C.Os revolver practice	S.C.
	29/11/16		Box resperator Drill "Wood fighting" Cleaning Guns etc Narratives to all Officers under Commanding Officer	S.C.
	30/11/16		Resperator and Physical Drill Tactical Scheme "Defense of Village" Lecture by Commanding Officer to Officers and N.C.Os (Co-operation of the Machine Gun in the attack)	S.C.

S. Crawford Major
O.C. 26th M.G. Coy

T2134. Wt. W708-776. 500000. 4/15. Sir J. C. & S.

26th Machine Gun 76 Company

Instructions regarding War Diaries and Intelligence Summaries are contained in F. S. Regs., Part II. and the Staff Manual respectively. Title pages will be prepared in manuscript.

WAR DIARY
or
~~INTELLIGENCE SUMMARY.~~
(Erase heading not required.)

Army Form C. 2118.

Vol XI

Place	Date	Hour	Summary of Events and Information	Remarks and references to Appendices
	1916			
	1st Dec		Company Route march	S.C.
	2nd		Physical exercise. Company inspected by Medical Officer for Scabies. Packing limbers ready to move	S.C.
	3rd		Company paraded at 2-30 PM and marched to LATTRE where it billeted for the night	S.C.
	4th		Moved from LATTRE at 2 PM marched to WANQUETIN where Company embussed for ARRAS arriving there at 6-30 PM. Relieved 104th Machine Gun Company in the line on the night of 4th inst. Sections took up positions as follows:	S.C.
			No. 2 Section. WOOD SECTOR. G.35. b. 3.5. / G.35 b. 75.15 / G.36 A. 1.7 / G.30 C. 7.2 — No 4 Section SAINT SAUVEUR G.29. d 9.5. 5.0. / G.29 d 75. 5.0. / G.29 d 8.5 / G.29 d 25.25 / ~~G.29 d 75~~	
			No 3 Section CEMETRY SECTOR G.29 b 75 / G.23 d.9.4 / G.23 d.75.45 / G.23 A 5.8.	
			Company HEADQUARTERS ARRAS. Transport lines AGNEZ-LES-DUIZANS	

26 MACHINE GUN COMPANY

WAR DIARY or INTELLIGENCE SUMMARY.

(Erase heading not required.)

Army Form C. 2118.

Instructions regarding War Diaries and Intelligence Summaries are contained in F. S. Regs., Part II. and the Staff Manual respectively. Title pages will be prepared in manuscript.

Place	Date	Hour	Summary of Events and Information	Remarks and references to Appendices
	Decr 1916 4th		Two teams of No. 1. SECTION at Company Headqrs ARRAR /remaining two teams at Course of instruction DIVISIONAL. FIGHTING SCHOOL, GIVENCHY-LE-NOBEL under 1 Officer	S.C.
	5th		Sections in the trenches. Cleaning emplacements, Clearing loopholes, laying duckboards	S.C.
	6th		Repairing emplacements and entrance to Shelters. Making Ammunition Recesses	S.C.
	7th		Rebuilding Gun platforms, levelling trench rounds Gun positions, making Gas alert boards, and range cards. Improving emplacements and dug outs. Commencing emplacement for Aeroplane firing	S.C.
	8th		Overhauling trench Stores. Making Screen for night firing. Working on new Cookhouse & Tunnel emplacement. Entrance to covered emplacement at no 10 blown in 1 Man slightly wounded.	S.C.
	9th		Indirect fire scheme carried out between 8.30 PM and 9.PM on road H31.b.0.3 to H.32.c 5.5. Ammunition expended 950 rounds	S.C.
	10th		Two teams of No1 Section under 2nd Lt Campbell moved up from Company Headqrs into reserve at G.29 a. 3.1. One Gun in reserve at G 29 a. 3.1. was ordered	S.C.

T2134. Wt. W708—776. 500000. 4/15. Sir J. C. & S.

Instructions regarding War Diaries and Intelligence Summaries are contained in F. S. Regs., Part II. and the Staff Manual respectively. Title pages will be prepared in manuscript.

78

WAR DIARY ~~or~~ ~~INTELLIGENCE~~ SUMMARY.

28th Machine Gun Company

(*Erase heading not required.*)

Army Form C. 2118.

Place	Date	Hour	Summary of Events and Information	Remarks and references to Appendices
	1916 Dec			
	10th		by Brigade to move into position at G 24. C 25. 85. This Gun took up position at 8.30 PM and came under the command of O.C. No 3 Section.	S.C
			Between 6.30 PM and 9.PM indirect fire was carried out on road H. 31. b. 1.1. to H. 32. b. 6.5. 1000 rounds were fired	
	11th		The Gun and team at G. 35. b 75. 15. was relieved by one Lewis Gun and an Infantry Section of the 10th Argyll & S. Hrs at 10. AM. This point being made into an Infantry Strong post. The Gun relieved came into position in reserve at G 29 a 3.1	S.C
			Between 6 PM and 9 PM indirect fire was carried out on ROAD H 31. b 1.1. to H 32. c 5.5. number of rounds fired 750	
	12th		Indirect fire positions have been completed at G 29. d 2.0 G 29. d 25. 35 and G. 28 d 9.0.15	S.C
			Indirect fire Scheme carried out on ROAD H 31 a. 9.2. to H. 32 c. 9.4 between 6 and 9 PM Ammunition expended 1000 rounds	
	13th		On ROAD G. 36 b. 6.7 to H 31 b. 2.1 and on trenches H. 31. C 95. to H. 31 Central. Indirect fire was carried out between 6.45. and 8 PM. 1000 rounds were fired	S.C.
	14th		In Co-operation with Artillery Scheme, indirect fire was brought to bear on ROAD. H. 31. C. 7.0 to H. 31. b 25. 05 and on trenches H. 31. C 3.0. to H. 31. Central. Ammunition expended 500 rounds.	S.C

Instructions regarding War Diaries and Intelligence Summaries are contained in F. S. Regs., Part II. and the Staff Manual respectively. Title pages will be prepared in manuscript.

79

26th Machine WAR DIARY Gun Company or ~~INTELLIGENCE SUMMARY.~~

(Erase heading not required.)

Army Form C. 2118.

Place	Date	Hour	Summary of Events and Information	Remarks and references to Appendices
	Decr			
	15th		Between 6 PM and 7.30 PM indirect fire was carried out on ROAD H.31 c 7.0 to H31 b.25.05 and between 9.30 AM and 10-30 AM on ROAD H.26 b 2.7 to H.32. a. 8.9 expenditure of Ammunition 1000 rounds	SC
	16th		Indirect fire was brought to bear on road H 32 a. 8.9 to H.26. b. 05.10. Rounds fired 1500 Three teams of No I SECTION relieved three teams of No 2 SECTION in the WOOD SECTOR Two teams of No 2 Section went to CAMBRAI ROAD in reserve, remaining teams came into Company reserve at the BARRACKS ARRAS.	SC
	17th		Between 5 PM and 8 PM indirect fire was carried out on ROAD H.32.a.8.9 to H 26 b.05.10. 1500 rounds were expended.	SC
	18th		On ROAD H.32.a 8.9 to H.26.b 05.10 between 5.45 PM and 7.30 PM 500 rounds were fired indirectly	SC
	19th		Nothing to report	SC
	20th		In co-operation with Artillery and Trench Mortar Batteries indirect fire was carried out between 2.PM and 2.30 PM on enemy COMMUNICATION TRENCHES H.25 b 4.1 to H26 a. 15.15. on H19a 9.5 75 to H19 b.48 and on H 13. c 35. 20 At night between 5.30 and 8 PM indirect fire was also carried out on ROAD	SC

T2134. Wt. W708—776. 500000. 4/15. Sir J. C. & S.

Instructions regarding War Diaries and Intelligence Summaries are contained in F. S. Regs., Part II. and the Staff Manual respectively. Title pages will be prepared in manuscript.

80/

26th Machine WAR DIARY Gun Company
or
INTELLIGENCE SUMMARY.
(*Erase heading not required.*)

Army Form C. 2118.

Place	Date	Hour	Summary of Events and Information	Remarks and references to Appendices
	1916 Dec			
	20th		H.32 a 8.9. to H 26. 13.05.10 Ammunition expended 3000 rounds	S.C
	21st		Nothing to report	S.C
	22nd		1 Gun in Company reserve at ARRAS moved up by orders of Brigade and took up position at G.23 b 5 0. Between 7 PM and 8.15 PM Indirect fire was carried out on ROAD H25 D 9 0 15 to H 26 a 1.0.10. rounds fired 1000	S.C
	23rd		Indirect fire was brought to bear on enemy COMMUNICATION TRENCHES between 9.15 PM and 11 PM Targets H25a9 0. to H 25 b. 4.5.10. H31 a 9.0.1.5 to H31 d.7.6 number of rounds fired 2250	S.C
	24th		Between 2 PM and 2 45 PM in Cooperation with Artillery on enemys COMMUNICATION TRENCHES. H 19 c.25.20. H 25 a 6.5 7.5 to H25a 9.5.7.5. – G.30 D.9.6 to H 25 c 0 5 . 65 and H26 a 35 50 to H26 a 85 50. Ammunition expended 1750 rounds	S.C
	25th		Indirect fire position at G 29 a. 05 completed and connected by telephone to Observation post at 29 d 9.0 3.5. Indirect fire was carried out on ROAD H31 b 11. to H31 d 7.8. 250 rounds were fired	S.C
	26th		The Gun at G 23 a 0.4. changed position to G 23 d 9.7. by orders of Brigade	S.C
	27th		The Personnel of 1 Section of the 197th Machine Gun Company was attached for 3 days	S.C

T2134. Wt. W708–776. 500000. 4/15. Sir J. C. & S.

81

Instructions regarding War Diaries and Intelligence Summaries are contained in F. S. Regs., Part II. and the Staff Manual respectively. Title pages will be prepared in manuscript.

26th Machine Gun Company WAR DIARY or INTELLIGENCE SUMMARY.

(Erase heading not required.)

Army Form C. 2118.

Place	Date	Hour	Summary of Events and Information	Remarks and references to Appendices
	Dec			
	27th	✓	to No 3 Section (2 Section, 4 Section) for individual instruction. Indirect fire was carried out as follows between 2 45 and 8 PM on enemy COMMUNICATION TRENCHES H 25 c 5.7 to H 25 9 on H 25 b 4.3. H 25 a 8 0.31 and on road H 32 a 8 9 to H 32 between 10 PM and 12 PM on CAMBRAI ROAD H 31 a 85 20. to H 32 c 80. 40. Ammunition expended 3000 rounds	S.C
	28th		Between 3.50 PM and 4 PM indirect fire was carried out on enemy COMMUNICATION TRENCHES H 25 c 90. 75. and on ROAD H 31 a 8.5 20 to H 32 c 80.40 between 10 PM and 12 PM ammunition expended 2250 rounds	S.C
	29		Personnel of team attached (199th Machine Gun Company) came out of the line Indirect fire was carried out on CAMBRAI ROAD H 31 a 85 20 to H 32 c 80 40 2000 rounds were fired	S.C
	30	✓	Four Guns of No 3 Section were relieved in the line by 4 teams of the 199th Machine Gun Company Indirect fire was carried out between 2 PM and 3 PM on enemy Communication trenches H19 c 00.65 to H25 a 8.2 on G25 b 8 to G25 8.0 and between 9 30 PM and 11 30 PM on CAMBRAI ROAD H 31 a 8.5 20 to H 32 c 80 40	S.C
	31		Indirect fire was carried out on enemy Communication trenches H 19 c 00 65 at 10 30 AM	S.C.

T2134. Wt. W708—776. 500000. 4/15. Sir J. C. & S.

82

26th Machine Gun WAR DIARY Company
or
~~INTELLIGENCE~~ SUMMARY.
(Erase heading not required.)

Army Form C. 2118.

Instructions regarding War Diaries and Intelligence Summaries are contained in F. S. Regs., Part II. and the Staff Manual respectively. Title pages will be prepared in manuscript.

Place	Date	Hour	Summary of Events and Information	Remarks and references to Appendices
	31/12/16		and between 9 30 PM and 12 PM on CAMBRAI ROAD H 31 a 5.2.0 to H32 c 8.0 40	S.C.

Sydney Crawford Major
O.C. 26th M.G. Coy
31-12-16

T2134. Wt. W708—776. 500000. 4/15. Sir J. C. & S.

83

26th Machine Gun **WAR DIARY** Company
or
~~INTELLIGENCE SUMMARY.~~
(*Erase heading not required.*)

Army Form C. 2118.

Vol 12

Instructions regarding War Diaries and Intelligence Summaries are contained in F. S. Regs., Part II. and the Staff Manual respectively. Title pages will be prepared in manuscript.

Place	Date	Hour	Summary of Events and Information	Remarks and references to Appendices
	1917			
	Jany 1st		Lieut A E Eberlin and 14 men with two Vickers Guns proceeded to the Divisional School of Infantry Fighting for course of instruction commencing 1st inst at GIVENCHY-LE-NOBLE.	
			Between 5 PM and 6 30 PM and 9.30 and 11 PM indirect fire was carried out as follows on ENEMY TRENCHES N.1.a 2.7 to N.1.C. 2.5. and on CAMBRAI ROAD. H 31 a 85.20. to H 32 C 84 2000 rounds were fired.	
	2nd		No 4 Section of the 197th Machine Gun Company relieved No1 Section of their Company in the CEMETRY SECTOR. Indirect fire was carried out between 9.30 – 11 30 PM on CAMBRAI. ROAD H 31. b 15. 10 to H 32 C. 10.70 Ammunition expended 2000 rounds	
	3rd		Between 9 And 9 30 PM indirect fire was carried out on ROAD H 31 a 85.20. to H 32. C. 80. 40 1000 rounds were expended.	
	4th		Between 8 and 11.30 PM indirect fire was carried out as follows on ENEMY COMMUNICATION TRENCH. N.1.a 80 45. to N.1.C 75. 50. and on CAMBRAI ROAD H 31 a 85. 20. to H 31 C 80. 40. 2000 rounds were fired. An enemy working party was seen at 12 30 PM our Machine Gun fire soon dispersed them.	

T2134. Wt. W708–776. 500000. 4/15. Sir J. C. & S.

Instructions regarding War Diaries and Intelligence Summaries are contained in F. S. Regs., Part II. and the Staff Manual respectively. Title pages will be prepared in manuscript.

WAR DIARY
or
INTELLIGENCE SUMMARY.
(Erase heading not required.)

Army Form C. 2118.

Vol 29

Place	Date	Hour	Summary of Events and Information	Remarks and references to Appendices
GONNELIEU	2nd Jan	8 pm to 12 m.	Battalion relieved in left Sub sector opposite GONNELIEU by 5th Btn Cameron Highlanders. Battalion marched to Brigade Reserve in Huts at Sheet 57c W2c.	
	3rd		Major W French assumed command of Battalion vice Capt J L Ewing	
	3rd to 6th		At Huts at W2c Baths, Anti Trench Foot Treatment, Sandbagging of of huts as Anti Bomb protection.	
	6th	5 pm to 8 pm	Battalion relieved 5th Cameron Highlanders in Left Sub. Sector relief passed without incident except that L/Campbell of D Company was wounded on route to line 2 O.R Killed & 2 O.R wounded. Companies were disposed as follows:- "D" Company Right. "A" Company Centre "B" Company Left. "C" Company in FLAG. RAVINE. in immediate Support. The weather up till now had been frosty but a decided thaw set in.	
	7th		Line very Quiet. Thaw Continues. Line Trench condition gradually getting worse.	

(A7092). Wt. W12839/M1293- 750,000. 1/17. D. D. & L., Ltd. Forms/C.2118/14.

Instructions regarding War Diaries and Intelligence Summaries are contained in F. S. Regs., Part II. and the Staff Manual respectively. Title pages will be prepared in manuscript.

WAR DIARY
or
INTELLIGENCE SUMMARY.
(*Erase heading not required.*)

Army Form C. 2118.

Place	Date	Hour	Summary of Events and Information	Remarks and references to Appendices
	8th.		Lt D. W. Ramsay rejoined Btn from England and assumed Command of "D" Company in Line. During the afternoon a heavy snow storm set in and at one time amounted to a blizzard. G.O.C. Division goes round line.	
	9th.		Snow Storm over leaving parts of line under 2 feet of snow. Frost again sets in. Line is very quiet.	
	10th.		Line very quiet. Frost still continuing.	
		8pm	Battalion is relieved by 5th Cameron Highrs. and A. B+C. Companies go back to Reserve line. "D" Company go to BEER ST. Relief took place without incident.	
	11th.		Shelters were found to be in bad condition and all men were at work improving same. Baths & Anti Trench Foot Treatment were proceeded with.	
	12th.		During afternoon enemy shelled a Battery in corner of GOUZEAUCOURT WOOD and WOODEN TRACK leading from Queens Cross & Deadmans Corner. Sgt GORDON Signalling Sergt. and a linesman were Killed.	
	13th.		Work on improvements of Billets continued. Shelling of previous day repeated. Captain E. W. Bannerman awarded D.S.O. and 2nd Lt A. Kew Wallace the M.C. for work during raid of 30th Decem.	

(A7092). Wt. W12839/M1293. 750,000. 1/17. D. D. & L., Ltd. Forms/C.2118/14.

Instructions regarding War Diaries and Intelligence Summaries are contained in F. S. Regs., Part II. and the Staff Manual respectively. Title pages will be prepared in manuscript.

WAR DIARY
or
INTELLIGENCE SUMMARY.
(Erase heading not required.)

Army Form C. 2118.

10 A & S H. [illegible]

Place	Date	Hour	Summary of Events and Information	Remarks and references to Appendices
	13th	-	Owing to withdrawal of South African Bde from line new disposition of Companies was made in front line causing "D" Company to take over Right of Reserve line from a company of South African Infantry.	[illegible]
	14th	8pm	Relieved 5th Btn Cameron Hrs in front line disposition (under new arrangement) "A" Company Right "C" Company left. "B" Company in support in FLAG RAVINE. "D" Company in RESERVE in BEER ST. Front line held by 3 posts or strong points on each Company front. Front and trenches in fair condition	[illegible]
	15th	3am to 5am	Thaw accompanied by rain set in and conditions of trenches became very Bad by midday were under 2 feet 6" of sticky mud and communication trench impossible. Line very Quiet.	[illegible]
	16th		Trenches still in very bad condition all communication done over open under cover of darkness. Individual enemy movement points to his line being in an equally bad state.	[illegible]
	17th	8pm	Slight improvement in trench condition. Inter Company relief. "D" Company to Left. "B" Company Right "C" Company BEER ST. "A" Company to FLAG RAVINE.	[illegible]

(A7092). Wt. W12839/M1293. 750,000. 1/17. D. D. & L., Ltd. Forms/C.2118/14.

Instructions regarding War Diaries and Intelligence Summaries are contained in F. S. Regs., Part II. and the Staff Manual respectively. Title pages will be prepared in manuscript.

WAR DIARY
or
INTELLIGENCE SUMMARY.
(Erase heading not required.)

Army Form C. 2118.

10th Argyll & Sutherland Hrs.

Place	Date	Hour	Summary of Events and Information	Remarks and references to Appendices
	18th	-	All available men employed in Carrying up RE Stores for works on posts in front line. Line very Quiet	JRO
	19th		More carrying of RE material. Working party of 20 OR put wire across CAMBRAI. RD.	JRO
	20		Steady improvement in trench conditions. Weather remains fairly dry	JRO
		8pm	Battalion is relieved by 5th Btn Cameron Hrs. relief passed without incident Btn returned to Huts at Sheet 57c W2c.	
	21st		Baths and Anti Trench Foot treatment and cleaning up.	
	22nd		Party of 100, O.R. working on Reserve line.	
	23rd		Working Party repeated.	
	24		Battalion relieved at Huts by 1st South African Infantry and moves by Decauville Railway to Camp in GURLU WOOD Sheet 62c D22 a+c	JRO
	25th		Camp sanitation & improvements	JRO
	26th		Working party of 300 on Section XII of Green Line.	JRO

A7092). Wt. W12839/M1293 750,000. 1/17. D. D & L., Ltd. Forms/C2118/14.

Instructions regarding War Diaries and Intelligence Summaries are contained in F. S. Regs., Part II. and the Staff Manual respectively. Title pages will be prepared in manuscript.

WAR DIARY
or
INTELLIGENCE SUMMARY.
(Erase heading not required.)

Army Form C. 2118.

10 · Argyll & Sutherland Hrs

Place	Date	Hour	Summary of Events and Information	Remarks and references to Appendices
	27th	-	Working Party of 300 men on Section XII of Green line.	
	28th		Working Party of 300 men in Section XII of Green line. Advance party left by motor for BRAY-SUR-SOMME	
	29th		Btn proceeded by route march to PERONNE and there entrained at 1.pm Proceeded to LA PLATEAUX railhead, and then by route march to BRAY-SUR-SOMME arriving about 4pm.	
BRAY-SUR SOMME.	30th		In Billets general cleaning up and Steady Drill.	
	31st		Inspection by C.O. and route march for about 10 miles.	
			The additional honours were awarded for the operation on 30th December last:-	
			No 2462 Private S. SHEARER 6356 Private N. McMARTIN 3260 Private J. BOYLAN } Military Medals.	

A5834 Wt. W4973/M687 750,000 8/16 D. D. & L. Ltd. Forms/C.2118/13.

Instructions regarding War Diaries and Intelligence Summaries are contained in F. S. Regs., Part II. and the Staff Manual respectively. Title pages will be prepared in manuscript.

WAR DIARY
or
INTELLIGENCE SUMMARY.
(Erase heading not required.)

Army Form C. 2118.

10 Argyll & Sutherland Highrs

Place	Date	Hour	Summary of Events and Information	Remarks and references to Appendices
			Officer Casualties During January	

Arrived		Departed		
Lieut David Mitchell Ramsay	6/1/18	2nd Lt Argyll Ferguson	Sick	23/1/18
2 Lt Jas Spiers Soutar	15/1/18	John Douglas Stafford Young	Sick	10/1/18
Roderick Mackenzie Walker	15/1/18	Agnew Wallace John Alexander MC	do	15/1/18
Robert McEwen	16/1/18	Jas Spiers Soutar	Sick	19/1/18
Capt Francis John Dobree Knowling	18/1/18	Lt Jas Dalgleish		13/1/18
2 Lt Maclean, Alastair	4/1/18	Lt Colin Campbell	Wounded	6/1/18
2 Lt James Percival McNicol	28/1/18	2 Lt Roger Geoffrey Hyde	Sick	9/1/18
Capt. R. Cavendish. rejoined from Div. H.Q.	30/1/18	" Jas Smith Thomson Russell		21/1/18

J H Scott?
Lt Col
Cmdg. 10. A & S. H.

A5834 Wt. W4973/M687 750,000 8/16 D. D. & L. Ltd. Forms/C.2118/13.

84

26th Machine Gun Company

Instructions regarding War Diaries and Intelligence Summaries are contained in F. S. Regs., Part II. and the Staff Manual respectively. Title pages will be prepared in manuscript.

WAR DIARY
or
~~INTELLIGENCE SUMMARY.~~
(Erase heading not required.)

Army Form C. 2118.

Place	Date	Hour	Summary of Events and Information	Remarks and references to Appendices
	1917 Jany 5th		Between 9PM and midnight indirect fire was brought to bear on CAMBRAI ROAD from H 31 a 85·20 to H 32 c 84 and on trench N 1 a 28 to N 1 c 2.5 Between 5.15 PM and 6.30 AM direct fire was carried out on enemy wire G 36.3.8 to G 36 a 75·10. Total expenditure of ammunition 6000 rounds	
	6th		Between 3.6 and 3.35 PM indirect fire was carried out in support of RAID on enemy trenches from H 31 c 4.4 to N 1.c.2.5 from N 1 a 2.7 to N 1.a 8.4. from G 36 c.65.20 to TILLOY to front line. Total ammunition expended 16750 rounds.	
	7th		Indirect fire was carried out between 9.15 and 10.45 PM on trench H 31 c 50·45 and on CAMBRAI ROAD H 31 a 85.20. between 9 and 10.30 PM Ammunition expended 2000 rounds	
	8th		Three Guns from reserve took up indirect positions G 28.d 47.88 G 28 b.73.07 and G 29 a 45.80	
	9th		4 Officers and 12 men of the 5th Cavalry Machine Gun Squadron visited all the Guns in the line. Between 9 and 10.30 PM indirect fire was brought to bear on enemy trench H 31 c.20.65 to H 31 c 50.45 and on CAMBRAI ROAD H 31 a 85·20. H 32 c 20·55 also on enemy wire throughout the night from G 36 c 30.80 to G 36.75.10. Ammunition expended 5000 rounds	

T2134. Wt. W708—776. 500000. 4/15. Sir J. C. & S.

85

Instructions regarding War Diaries and Intelligence Summaries are contained in F. S. Regs., Part II. and the Staff Manual respectively. Title pages will be prepared in manuscript.

WAR DIARY or ~~INTELLIGENCE SUMMARY.~~

26th Machine Gun Company

(Erase heading not required.)

Army Form C. 2118.

Place	Date	Hour	Summary of Events and Information	Remarks and references to Appendices
	1917 JANY	10th	Between 8 45 and 10 45 PM. indirect fire on CAMBRAI ROAD H 31 a 85 20 to H 32 c. 20. 55 and throughout the night on gaps in enemy wire from G 36 c 30. 80. to G 36. 75. 10. Ammunition expended 2500 rounds.	[initials]
	11th		3 Guns and teams of the 5th Cavalry Machine Gun Squadron relieved 3 Guns of No 1 Section in the line WOOD SECTOR G 35 b. 45. 45, G 36 a 00. 50 G 30 c 60. 15. One Gun and team of 5th Cavalry Machine Gun Squadron took over Indirect Fire position G 29 a. 05. Course at DIVISIONAL Fighting School at GIVENCHY-LE-NOBLE finishes	[initials]
	12th		Four guns and teams of the 5th Cavalry Machine Gun Squadron relieved No 4 Section in St SAUVEUR DEFENCES as follows. G. 29. d 95. 50 G 29 d 75 50 G 29 d 3 5 G 29 d 25. 25	[initials]
	13th		In the morning the 5th Cavalry Machine Gun Squadron relieved two guns and teams at G 24 c. 25. 85. and G 23 c 50. 7 Guns of the 37th Machine Gun Company relieved three Guns of the 26th Machine Gun Company in reserve Indirect Fire positions as follows G 29 d. 20 G 29 d 25. 35. G 23 d 90 15. and 4 Guns of the 197th Machine Gun Company in the following positions G 29. b 75 G 23. d 75. 45 G 23 d 9 4 G 23 c 85 65 Relief was complete at 11. 10 PM. Company marched to billets at MAROEUIL Transport lines ETRUN.	[initials]
	14th		At MAROEUIL. Cleaning Guns and overhauling ammunition	[initials]
	15th		At MAROEUIL. Kit and Smoke helmet inspections. Packing limbers.	[initials]

T2134. Wt. W708—776. 500000. 4/15. Sir J. C. & S.

Instructions regarding War Diaries and Intelligence Summaries are contained in F. S. Regs., Part II. and the Staff Manual respectively. Title pages will be prepared in manuscript.

WAR DIARY
or
INTELLIGENCE SUMMARY.
(*Erase heading not required.*)

Army Form C. 2118.

Place	Date 1917	Hour	Summary of Events and Information	Remarks and references to Appendices
	JANY			
	16th		The 26th Machine Gun Company relieved the 8th Canadian Machine Gun Company and 1st Canadian Motor Machine Gun Battery in the line L Sector. Sections took up positions as follows. Two Guns of No1 Section relieved two Guns of 1st Canadian MMG Battery in ECURIE DEFENCES. A27 b 8.4.	
			No 2 Section relieved 4 Guns of the 8th Canadian M.G. Coy in the right Sector and took up positions as follows A 29.a. 4.9. A 22 d. 80.15. A22 d. 4.3. A22 d 15.30	
			No 3 Section and 1 Gun and team of No1 Section relieved 5 Guns of the 8th Canadian M.G. Coy in the following positions A28 a 80.7½. A 22 c 95.35 A.22.c 5.2 A 22 c.1.6 A 28 a. 3.9.	
			Company advanced HEADQUARTERS A.28 a 5.5.	
			Transport and rear HEADQRS took over lines and billets of the 8th Canadian Machine Gun Company at ETRUN	[initials]
	17th		Nothing to report.	[initials]

87

Instructions regarding War Diaries and Intelligence Summaries are contained in F. S. Regs., Part II. and the Staff Manual respectively. Title pages will be prepared in manuscript.

26th Machine Gun Company WAR DIARY or ~~INTELLIGENCE SUMMARY~~

(Erase heading not required.)

Army Form C. 2118.

Place	Date	Hour	Summary of Events and Information	Remarks and references to Appendices
	1917 JANY 18th		The Brigadier visited Guns in left Sector and in consultation with the C.O. it was agreed that the two guns in ECURIE DEFENSES were of little use owing to the small field of fire. Two new emplacements for these guns were ordered to be constructed at A27 d 15·85 [A.27. d 3.3]. It was also decided that the Gun at A22C95·35 should be moved to position at A22.C. 3.6. to Co-operate with Gun at A22 C·1·6 in enfilading enemy front line, in A22 b and A23 a. A new emplacement at A28a 85·75 was also ordered for Gun at A28 a 80·75 to cover ground on right side of LILLE RD in a northerly direction	[illegible]
Y	19th		Between 8 and 9.45 PM indirect fire was carried out on LILLE ROAD A17a on C.T.A16 d 4.6 to A16.d.95.55. and C.T.A 23 a. 4.8. to A 17 c. 8.2. Ammunition expended 750 rounds	[illegible]
	20th		Indirect fire was brought to bear on LILLE ROAD between 7.30 and 8.30 PM. 500 rounds were fired.	[illegible]
	21st		Between 5.20 and 8.10 PM indirect on LILLE ROAD A17a 0.3 to A11.c.35.35 and on C.T.A16 B 65.45. to A10 d 95.20. Ammunition expended 1250 rounds	[illegible]

88

Instructions regarding War Diaries and Intelligence Summaries are contained in F. S. Regs., Part II. and the Staff Manual respectively. Title pages will be prepared in manuscript.

26th Machine Gun WAR DIARY Company

~~INTELLIGENCE SUMMARY.~~

(Erase heading not required.)

Army Form C. 2118.

Place	Date	Hour	Summary of Events and Information	Remarks and references to Appendices
	Jany 1917 22nd		Four teams of No 4. Section relieved four teams of No 2 Section in the right Sector. A new open emplacement was constructed at A28 a 85.75 firing in a northerly direction along east side of LILLE ROAD and cross firing with gun at A22. C 3.6. The Gun at A22C 95.30 was moved back to position at A22 C 3.6. New emplacements for the two guns in ECURIE DEFENSES were completed at A27 d.15.85 and A27 d. 3.3. Dug outs for these two teams at OC's HEADQRS ECURIE DEFENSES A27 a 75.10. The two guns defend ground SOUTH of ECURIE and would only take up positions in event of an enemy attack. The Guns are now numbered as follows;-	
			No. 1. A.29. a. 4.9. — No. 8. A.22. C. 5.2	
			No. 2. A.29. d. 80.15 — No. 9. A.22. C. 1.6.	
			No. 3. A.22. d. 4.3 — No. 10. A.27. d 2.8	
			No. 4. A.22. d. 15.30 — No. 11. A.27. d. 35.25.	
			No. 5. A.22. C. 3.6.	
			No. 6. A.28. a. 85.75	
			No. 7. A.28. a. 3. 9.	

T2134. Wt. W708—776. 500000. 4/15. Sir J. C. & S.

89

Instructions regarding War Diaries and Intelligence Summaries are contained in F. S. Regs., Part II. and the Staff Manual respectively. Title pages will be prepared in manuscript.

WAR DIARY
26th Machine ~~or~~ Gun Company
~~INTELLIGENCE SUMMARY.~~
(*Erase heading not required.*)

Army Form C. 2118.

Place	Date	Hour	Summary of Events and Information	Remarks and references to Appendices
	1917 JANY 22nd		Between 5.45 and 10 PM indirect fire was brought to bear on Enemy C.T. from A17. d. 4.6. to A.17.B 6.5. and on LIGHT RAILWAY A17 d 6.2. to A17 d 75.60 also on LILLE ROAD A 17 a. 0.3 to A11.C. 35.35. Ammunition expended 2000 rounds	
	23rd		Indirect fire between 5 30 and 9.30 PM on LILLE ROAD A17 a. 0.3 to A11 C. 35.35 1000 rounds were fired.	
	24th		Officer Commanding 197th M.G. Coy visited the line and informed our C.O. that the 26th MG Coy was to have the use of two of his Guns under the Command of 1 Officer. It was decided that these guns should take over Indirect Fire positions at A28 a 45.40 and A28 a 30. 85. Dug out accomodation was found for the two teams of 197 MG Coy at A21 d. 4.1.	
	25th		Between 8 and 9 30 PM Indirect Fire on Enemy LIGHT RAILWAY A17 d 6.2. to A17 d. 7.4. Ammunition expended 500 rounds. Two Guns and teams of the 197th Machine Gun Company came into the line under 1 Officer. These guns form a reserve in ECURIE DEFENCES and also carry out Indirect Fire.	

90

Instructions regarding War Diaries and Intelligence Summaries are contained in F. S. Regs., Part II. and the Staff Manual respectively. Title pages will be prepared in manuscript.

26th Machine Gun WAR DIARY Company

~~or~~ ~~INTELLIGENCE SUMMARY.~~

(Erase heading not required.)

Army Form C. 2118.

Place	Date	Hour	Summary of Events and Information	Remarks and references to Appendices
	1917 JANY 26th		Indirect Fire was carried out between 3.15 and 4 PM on enemy C.Ts A 16 b.7.4 to A.10 d 85.40. and A17 a.25.10. to A17 a.4.6. Ammunition expended 1250 rounds.	
	27th		Enemy was observed Carrying material down trench between A17 a 90.55 and A17 a.7.4 at 2.15 PM. Indirect Fire from A 28 a.45.40. was brought to bear on this trench. Enemy replied at 2.40 PM by Sending Several 4.2 Shells in direction of Gun. Fire however was maintained at intervals until 10 PM. Between 7 and 10 PM indirect fire on Enemy C.Ts A17 c 90.55 to A17 c 28. and A17 a 35.80. to A11.c 35.10. rounds expended 4500.	
	28th		No.3 Section and one team of No.1 Section Guns No 5.6.7.8.9 were relieved by No 2 Section and 1 team of No.1 Section. Indirect Fire was carried out between 7 and 10 PM on Enemy C.Ts A 16.b.7.4 to A.10.d 85.40. and A17.a.25.10 to A17.a.35.60. 1000 were fired.	
	29th		Between 7 and 10 PM Indirect Fire on JUNCTION OF LIGHT RAILWAY A.18 a.08.65 on C.T. A.11.c 50.15. to A11.c.85.95. and on SUNKEN ROAD B13 C.3.3 Ammunition expended 2000 rounds	

T2134. Wt. W708—776. 500000. 4/15. Sir J. C. & S.

Instructions regarding War Diaries and Intelligence Summaries are contained in F. S. Regs., Part II. and the Staff Manual respectively. Title pages will be prepared in manuscript.

91

26th Machine Gun WAR DIARY Company

~~or~~

~~INTELLIGENCE SUMMARY.~~

(*Erase heading not required.*)

Army Form C. 2118.

Place	Date	Hour	Summary of Events and Information	Remarks and references to Appendices
	1917 Jany			
	30th		Nothing to report.	[initials]
	31st		Between 7.15 and 10 PM indirect fire was brought to bear on JUNCTION OF LIGHT RAILWAY A.18.a.05.65 and on C.T. A17.d.45.60. to A17.b.7.4. 1500 rounds were expended.	[initials]
			While in rest Billets at ETRUN the following training was carried out Range practice Bombing Route marching and Box respirator drill.	[initials]

W. Chalmers Lt for
O.C. 26th Machine Gun Coy.

T2134. Wt. W708—776. 500000. 4/15. Sir J. C. & S.

Instructions regarding War Diaries and Intelligence Summaries are contained in F. S. Regs., Part II. and the Staff Manual respectively. Title pages will be prepared in manuscript.

92

26th Machine Gun WAR DIARY Company or ~~INTELLIGENCE SUMMARY~~

(Erase heading not required.)

Army Form C. 2118.

Vol 13

Place	Date	Hour	Summary of Events and Information	Remarks and references to Appendices
	1917 July 1st		Between 7.20 and 9 30 PM Indirect fire was carried out on LILLE ROAD A17a.15.65. to A17a.2.9 on Communication Trenches A17d.4.6 to A17 b.7.4 and on LIGHT RAILWAY A17.b 85.10. to A18a.05.65. Rounds fired 1750.	S.C.
	2nd		Rear Hqrs including 5 Guns in reserve, less Transport moved from ETRUN and took up new billets at ANZIN. Two Guns of the 197th M.G Coy went out of the line in accordance with instructions from 9th Division Between 3 and 4 PM Indirect Fire was brought to bear on enemy COMMUNICATION TRENCHES A17a.05.30. to A11.a 2 8.	S.C
	3rd		No 3 Section relieved No 4 Section in the line right Sector Guns Nos 1.2.3 and 4. Indirect Fire was carried out between 6.30 and 9 30. PM on LILLE ROAD from A.16.b 9.0. to A.11.c 35.10. Ammunition expended 2500 rounds	S.C.
	4th		Between 6.30 and 9.30 PM Indirect fire on LILLE ROAD from A16. b.9.0 to A.11.c 35.10 Ammunition expended 1000 rounds.	S.C
	5th		Nothing to report	S.C.
	6th		Indirect Fire was carried out between 7 and 10PM on JUNCTION of LIGHT.RLWY A18a.05.60. and on SUNKEN ROAD.B13.C2.3. Rounds expended 1500	S.C

1577 Wt.W10791/1773 500,000 1/15 D. D. & L. A.D.S.S./Forms/C. 2118.

Instructions regarding War Diaries and Intelligence Summaries are contained in F. S. Regs., Part II. and the Staff Manual respectively. Title pages will be prepared in manuscript.

Army Form C. 2118.

26th Machine WAR DIARY Gun Company
or ~~INTELLIGENCE SUMMARY.~~
(Erase heading not required.)

Place	Date	Hour	Summary of Events and Information	Remarks and references to Appendices
	July			
	7th		Between 7 and 10 PM Indirect Fire was carried out on LILLE ROAD A16.b9.0 to A11.C.3.1. and on COMMUNICATION TRENCHES A17.d.5.6. to A17.b.7.5. rounds fired 2000	S.C.
	8th		At 5.30 PM an enemy HEAVY TRENCH MORTAR got a direct hit on Concrete M.G emplacement at A22.d.4.3. corner of BIDOT and Support killing Sentry and completely smashing Gun and Equipment. This Gun was immediately replaced by one from reserve.	S.C
	9th		Nothing to report.	S.C
	10th		10 Guns of 152nd M.G.Coy relieved 10 Guns of the 26th M.G.Coy. No 5 Gun position was not taken over. On completion of relief the Company less Transport moved to Huts at L.3.C.	S.C.
	11th		The Company Route marched to Billets at CHELERS, arriving at 1.30 PM.	S.C
	12th		Overhauling of Guns and Equipment. Indents for deficiencies	S.C
	13th		Care and Cleaning of Guns. Interior economy. Haircutting etc.	S.C
	14th		Physical training, Squad Drill. Lecture. Map reading. Indirect and overhead Fire in billets. Judging distance, Demonstration of Indirect and Overhead fire.	S.C.

1577 Wt. W10791/1773 500,000 1/15 D. D. & L. A.D.S.S./Forms/C. 2118.

Instructions regarding War Diaries and Intelligence Summaries are contained in F. S. Regs., Part II. and the Staff Manual respectively. Title pages will be prepared in manuscript.

94

Army Form C. 2118.

26th Machine Gun Company WAR DIARY ~~or INTELLIGENCE SUMMARY~~

(Erase heading not required.)

Place	Date	Hour	Summary of Events and Information	Remarks and references to Appendices
	Feby 14th		Immediate action, Stoppages. Spare parts.	S.C.
	15th		2nd Lt Giles. No 1 Section complete with Guns and Equipment proceeded to day to join 8th BLACK WATCH to take part in Battalion training on 16th and 17th inst. 7.30 AM to 8. AM. Physical training under Orderly Officer. 9.30 AM to 11 AM Lecture on MAP reading and Indirect Fire (in billets). 11 AM to 12 30 PM. Judging distance. Explanation of methods of Indirect and Overhead fire. 2 PM to 4 PM Short ROUTE March and tactical Scheme viz defense of BAILLEUL VILLAGE without Guns.	S.C.
	16th		7.30 to 8 AM Physical training. 9 30 AM to 12.30 PM Route March to BAILLEUL. Tactical Scheme. Emplacements for defense of VILLAGE on N.E. sides. Range Cards. Judging distance. 2 PM to 4 PM Cleaning Guns and Overhauling Belts	S.C.
	17th		Training as above	S.C.
	18th		Church parade.	S.C.
	19th		Physical exercises. Tactical Scheme. Revolver practice	S.C.
	20th		The Company moved off at 9.15 AM to PENIN arriving in billets at 11 AM	S.C.
	21st		At PENIN. Handling Arms. Squad drill. etc.	S.C.

1577 Wt. W10791/1773 500,000 1/15 D. D. & L. A.D.S.S./Forms/C. 2118.

95

WAR DIARY

or

~~INTELLIGENCE SUMMARY~~.

(*Erase heading not required.*)

Army Form C. 2118.

Instructions regarding War Diaries and Intelligence Summaries are contained in F. S. Regs., Part II. and the Staff Manual respectively. Title pages will be prepared in manuscript.

Place	Date	Hour	Summary of Events and Information	Remarks and references to Appendices
	1917 Feby			
	22nd		Training	S.C.
	23rd		The Company moved at 10 15 AM to new billets at ORLENCOURT arriving there about 12.30 PM.	S.C.
	24th		Training at ORLENCOURT. A Class of instruction under Lt P.B. Duffus was formed for insufficiently trained men.	S.C.
	25th		No 4 Section with Guns and Equipment report to O.C 5th CAMERON HLRS at 10 AM. on Training area. Church parade.	S.C.
	26th		All Sections Tactical Scheme on Training Area, for practicing the Attack. Inspection of Smoke Helmets and Box Respirators	S.C.
	27th		Training in Conjunction with Battalions on training Ground	S.C.
	28th		Training Area Brigade Attack Scheme	S.C.

S. Crawford Major
O.C. 26th M.G.C.

96

Instructions regarding War Diaries and Intelligence Summaries are contained in F. S. Regs., Part II. and the Staff Manual respectively. Title pages will be prepared in manuscript.

26th Machine Gun Company

WAR DIARY
or
~~INTELLIGENCE SUMMARY.~~

(Erase heading not required.)

Army Form C. 2118.

Vol 14

Place	Date 1917	Hour	Summary of Events and Information	Remarks and references to Appendices
	March 1st		Training Practice in the Attack Preparing to move Overhauling Guns and Ammunition	
	2nd		Company paraded at 9 AM and marched to Y Huts L 2 C Arriving about 3 PM	
	3rd		Company less Transport and No 4 Section (this Section was isolated owing to an outbreak of German Measles) moved to ARRAS and relieved 9 Guns of the 28th M.G. Coy in the line taking up positions as follows 3 Gun of No 3 Section G 24. C 2.4 / G 24 C 15.40 / G 24 C 00.55 } 4 Guns of No 2 Section G 17 a 95.23 / G 17 a 75.30 / G 17 a 35.75 / G 11 d 20.03 } Two Guns of No 1 Section G 11 C 65 10 / G 11 C 15 68 } Remaining teams of No 1 and 3 Sections in reserve at Company Headquarters ARRAS	
	4th		On 9th Divisions instructions the two teams of No 1 Section in reserve relieved two teams of the 197th M G Coy taking over Anti Aircraft positions as follows G 17 C 35.85. and G 11 a 6.4.	C.V.B.

A5834 Wt. W4973/M687 750,000 8/16 D. D. & L. Ltd. Forms/C.2118/13.

97

Army Form C. 2118.

Instructions regarding War Diaries and Intelligence Summaries are contained in F. S. Regs., Part II. and the Staff Manual respectively. Title pages will be prepared in manuscript.

WAR DIARY or INTELLIGENCE SUMMARY.

26th Machine Gun Company

(Erase heading not required.)

Place	Date 1917 MARCH	Hour	Summary of Events and Information	Remarks and references to Appendices
	4th		Between 6 and 10 PM indirect fire was brought to bear on COMMUNICATION TRENCH H13 b 5.5 to H8 C.0.0 on SUNKEN ROAD and COMMUNICATION TRENCH G12 d 55.00 to G12 d.9.9 Ammunition expended 3000 rounds. One Section of the 28th M G COY was attached to the Company in reserve at Company Headqrs ARRAS	
	5th		Nothing to report 33 men worked from 10 AM to 3.30 PM on BARRAGE EMPLACEMENTS	
	6th		Between 2 and 11.00 PM Indirect Fire was brought to bear on the following targets ENEMY FRONT LINE G18 a 35.10 to G18 a 45.70 on COMMUNICATION TRENCHES G12 b.2.1 G12 d.5.0 to G12 d 95.90 H 7 a 9.9 to H1 d 30, G12 b 5.3 to G12 b 80.43 and on ROAD and LIGHT RLWY G18 b 90.32 to G13 b 4.5 Ammunition expended 3700 rounds. Work in progress on BARRAGE EMPLACEMENTS. Transport moved from Y HUTS to Transport lines at ETRUN.	
	7th		Between 7 and 10 PM. 4 AM and 5 AM Indirect Fire was carried out on the following targets SUNKEN ROAD and COMMUNICATION TRENCH H1C 5.5 to H.1.C.9.9. and on LIGHT RLWY G18 b 9.3 Ammunition expended 2000 rounds Work on BARRAGE emplacements Continued	
	8th		Nothing to report. Work continued as above	

C.H.R.

A5834 Wt. W4973/M687 750,000 8/16 D. D. & L. Ltd. Forms/C.2118/13.

98

Army Form C. 2118.

Instructions regarding War Diaries and Intelligence Summaries are contained in F. S. Regs., Part II. and the Staff Manual respectively. Title pages will be prepared in manuscript.

26th Machine Gun WAR DIARY Company

or

~~INTELLIGENCE SUMMARY.~~

(Erase heading not required.)

Place	Date 1917	Hour	Summary of Events and Information	Remarks and references to Appendices
	MARCH 9th		Indirect Fire was Carried out on COMMUNICATION TRENCH H7a 99. to H1d 30.05 H13 b. 4.5 to H.8.C 0.0 G6d 80.65 and on JUNCTION of TRENCHES and ROAD G12d 90.85 2750 rounds were expended. Work on BARRAGE EMPLACEMENTS Continued	
	10th		Between 7 and 8 PM and 4 AM and 5 AM Indirect Fire was Carried out on SUNKEN ROAD and TRENCH H1d 0.25 to H1d. 35 and on TRENCH H1d 0.25 to H1d 3.5 Work continued on BARRAGE EMPLACEMENTS.	
	11th		Between 6 and 8 PM Indirect Fire on BAILLEUL ROAD G6d. 30.25 to G6d 80.65 Artillery activity on Right Sector between 2.30 and 4 AM. Work on BARRAGE EMPLACEMENTS Continued	
	12th		During the day while the Garrison was on working party the REDOUBT was held by 4 Guns from reserve. Between the hours of 7 and 10 PM Indirect Fire was brought to bear on COMMUNICATION TRENCH and RAILWAY H14 a 1.3 to H7b 70 and on C.Ts H7a 9.9 to H1d 5.0 and G12 b 5.3 to G12 b 8 4. rounds expended 2500 Work on BARRAGE EMPLACEMETS Continued	
	13th		Between 630 and 10 PM Indirect Fire on ROAD and CT G12. d. 95 90 H7a. 47 97 and on ROAD G6d. 8.6 to H1C 39. Ammunition expended 2000 rounds. 27th MG Coy relieved 26th MG Coy in the line taking over 9 Guns. The two Anti Aircraft Guns were not taken over. On relief being completed the Company marched to billets at Y Huts L.C.2 Transport remaining at ETRUN	

A5834 Wt. W4973/M687 750,000 8/16 D. D. & L. Ltd. Forms/C.2118/13.

C.Y.R.

99

Instructions regarding War Diaries and Intelligence Summaries are contained in F. S. Regs., Part II. and the Staff Manual respectively. Title pages will be prepared in manuscript.

26th Machine Gun WAR DIARY or ~~INTELLIGENCE SUMMARY.~~ Company

(Erase heading not required.)

Army Form C. 2118.

Place	Date 1917	Hour	Summary of Events and Information	Remarks and references to Appendices
	MARCH 14th		At Y Huts. 4 Guns of No 3 Section relieved 4 Guns of the 28th M.G. Coy 2 Guns at Ammunition Dump BOIS-DE-HABARCQ. } on Anti Aircraft duty 2 Guns at Ammunition Dump LARESSET }	
	15th		Baths. Kit inspection	
	16th		Training Area. Lectures	
	17th		Training Area	
	18th		Church parades	
	19th		Physical exercise. Training area. Practice in the ATTACK Supply of AMMUNITION	
	20th		Owing to inclement Weather Sections training indoor. Technical instruction Lectures	
	21st		Preparing to move to the trenches. Two Sections and Headquarters moved to ARRAS. 26th Machine Gun Company relieved 6 Guns of the 27th Machine Gun Company in the line J Sector. Two Guns in Reserve at Coy Headquarters ARRAS.	C.V.R.

100

Instructions regarding War Diaries and Intelligence Summaries are contained in F. S. Regs., Part II. and the Staff Manual respectively. Title pages will be prepared in manuscript.

WAR DIARY or ~~INTELLIGENCE SUMMARY.~~

26th Machine Gun Company

(Erase heading not required.)

Army Form C. 2118.

Place	Date 1917	Hour	Summary of Events and Information	Remarks and references to Appendices
	March 22nd		Throughout the night. GAPS on enemy wire G 12 d 9 1. G 12 d 75 35 and G 12 d 75 95 were fired on. Between 5.30 and 6 30 PM two enemy Aeroplanes were fired on.	
	23rd		Between 5 PM and 6 PM two enemy Aeroplanes were fired on.	
	24th		Between 5 PM and 6 PM two enemy aeroplanes were fired on	
	25th		Nothing to report	
	26th		Nothing to report	
	27th		Nothing to report. No 4 Section returned to duty from Quarantine.	
	28th		Between 10 AM and 11-30 AM. 2 PM and 3 PM four enemy Aeroplanes were fired on. Indirect Fire was brought to bear on target H 7 b 7 0 to H 8 C 01 00 between 8.30 and 10 30 PM. Work continued on Barrage emplacements	
	29th		Nothing to report. Work continued on Barrage emplacements	
	30		Between 11 AM and 12 noon. 4 30 PM and 7 PM 6 enemy aeroplanes were fired on	
	31st		Between 3 and 4 PM. 6.30 and 7 PM two enemy Aeroplanes were fired on. Work continued on Barrage emplacement. No 4 Section moved from Y Huts to ARRAS	

C. W. Rigby Capt.
26th Machine Gun Company.

101

WAR DIARY for April 1917. Vol 15

or

~~INTELLIGENCE SUMMARY.~~

(Erase heading not required.)

26th M.G. Coy

Army Form C. 2118.

Instructions regarding War Diaries and Intelligence Summaries are contained in F. S. Regs., Part II. and the Staff Manual respectively. Title pages will be prepared in manuscript.

Place	Date	Hour	Summary of Events and Information	Remarks and references to Appendices
In the field	1/4/17.		Between 11.30 AM. and 1.15 PM 3.30 P.M. and 4 P.M. 5 and 6.30 P.M. enemy aeroplanes were fired on. Throughout the night Indirect fire was carried out on GAPS in enemy wire G.18.b. 3500 rounds fired. Section of 194 M. G. Coy relieved section of 26 M. G. Coy in the line	C.V.R.
	2/4/17.		Nothing to report. Working on Assembly trench east of FORESTIER REDOUBT. No. 4 Section relieved No. 2 Section in the line	C.V.R.
	3/4/17.		Between 1.30 and 1.35 p.m. enemy aeroplane was fired on. During the night Gaps in enemy wire G.18.b were fired on. Work continued on Assembly trenches. No. 1 Section moved to Y Huts.	C.V.R.
	4/4/17		Throughout the night Machine Guns fired on Gaps in enemys wire in Square G.18.b. Work continued on Assembly trenches	C.V.R.
	5/4/17.		Nothing to report	C.V.R.
	6/4/17.		Throughout the night Indirect fire on Gaps in enemy wire. Working on Assembly trenches	C.V.R.
	7/4/17.		Continuation of above	C.V.R.
	8/4/17.		The remaining gun and team of No 4 Section was moved up from reserve to position in in Redoubt Line, the idea being to hold the line with Machine Guns during the night of the 8th/9th while the Infantry moved into Assembly trenches. The remaining 12 Guns and teams of the Coy. with 4 Carriers per Gun moved up into position in assembly area. The Brigade attack scheme is as follows:—	C.V.R.

A5834 Wt. W4973/M687 750,000 8/16 D. D. & L. Ltd. Forms/C.2118/13.

102

WAR DIARY April 1917

~~or~~

~~INTELLIGENCE SUMMARY.~~

(Erase heading not required.)

Army Form C. 2118.

Instructions regarding War Diaries and Intelligence Summaries are contained in F. S. Regs., Part II. and the Staff Manual respectively. Title pages will be prepared in manuscript.

Place	Date	Hour	Summary of Events and Information	Remarks and references to Appendices
In the field	8/4/17		Reference TRENCH MAP ARRAS 1/10000 51B N.W 3. Intention, The XVII Corps is to capture the German 4th system of trenches and establish a line NORTH and EAST of FAMPOUX. The 9th Division is the right Division of Corps and the 26th Brigade the right Brigade of the Division. The 4th Division is in reserve and will pass through the 9th Division and capture the 4th German system, the 9th Divisions final objective being the 3rd system. 26th Brigade Boundaries:- Right the river SCARPE, Left; a line running from Enemy front line at G.18A.45.75 eastwards to Bridge at H.8 C.05.05 thence to H.15.A 35.65. Objectives:- First objective Enemy first system, THE BLACK LINE, a line running north and south along sunken road G.18.B 95.35 objective Enemy second system. (2.) THE BLUE LINE Railway Embankment H.13.D.7.3 to H.14A.05.95. 2nd objective (3.) THE BROWN LINE a line running from the SCARPE at H.21A.9.7 along the EASTERN edge of ATHIES to sunken road at H.15.A.15.30 thence northwards to H.15.A.35.65. Distribution of Brigade:- The 7th Seaforths on the right, the 8th Black Watch on the left, the 10th Argyle & Sutherlands in support and the 5th Camerons in Reserve. The Guns of the Company are distributed as follows:- 2 guns attached 7th Seaforths, 2 Guns attached 8th Black Watch, 8 Guns taking part in Divisional M.G. Barrage Scheme, 4 Guns in Reserve. In the Divisional Barrage Scheme 40 guns, 8 from each of the Brigade Companies and 16 of the Divisional Company are to be employed. These are divided into two groups of 20 each one group to open fire at ZERO on enemy trenches	

A5834 Wt. W4973/M687 750,000 8/16 D. D. & L. Ltd. Forms/C.2118/13.

103

Instructions regarding War Diaries and Intelligence Summaries are contained in F. S. Regs., Part II. and the Staff Manual respectively. Title pages will be prepared in manuscript.

WAR DIARY
or
~~INTELLIGENCE SUMMARY.~~
(*Erase heading not required.*)

April 1917.

Army Form C. 2118.

Place	Date	Hour	Summary of Events and Information	Remarks and references to Appendices
In the field	8/4/17		400 behind the front line for 4 minutes then lift on to BLACK LINE and finally form a protective barrage in front of BLACK LINE. The other group of 20 Guns to move forward at ZERO to BLACK LINE and open fire on BLUE LINE as soon as the advance from the BLACK LINE commenced. When our own troops get close up the guns lift and form a protective barrage 500 east of the BLUE LINE. 8 Guns of the Company were chosen for the latter group. The Company is alloted 68 men and 4 Officers as a Carrying party, this party is divided as follows:- 3 carriers per gun to the 4 guns allotted to Battalions, 4 Carriers per gun to 8 Barrage Guns under one officer, 4 carriers per gun to each of the 4 reserve guns under one officer, 8 reserve carriers at dump under one officer. __Ammunition Supply__. Three dumps are formed, one with the reserve guns and one on either flank of the Brigade. In the central dump with the reserve Guns and 8 reserve ammunition carriers, 98 filled belt boxes, 32 2 gallon tins of water, one gallon of gun oil and 10000 rounds of S.A.A. are stored. A belt filling machine is also fitted up. It is decided that pack mules loaded with filled belt boxes might be able to push forward to the barrage guns, the supply of ammunition to these guns being a big problem.	
	9/4/17		ZERO hour was fixed at 5.30 AM. __Disposition of guns at ZERO.__ 2 guns under 2nd Lt C.P. Rossi attached to 7th Seaforths in cellar close to Battalion HdQrs about C.H.D.7.4. 2 Guns under 2nd Lt S.S. Brown in assembly trenches behind Black Watch about G.19.B.4.3. 8 Barrage Guns under Lt J.S.R. Webster, Lt W.E. Ellerton, 2nd Lt A.W. Rider in assembly trenches in rear of 10th A & S. about G.M.A.9.4. 4 Guns in reserve in Shelters near Brigade Headquarters about	CWR

A5834 Wt. W4973/M687 750,000 8/16 D. D. & L. Ltd. Forms/C.2118/13.

104

Instructions regarding War Diaries and Intelligence Summaries are contained in F. S. Regs., Part II. and the Staff Manual respectively. Title pages will be prepared in manuscript.

WAR DIARY
or
~~INTELLIGENCE~~ SUMMARY.
(Erase heading not required.)

April 1917.

Army Form C. 2118.

Place	Date	Hour	Summary of Events and Information	Remarks and references to Appendices
In the field	9/4/17		G. M.A.Y.5. Company HdQrs with Brigade HdQrs. First Phase The attack on the BLACK LINE: At ZERO the barrage opened, the 2 guns under Black Watch moved forward to enemy third line behind the moppers up and from there to the BLACK LINE about H.13.A.05.Y5 taking up position to consolidate. The 8 barrage guns moved forward in rear of the front supporting Company of the 10th A & S. Hrs. One gun was put out of action, the barrel casing being pierced with shrapnell and the number 2 killed. 7 guns came into position in the BLACK LINE and took up positions ready to open barrage fire as soon as the advance on the second objective commenced. The 8 reserve carriers were sent up from dump to these guns with 16 belt boxes. These 8 carriers together with about 20 others attached to guns returned to dump and kept up the supply of SAA. At ZERO + 15 minutes the 2 guns attached to 7th Seaforths moved forward to positions about G.18.D.6.4 where a strong point was being formed. These guns got several good targets consisting of small parties of the enemy leaving village on south side. On the village of St LAURENT BLANGY being taken these guns moved to the BLACK LINE. One gun was pushed forward to obtain a better view of ground in front. This gun opened fire on several of the fleeing enemy. At ZERO + 2 hours the seven barrage guns opened an intense fire on the BLUE LINE which was maintained for 6 minutes. SECOND PHASE At ZERO + 2 hours 6 minutes the attack on the second objective commenced. The seven barrage guns lifted from the BLUE LINE and dropped a protective barrage 500 yds east of it, a steady rate of fire was maintained, about 14000 rounds were fired by the guns. By three hours after ZERO the pack mules got through and formed a dump of belt boxes on the right of the BLACK LINE about G.18.B.9.3. On the BLUE LINE being taken the 4 guns	

105

Instructions regarding War Diaries and Intelligence Summaries are contained in F. S. Regs., Part II. and the Staff Manual respectively. Title pages will be prepared in manuscript.

WAR DIARY

or

~~INTELLIGENCE SUMMARY.~~

(Erase heading not required.)

April 1914

Army Form C. 2118.

Place	Date	Hour	Summary of Events and Information	Remarks and references to Appendices
In the field	9/4/17		allotted to Battalions came into position on Railway embankment about H.14.A.05.20 and were prepared to give covering fire during the third phase (the [illegible] of the [illegible] and Camerons on the BROWN LINE). These guns got several small targets. One party of the enemy numbering about 20 seen leaving ATHIES on EAST SIDE was [illegible] dealt with two guns operating on it simultaneously at 1200 yds range. Third Phase. It was found unnecessary to give overhead (supporting) fire during the attack on the BROWN LINE; the enemy did not put up a fight. The 4 reserve guns had now moved up in rear of the Camerons and came into position in a strong point which was being formed at G.14.B.34 from which the whole front could be covered. Three of the barrage guns were now moved up to the BLUE LINE under Mr [illegible] and took up positions to consolidate. The 12th Brigade of the 4th Division passed through to the attack on the GREEN LINE. The final disposition of guns now was: 4 guns in BLACK LINE, 7 guns in BLUE LINE, 4 guns in STRONG POINT G.14.B.34, one gun out of action. These guns remained in position during the night. Company Head Qrs moved up to BLUE LINE. The whole attack went splendidly and the enemy seemed to be completely taken by surprise. He did not put up much of a fight except at ST LAURENT BLANGY where his bombers hidden in houses delayed the attack a little	C.W.R.
	10/4/17		The 4 guns in strong point were relieved by 4 guns of the 12th Brigade. These 4 and the 7 on the BLUE LINE moved back to the vicinity of the BLACK LINE. Coy. HQ Qrs established at G.18.B.8.1. All guns were now in reserve	C.W.R.

A5834 Wt. W4973/M687 750,000 8/16 D. D. & L. Ltd. Forms/C.2118/13.

106

Army Form C. 2118.

WAR DIARY
or
~~INTELLIGENCE SUMMARY.~~

(Erase heading not required.)

April 1917.

Instructions regarding War Diaries and Intelligence Summaries are contained in F. S. Regs., Part II. and the Staff Manual respectively. Title pages will be prepared in manuscript.

Place	Date	Hour	Summary of Events and Information	Remarks and references to Appendices
In the field	11/4/17.		Cleaned up and reorganised. One Section was sent up to BLUE LINE and came under the command of the Garrison Commander. O.C. Black Watch.	C.M.R.
	12/4/17.		Reference map - ARRAS 51.B.N.W.3. FAMPOUX. The Division was again ordered to attack. The enemy was holding a line from ROEUX through STATION in I.13 Central to H.12.D. and B. We held a line from the RAILWAY BRIDGE at H.18.D.25.15 running north west in front of FAMPOUX thence northwards to HYDERABAD WORK. The attack was divided into 2 objectives :- (A) First objective :- STATION and buildings in I.B. Central and the road from STATION to INN in I 7 A. (B) Second objective The CHEMICAL WORKS and BUILDINGS south of the RAILWAY - MOUNT PLEASANT WOOD - CEMETRY and VILLAGE of ROEUX. The 27th and SOUTH AFRICAN BRIGADES were ordered to attack the first objective and on it being gained the 26th BDE was to attack the second. The Machine guns of the 3 Brigades were detailed for barrage work and were in position along the line H.16.B.7.2 to H.11.A.6.2. The guns of the Divisional Coy were in readiness to move up and consolidate. ZERO was at 5 P.M. All Machine guns opened on enemy line on a front from I.13.C.9.0 to the INN at I.7.A.25.8. Intense fire was maintained until ZERO + 15 minutes when guns lifted on to the high ground behind. The infantry attack on the first objective failed owing to hostile Machine Gun and artillery fire, the guns of the Company fired 22000 rounds. The 15 guns of the Company were relayed on enemy line and orders given to fire in the event of enemy counter	

Instructions regarding War Diaries and Intelligence Summaries are contained in F. S. Regs., Part II. and the Staff Manual respectively. Title pages will be prepared in manuscript.

104

WAR DIARY
or
INTELLIGENCE SUMMARY.
(*Erase heading not required.*)

April 1917

Army Form C. 2118.

Place	Date	Hour	Summary of Events and Information	Remarks and references to Appendices
In the field	12/4/17		Attack. The Brigade relieved the 12th Brigade after the attack.	C.V.R.
	13/4/17		Company HdQrs and 9 guns moved back into reserve at ATHIES. 6 guns moved forward after dark and took up the following positions to consolidate, 2 guns in cellar of house at H.7.D.95.90, one gun H.18.A.3.7. one gun H.18.A.20.75, two guns H.11.D.7.3	C.V.R.
	14/4/17		The 8th BLACK WATCH holding the right of the Sector pushed forward the line on the right to H.18.D.70.35 thereby straightening it. One of the guns at H.17.D.955.90 was moved to H.18.D.2.2 to cover consolidation of new line.	C.V.R.
	15/4/17		The Company was relieved by the 153rd Machine Gun Company. On completion of relief Company moved to billets ARRAS	C.V.R.
	16/4/17		Company moved to Y Huts L 28	C.V.R.
	17/4/17		Cleaning up. Kit and Gun equipment inspection.	C.V.R.
	18/4/17		Inspection of men and gun equipment by Commanding Officer	C.V.R.
	19/4/17		Company in training	C.V.R.
	20/4/17		do. Gas Drill. Machine Gun Drill	C.V.R.
	21/4/17		The Company moved to MARQUAY. The Transport by road and remainder of Company by train	C.V.R.
	22/4/17		Company in training. Inspections	C.V.R.
	23/4/17		Physical Training. Cleaning of guns. Drill	C.V.R.
	24/4/17		Training. Elementary Tests	C.V.R.

A5834 Wt. W4973/M687 750,000 8/16 D. D. & L. Ltd. Forms/C.2118/13.

Instructions regarding War Diaries and Intelligence Summaries are contained in F. S. Regs., Part II. and the Staff Manual respectively. Title pages will be prepared in manuscript.

108

WAR DIARY ~~or INTELLIGENCE SUMMARY.~~

(Erase heading not required.)

April 1917

Army Form C. 2118.

Place	Date	Hour	Summary of Events and Information	Remarks and references to Appendices
In the field	25/4/17		The Company moved from MARQUAY to Y Huts the Transport by Road and remainder of Company by train	C.V.R.
	26/4/17		At Y Huts L.2.C. Training	C.V.R.
	27/4/17		The Brigade moved up into Corps Reserve at BLUE LINE H.7.D. Transport lines in ROCLINCOURT VALLEY G.16.A	C.V.R.
	28/4/17		At BLUE LINE. A reconnaissance of the 37th Divisional front was carried out 1.7.C.7.7 to 1.1.A.9.9	C.V.R.
	29/4/17		The 26th M.G. Coy relieved the 63rd M.G. Coy and the 112th M.G. Coy of the 37th Division in the line. 8 Guns took up positions as follows:- 1 Gun 1.7.A.5.5 } 1 " 1.7.A.0.2 } 1st LINE 2 " 1.7.A.2.6 } 2 guns in CHILI TRENCH H.6.b.8.1 } 2 " " H.12.C.9.9 } 2nd LINE 8 Guns in reserve at BLUE LINE. Company HQrs at H.4.D.7.3. It was now ascertained that our front line ran approximately from 1.7.A.6.9 through 1.7.B.1.6 southwards to 1.7.D.1.5. the enemy still being in possession of the southern part of the CHEMICAL WORKS in 1.13.	
	30/4/17		Building emplacements. Firing at aircraft.	C.V.R. [illegible]

C.V. Rigby Capt
O.C. 26 M.G. Coy

A5834 Wt. W4973/M687 750,000 8/16 D. D. & L. Ltd. Forms/C.2118/13.

109

Army Form C. 2118.

Instructions regarding War Diaries and Intelligence Summaries are contained in F. S. Regs., Part II. and the Staff Manual respectively. Title pages will be prepared in manuscript.

WAR DIARY or ~~INTELLIGENCE SUMMARY.~~

26th Machine Gun Company.

(Erase heading not required.)

Vol 16

Place	Date	Hour	Summary of Events and Information	Remarks and references to Appendices
	1917 May			
	1st.		Firing on enemy aircraft was carried out.	C.W.R.
	2nd.		The 8 guns in reserve at BLUE LINE moved up to positions for the attack on the following day.	
			The orders for the attack are as follows:- (Ref. ARRAS TRENCH MAP 1:20,000. The 9th Division is to take part in a general attack. The 26th Brigade is to attack on the right and the 27th Brigade on the left. One Brigade of the 17th Division is in reserve. The 4th Division is on the right.	
			Objectives The final objective is a line running from railway at 19.C.84 to 12.a.8.6. The Boundaries of the 26th Brigade are. (1) On the Right a line running from our front line at 17. D 05.45 eastwards to RAILWAY at 19c.22 thence along RAILWAY to 19.C.84. (2) On the left a line from front line in 11.C.55.20 eastwards to 13.C.4.3. The enemy holds a line of trench 60 to 200 yards EAST of our front line.	
			Disposition of the Brigade The attack is to be carried out by the 5th CAMERON HLRS. on the Right and the 8th BLACK WATCH on the Left. The 10th ARGYLL and SUTHERLAND HLRS. in Support and the 7th SEAFORTH HLRS. in Reserve.	
			Plan of Attack The Brigade is to attack in four waves. an interval of at least 100 yards being kept between each wave. One Company of the 10th ARGYLL and SUTHERLAND HLRS. and 4 Vickers guns and 2 Stokes Mortars	

1577 Wt. W10791/1773 500,000 1/15 D. D. & L. A.D.S.S./Forms/C. 2118.

110

Instructions regarding War Diaries and Intelligence Summaries are contained in F. S. Regs., Part II. and the Staff Manual respectively. Title pages will be prepared in manuscript.

WAR DIARY

26th Machine Gun Company

~~INTELLIGENCE SUMMARY.~~

(Erase heading not required.)

Army Form C. 2118.

Place	Date 1917	Hour	Summary of Events and Information	Remarks and references to Appendices
	May 2nd.		are to move immediately in rear of the right flank of the 5th CAMERON HLRS. and occupy the RAILWAY STATION to I.9.C.11 and will protect the right flank until the 12th Brigade on the Right has reached its objective. They will be prepared to cover the advance of the 12th Brigade with rifle and Machine Gun fire	
			Disposition of Machine Guns. 2 guns will advance with and under the Orders of O.C. 8th BLACK WATCH. 2 guns will advance with and under the orders of O.C. 5th CAMERONS. 4 guns with Company of 10th ARGYLL & SUTHERLAND HLRS. forming right flank guard. 4 guns to remain in and hold our original front line. 4 guns in Brigade reserve in HUSSAR trench. The guns of the 197th Machine Gun Company to be employed in indirect barrage fire.	
			The attack will be covered by a creeping barrage of field guns and 4·5 Howitzers.	
			Company Headquarters moved to sunken road at H.11.A.60.15.	C.W.R.
	3rd.		Zero hour was fixed at 3·45 a.m. The guns attached to Battalions moved forward on the flanks with the 4th wave. The four guns with the right flank Company of the 10th ARGYLL & SUTHERLAND HLRS. also moved forward with it. The attack broke down owing to the intense hostile Machine Gun fire. The two guns under 2nd. Lieut. ALLIN attached to the 5th CAMERONS got as far as the enemy front line and this officer shot two of the enemy with his revolver. All guns had, however, to withdraw,	

111

Instructions regarding War Diaries and Intelligence Summaries are contained in F. S. Regs., Part II. and the Staff Manual respectively. Title pages will be prepared in manuscript.

WAR DIARY
26th Machine Gun Company
or ~~INTELLIGENCE SUMMARY.~~

(Erase heading not required.)

Army Form C. 2118.

Place	Date 1917	Hour	Summary of Events and Information	Remarks and references to Appendices
	May 3rd.		with the infantry who suffered very heavily, to our own front line. The 4 guns in reserve in HUSSAR trench which had moved up to our front line also withdrew. One of the guns attached to the Black Watch was knocked out, as also was one of the four holding our own line. The original dispositions of guns for the defence of the sector was again taken up, six guns being held in reserve in HUSSAR TRENCH.	C.V.R.
	4th.		Nothing to report.	C.V.R.
	5th.		It was decided that the 197th Machine Gun Coy. which was available for duty with the Brigade should share the holding of the line with the Coy. They accordingly placed 8 guns in the following positions. 2 in CLASP TRENCH I.7.C.7.7. 2 in CLYDE TRENCH I.7.C.5.7. 4 in indirect positions along bank H.12A.8.9. These latter to be available for the protection of the left flank. The 6 guns in reserve moved back to the BLUE LINE.	C.V.R.
	6th.		Inter company relief of 4 forward guns.	C.V.R.
	7th.		Nothing to report.	C.V.R.
	8th.		At 7p.m. our artillery carried out a practice barrage. The enemy retaliated. His barrage was scattered, most of it fell well behind our front line on the ROEUX-GAVRELLE road.	C.V.R.
	9th		The 50th Machine Gun Coy. relieved the eight guns in the line. On completion of relief the Company	

Instructions regarding War Diaries and Intelligence Summaries are contained in F. S. Regs., Part II. and the Staff Manual respectively. Title pages will be prepared in manuscript.

112

WAR DIARY
or
~~INTELLIGENCE SUMMARY.~~
26th Machine Gun Company

(Erase heading not required.)

Army Form C. 2118.

Place	Date 1917	Hour	Summary of Events and Information	Remarks and references to Appendices
	May			
	9th		moved back to transport lines at G. 16. A.	C.W.R.
	10th		The other 8 guns were under orders to move up to the line to assist the 17th Division by doing indirect barrage work. The Coy. less 8 teams moved to "Y" huts L.2.c.	
	11th.		At "Y" huts cleaning up. The 8 guns attached to the 17th Division took up indirect positions as follows:- 4 in HALCYON TRENCH about H. 6.c. 35. 35. 4 in Old trench about H. 6. c. 2.2. During the night these guns searched the enemy trenches between C. 26. C 3.4 and I. 2. A. 5.2 to a depth of 600 feet. During the night the 17th Division captured the CHEMICAL WORKS.	C.W.R.
	12th.		ZERO hour for the attack of the 17th Division was fixed for 6.30 a.m. No Operation Orders showing the objectives of the attack were given to the Officers in Command of the 8 guns. The objective of the attack was the enemy trenches on the CUTHBERT and COD LINE in 1. 7. B; 1 8. C, and 1.14. A. During the attack, from ZERO to ZERO + 90 minutes the guns barraged the area C. 26 C 3.4 to I 2. A. 52 to I 2. B. 34 to c. 26 D1.8. in three lifts starting from the line C. 26 C 3.4 to I 2 A 5.2. and lifting 200 yards each time. The times of lifts were as follows:- 1st lift ZERO + 5 minutes 2nd lift ZERO + 16 minutes 3rd lift ZERO + 18 minutes. Intense fire was maintained from ZERO to ZERO + 18 minutes, and slow fire about 1500 rounds per gun per hour from ZERO + 18 minutes to ZERO + 90 minutes. At ZERO + 90 minutes the guns ceased fire but remained laid for protective	

1577 Wt. W10791/1773 500,000 1/15 D. D. & L. A.D.S.S./Forms/C. 2118.

113

Instructions regarding War Diaries and Intelligence Summaries are contained in F. S. Regs., Part II. and the Staff Manual respectively. Title pages will be prepared in manuscript.

WAR DIARY

26th Machine Gun Company

~~INTELLIGENCE SUMMARY.~~

(Erase heading not required.)

Army Form C. 2118.

Place	Date 1917	Hour	Summary of Events and Information	Remarks and references to Appendices
	May 12th		barrage along the line I. 2. B. 3.4. to I. 2A 5. 2. About 17000 rounds were fired. 2 guns were put out of action and four men killed by shell fire. The Attack was unsuccessful owing to Hostile M.G. and artillery fire. After dark the 2 Sections marched to ARRAS. The Company less 2 Sections in "Y" huts moved by route march to billets PENIN.	C.V.R.
	13th		The Company less 2 Sections moved to MARQUAY by route march. The 2 detached Sections moved by route march to "Y" huts.	C.V.R.
	14th		At MARQUAY Cleaning up and refitting. The 2 Sections joined from "Y" huts.	C.V.R.
	15th		Inspections, Baths	C.V.R.
	16th		Technical Training, Lectures	C.V.R.
	17th		Physical and Technical Training, Lectures.	C.V.R.
	18th		Inspections by Commanding Officer. Arms and equipment.	C.V.R.
	19th		Thorough inspection of Anti-Gas Appliances	C.V.R.
	20th		Church Parades	C.V.R.
	21st.		2 Sections on Range firing stoppages. 2 Sections Physical & Technical Training	C.V.R.
	22nd.		Company in Training, Sections on Range, Machine Gun Competitions	C.V.R.
	23rd.		Physical Training, Sections on Range firing stoppages. Route march in afternoon	C.V.R.

1577 Wt. W10791/1773 500,000 1/15 D. D. & L. A.D.S.S./Forms/C. 2118.

Instructions regarding War Diaries and Intelligence Summaries are contained in F. S. Regs., Part II. and the Staff Manual respectively. Title pages will be prepared in manuscript.

114

WAR DIARY
or
~~INTELLIGENCE~~ SUMMARY.

26th Machine Gun Company

(Erase heading not required.)

Army Form C. 2118.

Place	Date 1917	Hour	Summary of Events and Information	Remarks and references to Appendices
	May 24th		Baths for all men in Company. Thorough inspection of guns and equipment by Officer Commanding	CWR
	25th		Technical Training and sports.	CWR
	26th.		Range work.	CWR
	27th.		Church Parades for C. of E. R.C. and Presbyterian	CWR
	28th.		Preparing guns and equipment for action.	CWR
	29th.		Company moved from MARQUAY to ARRAS by bus. The Transport moved by road.	CWR
	30th.		The Company relieved the 154th M.G. Coy of the 51st Division in the line. Nos. 1 and 2 Sections with 8 guns took up the following positions. Ref. Map PLOUVAIN 1:10,000 I 19.d. 70.50, I 24 d. 85.95, I 19 c. 65.85. I 19 c. 60.95 I 19 d. 50.70. Guns in front line at I 20 a 32.55 I 20 a 32.98. I 14. c 10.25. Nos. 3 and 4 Sections with 8 guns in reserve at Ref. map 51B. N.W. in railway bank at H.23 central. Company Headquarters at H.23 b. 65.40.	CWR
	31st.		It was found that by day the enemy occupied CYPRUS and CARROT trenches which run through I 20 and I 14 d (PLOUVAIN map) and that by night he occupied Posts varying between 100x and 200x EAST of sunken road running through I 20 a and I 14 c. An enemy party of 200 were seen leaving HAUSA WOOD and entering a communication trench. They were fired on successfully. Two aeroplanes were driven off by our fire from I 24 d 85.95	CWR

A5834 Wt. W4973/M687 750,000 8/16 D. D. & L. Ltd. Forms/C.2118/13.

115

Army Form C. 2118.

Instructions regarding War Diaries and Intelligence Summaries are contained in F. S. Regs., Part II. and the Staff Manual respectively. Title pages will be prepared in manuscript.

WAR DIARY

26th Machine Gun Company

or ~~INTELLIGENCE SUMMARY.~~

(Erase heading not required.)

Vol 17

Place	Date 1917	Hour	Summary of Events and Information	Remarks and references to Appendices
	June 1st		Building anti-aircraft positions and firing at aircraft.	CWR
	2nd.		Nos. 3 and 4 Sections took over from Nos. 1 and 2 sections in the line. Nos. 1 and 2 Sections came back to Company Headquarters	CWR
	3rd.		Gun at I 19 b. 5. 7. moved up to COLOMBO. No. 1 Section moved down to Stirling camp (old blue line)	CWR
	4th.		New positions dug at I 20 a. 35.40. and I 20 a. 45.35. These two guns are to be used only in case of attack by enemy.	CWR
	5th		Guns from I 19 b. 50. 70. and from I 14 c. 10. 25 to two new positions mentioned above. The 27th Brigade on our left and the 34th Division on their left attacked at 8 p.m. Their object being to consolidate on a line running through CHARLIE, CURLY trenches in I 7. CUPID and SUNKEN ROAD in I 14. to COLOMBO at I 20. a. 30. 95. At ZERO Artillery put up a very excellent barrage. On 26th Brigade front barrage was only smoke. The objective was gained. Shelling on our front continued throughout the night	CWR
	6th		Much aerial activity. Enemy counter-attacked on 27th Brigade front at about 9.30 p.m. but was unsuccessful. Our 2 guns in COLOMBO fired on HAUSA and DELBAR WOODS where enemy was thought to be massing which afterwards proved to be correct. Heavy shelling continues throughout the night on our Communication trenches, support lines, ROEUX village and woods, tracks and approaches. Firing at aeroplanes was carried out. No. 2 Section relieved No. 3 Section in front line. One man was wounded.	CWR
	7th.		Guns now in position in COLOMBO at:— I 20. a. 30. 85. I 20 a. 30. 75. I 20 a. 25.55. I 20 a. 45. 45.	CWR

A5834 Wt. W4973/M687 750,000 8/16 D. D. & L. Ltd. Forms/C.2118/13.

116

Army Form C. 2118.

Instructions regarding War Diaries and Intelligence Summaries are contained in F. S. Regs., Part II. and the Staff Manual respectively. Title pages will be prepared in manuscript.

WAR DIARY
or
~~INTELLIGENCE SUMMARY.~~

26th Machine Gun Company

(Erase heading not required.)

Place	Date 1917	Hour	Summary of Events and Information	Remarks and references to Appendices
	June 7th		Enemy artillery very active at night on back area. Machine guns fired on HAUSA and DELBAR WOODS and area behind was searched during the night. No. 1 Section relieved No. 4 Section in Support trenches No. 3 Section went down to Sterling Camp, and No. 4 Section remained in reserve at Company Headquarters	CVR
	8th		Nothing to report	CVR
	9th		Two positions at I 19. c. 5. 0 taken over from 9th Machine Gun Company. Gun in CRUMP and most northerly gun in CUSP withdrawn to fill these positions. A Sub-Section of No. 2 Section took over two guns South of SCARP from 9th Machine Gun Company. These guns were in position at I 25 c 9. 5. and I 25 c. 9. 0. One Section from 28th Machine Gun Company was attached to 26th Machine Gun Coy. and took over positions at strong posts "K" "L" and "M". Remaining gun at Company Headquarters "K" strong point at H 30. c. 2. 8. "L" strong point at H 29 b. 5. 5. "M" strong point at H 23 d. 8. 7.	CVR
	10th		Gun and team of 28th Machine Gun Company at Coy. Headquarters took up a position under orders of O. C. 7th Seaforth Highlanders.	CVR
	11th		26th Machine Gun Company and one Section of 28th Machine Gun Company were relieved by 11th Machine Gun Company. 26th Machine Gun Coy bivouaced at Transport lines and Section of 28th Machine Gun Company marched to "Y" huts to rejoin their unit. Relief was completed at about 1 a.m. on 12/6/17.	CVR
	12th		Company moved by bus at 6 p.m. to CHELERS. Transport moved by road at 4 p.m.	CVR
	13th		Company in billets cleaning up guns and equipment	CVR

A5834 Wt. W4973/M687 750,000 8/16 D. D. & L. Ltd. Forms/C.2118/13.

Instructions regarding War Diaries and Intelligence Summaries are contained in F. S. Regs., Part II. and the Staff Manual respectively. Title pages will be prepared in manuscript.

WAR DIARY or ~~INTELLIGENCE SUMMARY.~~

117

26th Machine Gun Company

(*Erase heading not required.*)

Army Form C. 2118.

Place	Date	Hour	Summary of Events and Information	Remarks and references to Appendices
	1917 June 14th		Inspections and deficiencies by Section Officers. No 1 Section firing on MONCHY BRETON range 5 p.m. to 8 p.m. machine gun practice and No 2 Section revolver practice	CVR
	15th		Technical training	CVR
	16th		Technical training	CVR
	17th		Church Parades	CVR
	18th		2 Sections on Range at MONCHY BRETON. 2 Sections Technical Training	CVR
	19th		Company in Training	CVR
	20th		do do	CVR
	21st		Technical training. Baths. 1 Section on Range machine gun practice & 1 Section Revolver Practice.	CVR
	22nd		Company in Training	CVR
	23rd		1 Section on Range firing ab. flags. 1 Section Revolver practice. 2 Sections Technical training	CVR
	24th		Church Parades	CVR
	25th		2 Sections Technical Training 2 Sections on Range Machine Gun Practice & Revolver Practice	CVR
	26th		Company in Training combined drill. Fire Orders	CVR
	27th		2 Sections on Range firing Machine Gun practice and Revolver practice.	CVR
	28th		Technical Training	CVR
	29th		Company on the Range. 1 Section Tactical Scheme with Battalion.	CVR
	30th		Company moved from CHELERS to AVERDOINGT by march route. Started at 1.45 p.m.	CVR

C.V. Rigby
Commander 26th Machine Gun Coy

A5834 Wt. W4973/M687 750,000 8/16 D. D. & L. Ltd. Forms/C.2118/13.

H. 16.

"26th. Infantry Brigade"

Herewith Original Copy
of War Diary for month of
July 1917.

C M Rigby. Capt,
1/8/17 Commanding 26th Machine Gun Coy

118

WAR DIARY
26th Machine Gun Company
or
~~INTELLIGENCE SUMMARY.~~
(Erase heading not required.)

Army Form C. 2118.

Vol 18

Instructions regarding War Diaries and Intelligence Summaries are contained in F. S. Regs., Part II. and the Staff Manual respectively. Title pages will be prepared in manuscript.

Place	Date 1917	Hour	Summary of Events and Information	Remarks and references to Appendices
	July 1st.		Church Parades	C.W.R.
	2nd.		Company moved from AVERDOINGT to FOSSEUX by march route starting at 8 a.m.	C.W.R.
	3rd		Cleaning guns and equipment and Inspections by Commanding Officer	C.W.R.
	4th.		Company in Training, Tests of Elementary Training, Use of Packsaddlery	C.W.R.
	5th.		Technical Training	C.W.R.
	6th.		Company moved from FOSSEUX to BERNEVILLE by march route starting at 8.45 a.m.	C.W.R.
	7th.		Company on Training Area for Tactical Scheme in use of ground and cover	C.W.R.
	8th.		Church Parades.	C.W.R.
	9th.		Company on Range. Practice firing with Light Mounting	C.W.R.
	10th.		Company on the Training Area carrying out Tactical Section Exercises	C.W.R.
	11th.		Company paraded at 7.45 a.m. and marched to Brigade Sports, returning at 6 p.m.	C.W.R.
	12th.		Company on the Training Area carrying out practice in Selection and Occupation of positions Fire Direction & Control	C.W.R.
	13th.		Inspections Overhauling of Guns and Equipment Technical Training	C.W.R.
	14th.		Company Drill, Gas Drill & Inspection of Gas Appliances	C.W.R.
	15th.		Church Parades	C.W.R.
	16th.		Company on Training Area carrying out Tactical Scheme	C.W.R.

A5834 Wt. W4973/M687 750,000 8/16 D. D. & L. Ltd. Forms/C.2118/13.

119

WAR DIARY
or
~~INTELLIGENCE SUMMARY.~~

26th Machine Gun Company

(Erase heading not required.)

Instructions regarding War Diaries and Intelligence Summaries are contained in F. S. Regs., Part II. and the Staff Manual respectively. Title pages will be prepared in manuscript.

Army Form C. 2118.

Place	Date	Hour	Summary of Events and Information	Remarks and references to Appendices
	1917 July			
	17th.		Company carrying out Tactical Training on Training Area. Exercise in Map Reading and use of Compass	CWR.
	18th.		Company carrying out practice in Indirect Fire Barrage.	CWR.
	19th.		Company paraded at 8.30 a.m. for Route March.	CWR.
	20th.		Practice in Selection of positions and use of ground, use of Range finder on Training Area.	CWR.
	21st.		Company on Training Area carrying out Tactical Section Exercises.	CWR.
	22nd.		Church Parades	CWR.
	23rd.		Overhauling Guns and Equipment preparatory to going into the line. Inspection of Anti Gas Appliances. Anti-Gas Drill.	CWR.
	24th.		Company moved to entraining Station at SAULTY, leaving BERNEVILLE at 5.45 p.m. Arrived SAULTY at 9 p.m. and bivouaced in field at SAULTY STATION	CWR.
	25th.		Company Quarter Master Stores and Billeting Party left SAULTY at 2 a.m. with 1st Omnibus Train. Transport loaded on 2nd Omnibus Train at 5 a.m. and Company entrained at 7 a.m. and detrained at BAPAUME at 11.30 a.m. Dinners were cooked and eaten here and at 1 p.m. the Company moved by March route to NEUVILLE BOURJONVAL and took over tents from Town Major	CWR.
	26th.		Company at NEUVILLE BOURJONVAL making preparations for going into the line	CWR.
	27th.		Company relieved 215th. M.G. Coy in the line. HAVRINCOURT SECTOR. Brigade boundaries are right of Brigade, Q.3.B.9.6. left of Brigade K.26.c.7.0. Machine guns took over positions as follows	

A5834 Wt W4973/M687 750,000 8/16 D. D. & L. Ltd. Forms/C.2118/13.

120

Army Form C. 2118.

Instructions regarding War Diaries and Intelligence Summaries are contained in F. S. Regs., Part II. and the Staff Manual respectively. Title pages will be prepared in manuscript.

WAR DIARY
or
~~INTELLIGENCE SUMMARY.~~

26th Machine Gun Company

(Erase heading not required.)

Place	Date 1917	Hour	Summary of Events and Information	Remarks and references to Appendices
	July 27th		1 gun at Q.3.a.2.3., 1 gun at Q.2.b.8.6., 1 gun at Q.2.b.7.7., 1 gun at K.32.d.6.2., 1 gun at K.32.c.6.5., 1 gun at K.32.a.7.6., 1 gun at K.32.a.7.8., 1 gun at K.32.a.2.4. 4 guns in Reserve at Q.7.b.9.3, and 4 guns in Reserve at Transport Lines at NEUVILLE BOURJONVAL. Company Headquarters at Q.13.d.2.9.	CWR.
	28th		The 4 guns in reserve at NEUVILLE BOURJONVAL and Transport moved to YTRES at P.20.c.6.8. Positions for 4 guns in Reserve at Q.7.b.9.3. were selected as follows:- 2 guns at Q.8.a.3.9. and 2 guns Q.8.b.2.7.	CWR.
	29th		Construction of Emplacements and improving positions.	CWR.
	30th		Continuing work on Emplacements and deepening trenches near positions.	CWR.
	31st		Work carried on, on Emplacements and improvements to present positions	CWR.

C W Rigby Capt.
Commanding 26th Machine Gun Coy.

Army Form C. 2118.

Instructions regarding War Diaries and Intelligence Summaries are contained in F. S. Regs., Part II. and the Staff Manual respectively. Title pages will be prepared in manuscript.

WAR DIARY
26th Machine Gun Company
or
~~INTELLIGENCE SUMMARY.~~
(Erase heading not required.)

Vol 19

Place	Date 1917	Hour	Summary of Events and Information	Remarks and references to Appendices
	August 1st.		Two of the guns in reserve at Q.7.b.9.3. were ordered by the Brigade to move to and stay with Battalion in reserve at K.31.c.0.0. Positions for the remaining two guns were selected at Q.8.a.3.8 and at Q.8.b.15.85.	CWR
	2nd.		All quiet. At night Nos. 1 and 2 Sections relieved Nos. 3 and 4 Sections respectively. No. 4 Section on being relieved came into reserve positions occupied by No. 1 Section and No. 3 Section on completion of relief moved back to Divisional Reserve at YTRES	CWR.
	3rd.		Working on emplacements and trenches near gun positions. Improving shelters. Nothing to report	CWR.
	4th.		New emplacements under construction and improvements on existing emplacements.	CWR.
	5th.		All quiet. Work continued on emplacements, shelters and trenches.	CWR.
	6th.		Trenches deepened, cleaned and cleared, also constructing alternative emplacements.	CWR.
	7th.		All quiet. Continuing work on emplacements and shelters.	CWR.
	8th.		All quiet. At night Nos. 3 and 4 Sections relieved Nos. 1 and 2 Sections in the line. No. 2 Section on being relieved came into reserve positions occupied by No. 4 Section. No. 1 Section moved back to Divisional Reserve at YTRES. The relief was carried out at 9.30 p.m.	CWR

A5834 Wt W4973/M687 750,000 8/16 D. D. & L. Ltd. Forms/C.2118/13.

122

Instructions regarding War Diaries and Intelligence Summaries are contained in F. S. Regs., Part II. and the Staff Manual respectively. Title pages will be prepared in manuscript.

WAR DIARY
or
~~INTELLIGENCE SUMMARY.~~
26th Machine Gun Company

(Erase heading not required.)

Army Form C. 2118.

Place	Date 1917	Hour	Summary of Events and Information	Remarks and references to Appendices
	August 9th.		All quiet. Work continued on new emplacements. Trenches cleaned in vicinity of Gun emplacements and shelters rebuilt.	CMR.
	10th.		During the night 10th/11th. Our Machine Guns fired on the following targets. On Road K.27. b.7.7. to K.21.d.4.9. and Road K.27. d.4.4. to K.27. b.8.4. Road. K.27. [illegible] to K.22. C.3.2. 3500 rounds were expended. An enemy divisional relief was expected this night.	CMR.
	11th.		One gun fired on K.32.a.6.7. between 1.30 a.m. and 2.30 a.m. 250 rounds was fired. New emplacements built and present emplacements improved. Anti-aircraft position completed.	CMR.
	12th.		All quiet. Work carried on building new shelters and emplacements.	CMR.
	13th.		Work continued on M.G. Shelters and emplacements. Between 3 p.m. and 3.30 p.m. our medium Trench Mortars shelled WIGAN COPSE. About 14 of the enemy were seen to rush out and several were hit by a Lewis Gun which fired on them.	CMR.
	14th.		All quiet. Nos. 1 and 2 Sections relieved Nos. 3 and 4 Sections. No. 3 Section on being relieved came into reserve positions occupied by No. 2 Section. No 4 Section on completion of relief came back to Divisional Reserve.	CMR.

A5834 Wt. W4973/M687 750,000 8/16 D. D. & L. Ltd. Forms/C.2118/13.

123

Instructions regarding War Diaries and Intelligence Summaries are contained in F. S. Regs., Part II. and the Staff Manual respectively. Title pages will be prepared in manuscript.

WAR DIARY
or
~~INTELLIGENCE SUMMARY.~~
26th Machine Gun Company

(Erase heading not required.)

Army Form C. 2118.

Place	Date 1917	Hour	Summary of Events and Information	Remarks and references to Appendices
	August 15th.		All quiet. Work carried on making emplacements and improving shelters.	CMR.
	16th.		At night our machine guns carried out searching fire from points K.32.b.4.5. to K.26.d.3.9. to K.26.d.9.8 to K.32.b.9.8. and traversed from K.32.b.4.5. to K.32.b.9.7. Ammunition expended 3000 rounds. Working on emplacements and shelters.	CMR.
	17th.		One of the guns in reserve was moved to K.25.d.4.5. to fire on WIGAN COPSE in forthcoming operations.	CMR.
	18th.		Indirect fire was carried out on K.21.a.1.7. and K.21.a.1.4. At 10.55 p.m. the 10th ARGYLL & SUTHERLAND HLRS. carried out a raid on the EASTERN end of YORKSHIRE BANK and on DEAN COPSE. Strength of the raiding party was 4 Officers and 50 O.R. The objects of the raid were, (a) To search cutting at K.32.b.3.9. for suspected enemy dugouts or mining shafts, and to destroy any such works. (b) To clear the NORTHERN and EASTERN edge of YORKSHIRE BANK of the enemy. (c) To obtain an identification. (d) To kill Germans. Six of our guns cooperated with Artillery and Trench Mortars, firing on WIGAN COPSE, Enemy post at K.26.d.05.95, on enemy front line K.26.d.05.95 to SNOWDON and on trench K.27.c.1.4 to K.27.c.60.15. 14,990 rounds were fired as barrage from 10.55 p.m. to 11.25 p.m. The raid was entirely successful. A good number of the enemy being killed. One prisoner was brought back. The gun at K.25.d.4.5 was brought back to reserve.	CMR.

A5834 Wt. W4973/M687 750,000 8/16 D. D. & L. Ltd. Forms/C.2118/13.

124

Instructions regarding War Diaries and Intelligence Summaries are contained in F. S. Regs., Part II. and the Staff Manual respectively. Title pages will be prepared in manuscript.

WAR DIARY or ~~INTELLIGENCE SUMMARY.~~

26th Machine Gun Company

(Erase heading not required.)

Army Form C. 2118.

Place	Date 1917	Hour	Summary of Events and Information	Remarks and references to Appendices
	August 19th		All quiet. Work Done Filling belts, carrying S.A.A. to complete reserve. Building and improving emplacements.	CWR
	20th		All quiet. Sections 3 and 4 relieved sections 1 and 2 in the line. No. 1 Section on being relieved came into reserve positions occupied by No. 3 Section and No. 2 Section moved back to Divisional Reserve at YTRES and came under orders of O.C. Battalion in Divisional Reserve.	CWR
	21st		All quiet. Working on emplacements and trenches and carrying S.A.A. to gun positions.	CWR
	22nd		Between 5.30 p.m. and 7 p.m., our artillery shelled WIGAN COPSE and DEAN COPSE with incendiary shells, but no enemy showed themselves. Work was carried on on trenches and emplacements.	CWR
	23rd		Our Machine Guns fired 120 rounds in conjunction with Lewis Guns and Trench Mortars, at a line K.27.c.8.3. to K.27.d.3.3. The work on emplacements and deepening of trenches continued.	CWR
	24th		All quiet. Working on Emplacements and shelters.	CWR
	25th		At 6 p.m. Enemy Heavy Trench Mortar fired on the right of OXFORD VALLEY, from the direction of FEMY WOOD. A hostile air balloon was observing the fire and was seen to signal after each shot. Our T.Ms. retaliated. Work was continued on emplacements and shelters.	CWR
	26th		All quiet. A section relief took place at night. No. 1 and 2 sections relieving Nos. 3 & 4 Sections in the line.	CWR
	27th		All quiet. Work was carried on on emplacements.	CWR

125

Army Form C. 2118.

Instructions regarding War Diaries and Intelligence Summaries are contained in F. S. Regs., Part II. and the Staff Manual respectively. Title pages will be prepared in manuscript.

WAR DIARY
or
~~INTELLIGENCE~~ SUMMARY.

26th Machine Gun Company

(Erase heading not required.)

Place	Date 1917	Hour	Summary of Events and Information	Remarks and references to Appendices
	August 28th.		Situation Quiet. Work on improvements to emplacements and trenches.	CHR.
	29th.		All Quiet.	CHR.
	30th.		3000 rounds was fired this night in conjunction with artillery, during a raid which took place. Its object being to clear YORKSHIRE BANK of the enemy. The raid was entirely successful. The Infantry met with no resistance and posts were established, in YORKSHIRE BANK, on EAST END.	CHR.
	31st.		The Company was relieved by the 108th. Machine Gun Company. On completion of relief, the Company moved back to YTRES where it encamped for the night.	CHR

C. H. Rigby Capt.
Commanding 26 M.G. Coy.

A5834 Wt. W4973/M687 750,000 8/16 D. D. & L. Ltd. Forms/C.2118/13.

126

Instructions regarding War Diaries and Intelligence Summaries are contained in F. S. Regs., Part II. and the Staff Manual respectively. Title pages will be prepared in manuscript.

WAR DIARY
26th Machine Gun Company
or
~~INTELLIGENCE SUMMARY.~~
(Erase heading not required.)

Army Form C. 2118.

Vol 21

Place	Date 1917	Hour	Summary of Events and Information	Remarks and references to Appendices
	September 1st.		Company moved to GOMMIECOURT by train leaving YTRES at 8 a.m. The transport moved by road.	CMR
	2nd.		Church Parades.	CMR
	3rd.		Cleaning guns and equipment. Inspection of clothing, equipment & Anti-Gas equipment. Machine Gun Barrage Drill.	CMR
	4th.		Overhauling of gun equipment. Inspection by Commanding Officer.	CMR
	5th.		Technical training. Practice in coming into action from limbers.	CMR
	6th.		Anti-Gas Drill. Practice in coming into action from Pack Mules. Barrage Drill.	CMR
	7th.		Physical Training. Limber Drill, Barrage Drill.	CMR
	8th.		2 Sections in training with Battalions. 2 Sections Anti-Gas Drill, Physical Training and Limber Drill.	CMR
	9th.		Company firing on Range.	CMR
	10th.		2 sections in training with Battalions. 2 sections overhauling and filling belts. Cleaning limbers.	CMR
	11th.		Company took part in a Brigade Tactical Scheme. One half of the Company with the attacking force and one half with the force representing the enemy.	CMR

A7092). Wt. W12839/M1295 750,000. 1/17. D. D & L., Ltd. Forms/C2118/14.

Instructions regarding War Diaries and Intelligence Summaries are contained in F. S. Regs., Part II. and the Staff Manual respectively. Title pages will be prepared in manuscript.

127

WAR DIARY
or
~~INTELLIGENCE SUMMARY.~~
26th Machine Gun Company

(Erase heading not required.)

Army Form C. 2118.

Place	Date	Hour	Summary of Events and Information	Remarks and references to Appendices
	1917 Sept. 12th.		Thorough cleaning of all guns and gun equipment and packing limbers in preparation for move. Inspection by Commanding Officer of all guns, equipment, etc.	CMR.
	13th.		Company moved by march route to BAPAUME and entrained by 9 a.m. Train moved off at 9.30 a.m. and arrived at GODWAERSVELDE at 11 p.m. Company marched to WATOU AREA and encamped in the vicinity of TRAPPEST FARM	CMR.
	14th.		Company in camp cleaning up.	CMR.
	15th.		Company moved at 6.30 a.m. by march route to camp at G.8. b. 2.1 Ref. Map. France and Belgium, Sheet 28, 1/40,000	CMR.
	16th.		Church Parades 40 O.R. of the Company went up to the line C 30. C to construct barrage emplacements	CMR.
	17th.		Overhauling guns and equipment. The Company moved to TORONTO CAMP at G.18. A. 2.8. A party of 40 O.R. of the Company went up to the line at C. 30. C. (Ref. Map FREZENBURG 1/10,000) to construct Barrage Emplacements for coming operations. 10 O.R. per section were left with guns. The remainder moved back to TORONTO CAMP	CMR.
	18th.		Working on M.G. barrage emplacements. A Practice barrage was fired in conjunction with Artillery. 1 belt per Gun was expended.	CMR
	19th.		Another practice barrage was fired. 1 belt per gun was expended. Remainder of Gunner personnel and Company H.Q. moved into the line. Company H.Q. at I. 11. b. 3.3.	CMR

A7092). Wt. W12839/M1297 750,000. 1/17. D. D & L., Ltd. Forms/C2118/14.

128

Instructions regarding War Diaries and Intelligence Summaries are contained in F. S. Regs., Part II. and the Staff Manual respectively. Title pages will be prepared in manuscript.

WAR DIARY

26th Machine Gun Company

~~or INTELLIGENCE SUMMARY.~~

(Erase heading not required.)

Army Form C. 2118.

Place	Date	Hour	Summary of Events and Information	Remarks and references to Appendices
	1917 Septem 19th.		Transport lines remained at TORONTO CAMP	CWR.
	20th.		Ref. Map. FREZENBERG 1/10.000. The V Corps took part in offensive operations today. The attack was carried out by the 9th. Division on the right and the 55th Division on the left the 3rd and 59th. Divisions were in Corps reserve. The 2nd Australian Division was on the right. The boundaries of the 9th Division are on the right J.2.c.6.7. to J.3.A.05.70. on the left D.19.c.85.70. to D.20.d.2.7. The objectives were 1st. a line running from D.19.D.7.6. to J.2.B.2.1. Final Objective D.20.d.0.27. to J.3.A.05.70. The 27th Brigade is on the right and the South African Brigade on the left. The 26th Brigade being in support. The Machine Guns of the 26th Coy. and the 197th. Coy. (Divisional) were used for barrage work and were dug in and camouflaged by work work parties of these companies that had been sent up in advance. Each Coy was divided into two batteries of 8 Guns. These batteries were in position along the line C.30.d.3.0. to C.30.C.8.6. The 26th Company Group formed the two right batteries "A" and "B" and barraged the front of the 27th Brigade. The barrage table was as follows:—	
			ZERO to ZERO+20. 1 belt per gun in 4 minutes at J.2.b.85.45 to D.26.b.20.15.	
			ZERO+20 to ZERO+1hr. 20min. 750 rounds per gun per hour at do. to do.	
			ZERO+1hr. 20min. to ZERO+1hr. 45min. 1 belt per gun in 4 mins. at D.27.d.1.3. to D.27.a.65.60.	CWR
			ZERO+1hr. 45min. to ZERO+2hr. 45min. 450 rounds per gun per hour at do to do.	

A7092). Wt. W12839/M1293 750,000. 1/17. D. D & L., Ltd. Forms/C2118/14.

Instructions regarding War Diaries and Intelligence Summaries are contained in F. S. Regs., Part II. and the Staff Manual respectively. Title pages will be prepared in manuscript.

129

WAR DIARY

26th Machine Gun Company

or ~~INTELLIGENCE SUMMARY.~~

(Erase heading not required.)

Army Form C. 2118.

Place	Date 1917	Hour	Summary of Events and Information	Remarks and references to Appendices
	September 20th		ZERO + 2 hrs. 45 mins. to ZERO + 3 hrs. 20 mins. 1 belt per gun in 4 mins. at D.24 d. 1.5. to D.27. a. 65:60 ZERO + 3 hrs. 20 mins. to ZERO + 4 hrs. 750 rds per gun per hour. at do. to do After ZERO + 4 hours all guns remained laid in readiness to open fire on S.O.S. lines, being the final Barrage lines. Rate of fire for S.O.S. the Maximum for first 10 minutes and afterwards 500 rounds per gun per hour. ZERO hour was at 5.40 A.M. The Infantry attacked under cover of a very heavy barrage of field artillery. The Machine Guns carried out barrage as per table. The Infantry carried objectives to time. From ZERO to ZERO + 4 hrs. 110,000 rounds were fired. Between 4 p.m. and 9 p.m. fire was opened on S.O.S. line in conjunction with increased artillery activity, although no S.O.S. signal was fired. C. 36,000 rounds were fired. At 6 p.m. 2 of the guns of A battery moved up to positions about J.1.d.4.5. for direct fire defence.	
	21st.		5.30 a.m. to 5.45 a.m. in conjunction with artillery barrage guns fired on S.O.S. line, 8,000 rounds. At 6.55 p.m. enemy infantry were seen massing for the attack. The S.O.S. signal was fired and guns opened on S.O.S. line. 21,000 rounds were fired from Batteries and 6,750 rounds from guns at J.1.d.4.5. Nothing developed in the way of a counter attack, and it is thought that considerable casualties were inflicted on the enemy. At dusk 2 guns of 'B' battery moved up to direct positions at J.1.a.05.70 to take on any targets which might appear.	CWR

A7092). Wt. W12839/M1297 750,000. 1/17. D. D & L., Ltd. Forms/C2118/14.

130

WAR DIARY
or
~~INTELLIGENCE SUMMARY.~~
26th Machine Gun Company

(Erase heading not required.)

Army Form C. 2118.

Instructions regarding War Diaries and Intelligence Summaries are contained in F. S. Regs., Part II. and the Staff Manual respectively. Title pages will be prepared in manuscript.

Place	Date 1917	Hour	Summary of Events and Information	Remarks and references to Appendices
	Septem 21st.		The following is a note on the stoppages and breakages incurred during the firing:– 2 barrels bulged, 1 muzzle attachment smashed, one patch on barrel casing blown off, 1 lat spring broken, 1 lock spring broken, 1 tumbler broken, 2 firing pins broken, 1 crank handle knob broken, 1 fuzee spring broken. The new pattern muzzle cups were most satisfactory. All belts were filled by hand. It being impossible to fit up belt filling machines in the narrow slits. Had more time been available belt filling machines would have been fitted up.	CWR.
	22nd.		The Company was relieved by the 76th. M.G. Coy. and on completion of relief moved back to TORONTO CAMP.	CWR
	23rd.		Company cleaning up and packing limbers.	CWR.
	24th.		Company moved by bus to WINNEZEELE No. 2 Area and encamped at I.12.d. Central. The transport moved by road.	CWR
	25th.		Cleaning guns and gun equipment and indents for deficiencies.	CWR.
	26th.		Company less details moved by bus to TORONTO CAMP BRANDHOEK No 2. AREA in reserve to 3rd. Division. On night 26th/27th. 2 sub-sections were sent forward to RAILWAY WOOD and attached to 2 Battalions who had moved up into close support of 3rd Division.	CWR.
	27th.		No change.	CWR

A7092). Wt. W12839/M1297 750,000. 1/17. D. D & L., Ltd. Forms/C2118/14.

131

Instructions regarding War Diaries and Intelligence Summaries are contained in F. S. Regs., Part II. and the Staff Manual respectively. Title pages will be prepared in manuscript.

Army Form C. 2118.

WAR DIARY
or
~~INTELLIGENCE SUMMARY.~~

26th Machine Gun Company

(Erase heading not required.)

Place	Date	Hour	Summary of Events and Information	Remarks and references to Appendices
	1917 Septem			
	28th		2 sub-sections from forward area rejoined Company in TORONTO CAMP	CHR
	29th		Company less transport moved back to ZEGGERS CAPPEL Area by train. Transport moved by road to WINNEZEELE and bivouaced for the night.	CHR
	30th		Transport moved by road from WINNEZEELE and joined Company in ZEGGERS CAPPEL Area	CHR

CHRussell Capt.
Commanding 26th Machine Gun Company

A5834 Wt. W4973/M687 750,000 8/16 D. D. & L. Ltd. Forms/C.2118/13.

L. 29.

SECRET

26th. Highland Brigade.

Herewith Original War Diary
for the month of October 1917.

C W Rigby. Capt.

1/11/17 Commanding 26th. Machine Gun Coy.

132

Instructions regarding War Diaries and Intelligence Summaries are contained in F. S. Regs., Part II. and the Staff Manual respectively. Title pages will be prepared in manuscript.

WAR DIARY
or
~~INTELLIGENCE SUMMARY.~~

26th Machine Gun Company

(Erase heading not required.)

Army Form C. 2118.

Vol 21

Place	Date	Hour	Summary of Events and Information	Remarks and references to Appendices
	1917 October 1st.		Technical training and cleaning up.	CMR
	2nd.		Overhauling guns and gun equipment. Arms drill, Physical Training.	CMR
	3rd.		One Section on the Range firing stoppages. Three sections Physical Training, Barrage Drill and Technical Training.	CMR.
	4th.		One Section on the Range. Three Sections route march.	CMR.
	5th.		One section on the Range. Three sections Practice with Packsaddlery and Technical Training	CMR
	6th.		Company took part in Tactical Scheme along with Battalions	CMR.
	7th.		Church Parade. Transport moved off for SIEGE CAMP and halted for the night midway	CMR.
	8th.		Company moved by train from ESQUELBECQ STATION to SIEGE CAMP. Ref. Map. Sheet 28.	CMR.
	9th.		Company in Camp. Cleaning up.	CMR
	10th.		Company moved to REIGERSBURG CAMP. Reference map SPRIET 1/10,000. The Company relieved the 144th M.G.Coy. in the line N.E. of ST. JULIEN. 8 guns were placed in the front line in the following positions 2 at D.3.A.7.2., 2 at D.3.A. 4.4., 2 at V.26.d.5.7., 2 at V.26.C.0.5. 8 guns in reserve behind YORK FARM. D.2.A.0.3.	CMR.
	11th.		Preparation for the attack. On the 12th the 26th Brigade is to attack on a front D.3.c.8.8. to V.26.a.8.5. and capture 2 objectives, a first from V.28.c.9.1. to V.21.d.1.3. and a second from V.28.d.9.6. to V.22.a.2.1. The 27th Brigade when these objectives have been taken is to go through the 26th Brigade and capture further objectives.	CMR.

A5834 Wt. W4973/M687 750,000 8/16 D. D. & L. Ltd. Forms/C.2118/13.

133

Army Form C. 2118.

Instructions regarding War Diaries and Intelligence Summaries are contained in F. S. Regs., Part II. and the Staff Manual respectively. Title pages will be prepared in manuscript.

WAR DIARY
26th Machine Gun Company
or
~~INTELLIGENCE SUMMARY.~~
(Erase heading not required.)

Place	Date 1917	Hour	Summary of Events and Information	Remarks and references to Appendices
	October 12th.		At ZERO the Company was disposed as follows:- 8 guns holding the line in the following positions 2 at D.3A.6.2. and 2 at D 3.A.3.4. under 2nd. Lt. A.W. RIDER, 2 at BURNS HOUSE V.26.D.4.7. and 2 at V.26.A.9.1 under Lt. G.H. STOLTERFOTH. 2 guns with 8th BLACK WATCH under 2nd Lt. H.E. BROWNBRIDGE 2 guns with 7th. SEAFORTH HLRS. under Lt. S.S. BROWN. 2 guns with 10th. ARGYLL and SUTHERLAND HLRS. and 2 guns with 5th CAMERON HLRS. under Lt. A.S. FARR and Sergt. HARRISON. The 2 guns with each battalion formed up for the attack with the rear flank Company. Company H.Q. at HURNER FARM D.1.B.4.7. ZERO was at 5:25 A.M. The artillery barrage started very unevenly. The 55th Brigade on our left did not attack with the barrage and made no progress whatever. On the left the 5th CAMERON HLRS. and 10th ARGYLL and SUTHERLAND HLRS. were seriously handicapped by the very wet condition of the ground and were held up about 50 yards in front of our front line, by heavy rifle and Machine Gun fire from the front, from the high ground on our left, BEEK HOUSE, and from a pill box at V.26.A.8.1. The latter was taken about half an hour afterwards but by this time the 5th CAMERON HLRS. and 10th ARGYLL and SUTHERLAND HLRS. were all mixed up, and the 27th Brigade had also come into the battle. A line was formed about 300 yards in advance of our original front line and the 4 guns with the 5th CAMERON HLRS and 10th ARGYLL and SUTHERLAND HLRS. came into position about 7 a.m. 2 at V.26.D.5.9., 2 at V.26.D.9.9. These guns were able to give the infantry very little help owing to the shape of the ground, and merely consolidated. Only small targets of one or two of the enemy were seen.	

A5834 Wt. W4973/M687 750,000 8/16 D. D. & L. Ltd. Forms/C.2118/13.

134

Instructions regarding War Diaries and Intelligence Summaries are contained in F. S. Regs., Part II. and the Staff Manual respectively. Title pages will be prepared in manuscript.

WAR DIARY

26th Machine Gun Company

~~INTELLIGENCE SUMMARY.~~

(Erase heading not required.)

Army Form C. 2118.

Place	Date	Hour	Summary of Events and Information	Remarks and references to Appendices
	1917 October 12th		One of the guns at V. 26. D. 5. 9. was put out of action by a direct hit from a shell. One man being killed and three wounded of the team. On the right the 7th. SEAFORTH HLRS. and 8th BLACK WATCH were able to get on better and advanced about 500 yards. Lieut. BROWN with 2 guns pushed up to about V. 27. D. 3. 6. which was on the left flank of the right Battalion, and seeing that the infantry on the left were held up, got his guns into action and opened covering fire in the direction of the pill box at V. 26. B. 8. 1. Several small parties of the enemy were engaged with effect, but the guns had to cease fire owing to a limited supply of S.A.A. after expending about 3000 rounds. More ammunition was sent up later to these guns and a sufficient supply was maintained. Lieut. BROWN then withdrew them to about V. 27. D. 7. 6. where the infantry were consolidating. This officer also gave valuable assistance in organising the infantry and consolidating. There being at that time no infantry officer on the spot. The two guns under 2nd. Lt. H. E. BROWNBRIDGE got forward with the BLACK WATCH to a position on the flank about D. 3. B. 4. 4. There this officer got his guns into action and went forward to reconnoitre the exact position of our infantry. He could not find any of the BLACK WATCH officers but found O.C. 7th SEAFORTH HLRS. who ordered him to place his guns in position about V. 27. D. 1. 2. in front of INCH HOUSES and consolidate. This was done, very good positions being chosen which entirely covered the right front. About dusk several small reconnoitring parties of the enemy were engaged with good effect.	

A5834 Wt. W4973/M687 750,000 8/16 D. D. & L. Ltd. Forms/C.2118/13.

Instructions regarding War Diaries and Intelligence Summaries are contained in F. S. Regs., Part II. and the Staff Manual respectively. Title pages will be prepared in manuscript.

135

WAR DIARY
26th Machine Gun Company
~~or INTELLIGENCE SUMMARY.~~

(Erase heading not required.)

Army Form C. 2118.

Place	Date 1917	Hour	Summary of Events and Information	Remarks and references to Appendices
	October 12th.		The enemy appeared to be in force in trench in V. 27. B. and in BANFF HOUSES. The situation was in the evening still obscure. A line running from the CEMETERY in D. 4. a. to roadway about V. 27. D. 5.0. thence road to INCH HOUSES thence in front of INCH HOUSES to V. 26. a. 9. 1. thence to DOUNTY CROSS ROADS, was consolidated.	C.H.R.
	13th.		During the 13th the situation was cleared up a bit and the line was advanced a little on the left. The three guns at V. 26. D. 5. 9. and V. 26 D. 9. 9. were relieved by the 4 guns under Lt. G.H. STOLTERFOTH. These three under Lt. A.S. FARR and the 4 guns formerly under 2nd Lt. A.W. RIDER now came into reserve along the line D. 3. a. 8. 2. to D. 3. A. 4. 3. and were placed under the orders of O.C. 9th SCOTTISH RIFLES. This battalion being in reserve immediately north of KRONPRINZ FARM. The line was now well consolidated. Infantry was relieved on night 13th/14th.	C.H.R.
	14th.		Oxford Houses V. 26. B. and SHAFT V. 27. A. 1. 4. were occupied. The Company was relieved by the 28th. Machine Gun Company and moved back to SIEGE CAMP.	C.H.R.
	15th.		Company in camp cleaning up.	C.H.R.
	16th.		Overhauling guns and gun equipment	C.H.R.
	17th.		Kit inspection and indents for deficiencies. Cleaning arms clothing and equipment	C.H.R.
	18th.		Cleaning guns, Inspection of Anti-Gas Appliances & Gas Drill. Physical training	C.H.R.
	19th.		Packing limbers, cleaning guns and filling belts.	C.H.R.
	20th.		Company moved to IRISH FARM. At night company moved into the line and took up barrage	C.H.R.

A5834 Wt. W4973/M687 750,000 8/16 D. D. & L. Ltd. Forms/C.2118/13.

136

Instructions regarding War Diaries and Intelligence Summaries are contained in F. S. Regs., Part II. and the Staff Manual respectively. Title pages will be prepared in manuscript.

WAR DIARY
or
~~INTELLIGENCE SUMMARY.~~
(Erase heading not required.)

26th Machine Gun Company

Army Form C. 2118.

Place	Date	Hour	Summary of Events and Information	Remarks and references to Appendices
	1917 October 20th.		positions at about D. 1. b. 8.4. to barrage the area V. 21. a. 4. 8 to V. 20. b. 5.1 to V. 14. d. 8. 3. to V. 15. c. 6. 2. Line V. 21. b. 4.1 to V. 21. b. 5. 8. Line V. 21. b. 6. 5. to V. 15. d. 4. 4. The object of the barrage is to help the attack of the Division on the left. 10 guns of the Company are to be used. It was decided that owing to the state of the ground and the lack of weatherproof cover, not feasible to fill belts to keep pace with the barrage. The rates of fire ordered were ZERO to ZERO plus 1 hour 3000 rounds per gun per hour. ZERO plus 1 hour to ZERO plus 2 hours 500 rounds per hour. ZERO plus 2 hours to ZERO plus 3 hours 3000 rounds per gun per hour. The total rounds per gun required was 6500 for barrage and 2500 for S.O.S. 10 belts per gun were got up on the night 20th/21st.	
	21st.		Another 200 belts came up tonight by Carrying Parties but owing to casualties amongst the carriers only 160 of these belts reached the gun positions, thus giving each gun 26 belts.	CMR.
	22nd.		ZERO was at 5.35 a.m. The barrage was fired successfully, and after the barrage the guns were laid on the S.O.S. lines ordered. 8 belts per gun were cleaned as well as possible and refilled. This took sometime as great care had to be taken to prevent belts and ammunition from touching the muddy ground. The filling was done in small shelters made with tarpaulin sheets. No S.O.S. signal went up and the guns did not require to fire any of the filled belts.	CMR.
	23rd.		The Company moved from the line back to IRISH CAMP	CMR.
	24th.		Company in camp cleaning up. Repacking limbers	CMR.
	25th.		Company moved by train to ESQUELBECQ STATION and marched from there to WORMHOUDT where they billeted for the night. The transport moved from IRISH CAMP to WORMHOUDT by road.	CMR.

A5834 Wt. W4973/M687 750,000 8/16 D. D. & L. Ltd. Forms/C.2118/13.

134

Instructions regarding War Diaries and Intelligence Summaries are contained in F. S. Regs., Part II. and the Staff Manual respectively. Title pages will be prepared in manuscript.

Army Form C. 2118.

WAR DIARY
or
~~INTELLIGENCE SUMMARY.~~

26th Machine Gun Company

(Erase heading not required.)

Place	Date 1917	Hour	Summary of Events and Information	Remarks and references to Appendices
	October 26th		Company moved by bus to VENDERLEELE FARM Ref. Map. Sheet 19 C. 27. b. 8. 8. The transport moved by road	CWR
	27th.		Company in billets cleaning up. Overhauling guns and gun equipment.	CWR
	28th.		Company moved by bus to COXYDE-BAINS. Transport moved by road. Ref. Map sheets OOST-DUNKERQUE and BELGIUM 12. S.W. The Brigade relieved the 124th Brigade in the line NIEUPORT-BAINS sector. The Company took over the following positions. M.14. a. 8. 2., M. 14. d. 6.0., M. 21. a. 4. 2., M. 21. b. 7. 3. in front line by No. 4 Section, M. 21. d. 25. 95., M. 21. c. 25. 45., M. 26. b. 35. 95., M. 20. d. 25. 45. by No. 3 Section Right Reserve. 2 guns at M. 19. b. 5. 3., 2 guns at M. 20. a. 40. 45. by No. 1 Section. Left Reserve. 1 gun at M. 14. a. 60. 15., 2 guns at M. 13. d. 6. 4., 1 gun at R. 24. a. 0. 3. by No. 2 Section. Coast Defence. Company headquarters at R. 24. a. 4. 5., Transport lines W. 6. a. 3. 3.	CWR.
	29th.		Nothing to report. All quiet	CWR.
	30th.		Enemy shelled REGINA HOTEL and road behind our support line with heavy shells from about 6 p.m. to 9 p.m. Fairly quiet during the remainder of the day. Enemy machine guns fired occasionally throughout the night. Otherwise quiet.	CWR.
	31st.		From about 8 p.m. to midnight Enemy artillery shelled HOTEL REGINA and SUPPORT LINE from Y. 14 to BATH AVENUE with gas shells. Our Machine Gun position at M. 21. b. 2. 0. was shelled with heavy trench mortars in the early morning, and bursts of Machine Gun fire during the night were directed on it. The artillery positions in M. 20. d. and the road from M. 20. d. 5. 5. to M. 20. c. 9. 2. were heavily shelled. The remainder of the day was fairly quiet.	CWR.

1/11/17

CWRigby Capt.
Commanding 26 M. G. Coy.

"A" Form.

Army Form C. 2121.
(In pads of 100.)

MESSAGES AND SIGNALS.

No. of Message

Prefix .... Code .... m. | Words. | Charge.

Office of Origin and Service Instructions.

Sent
At .... m.
To ....
By ....

This message is on a/c of:

.... *Service.*

(Signature of "Franking Officer.")

Recd. at .... m.
Date ....
From ....
By ....

TO { 26th Infy Brigade.

Sender's Number.	Day of Month.	In reply to Number.	AAA
* C.R. 432.	30th		

Herewith War Diary for
month of November / AAA

From 26th M.G. Coy.
Place
Time

The above may be forwarded as now corrected.

(Z) C.K. Rigby Capt

Censor. Signature of Addressor or person authorised to telegraph in his name.

* This line should be erased if not required.

(3796.) Wt. W 492/M1647. 650,000 Pads. 5/17. H. W. & V., Ld. (E. 1187.)

138

Instructions regarding War Diaries and Intelligence Summaries are contained in F. S. Regs., Part II. and the Staff Manual respectively. Title pages will be prepared in manuscript.

WAR DIARY
or
~~INTELLIGENCE~~ SUMMARY.

26th. Machine Gun Company

(Erase heading not required.)

Army Form C. 2118.

Vol 22

Place	Date	Hour	Summary of Events and Information	Remarks and references to Appendices
The Field	1917 November 1st.		Enemy artillery shelled cross roads at M. 21. C. 35. 75 intermittently. Our ISLAND M.G. position at M. 21. b. 2. 0 was shelled with heavy Trench Mortars for about 3 hours, but no damage was done to the emplacement.	CMR
	2nd.		Enemy activity below normal. Enemy M. G's traversed front line at intervals during the night; otherwise all quiet.	CMR
	3rd.		Enemy artillery and trench mortars were active on our front line during the day. Our M. G's fired about 2000 rounds at hostile aircraft which crossed our front line during the day.	CMR
	4th.		Enemy Artillery active between 9 a.m. and 10 a.m., shelling vicinity of our M. G. positions at V.13 and V.14. From 1 p.m. to 2 p.m. Enemy Trench Mortars fired on Support line M. 20. b. 6. 8. to M. 14. d. 13. Enemy M. G's fired on point M. 21. C. 35. 75. and also traversed our front line throughout the night. Our M. G's fired on a suspected dump at M. 10. C. 35. 75. and traversing and searching fire was carried out on line from M. 15. b. 75. 85. to M. 10. d. 30. 75. from about 6.30 p.m. to 8.30 p.m. 1000 rounds were expended. 500 rounds were fired at enemy aircraft flying over canal between 7 a.m. and 9 a.m. The enemy sent up a small balloon at 8.30 a.m. believed to be for testing the wind.	CMR
	5th.		Enemy shelled front line and support line intermittently during the day. Enemy M. G's fired at cross roads at M. 21. C. 35. 75 during the night. Our M. G's quiet.	CMR

A5834 Wt. W4973/M687 750,000 8/16 D. D. & L. Ltd. Forms/C.2118/13.

Instructions regarding War Diaries and Intelligence Summaries are contained in F. S. Regs., Part II. and the Staff Manual respectively. Title pages will be prepared in manuscript.

139.

WAR DIARY
or
26th Machine Gun Company
~~INTELLIGENCE SUMMARY.~~

(Erase heading not required.)

Army Form C. 2118.

Place	Date	Hour	Summary of Events and Information	Remarks and references to Appendices
	1917 November			
	6th		Enemy artillery active on our support line between 4 p.m. and 1 a.m. Enemy M. Gs fired bursts on road running through M.20.d. into M.21.C. at intervals during the night and also traversed our front line. Our M. Gs quiet.	CWR
	7th		Enemy artillery fairly active against our front and support lines. M. Gs quiet.	CWR
	8th		The 28th M.G. Coy relieved the 26th M.G. Coy on the night 8th/9th. On completion of the relief 26th M.G. Coy moved back to reserve billets at R.32.d.5.6.	CWR
	9th		Company in billets cleaning up, overhauling guns, gun equipment and repacking limbers.	CWR
	10th		Physical Training, Belt filling.	CWR
	11th		Church Parades	CWR
	12th		7 guns of 26th M.G. Coy relieved 7 guns of 194th M.G. Coy in the Coast Defence Sector. Guns were disposed as follows:– 2 guns at No. 1 Post about R.27.b.5.2. 2 guns at No. 2 Post about R.32.a.4.5. 3 guns at No. 3 Post about W.10.b.2.5. 9 guns, Coy. H.Q. and remainder of Company remained at R.32.d.5.6.	CWR
	13th		Technical training, Anti-Gas Drill and Physical Training for Company in Billets. Coast Defence Sector, enemy shelled vicinity of R.28.c. and R.28.d. during morning and afternoon with shrapnel and gas shells. A few shells were also fired on the beach at R.28.a. about 5.30 p.m. Our M. Gs fired about 900 rounds at hostile aircraft flying over our positions between 10 a.m. and 11.30 a.m.	CWR

140

WAR DIARY
26th. Machine Gun Company
or
~~INTELLIGENCE SUMMARY.~~

(Erase heading not required.)

Instructions regarding War Diaries and Intelligence Summaries are contained in F. S. Regs., Part II. and the Staff Manual respectively. Title pages will be prepared in manuscript.

Army Form C. 2118.

Place	Date	Hour	Summary of Events and Information	Remarks and references to Appendices
	1917 November 14th.		Coast Defence Sector all quiet. Company in billets carried out Technical Training, Physical Training	CHR
	15th.		Coast Defence Sector all quiet. Company in billets Technical Training, Physical Training	CHR
	16th.		Coast Defence Sector all quiet. Company in billets cleaning up and making preparations for relief.	CHR.
	17th.		26th. M.G. Coy was relieved by the French and moved back by march route to TETEGHEM AREA and billeted for night in Distillery at I 21. b. 2. 8.	CHR.
	18th.		Company moved by march route to billets at WORMHOUDT. H.Q. at C. 10. a. 5.4.	CHR.
	19th.		Company moved by march route and billeted for night at about I. 29. b. 6. 6.	CHR
	20th.		Company moved by march route to BANDRINGHEM. and were billeted there for the night	CHR.
	21st.		Company moved to CAMPAGNETTE by march route and billeted for night there	CHR.
	22nd.		Company moved by march route to CREQUY and billeted there.	CHR.
	23rd.		Company in billets cleaning guns, cleaning and fitting up billets.	CHR.
	24th.		Technical Training. Cleaning guns. Overhauling belts. Kit Inspection	CHR
	25th.		Church Parades.	CHR
	26th.		Technical Training. Inspection of new drafts by G.O.C.	CHR
	27th.		Technical Training. Lectures on "Barrage Drill" Physical Training	CHR
	28th.		Technical Training. Physical Training + Lecture on "Use of Direction Dial + Clinometer	CHR
	29th.		Technical Training. Physical Training. Lecture on "Auxiliary Aiming Marks"	CHR
	30th.		Technical Training. Physical Training. Lecture on "Indication Recognition"	CHR

C H Rigby Capt. Commanding 26 M.G. Coy.

A5834 Wt. W4973/M687 750,000 8/16 D. D. & L. Ltd. Forms/C.2118/13.

L.215

[illegible]th Highland Brigade.

Herewith Original Copy of War Diary for the month of December 1917 please.

[illegible] Rigby Capt.

2-1-18. Commanding 2[illegible]th Machine Gun Coy

141

Instructions regarding War Diaries and Intelligence Summaries are contained in F. S. Regs., Part II. and the Staff Manual respectively. Title Pages will be prepared in manuscript.

WAR DIARY or INTELLIGENCE SUMMARY

26th Machine Gun Company

(Erase heading not required.)

Army Form C. 2118.

Vol 23

Place	Date 1917	Hour	Summary of Events and Information	Remarks and references to Appendices
	December 1st.		Company moved by march route from CREQUY to WAVRANS and billeted for the night there.	C.W.R.
	2nd.		Company entrained at WAVRANS STATION at 9 a.m. and detrained at PERONNE at 9 p.m. and billeted there for the night.	C.W.R.
	3rd		Company moved by march route from PERONNE to camp at HAUTEALLAINES. Sheet 62c. I.5. c. 5. 8.	C.W.R.
	4th.		Company moved by march route to HEUDECOURT and remained there for the night.	C.W.R.
	5th.		The Brigade relieved the 1st. Brigade of GUARDS in the line in front of GOUZEAUCOURT. Reference map GOUZEAUCOURT Ed. 2 Special Sheet. Parts of 57c S.E. and 57B. N.W., S.W. The Brigade boundaries are as follows:- Left Boundary from front line at R. 20. c. 6. 2. westwards to Q. 23. b. 9. 1. Right Boundary from front line at R. 32. a. 3. 3. westwards to Q. 29. c. 0. 0. The guns of the Company took over positions as follows:- No. 3 Section in front line between left boundary and R. 26. a. 9. 4. 4 guns. No. 4 Section 3 guns in front line about R. 26. b. 0. 2., R. 26. d. 0. 6. and R. 32. a. 5. 9. with one gun in support at R. 31. b. 8. 6. No. 1 Section (Flank Defence) 4 guns in following positions. R. 25. c. 5. 5., R. 25. c. 2. 8., Q. 30. d. 8. 8., Q. 30. d. 0. 7. No. 3 Section 3 guns in following positions in Reserve. Q. 23. c. 7. 8., Q. 23. c. 4. 9., Q. 23. a. 8. 0. Company Headquarters at Q. 22. c. 6. 5. Transport Lines at HEUDECOURT	C.W.R.
	6th.		It was decided at a conference with the Brigadier that there were too many guns in the front line, and that 4 of them should be moved to rear positions to assist the organization of defence in depth. The following changes were made. No. 3 Section was relieved by the 3 guns of no. 4 Section at R. 26. b. 0. 2. and R. 26. d. 0. 6. which took over 2 positions one at R. 26. a. 9. 9. and one at R. 26 a. 4. 9. No. 3 Section moved into Reserve line and took up the following positions:- 2 guns at Q. 35. a. 7. 8., 2 guns at Q. 29. c. 8. 6., Right Reserve. No. 2 Section also moved into Reserve line and took up the following positions:-	

2449 Wt. W14957/M90 750,000 1/16 J.B.C. & A. Forms/C.2118/12.

Instructions regarding War Diaries and Intelligence Summaries are contained in F. S. Regs., Part II. and the Staff Manual respectively. Title Pages will be prepared in manuscript.

WAR DIARY or ~~INTELLIGENCE SUMMARY~~

26th Machine Gun Company

(Erase heading not required.)

Army Form C. 2118.

Place	Date 1914	Hour	Summary of Events and Information	Remarks and references to Appendices
	December 6th.		1 guns at Q.29.b.1.3, 2 guns at Q.23.d.1.1. Left Reserve.	CHR.
	7th.		Overhauling belts, building emplacements etc.	CHR.
	8th.		Company H.Q. moved from Q.22.c.6.5 to Q.29.c.8.8. No. 2 Section relieved No 4 Section in the forward 4 positions. No. 4 came back to left reserve. 4 Guns of the 197th. M.G. Coy moved into Rear Reserve line about Q.29.a.3.6.	CHR.
	9th.		Overhauling belts, improving emplacements etc. No change in the situation.	CHR.
	10th.		Lieut. W. CHALMERS left to take over command of 235th. M.G. Coy. Lt. A.E. EBERLIN took over 2nd in Command. Hostile attack thought to be imminent. Situation unchanged.	CHR.
	11th.		Coy. Sergt. Major took over Command of No. 3 Section temporarily. No 3 Section relieved No 1 Section in flank defence positions. No. 1 Section took over positions in reserve vacated by No. 3 Section. Enemy did not attack. Some rounds were fired on Enemy Aircraft during the day. Anti-Aircraft position built at Q.29.c.90.85.	CHR.
	12th.		No. 4 Section relieved No. 2 Section in 4 front line positions. No. 2 took over 3 positions in left reserve vacated by No. 4 Section. Gun at Q.29.c.6.6. moved to position at Q.29.b.1.1.	CHR.
	13th.		Situation unchanged. Emplacement at R.26.a.9.9. repaired where blown in. Work on dugout and emplacement at R.25.c.55.80.	CHR.
	14th.		Gun at Q.29.c.9.2. relieved gun at Q.23.d.3.2. Gun at Q.30.c.95.55. transferred to No. 3 Section and No. 2 Section now becomes mobile reserve in dugouts in Q.24.c.	CHR.
	15th.		Alternative emplacement built at R.31.b.7.5. Position at R.26.a.8.3. improved. Situation normal.	CHR

2449 Wt. W14957/M90 750,000 1/16 J.B.C. & A. Forms/C.2118/12.

143

Army Form C. 2118.

Instructions regarding War Diaries and Intelligence Summaries are contained in F. S. Regs., Part II. and the Staff Manual respectively. Title Pages will be prepared in manuscript.

WAR DIARY
26th Machine Gun Company
~~INTELLIGENCE SUMMARY~~
(Erase heading not required.)

Place	Date 1917	Hour	Summary of Events and Information	Remarks and references to Appendices
	December 16th.		Anti-Aircraft emplacement at Q. 29. b. 22. built, also new emplacements at Q. 29. C. 9. 1. and Q. 29. C. 5. 8. Emplacement commenced in tent at R. 19. c. 60. 85.	CWR.
	17th		3 guns of No 1 Section relieved 3 guns of No. 3 Section in positions at GOUZEAUCOURT. 1 team of No 1 Section to mobile reserve. 1 team of No. 3. Section relieved 1 team of No. 2 Section in reserve line at Q. 23 d. 3. 2. No. 3 Section now became reserve line defence. Work was carried on building shelters.	CWR.
	18th		No. 2 Section relieved No. 4 Section in front line. 3 guns of No. 4 Section and 1 gun of No. 1 Section became mobile reserve.	CWR.
	19th		Building Anti-Aircraft position at Q. 35. b. 1. 7. No change in situation	CWR.
	20th		No. 2 Section were relieved in front line by Lewis Guns and came back to mobile reserve in road at Q. 24. C. No 4 Section took up defensive positions in POPE ALLEY Q. 30. b. and R. 25. a. and commenced making barrage position for 1 battery of 4 guns at R. 25. a. 1. 4. Anti-Aircraft position at Q. 35. b. 1. 7 was finished.	CWR.
	21st.		Position in tent at R. 19. c. 60. 85. was finished. Situation unchanged.	CWR.
	22nd		No. 2 Sections relieved No. 4 Section in defensive positions in POPE ALLEY and took up barrage positions at R. 25. a. 1. 4. 3 guns No 4 Section became mobile reserve along with 1 gun of No. 1 Section	CWR.
	23rd		No. 1 Section placed a gun in tent at R. 19. c. 55. 70. Work on barrage positions continued. Enemy artillery more active than usual, otherwise no change	CWR.

2449 Wt. W14957/M90 750,000 1/16 J.B.C. & A. Forms/C.2118/12.

1

Instructions regarding War Diaries and Intelligence Summaries are contained in F. S. Regs., Part II. and the Staff Manual respectively. Title Pages will be prepared in manuscript.

144

WAR DIARY
or
~~INTELLIGENCE SUMMARY~~

26th Machine Gun Company

(Erase heading not required.)

Army Form C. 2118.

Place	Date 1917	Hour	Summary of Events and Information	Remarks and references to Appendices
	December 24th		No. 3 Section relieved No 1 Section. 2 guns in GOUZEAUCOURT and 2 guns at 19. a. 2.5 and 19a. 2.3 (Ref. Map GOUZEAUCOURT sheet 57C N.E.)	CHR.
	25th		No change in situation. 2nd. Lt. P.E. BROWN took over temporarily the command of No 3 Section	CHR.
	26th		Situation normal.	CHR.
			Barrage positions and dugouts completed. Nothing to report. 4500 rounds were fired on R.27.a.9.1	CHR.
	27th			
	28th		Situation unchanged. Machine Guns fired on R.24. a. 9.1. during the night. 4500 rounds were expended.	CHR.
	29th		4000 rounds were fired from barrage positions on to R. 26. a. 95.50. during the night	CHR.
	30th		Enemy Artillery bombarded our trenches between 6.30 am and 7.15 a.m. Enemy raided right sub-sector of the Brigade, and succeeded in entering GIN sap, but was ejected. A heavy bombardment was put down at 3 p.m. and at 4.45 p.m. by the enemy but no further raids were attempted. Weather was very misty.	CHR.
	31st		4000 rounds were fired during the night on R 27 a. 6. 5 and 2000 rounds on R.33. b. 8.5. 3 guns of No 4 Section in Mobile Reserve at R.24.c. were withdrawn to Hutments at W. 2.C. and remained in reserve there. Gun of No. 4 Section at Q.30 d. 00.65, was relieved by gun of 194th M.G. Coy in reserve line and joined No. 4 Section in Hutments at W. 2. C. At intervals during the day our trenches were bombarded.	CHR.

C.H.Rigby Capt.
Commanding 26 M.G. Coy.

2449 Wt. W11957/M90 750,000 1/16 J.B.C. & A. Forms/C.2118/12.

~~2 Army Troops~~

9 DIV

26 BDE

26

TRENCH MORTAR BTY

1915 JUNE to 1915 NOV

~~1455~~

III Corps. G. H. Q. Troops 4th Div

IV & VI Divs

121/5931

26th Trench Howr Batty

Vol I 9 – 30.6.15.

a2

a/6

Instructions regarding War Diaries and Intelligence Summaries are contained in F. S. Regs., Part II. and the Staff Manual respectively. Title Pages will be prepared in manuscript.

Army Form C. 2118

WAR DIARY
or
INTELLIGENCE SUMMARY
(Erase heading not required.)

26th Trench How[r] Bty RGA.

Place	Date	Hour	Summary of Events and Information	Remarks and references to Appendices
IV and VI Div[ns]	June 9-30		Engaged Trenches, Houses, Mounds and other enemy strongholds. Fired 159 bombs at ranges from 80 yds to 325 yds, chiefly at night.	
			Guns & Amm[n] worked well except that about 15% of the fuzes were "blind".	
			Casualties - 3 NCOs and 2 Gunners to Hosp[tl] (2 wounded 1 injured 2 sick)	
			A Wilson 2nd Lt RGA Comdg 26 Trench Bty RGA	

1875 Wt. W593/826 1,000,000 4/15 J.B.C. & A. A.D.S.S./Forms/C. 2118.

Instructions regarding War Diaries and Intelligence Summaries are contained in F. S. Regs., Part II. and the Staff Manual respectively. Title Pages will be prepared in manuscript.

WAR DIARY
or
INTELLIGENCE SUMMARY
(Erase heading not required.)

Army Form C. 2118

Place	Date	Hour	Summary of Events and Information	Remarks and references to Appendices
12 Inf. Bde	11.6.15 to 13.6.15	✓	Two Howitzers to each Battalion in first line trenches Engaged enemy machine gun emplacements, sap heads, snipers' lairs, communication trenches, farms and houses – firing 46 bombs. NCOs & men are working in 24 hour shifts – resting 24 hours in billets. A. Wilson Lt. Comdg 26th Field How Bty 4th Div 13/6/15	

1875 Wt. W593/826 1,000,000 4/15 J.B.C. & A. A.D.S.S./Forms/C. 2118.

Instructions regarding War Diaries and Intelligence Summaries are contained in F. S. Regs., Part II. and the Staff Manual respectively. Title Pages will be prepared in manuscript.

IV
26 TI

WAR DIARY
or
INTELLIGENCE SUMMARY
(Erase heading not required.)

Army Form C. 2118

26 Trench Howitzer Battery RGA

Place	Date 1915	Hour	Summary of Events and Information	Remarks and references to Appendices
	1st July		Moved Battery from VI Div. to join IV Div. to assist in a special enterprise.	
	3rd to 5th		Dug guns in and reconnoitred targets vicinity of BOESINGHE - position as per rough sketch attached. The guns were placed in trenches branching from the main trench, not occupied by Infy, well concealed and protected.	
	6th	5.0 am	Battle opened by salvo from the four mortars - salvo ordered chiefly to screen breaking down of four parapet in front of 18/pr gun in fire trench. Then one gun (mortar) turned on to break up wire (W. in sketch) the other three fired into German trench distributing to 60 yds length of trench. Accuracy of fire good. Wire well broken up.	
		6.0 am	Bombardment ceased. Turned two guns on to German communication trench portion beyond which our assaulting Infy were ordered not to proceed, to engage German bombers and be ready for expected Counter-attack. This day fired 84 bombs. Casualties 1 killed 5 wounded	
	7th		Fired 17 rds at Germans in Comm: trench essaying counter-attack.	
	8th		——— do ——— ——— do ——— One wounded this day. Withdrew guns in the night.	
	10th to 23rd		Rejoined VI Division. Guns distributed along front of two Inf. Bdes. Engaged targets as under with good results — Redoubts. Barricades over roads and railway. Trenches, Saps and Sap-heads. Enemy's enfilading positions. Enemy digging. Fired fifty bombs. Casualties - 1 killed 1 wounded. Admitted to Hospital Sick during month - Five	
	13th		2Lieut. F.R. Watson R.H.A. joined.	

A Allitson 2Lieut
Comg 26 Trench How. Bty RGA

1875 Wt. W593/826 1,000,000 4/15 J.B.C. & A. A.D.S.S./Forms/C. 2118.

Instructions regarding War Diaries and Intelligence Summaries are contained in F. S. Regs., Part II. and the Staff Manual respectively. Title Pages will be prepared in manuscript.

WAR DIARY
or
INTELLIGENCE SUMMARY
(Erase heading not required.)

Army Form C. 2118

26th Trench How: Bty.

26 Trench How. Bty R.G.A

Place	Date July 15	Hour	Summary of Events and Information	Remarks and references to Appendices
S... H...	13	6 pm	Enemy annoying our Advanced Post with Rifle grenades. Silenced him by firing two light bombs - one short, one on his trench.	
W....	16	12.1 am	Enemy ~~had~~ was harassing this portion of our line with light shell fire. Fired 11 heavy and 3 light bombs at his Sap head, Road barricade, and Advanced Posts. He ceased shelling	
W.F....	16	12 noon	Working party of enemy digging new trench - spadefuls of earth being plainly visible as they were thrown up. Fired 3 light bombs, two of which dropped into the new trench. Party ceased working	
R....	16	10. pm	One Regiment suffered from German mortar attack. Asked for our assistance. Moved a mortar into their lines.	
R....	19 20 23 24	10.30 pm	Daily at request of O.C. Fire Trench fired 3 or 4 Heavy bombs into Redoubt Trench or Railway barricade. Enemy replied with light shells which fell harmlessly in our rear. Our position not discovered by ~~the~~ enemy.	
R....	25	5.0 pm	A German aeroplane was brought down in our lines. Our troops cheered. This caused enemy to fire at our support trenches with his Mortar. Our mortar at once replied by sending 3 heavy bombs at his Redoubt and 3 light at his (supposed) mortar emplacement. Silenced him.	
W....	26	2.0 am	Enemy troublesome with light shells. Opened on him with 3 mortars, firing severally into his listening post, machine-gun position, Sap head, main trench and Road barricade, our machine-gun meanwhile sweeping his parapets. Enemy replied briskly with two kinds of shell - light & medium, wounding three Infy. We fired 2 heavy 10 light bombs. Enemy fired about 50 shell. Our listening post shot two men of their listening post and captured their rifles.	

A. Wilson Lieut

1875 Wt. W593/826 1,000,000 4/15 J.B.C. & A. A.D.S.S./Forms/C. 2118.

26th T.M. Bty

Army Form C. 2118

Instructions regarding War Diaries and Intelligence Summaries are contained in F. S. Regs., Part II. and the Staff Manual respectively. Title Pages will be prepared in manuscript.

WAR DIARY
or
INTELLIGENCE SUMMARY
(Erase heading not required.)

26 T. M. Bty — 22nd to 26th Sept 1915

Place	Date	Hour	Summary of Events and Information	Remarks and references to Appendices
	22.9.15		Relieved 58 T.M. Bty. attached 17 I.B. 2 Guns in position at No Mans Cottage Sheet 28. I.5.0.4.7.	
			No firing done except on 24.9.15 in retaliation to German heavy mortar (approx 100 lbs) when 15 light bombs (5 blind) were fired at German 2nd line trenches at about 4.15.	
			These German mortars ~~to~~ appear to have a long maximum range, at a minimum 500x probably more.	
			These bombs fired were probably about 100 lbs, have comparatively little penetration power, but a ~~long~~ large lateral effect. Can easily be seen coming, unless painted white, which is a new German trick and which makes them very difficult to see when coming towards you.	
			J. Langhorne 2/Lt	

1875 Wt. W593/826 1,000,000 4/15 J.B.C. & A. A.D.S.S./Forms/C. 2118.

Instructions regarding War Diaries and Intelligence Summaries are contained in F. S. Regs., Part II. and the Staff Manual respectively. Title Pages will be prepared in manuscript.

WAR DIARY
or
INTELLIGENCE SUMMARY
(Erase heading not required.)

Army Form C. 2118

26th Trench Mortar Bty

Place	Date	Hour	Summary of Events and Information	Remarks and references to Appendices
			Good targets within effective range of heavy bombs which do great damage, breaking down German parapet. Pieces of wood often land in our lines even when firing at the range of 165 yds showing force of explosion; blinds not very frequent 6 in 29	
			Effect of light bombs longer range neutralised owing to No of blinds 8 in 17. If shrapnel effect (air burst) is wanted light bombs at short ranges will cause it, owing to long time of flight at short ranges being greater than the time fuze burns.	
			The position is very well hidden and from their shooting the Germans have no notion of the battery's position	
			After the 12th the Germans moved their position and only used on gun on 13th, thus it appears our searching rounds must have come near them, apparently their mortars are about 30-50 yds behind their front line and not close up 15 yds behind the front line as ours are.	
			The German mortars have longer range and can fire quicker than ours, but only fire about 8-10 lb bombs to our 33 heavy + 18 lb light Their large 200 lb mortar having gone elsewhere	
			An alternative position to cover our front line is being prepared in rear	
			Cause of blinds. Very hard to say, get them after all precautions are taken Some fault in fuzes.	
			J. Longbourne. 2/Lieut RFA Commdg 26 Trench Bty	K 20/6/15

1875 Wt. W593/826 1,000,000 4/15 J.B.C. & A. A.D.S.S./Forms/C. 2118.

Operations of 26 T H Bty
from 3 9 15 to 13 9 15

Instructions regarding War Diaries and Intelligence Summaries are contained in F. S. Regs., Part II. and the Staff Manual respectively. Title Pages will be prepared in manuscript.

WAR DIARY
or
INTELLIGENCE SUMMARY
(Erase heading not required.)

Army Form C. 2118

Place	Date	Hour	Summary of Events and Information	Remarks and references to Appendices
	3/9/15		Relieved 38 T.B. at 8 pm Back Billets on Canal Bank (28NW – C25 C42) First few days spent in consolidating position after wet weather 2 Guns 4 Beds at C 15 C 3.8 (No Mans Cottage) 1 Gun 1 Bed at C 22 a 11 (Forward Cottage)	
	4 9 15		Gun at C 22 a 11 fired 1 Heavy 2 Light with good effect. This gun was working under orders from Infantry (R Bde) at the time. Was moved to C 15 C 38 this night.	
	8+9th		Few ranging rounds fired from No Mans Cottage position 6 heavy + 1 light	
	10th		6 heavy bombs fired in reply to two German T.Ms which fired a few bombs of 8-10 lbs on our lines (1 Blind)	
	11th		Germans opened with two T Ms at about 1 pm on our trenches. Asked by Infantry (Royal Fusiliers) to retaliate did so with 5 Heavy and 10 light bombs good effect from the 2 guns used. Silenced Germans.	
	12th		Germans fired T Ms in course of evening. Effectively retaliated by suddenly opening at 6 15 pm with 3 Guns. Germans silenced. 7 heavy + 4 light bombs fired	20/9/15
	13th		Reset beds. Fired 4 heavy bombs to test Registrations. Germans replied with on T M fired about 8-10 bombs doing no damage so I did not engage them.	

J. Longbourne 2/Lieut RFA
Commdg 26 Trench Bty RGA

1875 Wt. W593/826 1,000,000 4/15 J.B.C. & A. A.D.S.S./Forms/C. 2118.

26th Trench Mortar Battery

Instructions regarding War Diaries and Intelligence Summaries are contained in F. S. Regs., Part II. and the Staff Manual respectively. Title Pages will be prepared in manuscript.

Army Form C. 2118.

WAR DIARY
or
INTELLIGENCE SUMMARY
(Erase heading not required.)

26 T.M. Bty — Period 18 – 29 Inclusive

Place	Date	Hour	Summary of Events and Information	Remarks and references to Appendices
	21		Handed over position at NOMANS COTTAGE to 42 T M B 49th DIV.	
	22.		Took over position held by 29 + 39 T M B at RLY WOOD (HOOGE)	
	22-28		Bombs Heavy & Light were fired into, and in neighbourhood of, the German Crater. Occasional bombs being fired by night as well as day	
	29		A position used as a bombing post on edge of German Crater was blown up. also a dugout near by, and from it a German was seen to be thrown up 15 ft into the air, presumably he had been resting inside.	
			Rounds fired During Period	
			Heavy. 33 — 17 blind — 51.51% (ammunition of very poor quality.)	
			Light. 26 — 13 blind — 50 %	
Jk 4/11/5			Germans used three T.M. of varying ~~sizes~~ weights (in reply) up to about 110 lbs	J. Ross Burns(?) Lt R.F.A. O.C. 26 T.M.B.
			NOTES	
			On 29th Oct the Germans were noticed to have erected during the night pieces of canvas about 3 ft square on two poles in various parts of their line. One such piece was on the bombing post which was blown up and in the afternoon our trenches was shelled by German heavies, as these flags were of the nature of those red ones used in our trenches for the benefit of our Gunners, it appears likely that the Germans use the same device.	

1875 Wt. W593/826 1,000,000 4/15 J.B.C. & A. A.D.S.S./Forms/C. 2118.

Instructions regarding War Diaries and Intelligence Summaries are contained in F. S. Regs., Part II. and the Staff Manual respectively. Title Pages will be prepared in manuscript.

WAR DIARY
or
INTELLIGENCE SUMMARY
(Erase heading not required.)

26th Trench Mortar Battery

Army Form C. 2118

Place	Date	Hour	Summary of Events and Information	Remarks and references to Appendices
ARMENTIERES	11/10/15		Battery at rest	
"	12/10/15		" "	
"	13/10/15		" "	
"	14/10/15		Placed 2 four pounder trench mortars in action. Emplacement of one had to be reconstructed. Under cover of Artillery bombardment which started at 2.30pm. fired. One shot burst in the air, one was a dud and the five burst in the enemy's trenches. There was no reply to our fire.	
"	15/10/15		Battery at rest.	
"	16/10/15		"	
"	17/10/15		Ten rounds were fired from 4 pr in new emplacement. 8 were duds 2 burst in enemy trenches. The enemy did not reply.	20/10

Army Form C. 2118

Instructions regarding War Diaries and Intelligence Summaries are contained in F. S. Regs., Part II. and the Staff Manual respectively. Title Pages will be prepared in manuscript.

WAR DIARY
or
INTELLIGENCE SUMMARY
(Erase heading not required.)

26 Trench Mortar Bty — October 5 – 14th (inclusive) 1915

Place	Date	Hour	Summary of Events and Information	Remarks and references to Appendices
	11th Oct.		Six light bombs fired. Test Rounds. (3 blind)	
	12th Oct		Germans opened ~~fire~~ hot fire with three mortars at 6–10 pm. They fired about 40 to 50 bombs altogether, backed up by light Shrapnel. Fired 25 light bombs in retaliation (2 blind)	
			Rounds fired during period = 31. Blinds 5 = 16%	
			Notes	
			German bombs very hard to see coming owing to the fog; also some were painted white to make them show less still.	
			J. Lory Lowrse 2/Lt R.F.A.	
			Comdg 26 Trench Howitzer Battery	

1875 Wt. W593/826 1,000,000 4/15 J.B.C. & A. A.D.S.S./Forms/C. 2118.

Further details of the German T.M bomb described as a rum jar in report.

Time fuze numbered up to 15 (presume in seconds)

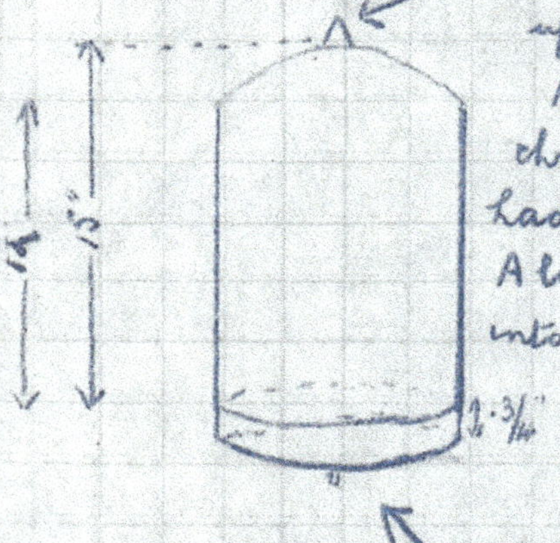

A safety pin going through fuze, in this case had not been removed.
Also a thin wire passes into fuze; use not clear but it is attached to the safety pin.

Screw holding on wood base.

Wood base of three ply wood, charred at base as a result of explosion.

Wt of bomb 25 – 30 lbs (approx)

Army Form C. 2118.

Instructions regarding War Diaries and Intelligence Summaries are contained in F. S. Regs., Part II. and the Staff Manual respectively. Title Pages will be prepared in manuscript.

WAR DIARY
or
INTELLIGENCE SUMMARY
(Erase heading not required.)

26 Trench Mortar Bty — Sept 26 – Oct 4th

Place	Date	Hour	Summary of Events and Information	Remarks and references to Appendices
	30 Sept		Fired 5 light bombs in reply to German T.M.	
	1st Oct		Germans opened at 6 A.M. with three T.M's. One firing a bomb whose appearance in the air is of the nature of a stone ream bottle. One the large cigar shaped bomb and the third a similar bomb but smaller. Retaliated with 24 light bombs using both guns with pretty good effect, on the German second lines. Later on both sides brought their light artillery into play, the Germans also using a 4·9 (approx). Damage done to S.20 and Canadian Trench by German fire.	
	4th Oct		Germans opened at 5.50 with T M's, light shrapnel + H E, and later on 4·9 H.E. concentrating their mortars + heavier H.E chiefly on S.20 and Canadian Trench and dugouts. Replied with both guns with light bombs; bombs fired 37; good effect obtained on German trenches just in rear of their fire trench. The battery worked very well under a pretty heavy fire of Shrapnel & light H.E.	
			Bombs fired during period 66, blinds Total 16 = 24%.	
			Best day on 4th only 5 blinds in 37 bombs = 13·5%	

10/15

1875 Wt. W593/826 1,000,000 4/15 J.B.C. & A. A.D.S.S./Forms/C. 2118.

Instructions regarding War Diaries and Intelligence Summaries are contained in F. S. Regs., Part II. and the Staff Manual respectively. Title Pages will be prepared in manuscript.

WAR DIARY
or
INTELLIGENCE SUMMARY
(Erase heading not required.)

Army Form C. 2118

26 Trench Mortar Battery

26 Trench Mortar Bty — Period from 12 noon Oct 30th to 12 noon Nov 7th 1915

Place	Date	Hour	Summary of Events and Information	Remarks and references to Appendices
X	X		During this period nothing of note to record.	
'B' Series. Sheet. 28. N.W.	30/10/15 to 7/11/15		Bombs heavy and light have been fired into, + in the neighbourhood of the German Crater by day + night.	
I.11.b.5.2. to I.11.d.6.8.			While the position is in course of reconstruction after recent wet weather.	
			Bombs fired — Heavy 15, blinds 53.3% = 8; Light 23, blinds 47.8% = 11	
			The German are using three mortars of various sizes, one being of their largest type firing a bombs about 120-200 lbs, + of very long range.	

J Longbourne 2/Lt R.F.A
Commdg 26 T M Bty

1875 Wt. W593/826 1,000,000 4/15 J.B.C. & A. A.D.S.S./Forms/C. 2118.

Army Form C. 2118

26th Trench Mortar Battery

WAR DIARY
or
INTELLIGENCE SUMMARY

Instructions regarding War Diaries and Intelligence Summaries are contained in F. S. Regs., Part II. and the Staff Manual respectively. Title Pages will be prepared in manuscript. 26 Trench Mortar Bty

(Erase heading not required.) Period 12 noon Nov 7th — 5pm Nov 11th 1915

Place	Date	Hour	Summary of Events and Information	Remarks and references to Appendices
I.11.b.6.3 to I.11.d.5.7	10/11/15 11/11/15		During period two portions of enemy trench were fired on near their crater on 10th and morning of 11th	
			Bombs fired 17 light Blinds 8 = 47.2%	
	11th		With-drew guns & beds during night on handing position over to 17th DIV Trench Mortars	

J. Longbourne 2/Lt RFA
Cmdg 26 T. M. B
14-11-15

www.ingramcontent.com/pod-product-compliance
Lightning Source LLC
Chambersburg PA
CBHW080815010526
44111CB00015B/2560